A JOHN DONNE COMPANION

GARLAND REFERENCE LIBRARY
OF THE HUMANITIES
(VOL. 1070)

A JOHN DONNE COMPANION

Robert H. Ray

GARLAND PUBLISHING, INC. • NEW YORK & LONDON
1990

Library of Congress Cataloging-in-Publication Data

Ray, Robert H., 1940–
    A John Donne companion / Robert H. Ray.
        p.   cm. — (Garland reference library of the humanities; vol.
    1070)
    ISBN 0–8240–4568–8 (alk. paper)
    1. Donne, John, 1572–1631—Dictionaries, indexes, etc. I. Title.
    II. Series.
PR2248.A3   1990
821'.3—dc20   90–31981
                                                                    CIP

Printed on acid-free, 250-year-life paper
Manufactured in the United States of America

CONTENTS

v

PREFACE

This book provides for the reader of John Donne a reference and resource volume similar to the companions, dictionaries, guides, and handbooks existing on several other major writers. I especially have modeled it upon F.E. Halliday's *A Shakespeare Companion*, Edward S. LeComte's *A Milton Dictionary*, and D. Heyward Brock's *A Ben Jonson Companion*. I am greatly indebted to these works, and, while learning much from their formats, criteria for sections and entries, and decisions on inclusions and exclusions, I institute modifications that seem more appropriate to Donne's life and work and more pertinent to my primary audience. Throughout the writing I have kept before me the kinds of questions I had when first reading, studying, teaching, and researching Donne. I attempt, then, a compendium of useful information for any reader of Donne to have at hand, especially information not easily accessible to the nonspecialist. I include key facts about his life, works, and times, to enhance understanding and appreciation, without being exhaustive. In fact, my citations, bibliography, and suggestions for further research direct the reader to those books, articles, scholars, and critics that can best satisfy curiosity stimulated herein on any topic or work related to Donne. Therefore, the book should be most helpful to the following groups: (1) general readers or undergraduate students coming to Donne for the first time for any extensive reading or study, (2) postgraduate students seeking both a basic background in Donne and some initial guidance to methods and tools for research in primary and secondary materials, and (3) nonspecialist teachers, particularly those teaching Donne's works commonly found in anthologies and covered in survey courses. I am assuming that the user of this *Companion*, especially in consulting entries in the "Dictionary" portion, has before him or her either an anthology with selections of Donne's works or an edition of Donne. This *Companion* is designed to be especially helpful to those with an edition or anthology having few or no notes or other aids in reading and understanding. I emphasize Donne's poetry over his prose, as well as the most frequently anthologized poems, prose pieces, and selections from prose over the more specialized pieces and the selections of lesser popularity and fame.

The preceding aims and primary audiences largely determine the precise sections included, as well as their lengths, divisions, content, format, tone, and language. "Research in Donne: Tools and Procedures" notes the most important tools for further research, as well as a step-by-step method of beginning with the "Selected Bibliography" at the end of this volume and then widening one's net to even more comprehensive and complex matters of criticism and scholarship. These steps allow the general reader to stop at the level most useful for his purposes, while the student or teacher eventually might wish to pursue more research into seventeenth-century originals and commentaries or into the complexities of text and scholarship: this brief section provides a way to begin. "A Donne Chronology" presents an overview of dated highlights of Donne's life and works in order to provide a perspective for absorbing the larger picture and further details in the succeeding "Donne's Life" and "A Donne Dictionary." The section "Donne's Works" provides a list of his major works by customary titles and groups, and the critical studies listed in the "Selected Bibliography" are classified according to these works. The lightly annotated "Selected Bibliography" is divided into major categories (with subcategories), such as editions of primary works, tools for research and reference, biographical studies, studies of Donne's reputation and influence, and criticism. The books, essays, and articles selected are those of first importance to anyone wishing to explore further the field represented within any given division or subdivision of Donne's life and works. The coverage of the bibliography extends to works published through early 1989. Compact annotations in brackets conclude those items of prime significance that need more description than is given in the titles.

The major portion of the volume, both in importance and size, is "A Donne Dictionary." Its entries are arranged alphabetically: they identify, define, and explain the most important and influential *persons* in Donne's life and works (mainly theologians, thinkers, family, friends, and aristocrats);

places either frequented by Donne or important in his life and works; *characters, allusions, ideas,* and *concepts* in his works and from his time; *words* and *phrases* of most importance and difficulty in his works, as well as those conducive to multiple meanings and puns in their interpretation; the most significant, famous, and frequently anthologized *books, poems,* and *prose works* of Donne; other important *writers* and *works* that are relevant to understanding portions of Donne's own life or works or his influence and reputation; and *literary terms* important to or arising from Donne's writing and influence. Maintaining my focus on the relevance of the content of each entry to Donne's life and works is uppermost: for example, I resist being led astray into too many details about an individual's life (e.g., King James's or Sir Francis Bacon's), but rather include only those facts that convey the essence to understand him or her and the role played by that individual in the course of Donne's career and in the content of his writings. Other reference works, biographies, and histories can provide additional matters for anyone interested in the full details of the lives of such individuals.

The format for the entries in "A Donne Dictionary" is designed to highlight and distinguish elements. The designation of each entry is capitalized and **Bold**: if it is a long work or book, it is also ***Italicized***; but, if it is a short work, it is in "**Quotation Marks.**" The same system of italics and quotation marks is employed within the content of an entry, but without the boldface. In addition, for any mention that appears elsewhere as an entry, I use ALL-CAPITALS as a cross-reference.

Other principles foster clarity and ease of reading. With the exception of the "Selected Bibliography," I modernize spelling and punctuation for all titles of books, prose works, and poems, as well as for any quotations from Donne's or others' Renaissance original editions, manuscripts, and letters. Through the entire volume I spell out fully the names of Donne's works, of professional journals, and of scholarly and critical books, rather than employ a lengthy list of abbreviations: for the nonspecialist reader, such abbreviations likely would be cryptic and frustrating, causing one continually to turn back to the key in an early part of the volume.

In writing this book, I have drawn from my own reading, teaching, and research of over twenty years, and I hope that some new perspectives in close readings of several of the *Songs and Sonnets, Holy Sonnets, Hymns,* "Meditations" in *Devotions Upon Emergent Occasions,* and passages from *Sermons* appear in the entries of the "Dictionary." I must acknowledge the study of works of reference, biography, history, philosophy, theology, scholarship, and criticism that enabled me to accomplish this task. Even though it is impossible to separate one's own readings at every point from the cumulative and mutual debts scholars and critics owe, I attempt to cite noteworthy readings that can be specified without burdening such a work as this with scholarly apparatus. I do, however, want my entire "Selected Bibliography" to be a grateful acknowledgment of and a granting of due credit to the authors of those works found to be most helpful as sources of knowledge and insight, both in my years of studying Donne and in composing this volume. In listing them I encourage readers to seek these items for fuller discussions and information on works and topics. Also, *The Oxford English Dictionary*, the *Dictionary of National Biography*, the *Cyclopaedia of Biblical, Theological, and Ecclesiastical Literature*, the *Encyclopaedia Britannica*, the *Dictionary of Phrase and Fable*, the *Gazetteer of the British Isles*, *An Encyclopaedia of London*, *The London Encyclopedia, and The Shell Guide to The History of London*, out of countless resources, have been of primary value and deserve singular mention. If I seem to have slighted or if I have been unaware of some work pertinent to my own readings and provision of information in this *Companion*, I apologize most deeply for the oversight.

I am indebted to many groups and their associated individuals for generous assistance. Garland Publishing has been exceedingly understanding and helpful, especially Phyllis Korper, Senior Editor. For continuing encouragement and generosity in allotting time and research sabbaticals for this work, I thank Baylor University and its administrators, especially James Barcus, John Belew, Robert Collmer, William Cooper, Herbert Reynolds, and William Toland. For her help in finding some articles on Donne, I thank my colleague, Paula Woods. I particularly am grateful to the College of Arts and Sciences Faculty Development Committee for its vital support in granting both the summer and long-term sabbaticals necessary to complete this project.

I wish to thank my family, especially my wife, Lynette, for unfailing encouragement.

R.H.R.
Baylor University

A John Donne Companion

RESEARCH IN DONNE:
TOOLS AND PROCEDURES

Although the "Selected Bibliography" concluding this volume provides key items for further study, researchers might wish to pursue Donne's life and works more thoroughly. The following discussion guides one in such a task.

Fortunately for students of Donne, two annotated bibliographies of criticism save labor and time. John R. Roberts's *John Donne: An Annotated Bibliography of Modern Criticism, 1912–1967* (1973) and his *John Donne: An Annotated Bibliography of Modern Criticism, 1968–1978* (1982) cover virtually every book, article, and essay of significance published on Donne between 1912 and 1978 (Roberts excludes dissertations). He arranges each volume chronologically by year of publication and alphabetically by author within each year. The annotations succinctly describe the content and nature of each item. Roberts also provides indexes to authors, subjects, and Donne's works. To survey the dissertations written on Donne, one should consult *Dissertation Abstracts* and *Dissertation Abstracts International* for the years desired. To find listings of books, articles, essays, and dissertations published from 1979 to the present (i.e., from the end of Roberts's coverage), the individual should employ the *MLA International Bibliography*, the *Annual Bibliography of English Language and Literature*, and the *Essay and General Literature Index*. Scheduled for publication in 1994 or soon after is Roberts's revised bibliography that is to contain all of the items in the first two volumes, with additions to them, as well as coverage extended through 1988.

The preceding references, then, provide ways to research almost everything written about Donne for the larger part of the twentieth century, and for many topics these will suffice.

However, if one wishes or needs to consult earlier books, articles, essays, and comments about Donne and his works, other reference tools provide the essentials. Geoffrey Keynes's *A Bibliography of Dr. John Donne* (4th ed., 1973) in its "Appendix V" cites biography and criticism chronologically arranged in sections covering 1594–1700, 1701–1800, 1801–1900, and 1901–1971. A selection of the most significant references to Donne from 1598 to 1889 is collected and edited by A.J. Smith in *John Donne: The Critical Heritage* (1975).

For even more comprehensive research that calls for the use of early editions and manuscripts, further tools are necessary. Keynes's *A Bibliography of Dr. John Donne* (already cited above) describes the important publications of Donne's works. Keynes's volume notes some libraries and collections possessing copies of these editions, but one can find additional locations in the various reference volumes known as the *Short-Title Catalogue of Books Printed in England* and the *National Union Catalog*. (The researcher unfamiliar with these tools should consult a reference librarian for help.) Actually, if one cannot physically hold and examine the original books because of limited access to them, seeing early publications of Donne's works (and those of writers who refer to and comment on Donne) is much easier than the researcher might think. Because of some microfilms made of English books by University Microfilms International, many libraries now possess Donne's works filmed from original editions. Armed with the number assigned to a particular book in the *Short-Title Catalogue*, the researcher can locate which reel of film that book appears on in a set of microfilms, by using the reel guides that accompany the collections. (Again, seeking a reference librarian's help in orienting oneself to this search is quite valuable.) If a person needs information on extant manuscripts of Donne's works (their contents and locations), the primary reference tool is the *Index of English Literary Manuscripts*, compiled by Peter Beal and others. Many of the modern editions of Donne cited in my "Selected Bibliography" also discuss the numerous manuscript sources for Donne's works, a complex matter indeed.

The researcher in Donne will be helped by a forthcoming work. *The Variorum Edition of the Poetry of John Donne*, Gary A. Stringer, General Editor, is to provide an authoritative text of the poetry from all known editions and manuscripts, as well as to condense hundreds of years of critical commentary on the poems.

The study of Donne's poetry should thereby be simplified, saving time for the researcher while increasing his accuracy.

The *John Donne Journal* specializes in articles on Donne and his age and is published twice a year. The editors are M. Thomas Hester and R.V. Young, Jr.

A DONNE CHRONOLOGY

1572   John Donne born between January 24 and June 19.

1576   Donne's father (John) dies. Mother (Elizabeth) marries Dr. John Syminges.

1584   Matriculates at Hart Hall, Oxford.

1587   Leaves Oxford?

1588   Dr. Syminges dies. Donne at Cambridge? On Continent with army? Traveling?

1591   Enters Thavies Inn to study law. Mother marries Richard Rainsford.

1592   Admitted to Lincoln's Inn to study law.

1593   Receives portion of inheritance.

1595   Leaves Lincoln's Inn?

1596   Sails with Essex in expedition against Cadiz.

1597   Sails with the Azores Islands expedition. Probably late in the year, begins service as secretary to Sir Thomas Egerton, Lord Keeper of the Great Seal.

1601   Serves in Parliament. Secretly marries Ann More, niece of Sir Thomas Egerton (December).

1602   Marriage made public. Egerton dismisses Donne from his
        service. After brief imprisonment of Donne, marriage is
        declared valid by the court of the Archbishop of
        Canterbury. Moves with Ann to Pyrford to live in the
        home of her cousin, Sir Francis Wolley.

1603   Daughter Constance born. Death of Elizabeth I and
        accession of James I.

1604   Son John born.

1605   Travels in France and possibly Italy. Son George born.

1606   Moves with family to Mitcham.

1607   Son Francis born. Donne's prefatory Latin verses in Ben
        Jonson's *Volpone* published. Thomas Morton, Dean of
        Gloucester, urges Donne to take holy orders. Donne
        refuses.

1608   Daughter Lucy born and baptized, with Lucy Harrington,
        Countess of Bedford, as her godmother. After serious
        illness, writing on *Biathanatos*. Unsuccessfully pursues
        secretaryship in Ireland.

1609   Unsuccessfully pursues secretaryship with the Virginia
        Company. "The Expiration" appears in Ferrabosco's
        Airs. Daughter Bridget born.

1610   Publishes *Pseudo-Martyr*. Receives honorary M.A. from
        Oxford.

1611   Daughter Mary born. *Ignatius His Conclave* and *An
        Anatomy of the World* published. "Upon Mr. Thomas
        Coryat's Crudities" published in *Coryat's Crudities*.
        Accompanies Sir Robert Drury to the Continent.

1612   Wife is delivered of a stillborn child (January). *The First
        and Second Anniversaries* published. Returns to England.
        Moves with family to a home in Drury Lane. "Break of
        Day" published in Corkine's *Second Book of Airs*.

1613   Visits Sir Henry Goodyer and Sir Edward Herbert. Son Nicholas born (died within a year). "Elegy on Prince Henry" published.

1614   Serves as a Member of Parliament for Taunton. Deaths of daughter Mary and son Francis.

1615   Ordained deacon and priest in Church of England. Appointed to be a royal chaplain. Accompanies King James I to Cambridge and is granted an honorary Doctor of Divinity degree by the King's command. Daughter Margaret born. Preaches at Greenwich (first of Donne's extant sermons).

1616   Granted rectories of Keyston and Sevenoaks. Preaches at Court for first time. Daughter Elizabeth born. Chosen Reader in Divinity at Lincoln's Inn.

1617   First sermon at Paul's Cross. Wife Ann dies after birth of a stillborn child. Ann buried at St. Clement Danes. Writes a "Holy Sonnet" and "A Nocturnal upon St. Lucy's Day," apparently in response to her death.

1618   Preaches at Court and Lincoln's Inn.

1619   Sermon of valediction at Lincoln's Inn. Accompanies, and serves as chaplain in, Viscount Doncaster's embassy to Germany. Writes "A Hymn to Christ, at the Author's Last Going into Germany."

1620   Returns to England.

1621   Preaches to the Countess of Bedford at Harrington House. Named and installed as Dean of St. Paul's Cathedral.

1622   Resigns Readership at Lincoln's Inn. Granted church living as rector in Blunham, Bedfordshire. Appointed Justice of the Peace for Kent and Bedford. Made honorary member of the Virginia Company. Appointed to serve as a judge in the Court of Delegates. Two of Donne's sermons published.

1623   Preaches at dedication of the new chapel at Lincoln's Inn.
        Seriously ill with fever in November and December.

1624   *Devotions Upon Emergent Occasions* published. Made
        vicar of St. Dunstan's-in-the-West. Preaches at St.
        Dunstan's and St. Paul's.

1625   Death of James I and accession of Charles I. Preaches at
        St. Paul's, St. Dunstan's, and Court. Living at Magdalen
        Danvers's home at Chelsea during time of plague in
        London. Her son, George Herbert, also there.

1626   Preaches at St. Paul's, St. Dunstan's, and Court. Serves as
        judge in Court of Delegates.

1627   Deaths of daughter Lucy, Sir Henry Goodyer, the Countess
        of Bedford, and Magdalen Danvers. Preaches memorial
        sermon for Lady Danvers at Chelsea.

1628   Christopher Brooke dies. Preaches. Serves as judge in
        ecclesiastical courts.

1629   Preaches at St. Paul's and Court and serves in judicial
        capacities.

1630   "The Broken Heart" and a portion of "Go, and Catch a
        Falling Star" published in *A Help to Memory and
        Discourse*. Illness. Makes will.

1631   Mother dies. Delivers his last sermon (at Court: published
        posthumously as *Death's Duel*). Poses for drawing of
        himself in his shroud. Dies March 31. Buried in St. Paul's
        April 3. Six of his twelve children survive.

1632   Monument of Donne completed for St. Paul's Cathedral.

1633   *Poems, by J. D. with Elegies on the Author's Death*
        published, the first collected edition of Donne's poetry
        (later editions published in 1635, 1639, 1649, 1650,
        1654, and 1669). *Juvenilia: Or Certain Paradoxes and
        Problems* published.

1640   *LXXX Sermons* published (containing also the first edition
        of Izaak Walton's *The Life of Dr. John Donne*).

1647   *Biathanatos* published.

1649   *Fifty Sermons* published.

1651   *Essays in Divinity* and *Letters to Several Persons of Honour* published.

1652   *Paradoxes, Problems, Essays, Characters* published.

1658   Walton's *The Life of John Donne* (revised and enlarged) published.

1660   *XXVI Sermons* published.

DONNE'S LIFE

John Donne's birth occurred in London between January 24 and June 19 of 1572. His father (John) was a prosperous hardware merchant and was descended from a respectable Welsh family. ("Donne" is pronounced as "dun" or "done": the poet himself puns on his name in some works.) His mother (Elizabeth) was a daughter of the dramatist and writer John Heywood and also a granddaughter of Sir Thomas More's sister. At his birth John Donne joined a staunchly Roman Catholic family with a history of members who had served as priests, had gone into exile from England, had suffered fines and loss of privileges enjoyed by Anglicans, and had even been martyrs for their faith.

Donne's father died when the son was only four years old, leaving a widow and children well provided for in his will. Elizabeth married a physician, Dr. John Syminges, six months after her first husband's death. Donne apparently was educated by a private tutor (presumably Roman Catholic) until he entered Hart Hall, Oxford, in 1584. Studying here until about 1587, he left (as was usual with Roman Catholic students) before taking a degree, since, to qualify for a degree, he would be required to swear to the Oath for the Act of Supremacy and to the Thirty-nine Articles of Religion in the Anglican *Book of Common Prayer*: the oath asserted that Queen Elizabeth was the head of the Church in England, a position in conflict with the claim of Papal authority. Donne's first biographer, Izaak Walton, contends that Donne then studied for a few years at Cambridge. Although no records survive to prove this, it may be true. But perhaps Donne spent a portion of the 1588–1591 period traveling or as a soldier. Without the discovery of further records, this period of Donne's life remains open to conjecture. During this period his stepfather

13

died, and his mother married her third husband (Richard Rainsford) in 1591.

Also in 1591 it is certain that Donne began the study of law that occupied him for some years. The Inns of Court are the law schools of England, but in the Renaissance they also were accepted as schools in which gentlemen could add polish to their education, forge social ties and friendships, and find entrees into influential families and the courtly circle. Donne found these facets of metropolitan culture particularly at Lincoln's Inn from about 1592 to 1595 or 1596, after a preliminary year at Thavies Inn. During this period at Lincoln's Inn he was helped in his role as a courtly gentleman of independence by receiving some of his inheritance, and he established lifelong friendships with several men, one of whom was Christopher Brooke. The writing of his early poetry began during these invigorating years: Sir Richard Baker later (*Chronicles*, 1643) refers to Donne at the Inns of Court as one "not dissolute [i.e., not negligent or careless in appearance], but very neat; a great visitor of Ladies, a great frequenter of Plays, a great writer of conceited [i.e., ingenious, witty, clever] Verses." In addition to the "Epithalamion at Lincoln's Inn," several verse letters, most of the elegies, and many of the songs and sonnets undoubtedly were written during this time at Lincoln's Inn. Donne himself, in a letter, acknowledged that he did not study law for a practical and professional purpose, for a career, but that he rather was attracted more by learning and languages.

Following his years at Lincoln's Inn, Donne volunteered his service to the Earl of Essex in military expeditions to be directed against the Spanish. A friend from his Oxford days, Henry Wotton, was one of Essex's secretaries; therefore, Donne had no problem of access to the Earl. Income, adventure, and possible prospects of advancement through Essex's influence may all have figured in Donne's motives for his stint as a soldier. He was accepted and thus sailed with two expeditions in 1596 and 1597, those against Cadiz and the Azores Islands. The Cadiz exploit was successful for the English, but the journeys to the Azores were plagued by bad weather and a failure to take the desired Spanish treasure. The latter expedition is the basis for Donne's verse epistles "The Storm" and "The Calm."

One of Donne's companions on the Azores expedition was the son of the Lord Keeper of the Great Seal (Sir Thomas Egerton). Through the commendation of the son Donne was made a secretary to Sir Thomas, a post that normally would offer significant public advancement in the future. The demands of the Lord Keeper's position meant that his secretaries were also quite

busy in attendance at legal and state matters, with Donne serving
well in this capacity through 1601: Egerton, in fact, chose him to
sit in Parliament for a borough that the Lord Keeper controlled
(Brackley, Northamptonshire). Service under Egerton assuredly
provided experience and education in public and courtly life, as
evidenced in Donne's satires, letters, and other works. Most of his
satires likely were written during the time he served Egerton. But
Donne's hopes for advancement through Sir Thomas ended in
1602 with the revelation of his secret marriage (in December,
1601) to Egerton's niece, Ann More. She and Donne had fallen
deeply in love during the few years prior to this when she had
been in Egerton's household. The couple knew, however, that her
father, Sir George More, was planning to secure Ann a husband of
much more substance, financially and socially, than John Donne.
When they married, Ann was seventeen (twelve years younger
than her husband). In not obtaining the father's permission,
Donne committed personal and social affronts, as well as an
offense against canon law. The secret lasted until its revelation in
early 1602, with a letter carried to Sir George by a friend and
emissary of the new son-in-law. Ann's father was extremely
angry, had Donne imprisoned, and then successfully urged that he
be dismissed from his position under Egerton. After writing
letters of penitential submission both to Sir George and Sir
Thomas, Donne was released from prison. After Sir George failed
in an attempt to have the marriage annulled, the Court of
Audience in Canterbury declared it a lawful marriage.

Ann's father refused to contribute any financial support to
the couple, leaving them without employment, without much of
Donne's inheritance remaining, and with debts incurred from the
imprisonment and legal proceedings. Ann did receive, however, a
legacy from her aunt, and the couple was offered a place to live in
the early years of their marriage: her cousin, Francis Wolley, took
them into his home at Pyrford. During their time here, the Donnes
had their first three children (Constance, John, and George).
Apparently during 1605 and early 1606 Donne spent some time
in France (and perhaps Italy) with Sir Walter Chute, maybe
sensing a means to find again some public recognition and
employment through men of influence.

In 1606 the Donne family moved to a house at Mitcham,
much closer to London, and lived there for a period of five years.
Donne spent time in London among friends of various social levels
and found patrons and patronesses. He was able to read in his
study at Mitcham what he refers to as "good Authors." Four more
children were born in the five years at Mitcham: Francis, 1607;

Lucy, 1608; Bridget, 1609; and Mary, 1611. Both the parents and children suffered numerous physical illnesses, frequently referred to by Donne in letters written over these years. Depression and melancholy apparently nurtured his writing on suicide in *Biathanatos* during these years living in what he calls his "hospital" at Mitcham. Nevertheless, Donne continued to pursue secular employment through the influence of such friends at Court as Sir Henry Goodyer and Lord Hay. But King James still recalled the scandal surrounding Donne's marriage and would not approve him for a secretaryship that Donne desired in Ireland. Similarly, the Virginia Company refused Donne as the Secretary of Virginia about a year later.

Even though secular employment continued to elude Donne, financial problems were alleviated by other means during the Mitcham years. In 1608 Ann's father finally agreed to pay a substantial dowry. Also by 1608 the Countess of Bedford had become a friend and patroness (even serving as godmother to the daughter Lucy) who gave financial support, respect, and influence to Donne, Ben Jonson, and other writers of the time. Donne addressed many poems to her and visited at her residence at Twickenham. His friendship with Mrs. Magdalen Herbert (later Lady Danvers) began in earnest in 1607, securing him another patroness, one to whom he sent *La Corona* (a series of sonnets or "hymns," as Donne terms them).

Donne's friendship with (as well as the respect given him by) other writers is evident in his Mitcham period. Edward Herbert, son of Magdalen Herbert, was an acquaintance to whom Donne addressed a poem. Donne also contributed verses commending Ben Jonson's play *Volpone*, and Jonson addressed and referred to Donne in several of his poems. Despite some begrudging and denigrating comments by Jonson that are related by William Drummond in his *Conversations*, on the whole Jonson valued Donne's abilities and poetic judgment. Drummond reports that Jonson said, "Donne, for not keeping of accent, deserved hanging," thus criticizing Donne's distortions of regular metrics and rhythm in much of his verse. Jonson also reportedly said that Donne, since his work is not understood, "would perish," implying the complexity, the obscurity of Donne's style and thought. On the other hand, Drummond also relates that Jonson "esteemeth John Donne the first poet in the world in some things."

During the Mitcham period Donne evidently began an intense concern with Christian matters, both generally and personally. The *La Corona* poems and most of his *Holy Sonnets* date from these years. As early as 1607 Thomas Morton, Dean of

Gloucester, urged Donne to enter the church. He apparently asked Donne's advice and opinions on some of his own writings urging Roman Catholics to quit being recusants—i.e., those who would not attend services of the Church of England. Donne himself was in the midst of moving toward larger allegiances with the Anglican Church and away from his Catholic faith, but he did not yet feel worthy of taking holy orders. Another motive, obviously, for not yet entering the church was that he still preferred secular employment. Ironically, Donne's own increasing reconciliation of his spiritual conflicts, a development that was propelling him toward the Anglican fold, led to his writing and publication (in 1610) of a prose work entitled *Pseudo-Martyr*. Because of the impressive quality of its spiritual argument on behalf of Anglican and King James's positions, Donne's hopes for secular advancement were doomed: the King felt his talents would be wasted. Donne argues that Roman Catholics could in conscience subscribe to the oath of allegiance, saying that Catholics must reject the belief that rulers excommunicated or deprived by the Pope may be deposed or murdered by their subjects. King James was so taken by Donne's work that he urged him to become an Anglican priest and saw to it that other routes to advancement were cut off. His work at this point was rewarded by an honorary Master of Arts degree conferred by Oxford University. Donne's prose satire against the Jesuits (*Ignatius His Conclave*) was published the next year.

Before Donne yielded to the wish of King James that he enter the church, the years 1611–1614 were spent in a variety of pursuits, several of which still testify to Donne's clinging to worldly patronage and hopes. In 1611 he published *An Anatomy of the World*, a lengthy eulogy of Elizabeth Drury, a girl of fourteen who had died a few months earlier (Donne already having written and presented to the parents a short elegy on her death). Donne had never met this daughter of the wealthy Sir Robert Drury, but the hyperbolic poems for her endeared him to Sir Robert, whom Donne obviously was appealing to as a potential patron. Sir Robert invited Donne to travel with the Drurys on a journey to the Continent: Donne accepted, giving up the Mitcham house and leaving his wife and children to stay at the home of Ann's sister on the Isle of Wight during his absence from England. While he was away, his wife had a stillborn child. Donne had written, meanwhile, a second long poem in memory of Elizabeth Drury, and both of these were published in 1612 as *The First and Second Anniversaries*.

By early autumn, 1612, Donne and the Drurys had returned to England. A further testimony to the high esteem in which

Donne was held is the offer to Donne and his family of a house owned by Sir Robert next to his own in Drury Lane, London, for only a small rent. Donne lived here from probably late 1612 to 1621 or 1622 (shortly after he became Dean of St. Paul's), worshipping at St. Clement Danes. A son (Nicholas) was born here in 1613 but died within a year. Donne visited his very good friend and frequent correspondent, Sir Henry Goodyer, during the spring of the year, eventually leaving Goodyer's home to visit Sir Edward Herbert, whose residence was sixty-five miles west of Goodyer's. The journey from one to the other occasioned Donne's "Goodfriday, 1613, Riding Westward." After serving a short time in Parliament in 1614, Donne felt that he had the support of several noblemen in proposing a state appointment for him to King James, but the King convincingly let it be known again that Donne should enter the Anglican Church for his career. By the end of 1614, two more of his children had died (Mary and Francis), and he, with additional gloominess from the utter loss of secular hopes, prepared himself for ordination.

In January, 1615, Donne was ordained as deacon and priest in the Church of England. Once ordained, honors and positions were granted him rapidly. He was appointed Chaplain-in-Ordinary to King James and, by March, had accompanied the King to Cambridge and been granted an honorary Doctor of Divinity degree by the King's Command. Donne began preaching to small parish churches but also preached at Court by April, 1616. From then on, he preached there regularly. In 1616 Donne was granted two benefices (and the consequent income), the rectories of Keyston and Sevenoaks. He was free to remain in London, however, and a curate or vicar residing in the parish would conduct the pastoral care. Further honor and income came from his being chosen Reader in Divinity at Lincoln's Inn, which entailed preaching about fifty sermons per year, but with the aid of a chaplain. By the spring of 1617 Donne's reputation as a preacher secured him an invitation to deliver a sermon at Paul's Cross, a covered pulpit outdoors within the precincts of St. Paul's Cathedral. Typically the sermons at Paul's Cross drew large audiences made up of every level of people, including nobility and those high in the government. The audience at Donne's first sermon there included, for example, Sir Francis Bacon (Lord Keeper) and the Archbishop of Canterbury.

During these early years after taking holy orders, Donne saw his family increase with the birth of Elizabeth (1616). But, tragically, complications from the birth of a stillborn child in 1617 led to the death of his wife five days later (August 15, 1617).

Donne grieved extremely, and, from this point, he turned even more intensely to his clerical calling, to his emotional and intellectual absorption in the Christian life generally. This new direction is clearly expressed in the "Holy Sonnet" beginning "Since she whom I loved," apparently written shortly after Ann's death. Many of his poems and prose pieces after 1617 support the transformation in spiritual feeling that the death of his wife initiated.

King James sent Donne in 1619 as chaplain to accompany Viscount Doncaster on an ambassadorial mission to Germany. Donne did not enthusiastically leave England, with all of his children there and feeling himself rather weak and ill as he prepared for the journey. In fact, many bits of evidence suggest that he foresaw a real possibility of his own death during the trip and that he was putting his worldly affairs in order at the prospect: he sent his unpublished manuscript of *Biathanatos* to Sir Robert Ker, saying to "Reserve it for me, if I live"; in a farewell to Lincoln's Inn he refers to meeting the members in the gates of heaven, if not again here on earth; and he pictures himself, in a letter to Goodyer, as going to face Jesuits, adversaries who hate him. These feelings clearly are concentrated and spiritually resolved in the poem based on this journey, "A Hymn to Christ, at the Author's Last Going into Germany."

Donne returned with the embassy to England in January, 1620, and resumed his normal duties at Lincoln's Inn. Because of his service to the King and new ties with influential men such as Doncaster, however, Donne expected elevation to a higher position in the church and indeed was mentioned during 1620 and 1621 as being among those considered for the position of Dean at Salisbury or at Gloucester, upon vacancy. In fact, Donne felt certain of being named Dean of Salisbury, having been practically assured of it by the now-powerful favorite of King James, George Villiers, Duke of Buckingham. When such did not develop, Donne wrote a rather self-pitying letter to Buckingham in August, 1621, expressing his great disappointment and referring to himself as a "poor worm" and "clod of clay" who wrestles with a "poor fortune" in this world. He reacknowledges his allegiance to Buckingham and submits to his direction for any future possibilities, reverting somewhat to the earlier Donne of courtly hopes, but now applied to ambitions within the English Church hierarchy. His loyalty reaped benefits soon, because the King proposed Donne as Dean of St. Paul's Cathedral in September, after the place had become vacant. Donne attributed this fortune to Buckingham's influence and wrote him a letter expressing his profuse gratitude. Donne

subsequently resigned his position at Lincoln's Inn: the resignation was accepted, with expressions of regret, thanks, and congratulations.

As Dean, Donne performed many administrative duties, but he also continued to preach at Court, St. Paul's, and other places to which he was invited or where he had a benefice. He apparently felt that he was effective as a preacher (a feeling supported by contemporary comments), and he carefully organized and polished his sermons. As he had time, he wrote out many of them fully from his notes after their delivery, and these became the bases for the publications of volumes of sermons printed after his death. Donne used his legal knowledge in several capacities during his years as Dean: he heard appeals at various times from the lower ecclesiastical courts, sat on the Court of Delegates for higher ecclesiastical appeals, served as a Justice of the Peace in some counties in which he held benefices, and sat on the busy and important Court of High Commission for examining ecclesiastical abuses. His personal life was also a full one: the deanery household contained his children, his mother, and several servants. With his new status and sources of income, Donne enjoyed financial bounty, but his letters and those of others show that he also was extremely generous and charitable during his tenure as Dean: he redeemed several from prison, gave charity to prisoners, supported poor scholars in the universities, and gave money to friends in need.

In 1623 Donne delivered the sermon dedicating a new chapel at Lincoln's Inn, one for which he helped raise funds. A contemporary describes the crowd at this sermon as a throng so large that a few people were almost crushed to death. The chapel still stands today. In late November and early December of this year Donne fell seriously ill to a fever that had developed into epidemic proportions in London. Recovery from the fever was lengthy, and Donne used this time to write the book occasioned by his serious illness and then published in 1624, his prose *Devotions Upon Emergent Occasions, and Several Steps in My Sickness.* He also wrote "A Hymn to God the Father" and probably "A Hymn to God my God, in My Sickness" during this same period of illness and recovery.

By March of 1624 Donne had regained his health and strength. At this time he also was made vicar of St. Dunstan's-in-the-West, a parish church near the Inns of Court and one frequented by lawyers and judges. Izaak Walton, the man later to become Donne's first biographer, was also a parishioner. Donne preached two sermons there in April, and he continued to preach

at St. Dunstan's frequently and to maintain a close interest in the matters of the parish, including necessary renovations in the interior of the church.

In March, 1625, King James died. Donne was called on to preach the first sermon to the new king, Charles I. He also preached a tribute by the body of King James on April 26 and walked a few days later in the procession to Westminster Abbey for his burial. That summer Donne visited the Danvers household at Chelsea, staying there much longer than he had intended because of the terrible outbreak of plague in London. In a letter written by Donne from Chelsea he refers to Lady Danvers's son, George Herbert, also being present. The next year, 1626, Donne delivered many sermons: more survive for this year than for any other.

Deaths of family members and friends saddened Donne's life in 1627 and 1628. His daughter Lucy died unexpectedly, followed by the deaths of Sir Henry Goodyer, the Countess of Bedford, Lady Danvers, and Christopher Brooke. Donne preached a memorial sermon on Lady Danvers at Chelsea a few weeks after her funeral. Izaak Walton was present at it, and he says that Donne did "weep, and preach" the sermon. The sermon was later printed, along with some Latin and Greek poems written by George Herbert in memory of his mother.

During 1629 and 1630 Donne continued to preach at various places and to perform his routine ecclesiastical and judicial duties. A government document in 1630 implies that he was one of a few in line for advancement to a bishopric, if such fell vacant; therefore, had Donne lived longer, he likely would have become a bishop. While visiting in the home of his daughter Constance, in the summer of 1630, Donne became ill with a fever. He had to remain there several months, employing some of the time in writing out more sermons from his notes. In December he made his will. In January, 1631, his mother died, and her funeral preceded his return to London.

Donne's haggard appearance shocked people when he returned. Izaak Walton tells how Donne's physician, Dr. Simeon Fox, prescribed milk for twenty days. After ten days Donne quit drinking it, telling Dr. Fox that he did not like milk, that he had drunk it to this point only to please Fox, and that he would have no more of it, even if he could be guaranteed that twenty years would be added to his life. On February 25, at Court, Donne preached his last sermon: witnesses said that he appeared to be an image of the mortification about which he preached and that it was his own funeral sermon (published after his death as *Death's*

Duel). According to Walton, the next day Donne told a friend that
he was full of joy and at peace as he thought over his life, which
he saw God providentially directing away from worldly
employment and into clerical service.   Walton also pictures Donne
saying to this friend, "But at this present time I was in a serious
contemplation of the goodness of God to me, who am less than the
least of his mercies."   Walton has, however, here attributed to
Donne the "motto" of George Herbert ("less than the least of his
mercies") that was not known until Herbert's poems were
published over two years after Donne died—and Walton did not
add this supposed statement by Donne until he revised his *Life of
Donne* in 1658.   Even though this insertion makes some of the
specifics of Walton's account suspect, suggesting that he perhaps
exaggerates Donne's saintliness with his own touches, there may
be a general tone of truth to Donne's preparation for death.

Part of this preparation entailed his own plan for a
monument to be set over his grave in St. Paul's.   Walton tells how
Donne had charcoal fires to warm his study while he posed,
wrapped only in his shroud with knots at head and feet, standing
on a wooden model of an urn, as if rising out of it and out of death
itself at the resurrection.   He closed his eyes and faced east (the
direction from which Christ is to appear at the Second Coming).
An artist sketched a life-sized drawing that Donne kept by his bed
until his death on March 31, 1631. His funeral was on April 3.

The sketch of Donne in his winding-sheet indeed provided
the basis for the marble monument sculpted by Nicholas Stone
after Donne's death (with over one-half of the money for it
donated anonymously by Donne's physician, Dr. Fox).   The
monument was completed in 1632 and put in its place, originally
facing east.   It is the only piece of the Cathedral that survived
intact the Great Fire of London in 1666.   It was preserved through
subsequent time and re-erected in the nineteenth century.   The
monument may be seen today in its niche in the south aisle of the
choir, an appropriate testimony to the endurance of interest in
Donne, himself a figure never scrutinized more than in our own
century.

(For fuller study of Donne's life, see the works cited in my
"Selected Bibliography," especially R.C. Bald's *John Donne: A Life*,
edited by Wesley Milgate.)

DONNE'S WORKS

As customarily classified by titles and/or groups, Donne's major works are as follows:

A. Poetry

> *The Anniversaries*
> 1. *The First Anniversary: An Anatomy of the World*
> 2. *The Second Anniversary: Of the Progress of the Soul*
> *Divine Poems*
> *Elegies*
> *Epicedes and Obsequies*
> *Epigrams*
> *Epithalamions*
> *Holy Sonnets*
> *Metempsychosis* (*The Progress of the Soul*)
> *Satires*
> *Songs and Sonnets*
> *Verse Letters*

B. Prose

> *Biathanatos*
> *Devotions Upon Emergent Occasions*
> *Essays in Divinity*
> *Ignatius His Conclave*
> *Juvenilia: or Certain Paradoxes and Problems*
> *Letters*
> *Pseudo-Martyr*
> *Sermons*

A DONNE DICTIONARY

A

Abednego. See "CHILDREN IN THE OVEN."

Abel. Second son of Adam and Eve. He was a keeper of sheep (foreshadowing Christ as the Good Shepherd). Abel was killed by his brother CAIN and thus suffered the first death after the fall and was the first martyr. See Genesis 4.

Abydos. City in which Leander lived: see HERO.

Accident. *Noun.* A special meaning (from ARISTOTLE) refers to the variable property of any material thing. Compare SUBSTANCE. In some contexts it refers to: (1) something nonessential, (2) anything that happens, (3) anything that happens unexpectedly or by chance.

Accidental. Adjective form of ACCIDENT (see above).

Adamant. *Noun:* magnet or lodestone (loadstone).

Admire. *Verb:* (1) to wonder, marvel, or be surprised; (2) to view with wonder or surprise; (3) to look upon with pleasure or approval or affection.

25

Admit. *Verb*: (1) to allow to enter, to let in; (2) to permit or allow; (3) to acknowledge; (4) to accept as true, to concede as fact.

Aesculapius. In mythology, son of Apollo and Coronis. God of medicine and healing. Restored many to health and raised Hippolytus from the dead: Zeus killed Aesculapius for the latter deed, since Zeus wanted none to have such power.

Aesop. Greek writer of fables in the 6th century B.C., possibly legendary rather than an actual person. The Greek historian Herodotus says that he was a slave on the island of Samos. His tales are anecdotal, usually with human-like animals as the main characters, and give a view of some typical human types. Each fable leads to a moral or lesson.

In one of his *EPIGRAMS* ("Mercurius Gallo-Belgicus") Donne alludes to the supposition that Aesop was a slave. He also refers there to a story that Aesop was purchased because two other slaves told the prospective owner that they knew everything, while Aesop told him that he knew nothing since the other two knew all. Donne refers to this same incident in a sermon preached on Ezekiel 34:19 (see Potter and Simpson edition, X, Sermon 7, p.172). In "Satire 5" (lines 88–91) Donne alludes to the truth of Aesop's fables and particularly to the one of the dog who held meat in his mouth, saw his reflection in the water, tried to grab the meat from the mouth in the reflection, and lost the meat he already had. In a sermon of 1628 (see Potter and Simpson, VIII, Sermon 14, p. 316) Donne refers to the reputed violent death of Aesop as analogous to that of ABEL. Also see FABLE OF KING LOG AND KING STORK.

Aetna. See ETNA.

Affect. *Verb*: (1) to aspire to or seek to obtain, (2) to like or love, (3) to frequent or inhabit, (4) to influence or act upon.

Affection. *Noun*: (1) emotion or feeling; (2) disposition, inclination, mental tendency; (3) fondness; (4) biased feeling.

Affects the metaphysics. See METAPHYSICAL.

Afford. *Verb*: (1) to perform or accomplish, (2) to grant or bestow or give of what one has, (3) to be capable of yielding, (4) to supply from resources or to yield naturally.

Agaric. *Noun*: a mushroom used as a medicine to reduce phlegm (one of the HUMORS) and to reduce fever.

Ague. *Noun*: a fever accompanied by chills and shaking.

Air. *Noun*: (1) one of the four ELEMENTS, (2) the atmosphere or space just above the earth, (3) breath or sigh.

"Air and Angels." One of the *SONGS AND SONNETS,* indeed one of the most complex and debated of the group. Its philosophical background, wordplay, paradoxes, shifting viewpoints, METAPHYSICAL CONCEITS, ambiguous pronoun references, and mingling of humor and seriousness all contribute to the puzzles that each reader ultimately must contend with and solve.

Paradoxically, the man speaking loved the woman addressed before he met her because she seems the abstract ideal of love in a woman that he had formulated in stages for himself (and that previous women did not fully qualify for?). The conceit compares this situation to the way one senses the immaterial presence of an angel before the angel itself appears materially (which it does by taking on a body of air, as medieval philosophy argued—see AQUINAS). But this particular woman herself appears to be a bodiless ideal, a spiritual manifestation, the angel itself (a "lovely glorious nothing"). In attempting to solve his problem of defining and expressing love, the man turns to some assumptions from Renaissance PLATONIC philosophy: as Bembo in Castiglione's *THE COURTIER* says, love originates in the soul and is the means by which the soul enjoys beauty; therefore, the man can say that love is the child of the soul. The child can do no more than its parent, and, since the soul has to act through a body to express itself, similarly the "child" (the speaker's feeling or idea of love) has to take on a body to express itself. One might note in lines 9–10 an example of Donne's ambiguous phrasing that fosters double meaning: (1) love must not be more subtle than its parent (the soul) is and thus must express itself through a body just as the soul does, and (2) love must not only be (i.e., only exist in an ideal of spiritual contemplation) but also do (communicate itself through bodily expression, through physical action). The body assumed by love, then, is the lady's body (her physical characteristics). He thinks that by enjoying her physical beauty his ideal of love will be fulfilled. Donne here cleverly shifts emphasis toward defining the angelic and spiritual entity (previously the lady herself) as now exclusively the speaker's own spiritual love. He attempts, then, to embody his spiritual love in her physical beauty.

But his little ship of spiritual love ("pinnace") is now overloaded with her tremendous physical beauty (the brief conceit centered around a ship at the beginning of the second stanza perhaps anticipated by one of the possible secondary meanings of "SUBTILE" in the first stanza, line 19: possessing the quality of slenderness, in reference to a ship). He discovers (middle of the second stanza) that love can embody itself neither in "nothing" (recalling line 6), the extremely insubstantial and spiritual ideal, nor in the extremely material of bodily, physical beauty. This implies that a combination of physical and spiritual is best, but he expresses it in a witty conceit of his love as the angel (that takes on a body of air and that, as an INTELLIGENCE, directs a Ptolemaic SPHERE) and her love as both the air taken on to serve as the angel's body and as the sphere in which the angel resides. Despite his joking comment at the end about the greater purity of the angel (man's love) compared to air (woman's love), her love for him satisfies the ideal that his love seeks. Their loves combine in a happy medium between the impossible extremes of physical and spiritual, in trying to experience love between body and soul, and, instead, their love partakes of both realms. Additionally, one partner will supply what the other lacks in such a mutual relationship in the real world of love.

Individual interpretation of and disagreement about this poem might center on determining Donne's tones and possible wordplay, especially the relevant multiple meanings from Donne's time of "AFFECT," "ALLOW," "ASSUME," "INHERE," and "SUBTILE," in the poem's context. Is it, for example, possible that Donne is having fun with one of several relevant meanings of "assume" in line 13, one of which might be that love "assumes" a body, when commonly it is the body that "assumes" food, drink, nourishment?

Alchemist. See ALCHEMY.

Alchemy. The "science" or "chemistry" of the Middle Ages and Renaissance that attempted to turn base metals into gold by the use of a "philosopher's stone." Also, these practitioners of alchemy, the alchemists (or "chemics"), wanted to concoct or extract an "elixir" (or "elixir vitae"), a miraculous medicine that supposedly would cure all disease and prolong life. This elixir was also referred to as the "quintessence" (or "fifth essence"), an absolutely pure substance that could purge impurities. It was believed by some to be latent in all matter but that it is what

makes up the heavenly bodies. *One must note that Donne and other writers commonly do not distinguish between the "philosopher's stone" and the "elixir" and the "quintessence," but use these terms interchangeably.* An important part of the combining and distilling apparatus used by the alchemists is the "alembic" or "limbeck," a womb-shaped retort with a rounded, bulbous bottom (referred to by Donne in "LOVE'S ALCHEMY" as the alchemist's "pregnant pot"): in this would be placed the chemicals to be combined, heated, and distilled into a smaller receiving vessel. In Donne's time, alchemy and alchemists were recognized as being fraudulent and as making claims that could not be supported by results—i.e., as the "imposture" designated in "LOVE'S ALCHEMY."
　　　Also see PARACELSUS.

Aldgate. A city gate of London that was rebuilt in 1609.

Alembic. See ALCHEMY.

Alexander's great excess. Phrase in line 252 of "Obsequies to the Lord Harrington," one of the *EPICEDES AND OBSEQUIES*. Alexander the Great mourned so excessively over the death of his friend Hephaestion that he pillaged walls and other defenses of towns to have material to build monuments to Hephaestion (see lines 253–54).

Alleyn, Edward (1566-1626). Respected actor who was Donne's son-in-law for the last three years of Alleyn's life. See DONNE, CONSTANCE.

Allophanes. Character speaking in one of Donne's *EPITHALAMIONS*, the "Epithalamion at the Marriage of the Earl of Somerset" (in the "Eclogue" and at the closing of the poem). The Greek name means "appearing otherwise" or "appearing like another" and thus seems to refer to Donne's friend Sir Robert Ker [see KER, ROBERT (1)] who has the same name as (and was a follower of) Robert Ker, Earl of Somerset, the bridegroom [see KER, ROBERT (2)]. Allophanes asks IDIOS (a character apparently representing Donne himself) why he is not at Court (with its light and warmth) at the marriage, instead having chosen to remain isolated in the cold countryside during Christmas (the marriage being on December 26, 1613). Allophanes speaks of the great generosity, justice, and virtue that Idios misses in the Court of the King (i.e., King JAMES). Idios responds that he knew of all of these qualities and implies that he rather shamefacedly withdrew, since he had "no grace to say" at such a "great feast" (line 96). But he did compose a "nuptial song" (line 99) to celebrate that great marriage and thus presents the "Epithalamion" itself to Allophanes to read. After this reading by his friend, Idios says that he will burn the "paper" now to complete properly his sacrifice, but Allophanes refuses to let him destroy the poem. Allophanes says that he will return to Court and present it to those who will "prize your devotion" (i.e., to Lord and Lady Somerset). (For another view of Allophanes, however, see first essay by Dubrow under "Critical Studies: *Epithalamions*" in "Selected Bibliography.")

Allow. *Verb*: (1) to praise or commend, (2) to approve of, (3) to accept as reasonable or valid, (4) to permit.

Allure. *Verb*: (1) to tempt, entice, charm; (2) to draw to oneself, to draw forth, to elicit.

Almoner. *Noun*: (1) an official who distributes the alms, the charity, of another—i.e., the King or Queen had such an official; (2) one who gives alms.

Amalgamating disparate experience. See DISSOCIATION OF SENSIBILITY.

Amber. *Noun*: (1) ambergris: waxy, oily substance secreted from a whale, used in cooking and in perfumes; (2) yellow translucent fossil resin, used for ornaments, and often found hardened around trapped insects.

Ambrose, Saint (339?–397). Bishop of Milan from 374 to 397. Gave all of his property to the Church and to the poor and advocated a strict way of life. Publicly rebuked and imposed penance on the emperor Theodosius and argued for the Christian emperor being subject to such actions by his bishop. Learned in Neoplatonic philosophy (see PLATONIC). Converted and baptized AUGUSTINE, influencing him in Catholic Neoplatonism. Strengthened Christianity among the nobility and generally in the western world. Famous for his sermons and hymns. He is one of the four traditional "DOCTORS" of the western church. Frequently referred to in Donne's *SERMONS*.

Amiens. City in France where Donne stayed with SIR ROBERT DRURY during their continental journey in 1611–12. While here he wrote one of the *VERSE LETTERS* ("A Letter to the Lady Carey, and Mistress Essex Rich, From Amiens").

Amorous evening star. Phrase (in line 61 of "Epithalamion Made at Lincoln's Inn") that refers to the planet Venus (associated with the goddess of love).

Anatomy. *Noun*: (1) dissection, (2) a body or corpse for dissection, (3) a skeleton, (4) a probing, detailed analysis.

Anatomy of the World, An. See *THE FIRST ANNIVERSARY*.

Anchor. Ancor or Anker River in Warwickshire that ran through GOODYER's estate. See line 25 of "A Letter Written by Sir H. G. and J. D.," one of the *VERSE LETTERS*.

Anchorit(e). A person who withdraws from the world in order to live as a religious recluse in a particular place.

Ancrum, 1st Earl of. See KER, ROBERT (1).

Angel. *Noun*: (1) spiritual beings, above man and below God in the hierarchy of creation, who attend God and serve as ministering spirits and divine messengers (see also HIERARCHY, THE HEAVENLY); (2) an English coin stamped with the image of the Archangel Michael piercing the Dragon (of Revelation). Writers of the sixteenth and seventeenth centuries, including Donne, frequently pun on the word.

Angelica. The heroine of Ariosto's *Orlando Furioso* who is the love object over which pairs of rival suitors fight. She escapes during the fights. Referred to in line 42 of "Satire 5."

Animal spirits. Vapors believed to result from the transformation of VITAL SPIRITS that are carried by the arteries into the brain. Associated with the INTELLECTUAL part of man's nature.

"Anniversary, The." One of the *SONGS AND SONNETS*. (One should not confuse this poem with *THE FIRST ANNIVERSARY* or *THE SECOND ANNIVERSARY*, together referred to as the *Anniversaries*.) The title, whether given by Donne or the compiler of one of the early manuscripts, reflects the passage of one year since the man speaking met the woman addressed. The emphatically-repeated and metrically-stressed "all" in the first several lines builds up impressively many worldly persons and values, only to contrast their ephemeral nature with the love possessed by himself and the lady. Even though a year has passed in their lives and in the lives of all those others being led to destruction by unstoppable mortality, their love is not decaying (and its uniqueness is underlined by the heavy stress on the first syllable of "Only"). Their love is constant and unchanging, with no past or future that can be distinguished from its present.

After booming forth eternal superiority, the poet shocks us with graves and corpses at the beginning of the second stanza. But this serves only to make the lady and other readers sharpen their distinctions: the lover is claiming immortality only for their *spiritual* love, not for their *physical* selves that must decay and die just as inexorably as do all the kings, courtiers, beauties, and others he mentioned previously. The insistence on two separate graves enforces the acceptance of their physical mortality in serious terms, but at the same time injects a bit of moderating humor: after all, if they were still physically together in one grave after death, they would be contradicting the truth inherent in the marriage vow in the Anglican service of matrimony (which he anticipates here that they will be taking?), a vow promising their togetherness only "till death us depart." This is the phrasing in the *Book of Common Prayer* of the Church of England in Donne's time. "Depart" means to sever, divide, separate--i.e., to "divorce." So, the anniversary of their meeting celebrated now may anticipate their future worldly anniversaries of marriage, but that physical togetherness will eventually be broken by death, the ultimate "divorce," he acknowledges. The larger implication, however, is that their spiritual union and undying love will not be destroyed by such physical separation.

In the second stanza, not only does the idea of "anniversary" grow from their one-year acquaintance to future wedding anniversaries, but it begins to accumulate the force of a METAPHYSICAL CONCEIT by implying also the anniversary of a ruler's, a king's, a "prince's" reign (foreshadowed by the mention of kings at the beginning of the poem). So, he and the lady also have governed each other for a year in their own MICROCOSM of a state composed only of themselves. Again, they are superior to ordinary rulers, not only in having a love not subject to decay, but also in possessing a compact world of themselves to exist in for each other exclusively. Lines 17–20 insist that their own souls house love as the only true resident therein (see INMATE), and their souls "then" (after physical death) will PROVE (experience

and/or show the validity of?) "this," a most ambiguous reference
that implies possible multiple interpretations. "This" may refer to
"this (spiritual) love" or to everything said in the first six lines of
the stanza or to the final statement in the stanza ("When bodies to
their graves, souls from their graves remove") or to all of these
assertions. Donne, of course, plays on "graves" in two senses: the
bodies go into literal burial places in the earth, but the bodies are
the burial places of souls out of which the souls arise to ascend to
heaven.

The final stanza asserts the lovers' own continuance
spiritually in heaven where they will be blessed as are all other
souls there. It is on earth that they are superior in status even to
kings, since they enjoy a state in which each is a ruler over and
subject of only one other person. There is fear of "treason" from
only one other citizen in their personal state. These "fears" of
"treason" (i.e., infidelity) are "false" ones, since inconstancy is
impossible in the perfect, mutual love they share. These false
fears and "true fears" will be restrained, held back by the lovers:
"true fears" seem to be those traditional Christian ones of death
and judgment. These fears are mentioned by the minister to the
couple in the Anglican marriage service: "ı require and charge you
(as you will answer at the dreadful day of judgment, when the
secrets of all hearts shall be disclosed) that if either of you know
any impediment why ye may not be lawfully joined together in
matrimony, that ye confess it."

So, even as fears of death and judgment are noted in the
midst of the larger joys of marriage, so does the man here
acknowledge the valid facts of physical death and judgment that
they both will face, only to be able to shove them aside in favor of
the larger spiritual love that exists for them both in this life and
the next. Thus, this first year of their relationship foreshadows
many more on this earth before death: he hopes that they are
able, in this finite life, to know and love each other for a total of
sixty (threescore) years. I feel that Theodore Redpath (see
"Works" in "Selected Bibliography") legitimately corrects
arguments by readers who contend that the speaker simply wants
to *live* sixty years: he wants to *love* sixty years. In fact, the
argument that Donne merely is thinking (as some editors and
critics have said) of "threescore" as the standard span of one's life
designated in the Bible is further undermined by the fact that the
Authorized (i.e., King James) Bible (specifically in Psalm 90)
actually says that our years are threescore and ten—i.e., seventy.
The lover, then, is looking toward fifty-nine more years of love
with the lady, in earthly measurement of time, as they are just

beginning the "second" year of their "reign" of each other (enforcing again the conceit of a king's continuing rule over his state after the celebration of one year on the throne—i.e., his anniversary). However, this ending on a very temporal note designating years in worldly terms seems deliberately transformed by Donne's ambiguity and wordplay into much more important implications: "this" in the last line most obviously refers to "year," and "second" refers to the year after their first one—i.e., "this year is the second year of our reign." But the phrasing might also suggest that "this entire expanse of earthly time, sixty years of loving each other until we physically die, is just a 'second,' only one-sixtieth of a minute, compared to eternal time and to our reign that will continue in the next life, with our love even possibly 'increased there above' (line 19)." Their love ultimately will escape all attempts to place physical and temporal limits on it, whether in the form of bodies, graves, years, or anniversaries.

Anniversaries, The. See *THE FIRST ANNIVERSARY* and *THE SECOND ANNIVERSARY.*

Annunciation. The announcement by the Archangel GABRIEL to MARY of Christ's incarnation, of Mary's selection to be the mother of Christ. A day celebrating the event is the Feast of the Annunciation on March 25.

Anon. *Adverb:* (1) at once, immediately; (2) soon, in a little while.

Antipodes. *Noun:* (1) those who dwell directly opposite to each other on the sides of the earth, (2) those who resemble dwellers on the other side of the earth, (3) places on the surface of the earth that are directly opposite to each other.

Antiquary. *Noun:* a person who studies and collects antiquities, relics of the past.

"Antiquary." See *EPIGRAMS.*

Anyan. A STRAIT referred to in "HYMN TO GOD MY GOD, IN MY SICKNESS" (line 18). Probably the modern Bering Strait that connects the Bering Sea and the Arctic Ocean between Siberia and Alaska.

Aphrodite. See VENUS.

Apostem(e). *Noun*: an abscess, supposedly caused by a collection of excess HUMORS in some part of the body.

Apothecary. *Noun*: a pharmacist, one who mixes and prepares drugs, medicines.

"Apparition, The." One of the *SONGS AND SONNETS*. The man speaking plays on the PETRARCHAN exaggeration that the lady's scorn or rejection would kill, would cause the "death" of the man wooing her. He rages against her scorn, then, by projecting a future in which he finally has been murdered by her unresponsiveness. With rather sadistic glee he imagines returning as a ghost (an "apparition") and terrifying her. The vision he presents of her character implies that she is a hypocrite and sensualist, since he expects her to be in bed with another man, all the while pretending to be a virgin (see FAIN). And he portrays her as having several lovers, one of whom just happens to be the one with her on this occasion ("he whose thou art then"). She seems wanton, too, by the ghostly lover's portrayal of her pinching the man in bed, calling for "more [sexual intercourse]." Part of the comedy in the poem is that the man in bed is imagined as sated and pretending to sleep, rather than willing to participate in "more." The "apparition" frightens her also by remarking that the candle (taper) will flicker, as an old belief says one will with a ghost present. The speaker derives great satisfaction in picturing the woman as pitifully trembling like a white aspen leaf and sweating profusely.

The paleness of her fearful self already has been foreshadowed, in fact, by the "sick," yellow light of the dimming candle and is climaxed by his self-consciously clever paradox that she will be an even truer ("verier") ghost than he. He also is rather viciously associating sickness and disease with the lady, since the candle is "sick" and since she will be in a "quicksilver" sweat: quicksilver is mercury and thus conveys drops of sweat rapidly coursing over her like fast mercury drops; however, the added connotation that a quicksilver sweat bath was the treatment commonly used for syphilis at the time can hardly be avoided here. (For the latter implication, see "Selected Bibliography: Critical Studies, *Songs and Sonnets*," article by Miller and Norton.)

With the speaker's implication that the lady may be the truer "apparition," the reader faces the problem of deciding just who or what is the "apparition"—most obviously it is the man speaking, but also the woman will have the appearance of one. A third "apparition," however, might well be the whole figment of imagination that the man projects for us. Are readers actually receiving a monomaniac's view—a situation real enough for him but lacking substance for us? The speaker's frustration may make us suspicious of accepting his view of the lady at face value: he allows her no defense against his implied accusation that she is a wanton hypocrite. Are his own wounded ego and frustrated desires impelling him to spin out this phantasm of the imagination? Of his ego there can be little doubt, since he pictures the man in bed as one with "worse arms" than his own to embrace the woman. The speaker's obsession also appears in his breathless spewing forth of assertions and images in what seems one lengthy sentence making up the whole poem: no period occurs until the end. The greatest slowing or pause comes after thirteen lines, but most editors still only use a semicolon at that point, just as in the first printed edition of 1633. Certainly the first thirteen lines seem, because of the punctuation, a consecutive presentation of images flooding uncontrollably out of his consciousness. But this unstopping feeling is also enforced by the many uses of "and" and "then" at the beginnings of lines and clauses—connectives that keep the images and reader continuing. Donne further conveys the extremely vivid, strange imaginings of the speaker by the METAPHYSICAL quality of colloquial language, seen best in "pinch" and "sweat."

In this poem, therefore, readers experience images, character slurs, and threats rushing, one after another, out of the speaker's imagination. The lingering question is whether or not the entire vision presented in the poem is the third and most important "apparition," a specter of the speaker's own making.

Approve. *Verb*: (1) to try, (2) to experience, (3) to corroborate or confirm.

Aquinas, Saint Thomas (1225–1274). The most famous and influential of the scholastic philosophers or SCHOOLMEN. Born of a noble family in Italy. Studied the philosophy of ARISTOTLE at the university in Naples and later became a Dominican friar. He taught at Cologne and Paris. Was made a Doctor of Theology at Paris. Later taught in several Italian universities, eventually remaining in Naples. His most famous and influential work is *Summa Theologica*, although it was unfinished at his death: his works reconcile Christianity with the philosophy of Aristotle (about whom he also wrote commentaries). This massive work analyzes parts of creation (including angels, men, the soul, and the body) and discusses righteousness, free will, original sin, the seven virtues (faith, hope, love are added to the four CARDINAL VIRTUES), the Incarnation, seven sacraments, the Word made flesh, and numerous other topics spanning theology, morals, and metaphysics. He argues that reason and revelation do not contradict each other, since God is the author of both reason and revelation.

Donne frequently alludes to Aquinas in the *SERMONS*, but the ideas of Aquinas appear in many of Donne's other works, as well. For example, the belief that angels assume bodies of air in order to manifest themselves to humans, as used by Donne in "AIR AND ANGELS," appears in *Summa Theologica*.

Archangels. See HIERARCHY, THE HEAVENLY.

Aretine (Aretino), Pietro (1492–1556). Poet who wrote the sonnets accompanying erotic paintings by Guilio Romano. Donne (as well as the English in general) mistakenly attributed the paintings also to Aretino; therefore, he refers to them as "Aretine's pictures" in line 70 of "Satire 4." He also is depicted as one of the pretended "innovators" in Hell in *IGNATIUS HIS CONCLAVE*.

Argus. The giant of Greek mythology that had 100 eyes and was appointed to guard Io. Also see MERCURY.

Aristotle (384–322 B.C.). Greek philosopher. Studied under PLATO for twenty years. Was tutor to Alexander the Great. Established a school (the Lyceum) in Athens and taught there for twelve years. His thought survives largely in his and/or his students' lecture notes, and his study covers all realms of knowledge in his time. His influence dominated thought for 2,000 years after him, reaching its height in the Middle Ages when he was idolized as the final word on all knowledge: he was particularly central to the SCHOOLMEN. In logic, his development of deductive reasoning held sway until the scientific advances following BACON and the rise of science and induction in the 17th century. Ultimately disagreed with and challenged Plato and PLATONIC thought, arguing rather for the reality of the physical and material world, and for the duality of body and spirit. In contrast to an idealistic mode of thought, Aristotle tends toward the pragmatic, the practical: *Nicomachean Ethics, Politics*, and *Poetics* treat conduct, government, and literature in this light.

Many of the assumptions underlying both NATURAL ORDER and the view of the universe ascribed to PTOLEMY have their sources in Aristotle, especially in his *Metaphysics*. He envisions a ranked, hierarchical nature that leads to the pure Unmoved Mover at the top that is the source of all energy in the universe. His philosophy was ultimately brought into agreement with major Christian conceptions and was embraced by the church.

The ideas of intelligences directing the SPHERES, of the human TRIPARTITE SOUL, and of the four ELEMENTS owe much to Aristotle, and they frequently appear in Donne and other writers of his time. Donne also refers to and uses Aristotle's conception of man as a MICROCOSM. Donne, as others, at times refers to Aristotle simply as "THE PHILOSOPHER."

Artist. *Noun*: (1) learned person, (2) astrologer, (3) ALCHEMIST, (4) astronomer.

As. Frequently means "that" and "since" (or "because").

"As due by many titles I resign." First line of one of the *HOLY SONNETS*. In the Italian SONNET form the speaker asserts and proves that he is God's (in the octave), and then he turns to the question of why Satan takes something that he does not own (the speaker) and urges God to fight for his property (the speaker). The dominating imagery through the sonnet is legal (contracts, property, things bought and sold).

In the first two lines the speaker asserts that he is God's because of the many "titles" (legal rights) by which God possesses him. In lines 2–8 he lists those titles: (1) he was made by and for God; (2) God's blood (through Christ's crucifixion) "bought" back (i.e., redeemed) his "decayed" (i.e., sinful) self—see also the reference to himself as a work that has decayed in the *Holy Sonnet* beginning "Thou hast made me, and shall thy work decay?"; (3) he is God's "sun" that should shine with God's light, including a serious play on "sun" as "son": just as Christ is the Son of God whose light came into the world, each human ideally should be the son of the Son and should shine with Christ's light; (4) he is God's servant whom God has always ("STILL") "repaid" for his work, as a good master should; (5) he is God's sheep (following the Good Shepherd); (6) he is God's image (created in God's image); and (7) he is the temple of God's spirit (in I Corinthians 3:16 St. Paul says, "Know ye not that ye are the temple of God, and that the Spirit of God dwelleth in you?").

After the relatively moderate, logical tone and feeling of the octave, the speaker becomes more emotional in the sestet. He is indignant at Satan but also at God. Satan has had the audacity to "usurp" (seize or overthrow) the speaker who belongs to God (i.e., sin has taken over the speaker). He not only "steals" God's property: the speaker says that he does also "RAVISH" the property (here the sense is to seize and carry it off violently). Line 10 conveys through harsh sounds (such as the repeated "s") and many heavy stresses the feelings of anger and forcefulness that the statement and imagery declare. The last four lines express his disappointment with and indignation at God whom the speaker takes to task for supposedly being so unconcerned about this piece of property: "EXCEPT" (i.e., unless) God rises and fights for His property against Satan's usurpation, then matters look bleak for the speaker. (As in much of Donne's Christian poetry and prose, this sinner seems helpless in his sinful state and has to rely on God's power and grace: the speaker cannot himself rectify his sinful state.) He ends on a resentful, sarcastic, and paradoxical note: it seems quite ironic and unbelievable to this speaker that God professes love for all of mankind but (or so it appears to the speaker) will not direct this love to this individual person speaking. Also, it is paradoxical that Satan hates any human and is out ultimately to destroy everyone, but is making a supreme effort to obtain each soul now on earth (the speaker's implied slap in God's face being that God is not showing that He either loves or wants the speaker and thus is doing much less than His old foe Satan is). The accusatory, argumentative, challenging, and questioning tones felt in this sonnet typify several of the *HOLY SONNETS*.

Ascapart (Askapart). A giant, thirty feet tall, in the medieval romance concerning Bevis of Hampton. Donne, in line 233 of "Satire 4," designates the guards at the Queen's chamber as "Ascaparts."

Aspersion. *Noun*: sprinkling or scattering.

Assume. *Verb*: (1) to adopt or take, (2) to receive into heaven, (3) to take food or drink into the body, (4) to take upon or put on, (5) to lay claim or usurp.

"At the round earth's imagined corners blow." First line of one of the *HOLY SONNETS*. In the octave of this Italian SONNET the speaker is a Christian ready for the end of the world and the

Last Judgment. He wants to see the four angels standing on the four corners of the earth blowing their trumpets (see Revelation 7:1) and the resurrection of all souls to be reunited with the scattered parts of their bodies around the earth in preparation for Judgment. He includes in his address for assembly all of those who died in the Old Testament flood, all who will die from the fire that will end the world (see II Peter 3:10), all who have died of every imaginable cause (which the speaker lists in lines 6–7, including "despair" [desperation in one to cause murder or suicide], "law" [death penalties through legal processes], and "chance" [misfortune, accident]), and even all those who will be alive at the Last Judgment (see Luke 9:27). Donne conveys the drama and grandeur of the unfathomable massiveness in such an assembly by the inclusive listings and by repetition and heavy stresses on "all." The speaker of this sonnet does not envision the soul ascending to heaven and leaving the body behind. Instead, he sees the soul and body both in a suspended state, a sleep until Judgment, at which time they both rise and then reunite and are judged. In the octave the speaker seems quite confident and eagerly anticipates and calls for Judgment and his seemingly-assured salvation.

The sestet, however, presents the speaker suddenly fearful and having misgivings, as if he has paused to think and has had second thoughts. The change in his attitude is evident in the word "But" that begins the sestet. He reverses himself by asking God to, after all, wait a bit longer before he causes the end of the world and the resurrection of the dead ("let them sleep"). He needs more time himself to feel sorrow and repent fully of his sins to be confident to face Judgment (the nasal sounds in "and me mourn" enforce the sense of melancholy mournfulness). He feels that his sins may be too abundant at present and that it will be too late to ask for God's abundant grace at the Last Judgment ("there" at the time and place one faces Christ). He wishes to have God teach him "here" and now on earth ("this lowly ground") how to repent truly and fully. Then he will be assured of salvation, of Christ's blood applying to him, of the cleansing of his sin, and of Christ's wish to SEAL personally the speaker's pardon. By wanting to know how to repent, this Christian has taken the first important step to overcome his fear of Judgment and to assure his salvation.

One should compare and contrast this sonnet with the one beginning "THIS IS MY PLAY'S LAST SCENE, HERE HEAVENS APPOINT."

Atlanta (Atalanta). In mythology, Atalanta wanted to remain a virgin, although her beauty attracted men. A fleet runner, she agreed only to marry a man who could beat her in a race. To distract her, Hippomenes threw down three golden apples he had acquired from APHRODITE. Atalanta paused to pick them up, lost the race, and married Hippomenes.

Attend. *Verb*: (1) to pay attention to or consider or listen to; (2) to apply oneself to; (3) to wait upon or serve or accompany; (4) to wait for or expect; (5) to wait or stay.

Augustine, Saint (354–430). Bishop of Hippo in Africa from 396 to 430. Recognized as one of the greatest thinkers, writers, and theologians in Christianity. His mother (Monica) was a devout Christian and continually wished Augustine to become one. He lived a rather dissolute early life, with a mistress and an illegitimate son. At the age of 28 he went to Milan as a teacher of rhetoric where he heard AMBROSE preach and was impressed by his use of Neoplatonic philosophy (see PLATONIC). He experienced a mystical conversion in Milan that was confirmed by a reading of St. Paul. He turned more ascetic and philosophical. He was baptized by Ambrose in 387. On his return to Africa his mother died, just after a conversation between mother and son on the ascent to heaven and its glories. After returning to Africa, he became assistant priest to the bishop at Hippo, and, after the bishop's death, Augustine was made Bishop in 395 and remained so until his death during the siege of the city by the VANDALS.

Augustine wrote sermons, commentaries, essays, and letters. Two of his works, however, are his most famous and influential. His *Confessions* detail his early life and conversion, expressing extreme guilt for the sexual and other sins of his youth. *The City of God* proposes that there are two cities in existence vying for man's adherence, Jerusalem and Babylon or the heavenly city and the earthly city or the city of God and the city of man. Although heavily influenced by PLATONIC philosophy and its ability to be reconciled with some facets of Christianity, Augustine increasingly saw the differences. He could agree that looking into himself at his own soul can reveal God and felt that he could find in God the author of all and the illuminator of truth. He is one of the four traditional "DOCTORS" of the western church.

Augustine's formulation of the concept of the BOOK OF CREATURES heavily influenced Donne in all of his works. It is in his prose (especially the *SERMONS*), however, where Donne's respect for and use of Augustine particularly appears: he is alluded to many times in the *SERMONS*. Donne refers to Augustine's *Confessions* frequently, probably perceiving parallels to his own life, especially his own early worldliness and the later change in direction and ultimate service for God. Donne also refers to *The City of God* and to Augustine's adaptation of Platonism. Donne primarily agrees with Augustine's views, such as the pervasiveness of original sin in humanity; however, he also refutes him on some major points (disagreeing, for example, with Augustine's [and with CALVIN's later formulations of such Augustinian thought] arguments for predestination and the elect, as opposed to the power of individual free will).

"Autumnal, The." See "ELEGY 9: THE AUTUMNAL."

Ave. Latin meaning "Hail!" Used for greeting or bidding farewell. The greeting of GABRIEL to MARY at the ANNUNCIATION.

Azores. Islands about 900 miles west of Portugal (also called St. Michael's Islands). In 1597 Donne sailed with an English expedition directed at the Azores to intercept Spanish ships from GUIANA, but a storm forced the ships back to port in Plymouth (see "The Storm," one of the *VERSE LETTERS*). Queen Elizabeth would not allow the expedition to sail directly to the West Indies to intercept the Spanish treasure. After sailing again and reaching the Azores, the ships encountered a calm that kept them immobilized for two days (see "The Calm," one of the *VERSE LETTERS*). Donne may have been on one of the ships under Sir Walter Raleigh's command this time, rather than on one under DEVEREUX. Although the expedition took a little treasure, most of it escaped capture: the expedition to the Azores was a failure. See also CADIZ.

B

B., B. Person addressed in one of the *VERSE LETTERS* ("To Mr. B.B."). The "poem" actually is made up of two sonnets, and they probably mistakenly were printed together originally. The recipient has not been certainly identified, but most editors and scholars feel that he is Beaupré Bell, a Cambridge graduate who proceeded to LINCOLN'S INN in 1594 while Donne was there. In the first sonnet Donne tells him to "wean" himself from "Cambridge thy old nurse" and now to "chew" and "digest" "volumes of our common law." In the second, Donne denigrates his own feeble attempts at rhymes which are "profane" and "imperfect."

B., C. See BROOKE, CHRISTOPHER.

B., S. See BROOKE, SAMUEL.

Babel, Tower of. The tower of brick erected by men who wanted its top to reach to heaven. God, seeing their pride, confounded their language so that they could no longer understand each other. They then ceased their building and scattered to various parts of the earth. See Genesis 11:1–9.

Bacon, Sir Francis (1561-1626). Studied and practiced law, served in Parliament, and held the position of Lord Keeper of the Great Seal under Queen ELIZABETH. His advancement was even more rapid under King JAMES, serving as Solicitor General, Attorney General, Lord Keeper, and Lord Chancellor. Knighted in 1603, created first Baron Verulam in 1618, and made Viscount St. Albans in 1621, Bacon accumulated many political enemies, and he was tried and convicted by the House of Lords in 1621 on the charge of accepting bribes as a judge. He was barred from holding public office: thus in public disgrace, Bacon retired to his estate to concentrate more on philosophical and scientific speculations and proposals and on writing. His *Essays* had first appeared in 1597, but subsequent editions through 1625 expanded their number. His most influential works are *The Advancement of Learning* (1605) and *Novum Organum* (1620), containing key proposals in his visionary plan to refute Aristotelian and medieval authority and means of reasoning. Bacon proposes the inductive (or scientific) method of arriving at truth, wishing to eliminate the human tendency to be misled by subjectivity. Bacon's works placed him in the vanguard of the rise of science, endorsing both an attitude of objective observation of physical matter outside of the individual and an increase of practicality and utility in outlook in the seventeenth century. His *New Atlantis*, proposing a type of scientific Utopia, appeared a year after his death.

Bacon had a close working relationship with SIR THOMAS EGERTON, and Donne undoubtedly knew Bacon through him. As revealed in a letter by Donne, Bacon was the one who introduced Donne to SIR JAMES HAY. Donne, as many others, was a bit bitter about how vociferously Bacon prosecuted ROBERT DEVEREUX, Earl of Essex, but apparently was able to establish a friendship again with Bacon in spite of this disillusionment: later Donne refers to Bacon's many "favors" for him. Bacon also attended Donne's first sermon at PAUL'S CROSS (March 24, 1617).

Bait. *Verb*: (1) to stop to refresh and rest, (2) to make a brief stop, (3) to furnish a hook or trap with a bait, (4) to use dogs to bite and annoy other animals (such as bulls or bears) for sport.

"Bait, The." One of the *SONGS AND SONNETS*. It, along with Sir Walter Raleigh's "The Nymph's Reply," is a response to and parody of Christopher MARLOWE's "The Passionate Shepherd to His Love" (which also begins "Come live with me, and be my love"). Marlowe's PASTORAL ideal of a shepherd and shepherdess described decoratively and with vivid sensuousness (beds of roses, buckles of gold) is undercut by Donne's bawdy, physically realistic play around the pastoral and PETRARCHAN conventions in the poem. The first two stanzas lull the reader into an apparently Marlovian world, with the sensuous appeal to gold, crystal, silk, and silver, as well as the picture of the apparently ideal Petrarchan lady whose eyes are brighter and warmer than the sun. The poem at first, then, seems a conventional one of compliment.

Beginning with the third stanza and the speaker's imagining of the lady swimming in the nude, however, Donne turns the surface ideal into covert bawdiness and sensuality by pressing his images with increasingly realistic and bawdy connotations. The speaker pictures "others" very unpleasantly freezing with cold and cutting their legs to catch fish, and some try to reach under the river banks to grab fish and pull them out of their "slimy" retreats—an appropriately METAPHYSICAL colloquialism to convey a vividly non-pastoral scene. But the amorous "fish" in these stanzas had already been used by writers for explicitly bawdy suggestions, specifically connoting the male sexual organ. Similarly, one strongly suspects Donne of employing "channel," "nest," and "banks" to connote elements of the female anatomy. The scene of hands groping for "bedded fish" in a "slimy nest" recalls Shakespeare's implications in *Measure for Measure* when Pompey points out a man being carried away to prison for "doing" a woman. Mistress Overdone then asks, "But what's his offense?" Pompey replies, "Groping for trouts in a peculiar river." Mistress Overdone immediately responds, "What, is there a maid with child by him?" (A similar suggestion about the bawdy undertones is made by Docherty, pp. 235–36: see "Critical Studies, Poetry: Miscellaneous" in "Selected Bibliography.")

In essence, Donne takes his poem quite far from Marlowe's prototype and wittily transforms the Petrarchan and pastoral world into one of ulterior sexuality and realistic physical motives in the man's invitation to love and in his attraction to the "bait" that will satisfy his own (his "fish's"?) appetite.

Bajazet(h). The Emperor of the Turks put into a cage by Tamburlaine, the former Scythian shepherd, where he is mocked. In MARLOWE's *Tamburlaine the Great, Part 1.* See "The Calm," line 33.

Ballast. *Verb*: to furnish or load a ship's hold with heavy material to make it steady.

Balm. *Noun*: (1) aromatic substance exuding from some trees and valued for fragrance and medicinal qualities, (2) a soothing and healing substance, (3) according to PARACELSUS, the life-preserving fluid existing in every living being, the absence of which means death.

Balsamum. *Noun*: same as BALM (3).

Banks, Mr. See WISE POLITIC HORSE.

Basilisk. Synonymous with COCKATRICE.

"Batter my heart, three-personed God, for you." First line of one of the *HOLY SONNETS.* The sinner speaking in this Italian SONNET calls on the TRINITY ("three-personed God") to exert all the power that can be mustered to free him from sin. In a METAPHYSICAL CONCEIT this idea is expressed in military, warlike terms as he calls on God to "batter" his heart, as if his heart were the gate to a walled city (himself) within which the soul resides. The impressive force placed by heavily stressing the first syllable of "batter" (reversing the expected iambic foot) and by the plosive "b" sound in the same syllable conveys the sense of power he is calling on from God, power like that of a battering ram to break open the gate. This military analogy of the sinner as a fortified city pervades the octave and is made most explicit in line 5 ("I, like an usurped town") The usurper of this town is Satan (God's "enemy" in line 10). So, the speaker himself being overcome by sin is expressed as a city belonging to God being overrun and taken over by Satan. The sinner (as in some other of Donne's Christian poems) berates God a bit to urge Him to further and more decisive action on the sinner's behalf: in line 2 the sinner says that "You" (God) "as yet but" (i.e., up to now "You" [God] "only") "knock, breathe, shine and seek to mend." The speaker implies that God must do more than these things, that these actions are insufficient to rescue him from sin. The three actions ("knock, breathe, shine") reflect the "three-personed God" of line 1: "knock" is the action of God the Father and his power, but this power must be intensified in order to break through this sinner's hard heart; "breathe" reflects the role of the Holy Spirit breathing grace; and "shine" connotes the light from Christ the Son (see TRINITY). These three actions can at best "mend," only partially or temporarily repair this town/sinner. What is needed, the speaker urges, is a complete destruction of the "old man" (the old town, the old sinful self as a MICROCOSM) so that a completely new, regenerated town/man can be constructed from the foundation up. This Christian idea of complete regeneration is expressed in the double paradox of lines 3–4: he needs to be "overthrown" in order to "rise and stand," and he needs to be broken, blown, and burned to be made "new." Destruction of the sinful generates the pure, in Christian terms. Donne constructs lines 2 and 4 carefully as parallels and contrasts. The sinner does not want merely to be mended by God, but to be made new. He does not want God the Father just to "knock," but to "break"; he does not want the Holy Spirit just to "breathe," but to "blow"; he does not want Christ the Son just to "shine," but to "burn." The sequence of three in both line 2 and line 4 reflects the Trinity, the three persons in the same order in each line. But the latter series presents intensifications in the actions of those persons. And "break, blow, burn" carries the full force of God in all three persons, especially with the added power from the three plosive "b" sounds beginning each word. This sinner needs all the power that all three persons can gather to free him from sin (Satan).

In lines 5–8 the speaker tells God that he himself is trying to admit God back into this town of himself but "to no end" (i.e., he is not able to accomplish the task). Personified "Reason" is God's "viceroy" within the town of himself (i.e., reason is man's Godlike quality within each individual that is to help the person choose both the true and the good), and Reason ideally should have defended the speaker from sin. But sin apparently is more powerful than reason, taking it captive or finding it to be a traitor to God's town (the individual person). So, as in several of Donne's Christian works, the role of faith is quite essential to ward off sin: reason alone cannot do it. And God's grace and power are essential to restore man to a sense of his redeemed status after he has fallen into sin. So, he has called on God's power in a military conceit primarily in the OCTAVE.

In the SESTET Donne shifts emphasis to another conceit or motif: the speaker addresses God as a lover and describes his wish to be reconquered by Him in terms of love, sexuality, and marriage. Commonly the soul was referred to as feminine (see discussion of "SINCE SHE WHOM I LOVED HATH PAID HER LAST DEBT"). The speaker loves God and would like gladly ("FAIN") to be loved in return. But the feminine soul feels that she has been forced into a marriage with the conqueror and usurper Satan (i.e., sin): the speaker feels "betrothed unto Your enemy." So, he calls on God to use his power to "divorce" the sinner from Satan, to "untie" or "break" the marital "knot" of the soul with Satan. And then God should take the soul to God: the sinner wants God to "imprison" and "enthrall" him: both words express enchantment and capture in a love relationship, but also both words can apply to military capture and enslavement; therefore, both conceits or motifs come together here. God's power and love are sought by the speaker. Line 13 expresses a paradox ("EXCEPT You enthrall me, [I] never shall be free"): unless God completely dominates and controls the speaker, then the speaker never shall be free. For restriction to give freedom seems quite contradictory, but Donne is calling attention to the Christian truth that true freedom is only enjoyed by the soul that is completely controlled by God. An even more shocking paradox is stated in line 14: "Nor [shall I] ever [be] chaste, EXCEPT [i.e., unless] You RAVISH [here, primarily meaning 'rape'] me." For a rape to give chastity is contradictory in ordinary physical terms, but being ravished by God (taken over completely) gives the soul purity. Spiritual purity comes to an individual's soul when God takes it completely.   This paradox is the high point of the love motif in the sestet.

So, the speaker asks for *spiritual* conquest by God in metaphorical terms as *military* and *sexual* conquest throughout the sonnet.   These conceits express his senses of deep entrapment by sin and the necessity for God's power and love to rescue him.

A sonnet such as this one also illustrates a recurring motif in some of Donne's Christian poems: the speaker describes his religion in terms of love (just as in some of Donne's secular poems the speaker describes his love in terms of religion).

(This particular one of the *HOLY SONNETS* probably is the most-debated of the nineteen—see, for example, only a sample of such studies noted in the "Selected Bibliography.")

Battery. *Noun*: (1) bombardment by artillery upon a fortress or city, (2) pieces of artillery.

Bays. *Noun*: leaves of the laurel, traditionally depicted as woven into a garland or wreath and used to reward poets and poetic achievement.

Bearbaiting. See BAIT (4).

Becomes. *Verb*: (1) comes to be, (2) befits or suits.

Bedford, Lucy Harrington (Russell), Countess of (1581–1627).   Patroness to Donne, JONSON, and other writers.   Was godmother to LUCY DONNE.   Married to Edward Russell, 3rd Earl of Bedford, in 1594, she possessed and frequented several residences, the primary one being the estate of Twickenham Park on the banks of the Thames River at TWICKENHAM, visited and referred to by Donne.   King JAMES and his Queen regarded the Countess highly, and she was made one of the Ladies of the Bedchamber at Court.

She was Donne's primary benefactor from 1607 to 1614, supporting him financially and socially.   In contrast, her husband referred to Donne as "that fool poet."   Donne greatly praised her intellect, charm, and beneficence in letters to his friends, as well as in seven *VERSE LETTERS* to her (most of them titled simply "To the Countess of Bedford").   In one (beginning "Reason is our Soul's left hand") he refers to her as "The first good Angel, since the world's frame stood, / That ever did in woman's shape appear" (lines 31–32).   In several of these verse letters he equates her with the shining essence of virtue and spirit, thus implying a serious play on her name *Lucy*, as originating from the Latin for *light*. In the one beginning "This twilight of two years" Donne attributes his poetic talent to her inspiration: he says that his verse is built of her praise (line 21). His most interesting and famous tribute is "TWICKNAM GARDEN," one from the *SONGS AND SONNETS*. By the time Donne was ordained he had secured other patrons and patronesses, a fact that weakened the strength of his former ties to Lady Bedford. Despite her statement that she wished to pay off his debts before he entered the Church, she was ultimately unable to do so because of her own financial obligations. Donne expressed in a letter to SIR HENRY GOODYER his disappointment and bitterness about the inadequate sum she did give. She also had come increasingly under the influence of a Puritan clergyman/physician (John Burges) who had criticized Donne's earlier life. Although their relationship was not as strong as before he entered the Church, Donne preached before the Countess on occasion and remained a friend until her death. See also: LADY MARKHAM, MISTRESS BOULSTRED, and JUDITH.

Bedlam. A hospital in London established specifically as an asylum for the insane. The name is a variant of "Bethlehem": the hospital was Bethlehem Hospital (actually St. Mary of Bethlehem). In Donne's time the original hospital, located in Bishopsgate, was still in use.

Bedstave. *Noun*: a stick used to hold bedsheets in place. Used in female masturbation, as well: see "Elegy 2: The Anagram," lines 53–54.

Behind. *Adverb*: (1) [spatially] in the back of or toward the rear of; (2) [temporally] following in time, later.

Bell(s). See DEATH BELL, FUNERAL BELL, and PASSING BELL.

Bell, Beaupré. See B., B.

Bench, the. The Court of Queen's Bench.

Benefit of Clergy. Legal claim that a literate criminal could make to save his life by being given a punishment lesser than capital. If he could read the opening of Psalm 51 (called the "neck-verse" because to read it would save one's neck) which asks for mercy, he would be spared under the assumption that he can still do some good in the future with his ability. Donne refers to the claim, for example, in lines 11–13 of "Satire 2."

Benight. *Verb*: (1) to involve in darkness, to darken, to cloud; (2) to blind, to dazzle.

Bernard, Saint, of Clairvaux (1091–1153). Born in a noble French family and was learned and devout. The first abbot of a monastery established at Clairvaux. In a controversy over the doctrine of the immaculate conception (i.e., that MARY, unlike all other humans, was free of original sin from her own conception), Bernard argued against the belief, feeling that only Christ enjoys such a distinction. Reputed to be one of the holiest of men, Bernard was regarded later by LUTHER as worthy of higher esteem than could be accorded all other monks and priests on earth. Luther's admiration is understandable, since Bernard saw corruptions in the Roman Catholic Church and worked for their correction, did not hesitate to berate the Pope, and believed in the doctrine of the real presence of Christ (rather than the doctrine of TRANSUBSTANTIATION) in the elements of the Eucharist.

Donne refers to St. Bernard frequently in his *SERMONS*. Bernard's writing emphasizes mystical experience, faith, God's grace, and ascension from bodily to spiritual love. His major works include sermons, meditations, and treatises.

Bethany. See BETHINA.

Bethina. Another name for Bethany, a place near Jerusalem that some traditions and Donne associated with the home of MARY MAGDALENE. It was the home of Mary, Martha, and Lazarus. In "To the Lady Magdalen Herbert, of St. Mary Magdalen" Donne associates MAGDALEN HERBERT with the saint by name, by devotion, and by inheritance of family land: in Mary Magdalene's case, he assumes that she inherits holdings in Bethina and Magdalo (Magdala, a town on the Sea of Galilee, more commonly regarded as the home of Mary Magdalene).

Betray. *Verb*: (1) to reveal or to disclose something or someone, (2) to place into the hands of an enemy by treachery, (3) to expose to punishment, (4) to be false or disloyal.

Bewray. *Verb*: to reveal, expose, or discover.

Beza, Theodore (1519–1605). CALVINIST theologian who translated the Greek New Testament into Latin. Referred to in line 55 of "Satire 4" and in several of Donne's sermons.

Bezar. A hard, stonelike substance taken from the intestines of mountain goats and used as an antidote against poison.

Biathanatos. Prose work by Donne written about 1607–1608 and described by him in a letter of 1619 to a friend [see SIR ROBERT KER (1)] as a "book written by Jack Donne, and not by D[octor] Donne." Donne also told Ker in the letter that the work is "misinterpretable" and should not be published: it remained only in manuscript during Donne's life and was not published until his son did so in 1647. Donne means the title to be the modern equivalent of "Suicide." The piece was written during the period in which he and his family were living at MITCHAM, a time of melancholy and depression from many illnesses and from general insecurity about Donne's prospects for a career and for financial stability. A kind of subtitle or comment on the title page following the title itself states the general thesis: "A Declaration of that Paradox, or Thesis, that Self-homicide is not so Naturally Sin, that it may never be otherwise. Wherein the Nature, and the extent of all those Laws, which seem to be violated by this Act, are diligently surveyed."

In his "Preface" Donne says that he has had often a "sickly inclination" to commit suicide, attributing this to several possible causes, including the fact that he grew up among Roman Catholics (of "a suppressed and afflicted religion") who were accustomed to despise death and to seek an "imagined martyrdom." He says that he has the "keys of my prison in mine own hand, and no remedy presents itself so soon to my heart as mine own sword." Meditating on this has caused him to interpret the acts of those committing suicide charitably and to attack the reasons of individuals that peremptorily judge those who kill themselves.

The book is divided into three parts and a brief conclusion. Part 1 ("Of Law and Nature"), Part 2 ("Of the Law of Reason"), and Part 3 ("Of the Law of God") cover the three areas in which and by which suicide ordinarily is condemned as a sin. Even though Donne ultimately grants that suicide, like the murder of another, should be condemned by law, he takes pains to point out that there are exceptional cases in each of the three areas that justify suicide. An animal killing itself to feed its young is an example of an exception to the general law of nature (Part 1); a person willing to let himself die to save another is an example of an exception to the general law of reason (Part 2); one who kills himself for God's glory (e.g., Samson) is an example of an exception to the general law of God. In the "Conclusion" Donne notes how he has shown through the work some of the justifications of and benefits from suicide, in the face of larger general rules and reasons against it. He says that part of his motive in the work is to counteract the attitudes that death is a horrible punishment and that one should love and cling to this earthly life as happiness. But, quite significantly, Donne implies that people who can easily distinguish proper suicide from sinful suicide (distinctions he calls "obscure" and "slippery") are unique and that our birth and death are best under "God's determination," rather than under "our election." Donne's sense of man's fallen nature (with its fallen reason) leads him, then, to agree that overall assent to law against suicide is best, although there are legitimate exceptions that the ordinary person cannot determine. And this conclusion to a lengthy work that seems to argue otherwise creates quite assuredly that "paradox" mentioned on the title page. (To study this work more fully and specifically, one should begin with the several separate editions of it [most with helpful introductions, notes, glossaries, etc.] cited in the "Selected Bibliography.")

Bill, the (plaguy). Bill of mortality. A sheet posted every week in London parishes during an epidemic of plague that indicated the number of victims who had died.

Bird-lime. *Noun*: a sticky substance used to smear on branches (lime-twigs) to catch and hold birds. Made from the sticky sap of the holly plant.

Blast. *Verb*: (1) to blow violently, (2) to wither.

Block. *Noun*: (1) a piece of wood, (2) a log, (3) a piece of wood on which beheading occurs, (4) a person of little or no intelligence, a blockhead, a numbskull.

Bloods, mingle. See MINGLE BLOODS.

"Blossom, The." One of the *SONGS AND SONNETS*. The man speaking foreshadows in the first stanza (with the picture of the flower) the fate of his own heart in the rest of the poem: the second stanza makes the analogy to his heart explicit. The naive optimism of his own heart's lofty expectations (as it faces the desired lady) will collapse because of her PETRARCHAN frosty rejection, just as a flower withers and falls in the face of a wintry blast. The METAPHYSICAL CONCEIT of the heart becomes complex, however, by being also secondarily pictured as a bird hovering and wishing to NESTLE in the tree. The tree that the poor, simple, innocent flowerlike and birdlike heart wishes to reside in is the lady, of course. But she is "forbidden" and "forbidding" like the Tree of Knowledge (here, physical knowledge?) in the Garden of Eden, representing the man's means of falling through passionate temptation. Literally, she may have the Petrarchan lady's typical pride or even may be married. The lady also is pictured as a sun, albeit a cold one, that makes the man and, ordinarily, his heart give up trying to bask in her nonexistent rays, in favor of leaving to follow the literal sun's course. But his heart is stubborn (stanza 3) and wishes to separate itself (as a representative of emotion and intellect) from the man's body (the physical, sensual, and lustful self).

The man speaks to his self-superior heart sarcastically in the fourth stanza, at the same time expressing his bitterness toward the lady by denigrating her and her unresponsiveness to him. He implies that she "wouldn't even know a heart if she were to see one": she has none herself and recognizes no semblance of real affection. Caustically, he implies that, even though she will not respond either to his own heart or body, she apparently does respond physically to other men: she has had experience with "some other part" of them, obviously their sexual part. He drives home his innuendo with the repetition of "KNOW," setting up the pun on its sexual connotation immediately preceding "some other part."

The last stanza gives the final admonition to his heart (his feeling, his emotional inclination): if it lingers in the vicinity of the lady, rather than accompanies him as he physically leaves, it is a fool and is destined to become only a shrunken blossom. In contrast, he himself will thrive in society: the play on "STILL" enforces his own refusal to continue to stagnate in an unmoving manner. He urges his heart at least finally to leave this garden of futility and rejoin him in London, thus reuniting his own body and mind. The final slap at this unresponsive lady comes with his prediction that there will be a "friend," a real woman, in London who will respond to him both physically and emotionally.

Blunham. Village in Bedfordshire where, beginning in 1622, Donne held a church living as rector, visiting the church and preaching there for a few weeks yearly. He gave the church an inscribed silver-gilt chalice, dated 1626, that it still possesses.

Board. *Noun*: (1) a thin piece or slab of wood, (2) a table, (3) food served at the table.

Book of Creatures. See BOOKS OF GOD.

Book of Life. See BOOKS OF GOD.

Book of Nature. See BOOKS OF GOD.

Book of Scriptures. See BOOKS OF GOD.

Books of God. The concept held by Donne and other Christians that God "wrote" two "books" which mankind can "read" and thus learn of God and truth. One is the "Book of Scriptures" (i.e., the Bible or Divine Revelation). The other is the "Book of Creatures" (i.e., everything God created in the universe or the "Book of Nature"). To Donne, both books testify of and lead to God the Creator. The phrases "Book of Creatures" and "Book of Scriptures" occur in Donne's prose and poetry.

Donne also at times refers to a third book, the "Book of Life": see especially the section "Of the Bible" in *ESSAYS IN DIVINITY* and "Expostulation 9" of *DEVOTIONS UPON EMERGENT OCCASIONS*. The "Book of Life" essentially is the roll or register of the Elect, the individual saved souls known only by God. Actually, Donne complicates the classifications a bit in *ESSAYS IN DIVINITY* by referring to the register of the Elect as the "First Book of Life," to the Bible as the "Second Book of Life," and to the creation as the "third book, the Book of Creatures."

Boot. *Verb*: to profit or to be of use or to do good.

Boreas. In Greek mythology, the north wind. He fell in love with Orithea, but her father and the people of Athens opposed the relationship. Boreas, however, swept down with his power and carried her away. Early versions of the story say that he had two sons by her, but PLATO says that Orithea was swept over a cliff by Boreas and died. See "ELEGY 16: ON HIS MISTRESS," lines 19–23.

Botch(es). *Noun*: boil(s) or pimple(s).

Bottle. *Noun*: bundle.

Boulstred, Cecilia. See BOULSTRED, MISTRESS.

Boulstred, Mistress. Two of the *EPICEDES AND OBSEQUIES* ("Elegy on Mistress Boulstred" and "An Elegy Upon the Death of Mistress Boulstred") memorialize Cecilia Boulstred (or Bulstrode) who died on August 4, 1609, at the age of 25. She was related to Lucy, COUNTESS OF BEDFORD, and died at TWICKENHAM Park. She is perhaps the dead companion of the Countess who is praised highly in the consolatory "To the Lady Bedford," one of the *VERSE LETTERS*. (See JUDITH.) Earlier BEN JONSON had written a poem ("Epigram on the Court Pucell") that he later said was about Cecilia Bulstrode. The implication of this poem and other comments was that she was a rather immoral, licentious young lady. However, by the period shortly before her death, she apparently justified higher opinion (possibly through a change in character), as evidenced by an epitaph written by Jonson, another by EDWARD HERBERT, the two poems by Donne, and some sincere expressions of concern for her in a letter by Donne to GOODYER. Also see KEPLER for Donne's apparent use of "new star" to symbolize her departed soul.

Bourse. See BRITAIN BOURSE.

Brahe, Tycho (1546–1601). Danish astronomer. In 1572 he discovered a "new star" in the constellation Cassiopeia. After a change of Danish rulers and withdrawal of state funds to support his work, Brahe went to Prague in 1599 after the emperor Rudolph II offered support. He died there in 1601. Brahe argued for a view of the universe that was a compromise between those of PTOLEMY and COPERNICUS: Brahe argued that the earth does not move but that the other planets revolve around the sun and that the planets and the sun revolve around the earth yearly. Although many of his views remained relatively conservative, several of his discoveries and accurate observations contributed to the full development of the "NEW PHILOSOPHY" under KEPLER and GALILEO.

Brass, Age of. See FOUR AGES.

Brave. *Adjective*: (1) courageous, daring; (2) splendid, showy, beautiful, handsome, grand; (3) finely-dressed; (4) worthy, excellent; (5) boastful.

Break. *Verb*: (1) to separate forcefully into parts; (2) to divide or part; (3) to wreck [a ship]; (4) to burst the surface; (5) "break on the wheel": to bind a criminal to a wheel or wheel-like structure and break his limbs or beat him to death; (6) "break the heart": to overwhelm with sorrow; (7) to demolish or ruin; (8) to ruin financially, to make or become bankrupt; (9) to dash against an obstacle [especially water or waves against a bank or wall, etc.]; (10) to cease or end; (11) to discipline, train, tame [especially animals, such as horses]; (12) to violate; (13) to penetrate; (14) to disclose, reveal, utter; (15) to escape confines, to emerge.

"Break of Day." One of the *SONGS AND SONNETS*, but it was first printed separately in Corkine's *Second Book of Airs*, 1612, with a musical setting. In contrast to the majority of Donne's poems, the speaker is a woman (see the last eight lines). The other poem in *SONGS AND SONNETS* with a woman speaking is "CONFINED LOVE." Traditionally, the poem is like many others in the Middle Ages and Renaissance in presenting two lovers parting at dawn. The woman's first words assume that the man has just said, in essence, "It's a new day, and I had better be going." Her argument is that daylight should not end love. She implies a clever question: "Just because the sun rises from its bed, do we have to rise from ours?" In a way similar to "THE SUN RISING" (but without its full development), Donne suggests both the superiority of love to time and its independence of time. To dissuade the man from leaving and from returning to the mundane scheduling of the everyday, the woman argues that they did not originally lie down because of the darkness and thus should not simply respond mechanically to the light: just as love urged them into bed, so it should motivate them to stay there. In the second stanza the woman tries to shame the man into staying by saying that she would not leave her own heart and honor that she has placed in him by going: the implied question is why he is doing so. If the man attempts to use his worldly business as an excuse, she has her answer, as is evident in the final stanza. She argues that love cannot coexist at all with business: they are like fire and water. If business takes precedence over love, the situation is similar to a married man always returning to his wife over his lover (and one notices that this speaker clearly implies that marriage and wooing are quite different): from the perspective of this woman, such obligation in the world of normal time (involving either business or marriage) destroys the separate world of real love potentially there for these lovers. Time will then be superior to and destructive of love (rather than the reverse, earlier argued by the lady), and she wishes to prevent such an unacceptable situation from occurring.

Bright. *Adjective*: (1) shining, (2) beautiful, (3) of vivid or brilliant color, (4) glorious or splendid.

Britain Bourse. Britain's Bourse was a stock exchange that opened in 1609.

"Broken Heart, The." One of the *SONGS AND SONNETS*, but it was first printed separately in *A Help to Memory and Discourse*, an anonymous publication of 1630. Donne revitalizes the trite expression of a lover's "broken heart" with his unique treatment. The speaker first leads the reader into the trap of thinking that the man is arguing that one's love cannot even last an hour, that his own feeling of love is ephemeral, transitory. But then the speaker says that it is wrong to think that: he asserts that what he really means is that love can actually destroy "ten" (men? hearts?) in less than an hour. Therefore, love (implying also the powerful god of love, Cupid), like an all-powerful animal, viciously overwhelms and destroys the lover. Through METAPHYSICAL analogies the poet argues that love is not like a lingering disease, but rather like the rapid bubonic plague, or it is like a fast explosion of gunpowder. The METAPHYSICAL CONCEIT of Love as a gluttonous beast continues in the second stanza, with the pictures of the animal that will not allow other animals to share the food and the large fish that devours the smaller ones. The specific occasion to which he compares all in the first half of the poem is made clear in the last half. The PETRARCHAN lady with her cruel rejection and lack of "pity" has shattered his heart like a mirror being broken into many pieces. This lady's nature is highlighted by the equating of her with the cruel Cupid, "Love." The pun on "alas" in line 23 further specifies that the "love" is indeed "a lass" with the power of destruction beneath her deceptively beautiful exterior.

Donne pursues the conceit of the heart as a mirror to its limit in the final stanza, strangely bolstering his arguments by bringing in the scientific impossibilities of destroying matter completely and of establishing an absolute vacuum. His conclusion is that his heart must still exist in his breast, even though the powerful emotional blow has caused it to change its form. It is now in pieces, and, just as pieces of a shattered mirror still reflect things, his heart can still reflect (and relate to) both lesser faces (women inferior to this one lady) and lesser emotions (liking, wishing, and adoring, rather than truly loving) in the future. The originally unified mirror connotes, then, his unified heart that focused on one lady and one love. Surprisingly, the lady that so disappointed him by her unresponsiveness is still complimented in her beauty and in the power of emotion she could generate in a way that no other women seem able to do.

Bronze, Age of. See FOUR AGES.

Brooke, Christopher (about 1570–1628). Studied law at LINCOLN'S INN, where he shared chambers with Donne. He was a witness to Donne's secret marriage to ANN MORE, his brother SAMUEL BROOKE performing the ceremony. Both Brookes, along with Donne, were imprisoned upon the revelation of the secret. Became a bencher at Lincoln's Inn, served in Parliament, wrote some minor poetry, and maintained friendships with such literary figures as Donne and JONSON. He was one of those dining at the MERMAID TAVERN regularly. One of Donne's *VERSE LETTERS* called "The Storm" is addressed to Brooke, and it is likely that "The Calm" was sent to him, as well. The verse letter "To Mr. C. B." speaks of Donne's enforced separation from two that he loves ("thee" and the "Saint of his affection"), Brooke and an unnamed lady, perhaps Ann More: the poem may either refer to an early love relationship in PETRARCHAN terms or to the close relationship between the two men that was forged even more tightly by their shared punishments (imprisonment, but in separate prisons) after the marriage, and it may speak of his own separation from his wife for a time, forced by her father. The "ice" that "walls her heart," if the marital interpretation is pursued, could be Ann's father and the literal walls in which he has enclosed and separated her from Donne, rather than the Petrarchan chill that might usually be associated with an unresponsive lady.

Brooke, Samuel (about 1575–1631). Probable recipient of "To Mr. S. B.," one of the *VERSE LETTERS*. He was the brother of CHRISTOPHER BROOKE. He was ordained in 1599, performed the marriage ceremony of Donne and ANN MORE, and was imprisoned with his brother and Donne for a brief period afterward. Later became a Royal Chaplain and Master of Trinity College at Cambridge.

Buckingham, 1st Duke of. See VILLIERS, GEORGE.

Bull. Refers in some contexts to Taurus, one of the twelve signs of the ZODIAC.

Bulstrode, Cecilia. See BOULSTRED, MISTRESS.

Busk. *Noun*: corset.

C

C., L. See L. C.

Cabinet. *Noun*: (1) a small chamber or room; (2) a case in which to keep jewelry, letters, documents, or other valuable items.

Cadiz. City in Spain (also called Cales) successfully sacked by the English in 1596. Some wished to go on after this event to the West Indies to take the Spanish silver being transported from GUIANA to Spain, but the fleet was ordered not to do this (see one of the *EPIGRAMS*, "Cales and Guiana," as well as one of the *VERSE LETTERS*, "To Mr. R. W.," beginning "If, as mine is"). Another of the *EPIGRAMS*, "Sir John Wingfield," memorializes WINGFIELD, an English commander killed in the attack on Cadiz. Donne participated in this expedition, serving under DEVEREUX (Earl of Essex). Also see AZORES.

Cain. First son of Adam and Eve. He was a tiller of the ground. God respected the offering brought to him by Cain's brother (ABEL) but not that brought by Cain. Out of envy Cain murdered Abel. God then cursed Cain by making it impossible for him to secure fruit from tilling the earth and by making him a fugitive and vagabond on earth. God also pronounced sevenfold vengeance on anyone who would kill Cain, and He put a mark on Cain so that he would be recognized. Cain dwelled in the land of Nod, east of Eden. Donne, following non-scriptural tradition, designates THEMECH as Cain's wife. Cain had a son named Enoch. From his descendants arose tent dwellers, keepers of cattle, players of the harp and organ, and artificers in brass and iron. See Genesis 4.

Calenture. *Noun*: a tropical fever, formerly thought to be caused by heat, that engenders delirium in sailors so severe that some jump off a ship at sea.

Calepine, Ambrose (1455–1511). Italian friar who published a polyglot dictionary. Referred to in line 54 of "Satire 4."

Cales. Another name for CADIZ.

"Calm, The." One of the *VERSE LETTERS*. Probably written to CHRISTOPHER BROOKE (the companion poem "The Storm" being specifically addressed to him). Describes an incident when Donne served on the expedition proposed for the Azores Islands in 1597 under ROBERT DEVEREUX, Earl of Essex. See above, p. 14 (in "Donne's Life").

Calvary. See GOLGOTHA.

Calvin, John (1509–1564). Jean Cauvin, French theologian and Protestant reformer. Studied law, logic, Latin, Greek, and Hebrew. After accepting many of LUTHER's beliefs, he was forced to flee Paris during a royal proscription of Lutherans. In 1536 he published *Institutes of the Christian Religion* in which he criticizes many facets of Roman Catholicism and promotes reformed Protestantism. Soon after its publication he took up residence in Geneva, Switzerland. The beliefs of Calvinism emphasize human depravity resulting from original sin, salvation only through God's grace (Calvin agreeing with Luther concerning the inability of good works to gain salvation, but emphasizing God's grace more than the individual's faith emphasized by Luther), and the doctrine of the Elect (those predestined by God for salvation). Calvin argues that Christ "imputes" righteousness to the believer (see Donne's use of this word and idea in line 13 of "THIS IS MY PLAY'S LAST SCENE, HERE HEAVENS APPOINT," one of the *HOLY SONNETS*). Calvin argues that the two sacraments are Baptism and the Lord's Supper. These beliefs of Calvin, along with his insistence upon the church being governed largely by individual congregations (rather than by an episcopal hierarchy) and on the Bible as the true and authoritative one of the BOOKS OF GOD, became most important in the thinking and practices of the English PURITANs of the 16th and 17th centuries. Donne refers to Calvin and his arguments many times in the *SERMONS*.

Calvinism. The doctrines and practices of the Calvinists, following John Calvin. See CALVIN.

Calvinist. A proponent of Calvinism, the doctrines and practices subscribed to by John Calvin and his followers. See CALVIN.

Canaries. (1) The Canary Islands, (2) canary wines.

Canker. A special use of the word is to describe a type of cancer that eats away portions of the body.

"Canonization, The." One of the *SONGS AND SONNETS*. The title reflects the most fully-developed METAPHYSICAL CONCEIT in the poem, the detailed and farfetched analogy of two lovers and two saints.

The colloquial language (cursing) and irregular metrical pattern in the first line illustrate some of Donne's METAPHYSICAL characteristics. The emotional outburst by the man speaking to (apparently) another man conveys his anger at someone who has criticized and ridiculed the speaker for taking love too seriously. The first stanza, in fact, sarcastically lists matters for the other man to criticize or to do himself, rather than bother the lover any further. If the other man wishes to criticize the speaker, he should criticize his physical and economic afflictions and flaws (palsy, gout, gray hairs, and bankruptcy): by sarcastically proposing this action for the critic of love, the speaker implies that the critic's values are askew, since one should not criticize someone for physical and economic weaknesses, and further implies that the critic sees love itself as an infirmity (when it really is a strength). Better than criticizing someone else, though, is to mind one's own business; therefore, the speaker suggests that the other man should occupy himself with making money, improving his mind, deciding on a course in life or a career, securing a lucrative position by fawning around someone of the aristocracy, royalty, or of high position in government or church ("his Honor or his Grace"), or being attentive to the King himself at court or to the King's face stamped on coins. His exasperated summary ending the stanza emphasizes his primary point: just do whatever you want to in your own worldly interests, but leave me alone to enjoy my experience in love. The values of the world are thus embodied in the critic being addressed, and the values of love are in the man speaking: the clash of these is already suggested, and this conflict becomes central to the development of the rest of the poem and to the kind of "canonization" portrayed therein.

The second stanza presents the speaker defending his right to love, since his love harms no one else. Merchants can still carry on their trade by sea, and farmers can still plant and grow crops: ships will not be capsized by this lover's PETRARCHAN stormy "sighs," and cropland will not be flooded by his PETRARCHAN tears (obviously, his is not a ridiculous Petrarchan love relationship with his lady). Similarly, he has no Petrarchan cold and heat (the extremes of rejection and sheer passion) tainting his love. Winter will not be prolonged, spring can arrive on time or early ("forward"), and no one is given plague in a time of extreme heat that this lover might cause (plague thrived in warm weather, and its victims were listed in weekly "BILLS" or notices). In a satirical parallel with each other, soldiers and lawyers fight their battles and make their money by taking advantage of violent, destructive passions in men and the world: the speaker again insists that he, his lady, and their love do not harm the lives of these men. The ways and people of the frivolous world can continue unaffected by the ways and the people of serious love, then.

The third stanza turns from the emphasis on the worldly to a more emphatic and detailed presentation of love, particularly that of the speaker and his lady. The change is reflected as well by almost a curt dismissal of the worldly man being addressed—his criticism now seems ineffectual ("Call us what you will": whatever you want to say is fine, since it does not bother us—we are above such ridicule). The speaker is surly enough now, in fact, even to suggest possible analogies that would be apt. He and the lady each could be called flies (moths), since the fly's attraction to a taper (candle) symbolizes each lover's physical attraction to the other. And, thus, each lover could also be compared to the taper that attracts the other. The ingenuity of this METAPHYSICAL CONCEIT appears in the fact that both the fly and the taper "die," the fly being consumed in the flame and the candle itself being shortened as it burns up. Their consuming (playing on the idea of sexual consummation) does "cost" the lives of the fly and candle, and this play on "DIE" suggests the lovers' physical consummation with the shortening of their own lives believed in Donne's time to be the result of sexual intercourse. This conceit emphasizes their physical attraction for each other and the expression of their love physically. They also can be said to be like the eagle (implying the larger size and strength of the male) and the dove (implying the smaller size and weakness of the female), yet these opposites attract and combine. The imagery of birds and flames is then given its climactic expression in the analogy (another METAPHYSICAL CONCEIT) of the PHOENIX, the single bird that lived hundreds of years, built its own funeral pyre, destroyed itself, and arose a new phoenix from the ashes. This point of the conceit takes the all-important step from "two" into "one": the sense of two lovers, two flies, two candles, two birds, male and female, etc., has been obliterated by the sense of union in a single bird, physically "dying" (compared again, by implication, to the two lovers as one sexually "dying") and then rising out of that "death" unchanged, with love unabated by the sexual expression of it ("We die and rise the same"). Their love is not merely

physical passion that declines. Since the phoenix is a traditional
symbol of immortality and the spirit rising out of the body at
death, Donne here transfers this spiritual nature to their love: it is
not simply a physical love, but it is ultimately a spiritual one that
is, paradoxically, undying. The mystery of the phoenix, then, is
understandable if it is seen to be exemplified by the speaker and
his lady: it is a spiritual mystery comparable, by implication, to
the physical death but spiritual immortality of saints.
Significantly, the phoenix analogy occurs in the middle line of the
middle stanza and becomes the fulcrum on which the whole poem
turns. It provides the transition from the physical to the spiritual.
     The fourth stanza emphasizes that these two lovers both live
and "die" (the pun continues) by love. But beyond the physical,
sexual "death" is even more audaciously developed the conceit of
these two as comparable to saints, to martyrs in the church who
live and die by their Christian faith. Thus, these two lovers exist
entirely for their religion of love and are thus removed from the
worldly realm emphasized in the first two stanzas. Just as the
otherworldliness of self-sacrificing believers qualify them for
Christian sainthood, so are the speaker and the lady qualified for
love's sainthood. Their "legend" (a saint's life) will be related in
compact verse, rather than in a lengthy prose account
("chronicle"). The story of themselves will be told in "sonnets"
(simply short lyric poems—see *SONGS AND SONNETS*), the irony
being that it is indeed being told in this very "sonnet" entitled
"The Canonization." The speaker asserts that this is a more
appropriate memorial than any huge physical monument ("tomb")
or long prose piece. Then, pursuing this further in a
METAPHYSICAL CONCEIT, he compares a beautifully-rendered
sonnet to a finely-wrought, small burial urn: the beautiful urn
holds ashes just as effectively as a gigantic tomb in a way similar
to a beautiful lyric poem compactly memorializing a person as
well as a long prose account does. And the "rooms" in "half-acre
tombs" are no finer than the structural divisions (lines, stanzas,
etc.) in a beautiful lyric poem. By calling these love poems about
himself and his lady "hymns," the speaker further develops the
conceit of love as a religion for which these two live, die, and are
praised. They qualify, with the approval of all succeeding lovers
on earth, to be canonized as the saints of love.
     Once the lovers have been made comparable to saints, the
speaker asserts in the fifth stanza that all other lovers can
"invoke" (pray to and call on for aid) them as the saints of love,
just as worshippers in the church can invoke Christian saints.
Except for the first four words, this entire stanza is what the

speaker imagines all other people saying in their invocation of the two saints of love ("You"). These two lovers made each other a "hermitage"—a retreat in which they would worship each other, in their faith of love, in isolation from the world outside. The love that these two had will seem a peaceful, harmonious, perfect one in contrast to the "rage," the passionate, violently physical and lustful type that seems to prevail in everyone else's experience and/or after these two lovers' "death." Their perfect blend of physical and spiritual elements is lacking in others' loves. Their spiritual, heavenly love contrasts with worldly love in a way similar to the speaker early in the poem who values love contrasts with the man who values the world. Now the world is begging true love for help, rather than criticizing it. These two lovers who retreated into a worship of each other comprised their own superior world, a MICROCOSM superior to the MACROCOSM: they contracted (squeezed into little space compactly) the entire soul or essence of the world outside simply by looking at each other. They "drove . . . countries, towns, and courts" into their eyes by looking into each other's eyes: all realms of the earth, then, were compactly represented simply by the faces of the two individuals reflected on the eyes ("glasses," mirrors) as they gazed at each other. They saw "all" that existed of any importance on earth by looking at each other. These saints, then, have the key to perfect love, and others want them to intercede with God "above" (Cupid as the God of Love, but also either implied in or analogous to the Christian God in heaven) for a pattern, a model to follow by which they might also attain this perfect, immortal love. The intercessory role of the "saints" completes the metaphysical conceit of canonization uniting the poem.

    This poem tempts some critics to see matters of autobiographical importance, suggesting Donne's own conflict between his worldly ambition and his love for ANN MORE. Various readings have seen Donne asserting the primacy of his own love over trivial worldly concerns or scornfully dismissing the failure of his own secular hopes. But, on the other hand, the poem has been related to Donne's own persistence toward gaining governmental, courtly positions and thus seen as a paradoxical, self-biting regret of his being barred from such positions by his tragic choice of love and secret marriage. Some of these personal, subjective elements possibly are present, but they are not necessary to appreciate the poem as an objective drama in itself, and we have no evidence of the specific date of the poem or the circumstances under which it was written. For further analyses and speculations on this much-discussed and much-debated work, one should consult the many books, articles, and essays concerning Donne (and this poem in particular) listed in "Selected Bibliography: Critical Studies, Poetry." Especially valuable starting points are the studies by Brooks (see under *Songs and Sonnets*) and Hunt (see under "Miscellaneous").

Capuchin. A new rule of Franciscan friar developed in 1528. The name arose from the wearing of a capuche, a pointed hood. A Capuchin was vowed to poverty and wore a habit without pockets to hold money.

Cardan, Jerome (1501–1576). Italian physician, mathematician, and astrologer. Gave the first clinical description of typhus fever, published the first book on computation of probabilities based on games of chance, and published a book important in the history of algebra. Argued against the existence of a layer of the element of fire in the universe: see NEW PHILOSOPHY.

Cardinal Virtues. Justice, prudence, fortitude, and temperance.

Carew, Thomas (1594?–1640). "Carew" is pronounced "Carey." Poet and courtier. Took his B.A. at Oxford in 1611, studied law, served as secretary to Sir Dudley Carleton (ambassador to Venice and later to the Netherlands), served as secretary to EDWARD HERBERT, and eventually held some positions at Court under CHARLES I. Most of his poetry was published after his death.
    Carew is primarily a follower of JONSON and the CLASSICAL line in poetry (and is usually grouped with the "Cavalier Poets"), but he also reveals some influences from Donne and the METAPHYSICAL strain. He is one of the most polished and impressive literary craftsmen of the minor poets during the first half of the 17th century. His "An Elegy Upon the Death of the Dean of Paul's, Dr. John Donne" was first published in the 1633 edition of Donne's poems, along with several others contributed by other poets. Carew's is by far the best of them and indeed is one of the most perceptive critical assessments of Donne ever written. His poem is carefully crafted, at points imitating Donne's own style. Among many of his memorable comments on Donne's contributions to English poetry are the following: (1) Donne "purged" the Muses' garden of its "pedantic weeds," (2) Donne's "imperious wit" caused the "troublesome language" to bend in "awe" of it, (3) Donne exiled the "goodly train of gods and goddesses" from noble poetry, and (4) Donne was like a king that ruled the "universal monarchy of wit."

Carey, Lady (the former Lettice Rich). Sister to Mistress Essex Rich and recipient with her of Donne's "A Letter to the Lady Carey, and Mistress Essex Rich, from Amiens," one of the *VERSE LETTERS*. Written during Donne's trip to France with Sir ROBERT DRURY, it is, as far as is known, the only English poem surviving in his handwriting. Donne did not know the two ladies but did know their brother (Sir Robert Rich), who might have suggested to Donne that he write the poem.

Carlisle, 1st Earl of. See HAY, JAMES.

Carr, Robert. See KER, ROBERT.

Carthusian. *Adjective*: Refers to an order of monks noted for its strict, severe way of life.

Cary, Henry. See L. C.

Castiglione. See *COURTIER, THE.*

Cecil, Catherine. See SALISBURY, COUNTESS OF.

Cecil, Robert (1563–1612). 1st Earl of Salisbury. Son of William Cecil, Lord Burghley. Secretary of State under Queen ELIZABETH and succeeded his father as her chief advisor in 1598. During the trial of ROBERT DEVEREUX, Earl of Essex, in early 1601, Essex accused Cecil of saying that the INFANTA of Spain was the rightful heir to the throne of England. The charge proved to be without foundation. Cecil was the primary force in arranging for King JAMES to succeed Elizabeth and for the succession occurring peacefully. King James retained him as Secretary, giving him many titles and honors. Until his death he was the primary administrator of the government. His power and influence under both Queen Elizabeth and King James caused much resentment and envy, particularly from the adherents of Essex and other would-be powers.
    Donne might well have aimed his satirical *METEMPSYCHOSIS* at Cecil, since Donne apparently wrote the poem in 1601 after the trial and execution of Essex. The followers of Essex largely blamed Cecil for scheming to bring about Essex's fall. Donne, in fact, had allegiances to friends of both Essex and Sir Walter Raleigh, most of whom hated Cecil. (See especially the essay about the poem by M. van Wyk Smith cited in the "Selected Bibliography.")

Celebrate. *Verb*: (1) to perform publicly [a marriage or funeral or other ceremony]; (2) to proclaim publicly; (3) to praise, to extol.

Centric (Centrique). *Adjective*: (1) central, i.e., most important; (2) central, i.e., located at or in the center or middle.

Certes. Certainly.

Chain(ed) shot. Cannon balls chained together.

Cham. Also called Ham. One of Noah's three sons who repopulated the world after the Flood. The others were JAPHET and SHEM. (See Genesis 9 and 10.) Cham's descendants were believed to dwell in Africa. See "HYMN TO GOD MY GOD, IN MY SICKNESS."

Character. A literary form popular in Donne's time. Most are sketches of types of people, such as pedant, scholar, courtier, PURITAN, or actor: Donne himself wrote "THE TRUE CHARACTER OF A DUNCE." But some also characterize places (a tavern, for example). Particularly influential in the development of the form are JOSEPH HALL's *Characters of Virtues and Vices* and the collection of pieces by various hands in the book first published as *A Wife: Now the Widow of Sir Thomas Overbury* (1614) and its later appearance with many additions as *Sir Thomas Overbury His Wife* (1622): see "THE TRUE CHARACTER OF A DUNCE" for Donne's relationship to the Overburian characters. The best of the writers of characters is John Earle who published *Microcosmography* in 1628.

Charing Cross. A large cross erected by King Edward I. It existed in Donne's time but was later removed (in 1647).

Charles I (1600–1649). King of England, 1625–1649. Son of JAMES I. Donne dedicated *DEVOTIONS UPON EMERGENT OCCASIONS* to him while he was still Prince of Wales. Donne preached the first sermon after his accession, one that was soon published with Charles's approval. Thereafter Donne gave many sermons before Charles, some of which endorse church ritual, vestments, and ceremony (over against Puritan arguments for plainness) in ways that pleased the King. After Donne's death, increasing conflicts between King and Parliament, as well as among factions in the Church, developed into the Great Rebellion

(English Civil War) with Parliamentary and Puritan forces pitted against those of the King and Court. Charles surrendered and eventually was beheaded.

Chaw(e), Chawes (Chaws). Chew, chews.

Chelsea. Area on the banks of the Thames River a few miles southwest of central London. MAGDALEN HERBERT (Lady Danvers) lived here in the home (with its impressive grounds and garden) of her husband Sir John Danvers. Donne visited them frequently, once for six months in the summer and fall of 1625 when an epidemic of plague in London prolonged his stay. GEORGE HERBERT was present at the same time. While staying here, Donne spent some of the time writing out previous sermons from notes, thus preparing them for later publication. Donne preached a memorial sermon in Chelsea Church for Lady Danvers after her death in 1627.

Chemic, chemique. See ALCHEMY.

Cherbury, Lord Herbert of. See HERBERT, SIR EDWARD.

Cherubim. See HIERARCHY, THE HEAVENLY.

Cherubin. Also "cherubim." See HIERARCHY, THE HEAVENLY. Also see "MOSES' CHERUBINS."

Chest(s). *Noun*: (1) a box or coffer; (2) a coffin; (3) metaphorically, a chamber or room or study [see "Satire 1," line 2]; (4) the portion of the human body enclosed by the ribs and breastbone; (5) [plural] game of chess.

Children in the oven. Phrase used by Donne in line 24 of "SATIRE 3" to refer to Shadrach, Meschach, and Abednego, the three Jewish men (i.e., children of God) who did not worship the golden image constructed by Nebuchadnezzar, were cast into the fiery furnace as punishment, and were miraculously untouched and unharmed, protected by an angel of God. They are referred to in lines 27–28 of "The Calm" as "walkers in hot ovens." See Daniel 3.

Chimera. *Noun*: (1) a fire-breathing monster of Greek mythology with a lion's head, goat's body, and serpent's tail; (2) in art and architecture, a grotesque monster formed from various parts of various animals; (3) an unreal creation of the imagination.

Choler, choleric. See HUMOR.

Chrysostom, Saint John (about 345–407). Born in Antioch, Syria, where, after some time as a monk and in solitude, he later was ordained and gained the reputation of a great preacher. Noted for his ability to apply the scriptures to everyday life, for his humor, his compassion, and his eloquence (he was called "golden-mouthed"). In 398 he became Archbishop of Constantinople. Here he alienated some of the wealthy and powerful by his criticism of the misuse of wealth, and charges were trumped up against him, leading ultimately to his banishment and exile in Cucusus. Since he still wrote powerfully and communicated with Constantinople, he was ordered to be moved to an area farther away, but he died on the journey. His remains were returned to Constantinople about thirty years later. His influential writings survive in his sermons, famous for their commentaries on the Bible and for their practical advice. He also wrote essays, treatises, and letters. St. Chrysostom is one of the four traditional "DOCTORS" of the eastern church. Donne refers to Chrysostom frequently in his prose, especially in the *SERMONS*.

Church, Militant; Church Militant. The band of Christians battling sin on earth.

Church, Triumphant; Church Triumphant. The souls of Christians who have reached salvation in heaven.

Cicero, Marcus Tullius (106–43 B.C.). Roman orator, statesman, and prose writer. Studied philosophy, literature, rhetoric, and law. Practiced law. Elected Consul in 63 B.C. He discovered Catiline's conspiracy to overthrow the government and suppressed it. After the assassination of Julius Caesar, Cicero made speeches attacking Antony. After the Second Triumvirate of Antony, Octavian, and Lepidus assumed power, Cicero was killed by Antony's army. Speeches, treatises, and letters by Cicero survive. He is influential in the rhetoric, politics, and philosophy of his prose works, as well as the primary model for the polished, lengthy clause or sentence known as the Ciceronian prose style. Donne refers to him many times in the *SERMONS*, calling him "the great Master of Latin language" and "the Father of Orators." He also refers to him in line 287 of *THE SECOND ANNIVERSARY*.

Circe. In Greek mythology, the sun god's daughter who was exiled to the island of Aeaea after murdering her husband. She was an evil enchantress. The companions of Odysseus ("Circe's prisoners" in line 129 of "Satire 4") were changed into swine when they visited her island. Odysseus himself was not changed, having been given an herb by Hermes to resist Circe's power. After seeing Odysseus unchanged, Circe transformed the men back to their normal state, entertained them and Odysseus lavishly as her guests for a year, and bore Odysseus a son.

Circle. Frequently used by Donne (and many other writers) as the symbol of perfection, infinity, immortality, and God.

Classical. As used in this "Dictionary," "classical" refers to the particular style and content of poetry stemming from "classicism," especially as viewed and practiced by BEN JONSON and his followers in the late 16th and early 17th centuries. The assumptions of such classical verse arise from similar assumptions in works of ancient Greece and Rome that provide the major models for Renaissance classicism. The term "classical" is extremely complex and is applied in numerous ways, but the following working definition, albeit a greatly simplified one, may serve to illustrate the major characteristics of it, especially those that differ in important respects from those of Donne's poetry and of much other METAPHYSICAL poetry.

As far as content, many classical poems are complimentary in nature, praising certain individuals. Praises for the country life and for good food and drink also are common. The *carpe diem* theme (literally, "seize the day": urging one to live and love fully and actively now, for time is passing rapidly and death is approaching) is a recurring one. Epitaphs (compact poems memorializing individuals who have died) appear frequently in classical verse. In many (especially in JONSON) the poet is in a public role as a social, moral, and ethical critic. Generally the speaking voice is rather formal and polite in word choice and tone, with emotion kept restrained.

In style and structure a classical poem is overtly well-organized, displaying strict divisions, logical progressions, and stages clearly defined from beginning to end. The structure and style of the poem, stanzas, and lines employ careful balance, parallelism, and symmetry. The metrics generally are regular, avoiding excessive variations. Frequently the classical poet writes in couplets, many of which have carefully placed and clear caesuras. All in all, clarity is valued in syntax, word choice, and thought. ˙Some relevant examples of classical poetry in which one can see these characteristics are the following by Ben Jonson: (1) the song beginning "Still to be neat," (2) the song beginning "Come, my Celia, let us prove," (3) No. 4 of "A Celebration of Charis," (4) "To William Camden," (5) "To Penshurst," (6) "On My First Son," and (7) "Inviting a Friend to Supper."

Clifford, Lady Anne (1590–1676). Married to RICHARD SACKVILLE, 3rd Earl of Dorset, when Donne was rector of Sevenoaks. She heard him preach there and, as Countess of Dorset, was hostess to Donne on occasions at Knole, their residence. After Sackville's death she later married Philip Herbert, 4th Earl of Pembroke (son of MARY SIDNEY). She then was Countess of Pembroke and resided at Wilton House during the same time that GEORGE HERBERT served his parish at Bemerton, with the church and parsonage quite close to Wilton House. George Herbert visited her there. So, Donne and Herbert both knew and respected this intelligent and learned lady. She wrote of herself that she made good books and virtuous thoughts her companions. Her library contained Donne's and Herbert's poems and some of Donne's sermons, a fact evidenced by a large portrait of her with those volumes prominently displayed in the background. She also erected the monument to EDMUND SPENSER in Westminster Abbey.

Clog. *Noun*: (1) a block or heavy piece of wood or other material that is attached to the leg or neck of a person or animal to prevent escape or to slow movement; (2) figuratively, any impediment or hindrance.

Cloister. *Verb*: (1) to enclose; (2) to place in a monastic house or cloister. *Noun*: (1) an enclosure; (2) a place of religious seclusion, such as a nunnery, convent, monastery.

Clyster. *Noun*: enema.

Cochineal. *Noun*: dried bodies of insects imported from South America that were used to make an expensive red dye. Also called "cutchannel."

Cockatrice. *Noun*: basilisk, a serpent reputedly able to kill by a glance and supposedly hatched from a cock's egg.

Cokayne, Sir William (1561?–1626). Merchant and alderman in London. King JAMES had dinner at his house on June 8, 1616, and there made him a knight. Served as Lord Mayor of London in 1619–20. Was in the Merchant Adventurers' Company that equipped explorers (such as William Baffin) for voyages. Accumulated great wealth and purchased several large estates in England. One of Donne's *SERMONS* was preached at his funeral on December 12, 1626, and Cokayne was buried in ST. PAUL'S CATHEDRAL.

Colossus. The Colossus at Rhodes (Rhodian Colossus) was a huge statue of Apollo, the legs of which stretched across the harbor on the island of Rhodes in the Aegean Sea. It was constructed about 280 B.C. with a height of 120 feet and became one of the Seven Wonders of the ancient world. It was destroyed by an earthquake in 224 B.C.

Combination of dissimilar images. See METAPHYSICAL CONCEIT.

Come. *Verb*: (1) to move towards, to approach; (2) to be derived [from]; (3) to arrive [in course of time]; (4) to happen; (5) to approach for sexual contact; (6) to experience sexual orgasm.

"Community." One of the *SONGS AND SONNETS*. With consciously masculine ego the speaker justifies male promiscuity through some of Donne's famous illogical logic and witty manipulation of "philosophical" assertions. What begins as an ethical and moral argument that "we" (apparently only "men") must love good and hate evil, the difference between the two being quite apparent, ultimately leads to rationalizing a flippant and immoral attitude by the end of the poem.

The "things indifferent" that cannot be easily assessed as clearly good or clearly evil are revealed to be women. The man says that since "Nature" (Mother Nature) did not create her daughters to be so easily figured out (and thus being partial to her own sex in a sly ["wise"] way?), then all men are forced to "prove," to test, all women by "using" them (especially to "USE" sexually) to find out if they are good or bad, whether to be loved or hated. The definition of "good" here becomes disturbingly close to "ability to give men sexual pleasure," rather than the moral goodness we might have expected. The satisfaction of men's appetites as the real purpose of women as designated by this speaker becomes quite explicit in the last stanza in which he compares women to fruit eaten by men.

The tone and multiplicity of feeling in the poem depend somewhat upon the various meanings of "INDIFFERENT." For instance, one common meaning in Donne's time was something of neutral quality, neither good nor bad. But also it could imply something of no consequence, or indeed unimportant. The latter sense in the first stanza anticipates the eventual denigration of women to unimportant objects of pleasure for men in the last stanza. Men, he says, should feel free only to "taste" a woman, "devour" her fully (if she is "good" by his definition), or avoid her completely. Women are fruits for the plucking and can be disposed of as men desire. By sampling a variety of women, as if they were different fruits, a man can find the one that is "good" for him. The variety is a shared variety of "all" women that may be sampled by "all" men: women are, then, like "commons," common land to be farmed by many men or' like a shared community of goods or like a shared orchard of fruit—the title reflects this idea developed through the poem. Other meanings of "USE" in line 12 (in addition to that of having sexual intercourse) are implied through the poem, especially that of making use of land by tilling or occupying it and that of partaking of food (both frequently-employed definitions in the early seventeenth century).

An interesting comparison of this poem with "CONFINED LOVE" might be made: there a woman justifies female promiscuity with an argument that women are created "good" and that "good" is to be used. Possibly Donne deliberately wrote these two as companion poems.

Compass(e), compasses. *Noun:* (1) an instrument for drawing circles and taking measurements, consisting of two legs (or "feet") that are joined at one end only; (2) a mariner's instrument for guiding the course of a ship at sea, consisting of box, card, and magnetized needle; (3) circle or anything circular; (4) circumference or boundary or any limits of an area.

Complexion. *Noun:* (1) the type of physical appearance, personality, disposition, and temperament resulting from the dominance of a particular HUMOR in the body: choleric, sanguine, phlegmatic, or melancholic. See also ELEMENT and GALEN.

"Computation, The." One of the *SONGS AND SONNETS.* The title suggests the mathematical concern in the poem, and the first line presents both the first figure to be added and the central paradox: the first "twenty years, since yesterday." He implies the feeling that lovers have while apart—minutes seem hours, and hours seem years. "Twenty years" in itself would appear to be METAPHYSICAL exaggeration enough, but Donne makes even this period only a small amount of the total time that seems to have passed since yesterday. By the end of the poem, the years total 2,400. Since it has been one day since the speaker parted from the lady addressed, 24 hours seem to be 2,400 years; therefore, each hour has seemed to be 100 years to the lover.

After realizing that she actually had left, the man reminisced on her past favors to him, and then he spent an equal amount of time hoping that she will continue to show such favors to him in the future. He wept for 100 years (i.e., one hour) and sighed for 200 (i.e., two hours), echoing some traditional PETRARCHAN elements. For the next 1,000 years (i.e., ten hours) he became absolutely insensible, dead to the world, dead to thinking and doing anything other than thinking of the lady—and even in this he could not distinguish ("divide") thought from action. Line 8 is the most ambiguous in the poem: for the next 1,000 years he forgot "that" (the previous 1,000 years? or thought of the lady?). At any rate, the implication of his complete "deadness" at being apart from the lady is apparent, and this logically leads to the overt assertion in the last two lines that he is "dead." One of the many Renaissance meanings of DIE applies here—specifically, parting as dying. Continuing to play on paradoxes and stereotypes regarding lovers, Donne presents the speaker concluding that these 24 hours as 2,000 years do not argue a long worldly "life" for him, since he was killed at parting from her, is so desolately dead to the world, and is now spiritually "immortal" as a ghost (the period apart from each other is like an eternity to lovers). Since he already is dead, there can be no other death for him, a "ghost."

Underneath the witty play, the speaker implies his deep feelings of loss and desolation at being parted from the lady. His deadness to life appears through the picture of himself as a ghost, and the hyperbole of the poem functions to convey his feelings as one of the living dead when he is without the lady.

Conceit. See METAPHYSICAL CONCEIT.

Conclave Ignati. See *IGNATIUS HIS CONCLAVE.*

Concoction. *Noun*: (1) digestion; (2) a late stage of digestion that appears in a late stage of illness, signs of which appear in the urine, sweat, tears, and saliva and thus indicate separation of the HUMORS from corrupting elements; (3) ripening, bringing to a state of perfection.

"Confined Love." One of the *SONGS AND SONNETS*. In contrast to the majority of Donne's poems, the speaker is a woman (see lines 6 and 14). The other poem in *SONGS AND SONNETS* with a woman speaking is "BREAK OF DAY."

"COMMUNITY" presents a man justifying male promiscuity because "good" is not apparent in women from their manner of creation, and this poem presents a woman justifying female promiscuity because women are created "good," and "good" is to be "USED." It is possible that Donne deliberately wrote these as companion poems. The female speaker blames "some man" in the past for formulating a law that a woman is permitted to "KNOW," to have sexual intercourse with, only one man. The lady attributes this attitude and law to the anger that this man had against women in general, implying that this man was unworthy to "POSSESS" (both "own" and "sexually interact with") either a love(r) he already had or a new one he might seek. He was unworthy because he was "false" (unfaithful) to a previous love and "weak" regarding any new love he might desire—i.e., he was easily tempted by women or he was ineffectual in being able to woo other women, but also the implication is that his frustrations were increased by his becoming "weak" in the sense of being sexually impotent (the latter meaning particularly enforced by his consequent "shame"). Rather than accept personal responsibility, this man (according to the woman speaking) shifted blame to all women and meted out a punishment in the form of his "law": this "law," in essence, is the double standard, setting up one standard of conduct for men (they may be promiscuous and "know" many women) and another standard for women (they may not be promiscuous and must "know" only one man). This double standard assumed by all males (represented by "some man") is what the woman speaking argues against: she does not accept this "confined love" for women because no other "CREATURES" (creations of God or Nature) are so restricted in sexual partnerships.

The second stanza presents examples of elements in creation that are not restricted in a way that this "law" restricts women. The sun, moon, and stars are personified to serve the speaker's purpose: these elements may "smile" (i.e., give flirtatious looks) freely, and they may give away their "light" (i.e., physical love), but women cannot. Birds paired with mates may still spend nights with other partners, may "LIE" sexually with others, but women who would do so would be criticized or divorced. Animals who vary their sexual partners do not lose their "JOINTURES" (their marriage or their sexual union in marriage or their rights to hold property jointly with the marriage partner). Women ("we") do not have these privileges, the speaker argues.

The last stanza compares a beautifully-created ("good") woman to a beautifully-prepared ship that wastes away in a harbor if not used for the purposes for which it was built. The ship should "seek new lands," implying that the woman should be able to "sail" to new men and should not be kept confined in "harbor," to one man alone. As the ship carries on trade ("deals"), the woman should be able to exchange sexual favors with several different men. (An explicit meaning of "DEAL" in Donne's time as "having sexual intercourse" is quite pertinent here.) Beautiful houses, trees, and arbors that are unseen, unused, and left to waste away are other symbols for women regarded and treated so. The final argument is driven home in the last three lines: "good" unused is not "good." "Good" is only "good" if "a thousand it possess," a deliberately ambiguous statement with two relevant ways to be read (both "it must possess a thousand others" and "a thousand others must possess it"). The implication for the case of the woman as the "good" to be "used" is that the woman should have a thousand lovers and that a thousand lovers should have the woman, with the clearly sexual connotation of "POSSESS" applicable here. If a woman is not so used, she "doth WAST[E]" (wastes away) with "GREEDINESS." In other words, the "greediness" of a man's "possessiveness" in "owning" a woman and not allowing her to be used causes her to waste away. But equally relevant is the interpretation of "greediness" as the woman's "sexual passion or desire" that she feels but is frustrated in not being allowed to express fully in action: both interpretations of "greediness" reflect the "confined love" of the title.

Conjurer. *Noun*: magician.

Conqueror, William the (1027–87). Norman who conquered the English at the Battle of Hastings in 1066. Ruled England from 1066 to 1087. Upon his death at Rouen his attendants fled to their own estates after stripping his body and the room of everything of value, disrespectfully leaving his body almost naked and unguarded.

Consummatum est. Latin phrase meaning "It is finished." The last words of Christ on the cross (John 19:30).

Consumption. *Noun*: (1) action of consuming or destroying; (2) evaporation of moisture; (3) decay or wasting away; (4) pulmonary consumption, tuberculosis.

Convenient author, a. In "Meditation 16" of *DEVOTIONS UPON EMERGENT OCCASIONS* Donne refers to HIERONYMUS MAGIUS as "a convenient author, who writ a discourse of bells when he was a prisoner in Turkey."

Copernican. Referring to Copernicus and/or his concept of the universe. See COPERNICUS.

Copernicus, Nicolaus (1473–1543). Polish astronomer. Studied in Poland and Italy. Well-versed in astronomy, mathematics, law, medicine, and theology. Increasingly disagreed with the theories of PTOLEMY, and he formulated a heliocentric theory for the structure of the universe (i.e., one with the sun as the center, rather than the earth). Argued that the earth and other planets move around the sun in orbits. His work profoundly influenced later astronomers such as KEPLER and GALILEO and others of the "NEW PHILOSOPHY" referred to by Donne.

Cordial. *Noun*: a medicine, food, or drink that invigorates the heart.

Corinna (early 5th century B.C.). Greek lyric poetess in Thebes, where she was reputed to have defeated PINDAR five times in writing contests. Referred to in "A VALEDICTION: OF THE BOOK" as "her who from Pindar could allure."

Corn. *Noun*: (1) grain, (2) seed. [Does not designate Indian corn, as in later American usage].

Corse. Common spelling of modern "corpse." Also spelled "coarse" in Donne's time.

Coryat, Thomas (1577?–1617). A traveller who was a member of a dining club that met at the MERMAID TAVERN in London, with Donne and JONSON apparently participants in it. He was felt to be eccentric, but convivial and entertaining. Published in 1611 an account of some of his travels, with the title *Coryat's Crudities.* Among the many mockingly commendatory poems contributed to this volume was Donne's satirically playful "Upon Mr. Thomas Coryat's Crudities."

Coscus. Character in "Satire 2," the bad poet who became a bad lawyer. Uses tricks to satisfy his greed.

Council of Trent (1545–63). Roman Catholic Council convoked by Pope Paul III that met at Trent in northern Italy, with various sessions occurring over the years. Among many decrees, one of the most important was the attempt to answer the Protestant doctrine of justification by faith alone (see LUTHER): the Council said that only after man's cooperation with free divine assistance is he justified by sanctifying grace, which makes him capable of meriting by good works. The Council also defined the doctrine of the real presence of Christ in the Eucharist by transubstantiation (see TRANSUBSTANTIATE). In addition, the Council said that a book on sacred matters is not to be published anonymously and that an Index of prohibited books would be instituted (see Donne's reference in the "Epistle" to *METEMPSYCHOSIS*).

Courage. *Noun*: (1) spirit, vigor, energy; (2) boldness or bravery; (3) sexual desire or lust.

Courtier, The. Book written originally in Italian (entitled *Il Libro del Cortegiano*) by Baldassare Castiglione (1478–1529). Castiglione was himself a courtier and diplomat and received a humanist education. The book essentially was written during 1513–16, but Castiglione continued revising it until it was published in 1528. It is the epitome of a "courtesy book," one that delineates the ideal qualities of a gentleman (and thus forms the basis for the ideal, well-rounded Renaissance man). It is structured as a dialogue in four books (representing four discussions on four evenings), with Pietro Bembo (a man Castiglione knew) as the primary speaker. Other real individuals are also made participants in the discussions with Bembo. The work immediately became popular and influential and was translated into several languages in the 16th century. The first English translation (by Sir Thomas Hoby) was published in 1561 and influenced the English court and major writers such as Sir Philip SIDNEY, SPENSER, Shakespeare, and Donne.

The ideal courtier is presented as one who is graceful, modest, learned, skilled in many areas, ethical, and cultivated.

The most important part of the work is the fourth book, in which Bembo specifies such central matters of Renaissance philosophy (especially from the perspectives of Christian humanism and Christian Platonism) as the natures of the universe, the soul, beauty, and love. Beauty is described as a circle with goodness at its center. The individual as a MICROCOSM and as a partaker of both angelic and animal characteristics and potentiality is an important consideration. The conflicts of reason and passion, the spiritual and the physical are discussed. For some of the other fundamental concepts embodied in this book, see PLATONIC.

Donne's awareness of *The Courtier* and its ideal doctrines is apparent throughout his work. Most specifically, however, he refers to Castiglione (without naming him) as "he which did lay / Rules to make courtiers" in lines 2–3 of "Satire 5." The ideal of the kiss as a union of souls is found in *The Courtier* and seems echoed by Donne at the opening of one of his *VERSE LETTERS* (one to Sir HENRY WOTTON that begins "Sir, more than kisses, letters mingle souls"). "Elegy 10: The Dream" employs the idea from *The Courtier* and other Neo-Platonic writings that a lover can form an image of his lady in his imagination that is superior to the physical vision of her with his senses. Also see "WHAT IF THIS PRESENT WERE THE WORLD'S LAST NIGHT," one of the *HOLY SONNETS*.

Covetize. *Noun*: covetousness.

Cozen. *Verb*: to cheat, deceive, defraud.

Crab. One of the twelve signs of the ZODIAC. Also called Cancer. Refers in some contexts to the summer solstice.

Cranfield, Lionel. See L. C.

Crants (Crantz). Personified character in "SATIRE 3" who represents an adherent of Protestant CALVINISM, loving the plain, simple, unadorned church as found in GENEVA.

Creature. *Noun*: (1) a created being, animate or inanimate; (2) an animal; (3) a human being; (4) anything created; (5) a person who owes his position, wealth, or power to another person [including a patron] and who is willing to carry out the will of the benefactor.

Crier. Town crier, one who would announce and advertise as he walked, like a human loudspeaker.

Cross-armed. Conventional pose of the melancholy lover. See line 22 of "To the Countess of Huntingdon" (beginning "That unripe side of earth").

Crown. A common reference in Donne's time to a coin worth five shillings.

Crowns of France. French coins—but a common pun in Donne's time involved "French crowns" as bald heads that result from syphilis (called the "French disease").

Crystal glass. A magnifying glass.

Curious. *Adjective*: (1) carefully or skillfully made, (2) ingenious, (3) inquisitive. *Adverb*: (1) exquisitely, (2) elaborately.

"Curse, The." One of the *SONGS AND SONNETS*. This is Donne's version of an ancient form of poetry, anathema, in which the speaker places a curse on his enemy. Donne's speaker is directing his curse to any man who thrives on gossip and rumor, to warn such a man not to try to discover and talk about the identity of the lady that the speaker loves ("MISTRESS"). It is tempting to relate this to Donne's own secret love for ANN MORE, but no evidence makes it explicit that such an autobiographical circumstance is indeed the motivating force behind this poem.

　　The first portion of the entire curse (or the first of many curses in the poem) is that such a man "wither," foreshadowing many types of witherings (shrivelings and declinings) wished on him in the rest of the poem—withering bodily, financially, emotionally, socially, and spiritually. The suggestion by Shawcross (see "Works" in "Selected Bibliography") that "wither" is also a sexual pun seems quite valid: i.e., he is cursing this would-be busybody about another's love with sexual impotence in his own. From this point on, curses are wrapped within curses in a seemingly endless stream. The speaker wants some dull, cold, unresponsive woman to love the man's only purse of money and to love him for no other reason than his money. But that is not all: let her be sexually unresponsive to the cursed man but to be sexually receptive ("YIELD") to his personal enemies. This man is also doomed to be scorned by a woman that no other men will even touch (i.e., he will not even be able to attract a woman who is universally rejected by other men—the ultimate shame). He will be forced to lie by denying ("forswear") to others the things that he actually has told this woman whom no one else will have, since he is torn between "missing" (not winning) her and "getting" (winning) her—i.e., between the fear of not at least having some sexual partner and the shame of having this particular partner that no one else will have.

The second stanza curses the man with madness (growing from sorrow) and gout (growing from cramps), both resulting from his lowly illicit love. He will not be disturbed ethically or spiritually by his sinful love, but only by the danger to (and the "withering" of) his own reputation ("fame") in degrading himself to this lowly woman. Through this sexual relationship with a woman closely related to him, he will (so the curse goes) beget an heir that will have a better claim to land that he himself would have inherited; therefore, he will doom himself to poverty ("scarceness"—another form of "withering"—both bodily and financially).

The third stanza presents alternative curses—either one will be satisfactory. This prying man will imagine committing treason so vividly that he will believe he did, then confess his crime, and be executed: no record will survive to vindicate his reputation with the truth, thus leaving his sons (all illegitimate ones) to inherit only the bad reputation of their father (since traitors' property was confiscated by the state). Or, equally satisfactory to the speaker, the man will so long have supported "parasites" (subservient, fawning hangers-on who have fed monetarily on the supporter) that he will have spent all of his money on them and be forced to turn to them to request support and thus become their parasite: they will not support him in turn, forcing the man to renounce his Christianity and become a Jew ("be circumcised") just to be able to join the Jewish communal fellowship in order to have a meal.

After such extreme curses, it would seem that none could be worse, but apparently the speaker feels that the climactic, most terrible ones have been saved for last, not the least of which is the venom of all stepmothers ("stepdames"). All the bad that can come from gamblers, tyrants, subjects of tyrants, plants, animals, minerals ("MINE[S]"), prophets, poets, and of anything else he can think of later to add to this curse ultimately is wished on the man who is the object of attack in the poem. To cover all possibilities, including the fact that a woman (a "she") rather than a man could also try to discover and talk about the identity of the speaker's lover, the speaker wittily and satirically implies that he does not have to bother formulating a lengthy curse for her, since Nature has already outdone him in curses placed on her just by creating her to be a woman.

Cusco. Cuzco in Peru.

Cutchannel. See COCHINEAL.

Cynthia. (1) Goddess of the moon, hunting, and chastity; (2) the moon.

Cyprian, Saint (about 200–258). Born at Carthage in Africa. After he was converted to Christianity, he sold all of his property to help the poor and adopted chastity for himself. Became Bishop of Carthage in 249 and served during the period of the persecution of Christians by the Roman emperor Decius. He was beheaded during the persecution under the emperor Valerian, thus becoming a Christian martyr. A professed follower and admirer of TERTULLIAN, whom he called his "master." Cyprian's writings are letters and treatises. He argues for the authority of bishops and against the baptism of heretics and schismatics. Donne refers to Cyprian frequently in the *SERMONS*.

D

Damp. *Noun*: (1) A noxious exhalation, vapor, or gas, including that from mines; (2) visible vapor, such as fog or mist; (3) moisture, dampness, humidity; (4) stupor or loss of consciousness; (5) a state of dejection; (6) a discouragement.

"Damp, The." One of the *SONGS AND SONNETS*. As in many others, Donne employs several elements of the PETRARCHAN love convention, ultimately only to satirize it, exaggerate it, and transform it into an extremely bawdy application.

The man speaking (to the lady whom he would like to seduce) projects by imagination to the time and circumstance after he is "dead"—already hinting to the reader who is aware of the Petrarchan convention that this man might be taking the lady to task for rejecting his amorous advances (see DIE). This, in fact, turns out to be the case: our "curiosity" is satisfied (just as is that of his "friends") when we discover through the rest of the first stanza that the lady's image has speared through his eyes and is implanted in his heart and that he is not so subtly accusing her of his own "murder." During his autopsy he imagines a "DAMP" of love engulfing the senses of all those men (the doctors and any friends) who are standing around the table on which his corpse is being "cut up." Since the "damp" is said to move through all their senses, the primary meaning from Donne's time applicable in line 5 and in the title of the poem seems to be "stupor" or "loss of consciousness." However, secondarily Donne seems to present it arising out of the man's heart as a "noxious vapor or killing gas from a mine," another valid definition in Donne's time (see DAMP for these and other possible connotations of the word in Donne's works). The man speaking presents the lady as sadistically having plotted the murder of the other men ("You think . . . damp . . . will move . . . and work"). It is as if she has created a death-trap in the body of the speaker in order to "prefer" (promote, raise, expand) her destruction of only one man (a mere single "murder") into a much more impressive "massacre" of many men, thus illustrating her great power. The language and imagery here begin to be more violent and suggestive of armies, clever weapons of destruction, and assertion of military might. This becomes a unifying METAPHYSICAL CONCEIT through the poem: the battle of the sexes here is like armies struggling for "victories," "conquests," control, and boastfulness.

The speaker in the next stanza denigrates these victories as of low quality, inferior. But if the lady really wants to be "BRAVE" (both "courageous" and "showy, boastful") and ultimately have more joy in her conquests of men's hearts, the speaker is ready to spell out the process that she can employ to achieve this "PLEASURE" (this word taking on multiple meaning, one being personal sexual satisfaction). The man presents the process in a miniature allegory: she should first "kill" the symbolic powerful giant, her Disdain (i.e., dispense with her typically Petrarchan scorn and rejection of men—a deliberately witty and paradoxical action as phrased, since that very Disdain is what she usually employs to "kill" men). Then she must dispense with concern for her "HONOR," specifically the meaning implying protecting her chastity: this "honor" is another quality that keeps men away. Next, she should even further rise up and rebel against herself, expressed by Donne in a METAPHYSICAL CONCEIT (coming within his larger one of battle that unites the poem) of the lady like the staunch Roman Empire suddenly being overrun by the barbarian tribes (GOTHS and VANDALS) that sacked Rome and destroyed many records of its history, art, and culture. Just so, she should erase her personal empire and past history of aloofness with men, bending now to her own passions and senses, giving them free reign to forge a new life of sexual pleasure in the MICROCOSM of herself. By disposing of such aids and weapons (catalogued in this stanza) the woman can be more "BRAVE" by attempting to "KILL" the man, and the man urges her to do so, since he now means that she should "kill" him sexually by agreeing to intercourse (as opposed to the earlier meaning in the first stanza of "killing" him by her rejection).

The third stanza presents the speaker, on his side of the battle, threatening to "muster" his troops, his allegorical warriors Constancy and Secretness: he could promise her, if he wished to, that he will remain faithful to her and will keep their affair a secret (implying that this promise would make her more willing to yield herself to him). But, significantly, the man says that he will not make such promises: he will not profess to have or to employ these qualities himself and will not demand ("look for") such qualities in her. So, he would rather that their sexual encounter be one only for mutual and transitory sexual pleasure, with no commitments implied. Even more explicitly he wants to be "killed" and to "die" sexually at her hands, by her using only her sexual weapons as a physical woman. If she will "TRY" (test) her "passive valor" (i.e., her passive acceptance of the man being the active partner, the aggressor in sexual consummation), she will show her bravery and greater power to "kill" the man and win a "conquest" that gives herself greater "pleasure" than when she earlier actively and aggressively rejected the man. With this recommended new military tactic the woman has the greater odds for victory over any man, according to the speaker who will willingly himself accept this kind of "defeat."

Danow. Danube River.

Dante Alighieri (1265–1321). Italian poet, soldier, and politician whose greatest work is *The Divine Comedy*, a part of which is *Inferno*, portraying hell. In line 158 of "Satire 4" Donne refers to Dante (without naming him) as the one "who dreamed he saw hell."

Danvers, Lady. See HERBERT, MAGDALEN.

Danvers, Sir John. See HERBERT, MAGDALEN.

Dard. Dared.

Deal. *Verb*: (1) to share or distribute, (2) to deliver blows, (3) to do business or to trade, (4) to associate with or to have to do with a person or thing, (5) to have sexual intercourse, (6) to take action.

Dearth. *Noun*: (1) famine, (2) a condition in which food is scarce, (3) scarcity or lack of anything.

Death. See DIE.

Death bell. Bell tolled in a "death knell" after someone has died. Compare FUNERAL BELL and PASSING BELL.

"Death, be not proud, though some have called thee." First line of one of the *HOLY SONNETS*. The speaker of this sonnet is a Christian with absolute confidence in his eternal salvation and triumph over physical death. His assertive confidence is evident from his opening address to personified Death in his command for it not to be proud, but the feeling of the speaker also is conveyed by the four consecutive, booming heavy stresses on the first four single-syllable words in that opening. In lines 1–2 he goes on to say that although Death is commonly regarded as "mighty and dreadful," it really is not: the speaker's confidence appears in yet another emphatic and heavily-stressed series of four words ("thou art not so"). The remainder of the sonnet is the speaker's proof, through a series of reasons, why Death is not "mighty and dreadful" and should not be "proud."

In a contemptuous address to "poor Death," lines 3–4 say that Death thinks that he conquers people (i.e., with physical death), but the speaker says that Death does not really kill (i.e., he cannot deal out spiritual death to those of Christian belief, those like the speaker). Lines 5–6 propose as the next reason (why Death is not powerful, not to be feared, and should not be proud) the fact that a human secures pleasure from rest and sleep and, since rest and sleep are common images or symbols ("pictures") of Death, then a human should secure even more pleasure from Death itself. He supports this assertion with the following two lines (7–8): even the best of men on earth readily ("soonest") die to achieve both this rest after earthly pain and freedom for their souls. Line 9 emphasizes the essential weakness of Death (in contrast to the common view of its great strength) by listing and placing heavy stresses upon all of the things that Death has to depend upon for its operation: death happens through providential determination ("fate"), quirks of fortune or accident or bad luck ("chance"), such actions of "kings" as sending men to war or ordering executions, and "desperate men" (who commit murder or suicide because of their despair). So, Death is subservient to and dependent upon all of these for any power it has. The speaker further belittles death in line 10 by sarcastically suggesting that its common companions ("poison, war, and sickness") are not very respectable, in addition to the continued implication that Death kills through their agency, not through his own. The extreme cataloguing of things in this portion of the sonnet emphasizes the very many things that Death is inferior to. And if Death were to claim that it can suddenly, with one stroke, put people to "sleep," the speaker already has an answer: a drug such as opium (from the "poppy") or magic, hypnotic spells or enchantments ("charms") can do so as well or better. The question "why swell'st thou then?" implies a return to the command for Death not to be proud, not to swell up with pride. But it also plays a bit, in a grimly humorous pun, on the image of Death as seen in a corpse that is swollen: the speaker sees the effect of physical death on a dead body as exemplifying the pride in Death personified. But it is pride without justification, as he has shown.

The Christian confidence and final deflating of death is in the last two lines. The short words making up the first four syllables of line 13 ("One short sleep past") move rapidly with regular rhythm, conveying the shortness (and thus insignificance) of the sleep of physical death ending earthly life. The important fact is that this brief sleep allows us to awake into eternity with death obliterated. The last four words ("Death, thou shalt die") create a parallel and contrast to the opening four words of the sonnet. The final four, in fact, provide the definitive answer, the epitomized reason why Death should not be proud: Death itself, paradoxically, will die, since, with spiritual life for the Christian in heaven, all death will end. This parallel and contrast brings the reader full circle in the poem, just as the CIRCLE symbolizes (for the Christian speaker) the infinity that ends death.

Death's Duel. The title given to Donne's last sermon when it was separately printed in 1632: see *SERMONS*, discussion of the sermon preached in 1631.

Death's Head. See MEMENTO MORI.

Deign. *Verb*: (1) to condescend to bestow or grant; (2) to condescend to accept, to take or accept graciously; (3) to treat someone as worthy, to dignify someone.

Descry. *Verb*: (1) to declare, make known, reveal; (2) to reveal something hidden or secret; (3) to cry out against or denounce; (4) to see or perceive; (5) to explore or investigate.

Destiny. *Noun*: (1) whatever is fated to happen, (2) the power or agent that determines events, (3) supernatural or divine preordination, (4) God's divine providence, (5) mythological goddess of destiny.

Devereux, Robert (1566–1601). 2nd Earl of Essex. A favorite of Queen ELIZABETH. The commander whom Donne served in the Cadiz and Azores Islands expeditions of 1596 and 1597. The latter military experience served as the occasion for "The Storm" and "The Calm." After disagreeing with the Queen and fomenting a minor rebellion against her, Essex was prosecuted and executed in 1601.

Devotions Upon Emergent Occasions. Prose work by Donne published in early 1624. In late November of 1623 Donne was seriously ill with a fever, then of epidemic proportions in London. During his lengthy recovery through December he wrote this work based on his illness and published it in early 1624, with a dedication to Prince CHARLES. The same sickness led to his writing of "A HYMN TO GOD THE FATHER" and probably "A HYMN TO GOD MY GOD, IN MY SICKNESS." The work presents Donne's personal experiences during the stages of his illness, but of greater import is the expansion of his sickness into a commentary on the human condition and man's relationship to God. The "emergent occasions" are the unplanned occurrences during his illness that simply emerge (or appear or arise). There are twenty-three separate Devotions in the work, each one consisting of "Meditation," "Expostulation," and "Prayer" in that order. The "Meditation" ponders and expounds upon his own and the general human condition; the "Expostulation" addresses questions to and debates with God; and the "Prayer" prays to God. Each part is numbered according to the Devotion in which it appears. Certain of the "Meditations" traditionally have been the most popular and frequently-anthologized portions of the work, and they are emphasized in this entry (and in others that relate to this work) in this "Dictionary."

Principles of structure may be found in the simple chronological progression through Donne's illness from onset to recovery and in recurring images and emphasis on major motifs of imagery through the work or in large portions of it. But also critics see unity in the embodiment of meditative procedures (especially from the influence of IGNATIUS LOYOLA's work), the philosophical vision of the entire work, and in the expansion of the literal into metaphorical and symbolic dimensions through the work.

Devotion 1 is titled "The first alteration, the first grudging of the sickness," and "Meditation 1" begins "Variable, and therefore miserable condition of Man; this minute I was well, and am ill this minute." His personal experience of change from health to sickness causes him to see change as typical of the human condition: to him, man is "miserable" because he is subject to change. This is rather different from, or a variation of, the traditional Christian view that man is miserable because of his fallen state: i.e., Donne is assuming that man is subject to change because of his fallen condition. In fact, he goes on to say that "we" (mankind) brought our own changeable condition upon us by blowing out the flame of immortality that God gave us: we forfeited our chance of life without change when we committed the original sin. And change means life subject to sickness, decay, and death, an end which his own ill health might bring. Sickness and change are inherent in the "miserable condition of man," a phrase emphatically used three times in this meditation, including occurrences in the first and last sentences of it. "Meditation 1" also begins the recurring and central reference through the work to man as a "little world," a MICROCOSM. He sees dangerous disruptions ("earthquakes," "thunders," "noises," etc.) in himself at the onset of his sickness that may bring destruction to the world of himself. So, he and (by implication) all people suffer under the penalty of the Fall, continually see its consequences reenacted in themselves, are subject to change, and are in the "miserable condition of man" in this fallen world.

Devotion 2 ("The strength, and the function of the senses, and other faculties change and fail") presents the rapid weakening of Donne by the illness, with the fever causing him to sweat: in "Meditation 2" he relates this to the punishment placed on Adam (Genesis 3:19) to eat bread by the sweat of his brow, but in Donne's case he has no desire for food. His taste and sight rapidly fail him. In "Expostulation 2" he concentrates on God's mercy and acknowledges that the haste God will use to reunite his body on Resurrection Day is more important than the rapidity with which his body dissolves by the power of this disease.

Devotion 3 ("The patient takes his bed") begins (in "Meditation 3") with "We attribute but one privilege and advantage to man's body above other moving creatures, that he is not as others grovelling but of an erect, of an upright form naturally built and disposed to the contemplation of heaven." This traditional view of man above other animals and walking upright connotes man's dignity and value. So, Donne uses this view to begin the meditation and then elaborates on it: man's form raises his soul closer to heaven, and it allows man to contemplate better his ultimate home. But suddenly Donne reverses these feelings, based on his personal experiences in this sickness: ". . . but what state hath he in this dignity? A fever can fillip him down, a fever can depose him; a fever can bring that head which yesterday carried a crown of gold five feet towards a crown of glory as low as his own foot today." Suddenly, he insists on man's essential weakness (as in many of the *HOLY SONNETS* and *DIVINE POEMS*). Man is portrayed as a king (including a literal king in his imagery), but any individual (including a king) can be knocked from his supposedly high position even by "a fever" (the power of which is emphatically conveyed by Donne's repetition of the phrase, with heavy stress on it in pronunciation). The METAPHYSICAL CONCEIT in this passage of poetic prose centers on the analogy developed around the state and regality ("prerogative," "state," "depose," "head," "crown"). Donne even employs a witty pun on "feet" and "foot" (measure and human anatomy) with some sarcasm directed at man's pompous view of himself and at man's delusion about his own power and dignity. From this point on in the meditation, Donne emphasizes lying on the ground and in the bed as postures more indicative of man's true state, that of weakness and lowliness. He first states what becomes a central image and symbol through the work: "A sickbed is a grave. . . ." At the end of the meditation Donne says, "Miserable and (though common to all) inhuman posture where I must practice my lying in the grave by lying still and not practice my resurrection by rising any more!" Donne in the sickbed, then, exemplifies the posture of every human—weak, unable to help himself, and foreshadowing his ultimate lying in the grave.

Devotion 4 ("The physician is sent for"): "Meditation 4" is another that at first exalts man ("It is too little to call man a little world; except God, man is a diminutive to nothing"). The idea of man as a MICROCOSM ("a little world") does not do justice to man. Man seems to have more parts than the MACROCOSM. If all of man's parts were stretched out proportionately to the sizes of those correspondent things on earth, the result would be a world greater than the earth. So, paradoxically, Donne argues that man (the microcosm) is greater than the world (the macrocosm)! The little is bigger than the big! And, if the creatures of this microcosm, man's all-reaching thoughts, were added, the immensity is beyond comprehension. So, until the middle of the meditation, man seems greater than the world. But at about mid-point Donne begins steadily to tear down this impressive structure when he returns to the fact of disease so easily infecting this microcosm: then man's supposed "abundance" is "miserable," and his supposed "riches" are "beggarly." In fact, man cannot even cure his own diseases, as some animals are able to do. Some animals seem to be their own physician and pharmacist ("APOTHECARY"). But man has to rely on his "HERCULES," the physician, to combat these monsters. Even though the "drugger" (the seller, the provider of the apothecary's drug) might be near to us, we do not perceive it. We call on the physician for help, but we are not the physician himself; therefore, since man is essentially helpless, Donne retracts his earlier view by saying, "Call back therefore thy meditation again and bring it down." By the end of the meditation man seems only a "handful of dust" (not even, perhaps, on the level of Hamlet's sense of man as the "quintessence of dust"). His "soaring thoughts" taste only of ashes in confronting the fact of the grave. With this meditation Donne has taken the first step in expanding the physician symbolically in the *Devotions*. Just as man calls the physician for help to raise him from the sickbed, so does man have to call God to raise him from the grave. In fact, in "Prayer 4" Donne refers to God as the Lord of both spiritual health and bodily health and says, "thou in thy Son art the Physician, the applier of both."

Devotion 5 ("The physician comes"), Devotion 6 ("The physician is afraid"), and Devotion 7 ("The physician desires to have others joined with him"): Donne considers in Devotion 5 the sick man's solitude (friends are afraid to visit him) that seems worse even than that in hell (there is society there!). He notes that even God is not alone (there are three persons in the TRINITY) and that there are orders of angels. In his bed he knows he is alone, but in the grave he will not be conscious of his solitude. Fear itself is explored (the word is almost endlessly repeated) in Devotion 6. In 7 a consideration of having many physicians in consultation about his own illness leads Donne to feel compassion ultimately for those in an even more fearful and miserable condition—the poor people who are sick, who cannot afford to be treated privately by physicians (and rather are "thrown" into hospitals, languishing and waiting for the physician's attention). But even worse are those who die on the flint of the street as their bed, passed by people with ears and eyes "harder" than the flint (i.e., implying their lack of compassion).

Devotion 8 ("The king sends his own physician"), Devotion 9 ("Upon their consultation, they prescribe"), and Devotion 10 ("They find the disease to steal on insensibly, and endeavor to meet with it so"): Devotion 8 (in "Meditation 8") moves from the pitiable literal and physical sickness of the poor in the world (in Devotion 7) to both literal and symbolic sicknesses possessed by all humans of any level, even by kings ("Scarce any misery equal to sickness, and they are subject to that equally with their lowest subject." Donne goes on to say, "They [kings] are gods, but sick gods . . . . God is called angry, and sorry, and weary, and heavy; but never a sick God: for then he might die like men, as our gods do." So, sickness now signifies a characteristic of the human condition: it symbolizes inherited original sin that leads to inevitable death for any human. Sin infects all men and will kill all mortal bodies. Devotion 9 extends the analogy of the physician(s) compared to God: in "Meditation 9" he sees in the consultation by the physicians that there is hope of remedies, and he (in "Expostulation 9") comprehends that the persons of the

TRINITY are in consultation over both his body and soul. In "Prayer 9" he prays for God to raise him out of his sickness of sin and to provide him spiritual PHYSIC. Devotion 10 relates the disease in Donne's body to the inherent decay in the earth: the world had its sickness ("dropsy") in the Flood and will have its ultimate destructive disease ("fever") in the Fire to end the world. Just as his fever works secretly and unpredictably, the final Fire for the world cannot be foreseen, except by the ultimate Physician, God. (The MICROCOSM/MACROCOSM concept is extended even further in Devotion 10 by Donne's relating of similar natures and undermining processes occurring in cities and states, in addition to men and the earth.)

Devotion 11 ("They use cordials, to keep the venom and malignity of the disease from the heart"), Devotion 12 ("They apply pigeons to draw the vapors from the head"), Devotion 13 ("The sickness declares the infection and malignity thereof by spots"), Devotion 14 ("The physicians observe these accidents to have fallen upon the critical days"), and Devotion 15 ("I sleep not day nor night"): "Meditation 11" calls an individual's heart the "King of man," relating the MICROCOSM to the MACROCOSM again. Both the heart and a king receive "venom and poison" directed at them. In "Expostulation 11" and "Prayer 11" Donne relates the CORDIALs given by his physicians to spiritual cordials given by God the Physician, those such as God's peace, the water of baptism, Christ's blood in the Eucharist, and obedience to God's will. Devotion 12 relates the VAPORS within the little world or state of Donne to the "venomous rumors" that wound a political state. Medicine in Donne's time used pigeons (either eaten or applied to the feet) to try to draw the harmful vapors away from the head, and Donne relates these pigeons to "virtue" and "power" in the political state to rid it of noxious vapors. On the spiritual level, Donne compares the pigeons to the "Dove" (i.e., the Holy Spirit: see TRINITY) provided by God and to the Sacraments as "doves" to rid us of sins. Devotion 13 argues that man partakes of more misery than happiness and that many times one must suffer more to be able to achieve happiness thereafter: his specific experience of this paradox is the fact that the spots appearing on his body show that he is in worse health than he already was sure of being in and that this stage of the disease is a "poor step toward being well" (end of "Meditation 13"). Devotion 14 parallels the critical days of Donne's illness with the critical days of man's "false happiness" in this world generally and ultimately compares mortal time to eternity. Devotion 15 contends that God originally wanted sleep to refresh man bodily but that, after man himself brought death into the world with the Fall, God now uses sleep to suggest that death also will be pleasant and like sleep. But Donne cannot partake of this pleasure at this stage of his disease and suggests that his staying awake perhaps should be interpreted as a foretaste of his existence in eternity where no sleep exists.

Devotion 16 ("From the bells of the church adjoining, I am daily remembered of my burial in the funerals of others"), Devotion 17 ("Now, this bell tolling softly for another, says to me, thou must die"), and Devotion 18 ("The bell rings out, and tells me in him, that I am dead"): these three devotions concern three bells that Donne hears ringing for others—(1) while they are dying (the passing bell in Devotion 17), (2) after they die (the death bell in Devotion 18), and (3) at their funerals (the funeral bell in Devotion 16). Donne, himself sick and possibly dying, ponders the meaning of these bells for himself, for his relation to other humans, for his relation to the church as a whole, and for his relation to God. (The most famous and frequently-quoted of all of Donne's prose writings is "Meditation 17," in this particular group of devotions.) Devotion 16 refers to Donne hearing from his sickbed the bells of ST. PAUL'S CATHEDRAL or another neighboring church that never seem to cease ringing for the funerals of people of the area: he regards this as a promised "comfort" whenever his own funeral comes. Devotion 17 portrays the bell "tolling softly for another": this is the passing bell tolled slowly and softly when an individual is dying. In "Meditation 17" Donne says that hearing this bell tells him that he too must die, and it convinces him that he has ties with all other humans in that all are subject to mortality. He is related to all humans in the universal Church: all are "members" of one "body" controlled by a "head" (the separate individuals are like parts of a body that are connected and interrelated into a unified whole). From the conceit of individuals unified like parts of a body, Donne proceeds to all men as connected parts of a book, a "volume," written by "one author" (i.e., God). Each man is like a "chapter," and physical death is being merely "translated into a better language" (playing on "TRANSLATE" as change in language, transformation in form, and transference in place [i.e., from earth to heaven]), rather than being "torn out" of the book. Pushing the METAPHYSICAL CONCEIT even further, Donne pictures God's "translators" as "age," "sickness," "war," "justice," etc. And God will rebind all the scattered "leaves" of the volume of mankind in that ultimate "library" of heaven. Anyone hearing the passing bell, Donne says, is hearing "that bell which is passing a piece of himself out of this world." This sense of unity with all of humanity leads to another

conceit in the most famous passage of Donne's prose: "No man is
an island entire of itself; every man is a piece of the continent, a
part of the main; if a clod be washed away by the sea, Europe is
the less, as well as if a promontory were, as well as if a manor of
thy friend's, or of thine own were; any man's death diminishes
me, because I am involved in mankind; and therefore never send
to know for whom the bell tolls; it tolls for thee." Mankind is like
a continent (the "main," the mainland), and each man is a part of
it, rather than an island unto himself. Any man's death subtracts
from the totality of that continent of humanity. The passing bell
tolls for a part of one's self as united in all of humanity, then. One
should notice, however, that to Donne this unity is in a spiritual
and Christian context: all men are created by God, are part of one
church, are mere men, and are subject to the same miseries,
diseases, and death. Donne is not concerned here with human
interrelatedness in political and social realms, although many
modern quotations of this passage out of its context imply these
senses. Donne's primary concerns with man as God's creation, as a
fallen creature in earthly misery, and as a Christian that must
properly respond to misery are reinforced by the conceit that he
immediately introduces following this famous passage: " . . .
affliction is a treasure, and scarce any man hath enough of it. No
man hath affliction enough that is not matured and ripened by it
and made fit for God by that affliction." Suffering is not primarily
valuable in that it teaches one about this world and this life: its
value is that it convinces one that he is merely a weak human and
prepares one for God and the next life and the important spiritual
goal of reaching "home" in heaven. Affliction is like gold made
into coins to be spent, gold that is only useful on the journey
through earthly life if it allows an individual to progress
spiritually "nearer and nearer our home, heaven, by it." By the
end of "Meditation 17" Donne makes the "bell" analogous to a
shovel that "digs out" the gold of the dying man's affliction and
applies it to Donne himself who better sees that God is our "only
security," thus ending the conceit of monetary matter as spiritual
treasure. Devotion 18 presents Donne hearing the death bell rung
loudly (as opposed to the soft sounds of the passing bell) after the
person has died: Donne makes the louder and more rapid ringing
represent a quickened "pulse" that indicates "stronger" and "more"
and "better life" (i.e., the dead person's eternal, spiritual life has
begun now). Donne cites in "Meditation 18" some opinions
(especially of ST. AUGUSTINE and ST. JEROME) about the origin
and nature of the soul, concluding that most important is its
ultimate destination, which no one left on earth can know: Donne's

"charity" tells him that the soul of the person who has just died has gone to "everlasting rest, and joy, and glory."

Devotion 19 ("At last, the physicians, after a long and stormy voyage, see land; they have so good signs of the concoction of the disease, as that they may safely proceed to purge"), Devotion 20 ("Upon these indications of digested matter, they proceed to purge"), Devotion 21 ("God prospers their practice, and he, by them, calls Lazarus out of his tomb, me out of my bed"), Devotion 22 ("The physicians consider the root and occasion, the embers, and coals, and fuel of the disease, and seek to purge or correct that"), and Devotion 23 ("They warn me of the fearful danger of relapsing"): "Meditation 19" and "Expostulation 19" present Donne's disease as a storm at sea in which he and the physicians look for some land on which to end the turbulent journey. Donne speaks of God as using both literal and metaphorical language in his Word (using TYPES and other forms of symbolism): by God's example Donne, being "bold," speaks of his illness with metaphors that extend even to relating this "sea" to God's "waters" that are afflictions and sins in this earthly life. But, paradoxically, God fights these sinful and calamitous "waters" with "waters" such as baptism. "Expostulation 19" becomes a CONCEIT that is almost an endless sea itself of interconnected images and extensions metaphorically from notions of the "sea": for example, in Donne's "sea" of illness, the saving ship is the physician (who thus is comparable to Noah's ark). Near the end of "Expostulation 19" Donne seems to pun on his name (as he does in "A HYMN TO GOD THE FATHER," apparently written on the same occasion as this prose work): "Every thing is immediately done, which is done when thou [i.e., God] wouldst have it done. Thy purpose terminates every action, and what was done before that, is undone yet." In Devotion 20 "Meditation 20" considers the irony that in any ordered entity, including man, all pieces need to be present to yield happiness, yet he must now be purged by his physicians, to have matter withdrawn from him to beget his own health and happiness: to Donne, this represents again the "slippery condition of man." Then "Expostulation 20" expands further the early implication that God is the ultimate physician, as Donne sees an analogous situation: as his earthly physician purges him physically for bodily health, so does God use "purgative PHYSIC," the "evacuation" of his soul by "confession" to attain spiritual health. As he submits by faith to strange bodily medicine from earthly physicians, so does he agree to submit to God's GALENIST "contrary" physic for his soul. The development of God as the Physician reaches its climax in Devotion 21,

"Meditation 21": "I cannot rise out of my bed till the physician enable me, nay, I cannot tell that I am able to rise till he tell me so. . . . Another tells me I may rise; and I do so." Literally the earthly physician "enables" and "tells" him to "rise" out of the sickbed, but the larger implication is that God will spiritually "enable" and "tell" him to "rise" out of his grave at the Last Judgment. When Donne stands up, he is dizzy: "I go round; and I am a new argument of the new philosophy that the earth moves round." Thus, Donne adapts the new ideas stemming from COPERNICAN astronomy, from the NEW PHILOSOPHY, to his personal situation in a humorous, but serious way. He can believe that the earth moves when it seems to him to be standing still, if he can seem to be standing but also be carried in a "giddy and circular motion." The MICROCOSM again illustrates the MACROCOSM. Previously the earth seemed to be the fixed center of the universe, but now scientists claim that it is not, a fact that leads Donne to assert (now making the MACROCOSM illustrate the MICROCOSM!), "Man hath no center but misery; there, and only there, he is fixed and sure to find himself." The emphasis on man's "misery," then, continues as a keynote even from "the miserable condition of man" introduced in "Meditation 1." Donne ends "Meditation 21" on this note of misery, but with spiritual hope from spiritual preparation as an antidote: "Everything serves to exemplify, to illustrate man's misery. But I need go no farther than myself. For a long time I was not able to rise; at last I must be raised by others; and now I am up, I am ready to sink lower than before." His physicians are those "others" that raise him out of his miserable sickbed, and this makes him ready to "sink lower" than the sickbed by going into the grave itself when he dies, because he knows that he will be raised out of it by God the Physician. His soul is able to rise out of both man's sinful condition (the sickbed) and death (the grave). In Devotion 22 Donne develops a conceit of the body as a farm that is weed-covered, sterile, unprofitable, and expensive. He also says, "to cure the body, the root, the occasion of diseases, is a work reserved for the great Physician, which he doth never any other way, but by glorifying these bodies in the next world." Devotion 23 takes the literal physicians' warnings of a possible relapse of Donne's fever and applies it to the danger always of man relapsing into spiritual carelessness and then into sin as a sickness. In "Expostulation 23" he fervently expresses to Father, Son, and Holy Spirit the hope that he will not overthrow all of the PHYSIC that they have applied to him and "relapse into those spiritual sicknesses from which your infinite mercies have withdrawn me." The last sentence of the *Devotions* (at the conclusion of "Prayer 23") prays "against . . . a relapse into those sins which I have truly repented and thou hast fully pardoned." Ultimately, then, it is the sickness of sin, not of fever, that concerns Donne. His physical sickness itself is indeed only an "occasion" out of which his and all humanity's spiritual and bodily natures in relation to God are analyzed.

Diana (Dian). See CYNTHIA and DIAN'S FANE.

Dian's fane. Dian's temple. In line 14 of "To the Countess of Bedford" (beginning "To have written then"), one of the *VERSE LETTERS*, Donne refers to the belief that ST. PAUL'S CATHEDRAL in London was built on the site of a temple to Diana (i.e., CYNTHIA).

Die. *Verb* used in various senses by Donne (and other writers of his time), but particularly in the following: (1) to cease living; (2) to experience rejection by a lady (in the PETRARCHAN love convention); (3) to part from a loved one; and (4) to experience sexual intercourse, orgasm (since each sexual consummation was believed to subtract some moments from a person's life)—see "THE CANONIZATION," "THE DAMP," "THE FLEA," "THE PARADOX," and many other works for occurrences of the word in this sense.

Dildo(es). *Noun*: artificial penis(es).   Used for female masturbation.

Diocis. Diocese.

Diocletian (Dioclesian) (245–313).   Roman emperor from 284 to 305 who persecuted Christians (303–305) and is thus the epitome of a persecutor.

Diogenes the Cynic (about 412–323 B.C.).   Greek philosopher who lived in a tub to illustrate scorn for luxuries and who, with a lantern during the day, searched for an honest man.

Dionysius the Areopagite. See HIERARCHY, THE HEAVENLY.

Dionysius the Elder (430?–367 B.C.).   Greek tyrant who ruled in Syracuse (405–367 B.C.).   He wrote a play that was given an award, and in the celebration of it he died from excessive drinking. Donne alludes to him in *DEVOTIONS UPON EMERGENT OCCASIONS* ("Meditation 7"), but Donne also confuses the Elder with his son Dionysius the Younger (395?–343 B.C.), the tyrant who was deposed in 357 because of misrule.

Discover. *Verb*: (1) to uncover, (2) to disclose or reveal, (3) to show, (4) to manifest or display, (5) to find out, (6) to see.

Discovery of occult resemblances in things apparently unlike. See METAPHYSICAL CONCEIT.

Disgest (digest). *Verb*: to discharge or disperse.

Disparate experience. See DISSOCIATION OF SENSIBILITY.

Disport. *Noun*: recreation, entertainment, amusement.

Disproportion. *Verb*: to make out of due proportion or to make inappropriate or to mismatch.

Dissociation of sensibility. A famous phrase used by the poet and critic T.S. Eliot in a 1921 *London Times Literary Supplement* review of H.J.C. Grierson's 1921 volume entitled *Metaphysical Lyrics and Poems of the Seventeenth Century.* Eliot says that later in the 17th century (after Donne and the other major METAPHYSICAL poets) a "dissociation of sensibility set in." He apparently means a separation of thought and feeling or of thought and experience in verse, since he praises Donne by saying that "a thought to Donne was an experience." He also asserts that "When a poet's mind is perfectly equipped for its work, it is constantly amalgamating disparate experience." He also calls sensibility "the feeling" in verse.

Dissolution. *Noun*: (1) reduction of any body or mass to its constituent elements; (2) destruction of an existing condition; (3) disintegration or decomposition; (4) undoing of a tie, bond, union, or connection; (5) death.

"Dissolution, The." One of the *SONGS AND SONNETS.* Scholars and critics have tried to identify the occasion of the poem with the death of a particular loved one in Donne's life. Even though specific evidence has not been discovered, speculation centers on LUCY, COUNTESS OF BEDFORD, or, even more plausibly, on ANN MORE. (Marotti [see "Critical Studies: Poetry, Miscellaneous" in "Selected Bibliography"] argues for possible puns on "More" in lines 18 and 24, although he feels that the poem probably was not written about her death.)

The speaker, the man in mourning, asserts that with the death of his beloved all of her bodily, physical matter (that which dies, as opposed to the soul that still lives) returns, dissolves to its "first ELEMENTS"—i.e., to fire, air, water, and earth. Everything mortal must die and return to its constituent elements, and her body is no exception. But the speaker claims that he and the lady were united as two beings in one and thus their elements constituted one MICROCOSM made of two. Since this is so, her soul's departing leaves her body to turn back into the elements that made it up, back into him. He is almost overburdened by the smothering, physical elements from her now accumulated in him (symbolically, these elements are his extremely painful, worldly, physical existence and grief after her death and her spiritual release—a release he too would like). During his love with her while she was alive, the man manifested his four elements in the forms of passion (fire), sighs (air), tears (water), and despair (earth), like an unsatisfied PETRARCHAN lover, but she was able to calm these elements, and she indeed almost had extinguished ("worn out") these elements by reciprocating his love (in contrast to the Petrarchan lady who would not reciprocate). This secure love was removed with her death and thus regenerates, replenishes, reinstates ("doth repair") these four elements and their restlessness as he now has to long for her again after she has died (paradoxically, this "repair" actually is a "loss" of security, love, and the lady's presence). This reinstatement of the four elements in him plunges him into what seems a hopeless prospect for a wretched, emotion-torn existence.

Line 15, however, begins his hope for a solution that consequently is outlined in the remainder of the poem. He sees that his "fire" (again, passion or emotion) is increasing with the added fuel (air, water, earth as sighs, tears, despair): i.e., his extreme grief and mournfulness and the elements expressing them increase his longing, desire (fire) to be reunited with the lady. This develops into a METAPHYSICAL CONCEIT by the end of the poem: the elements that serve as fuel are like a stockpile or "STORE" of munitions or "POWDER" (gunpowder) that, through his "fire" (passion) ignites and explodes. Thus, in the speaker's own death his soul (like a bullet) will be propelled so forcefully that, even though her soul (also a bullet) left earlier, his soul will overtake hers, and he will be reunited with her and have again that secure love, now established in the spiritual realm. Within this conceit, however, Donne develops a subsidiary one (lines 16–

21): the speaker is like a king who has conquered another state and brought home its treasure, implying that the lady's love and whole being have been deposited in him at her death. But with more wealth accumulated the king spends more of it and very soon must "break" (be bankrupt). Here "STORE" implies a stockpile of wealth, treasure. But the man, like the king, tends to increase spending ("use") of the elements accumulated within him from her: i.e., a true love is "active," just as the king who is more than a nonentity or figurehead is "active." The man's active expression, his use of his love does not end, then, with the lady's death, but rather increases to such an extent that he is assured of reunion (or remarriage after their earthly marriage was parted by death?) in the hereafter.

By the end of the poem the title and the idea of "DISSOLUTION" thus accumulate multiple implications. The overall conceit depends upon the dissolving of the lady's body (or any mortal creation) into its physical elements, into its components at death. There is also a dissolution of the physical, earthly love of the couple occurring at the death of one partner. And, if the poem is interpreted autobiographically as concerning the death of ANN MORE, then the Anglican marriage vow of the two being together until death parts them might well suggest that the dissolution is that of Donne's own marriage. There is also metaphorically present a financial dissolution, "breaking," bankruptcy. And there is dissolution of powder and the elements by their explosion with "fire." The final dissolution is the physical death of the speaker himself and consequently the dissolving of his own earthly existence. The final irony, however, rising out of all these "dissolutions" is that ultimately there is regeneration and new life optimistically projected for formation in the spiritual world—remarriage of the lovers in a union of their spirits.

Disuse. *Verb*: (1) to make one unaccustomed to anything, (2) to discontinue the practice or use of something.

Disused. *Adjective*: unaccustomed.

Divine Poems. Traditional title for the grouping of Donne's religious poems, including the subdivisions *LA CORONA* and *HOLY SONNETS*, as well as separately-titled hymns and other poems. Such a division generally appears in editions after the second one (1635), in which such a section is designated by the running head on the pages. Twenty-seven of these poems (although not included in a grouping with this title) were published in the first edition of 1633, and later editions added further ones. These Christian poems were written at various times in Donne's life, and many cannot be precisely dated. A few poems have dates specified or can be dated rather accurately by the occasion depicted. Some are late, coming after Donne's entry into the church in 1615 and some after his becoming Dean of ST. PAUL'S CATHEDRAL in 1621. But others clearly come before he was ordained: obviously so in "GOOD FRIDAY, 1613. RIDING WESTWARD," most likely so in the case of *LA CORONA*, and suspected so in several of the *HOLY SONNETS*.

In this "Dictionary" ten of the most famous and frequently-anthologized *HOLY SONNETS* are entered individually, using the first line of each as a title. Also, the three hymns and "Good Friday, 1613. Riding Westward" are entered separately by their titles. The content of all the remaining poems of *Divine Poems* has been examined for elements to make up other entries.

Do. *Verb*: (1) to put forth action or effort; (2) to perform or carry out; (3) to accomplish or finish; (4) to copulate, have sexual intercourse [see, for example, the wordplay in "THE GOOD-MORROW" and "THE INDIFFERENT"].

Dr. Faustus. Play (the full title is *The Tragical History of Dr. Faustus*) by MARLOWE. The tragic hero (Dr. Faustus) sells his soul to Lucifer, acquiring in the bargain twenty-four years of life filled with worldly pleasure and magical power. At the end of this period of time (and at the end of the play), the compact expires at midnight, and Lucifer takes Faustus to hell. Donne makes numerous references to the play: see, for example, several of the *SERMONS*, especially one of 1628, no. 48 in *LXXX Sermons* [see R.C. Bald, *John Donne: A Life*, p. 73, footnote 3 for other allusions to the play in the *SERMONS*].

Doctors. (1) Teachers; (2) learned men; (3) eminently learned early Church FATHERs who were given the special title of "Doctor": e.g., AUGUSTINE, AMBROSE, JEROME, CHRYSOSTOM, and NAZIENZEN; (4) eminent SCHOOLMEN; (5) physicians or medical practitioners.

Dog-star. Sirius, supposed to cause heat on earth when it is ascendant and the sun is in Leo (during the "dog-days" of summer) and to bring ill health and fever.

Dole. *Noun*: (1) portion or share, (2) gift of food or money, (3) grief or sorrow.

Dominations. See HIERARCHY, THE HEAVENLY.

Doncaster, 1st Viscount. See HAY, JAMES.

Donne, Ann(e). See MORE, ANN(E).

Donne, Bridget. Daughter of Donne. Born in 1609. Married in 1633.

Donne, Constance. First child of John and Ann Donne, born in 1603. Married (in 1623) Edward Alleyn, a famous and accomplished actor who had played such roles as the hero in *DR. FAUSTUS*. Alleyn, six years older than John Donne, was retired and wealthy. Relations between the father and son-in-law were strained in 1625 by Donne's refusal to lend Alleyn a sum for ready cash needed temporarily because of Alleyn's complex financial obligations. With a settlement of leases for Constance shortly before Alleyn's death in 1626, however, the differences were reconciled. Constance married Samuel Harvey in 1630. Donne visited their home in 1630, where he contracted the illness that led to his death in 1631.

Donne, Elizabeth. (1) Mother of Donne. From a strongly Roman Catholic family. As a widow, she lived with Donne for some years in the deanery at ST. PAUL'S CATHEDRAL. Died in 1631, preceding her son in death by only two months. (2) Daughter of Donne, born in 1616. (3) Sister of Donne, died in 1577.

Donne, for not keeping of accent, deserved hanging. See JONSON and METAPHYSICAL.

Donne, Francis. Son of Donne, born in 1607, died in 1614.

Donne, George. Son of Donne, born in 1605. Soldier, imprisoned in Spain for some years, and died on his way to Virginia in 1639.

Donne, John. (1) The writer, clergyman, and Doctor of Divinity (1572–1631). (2) The writer's oldest son (1604–1663). Took holy orders and held church livings. Secured some manuscripts of his father's works and published them, the most significant volumes being *LXXX Sermons, Fifty Sermons, XXVI Sermons,*

BIATHANATOS, Letters to Several Persons of Honor, ESSAYS IN DIVINITY, and *Poems, By J.D.* (1650). (3) The writer's father (1535?–1576). Prosperous ironmonger (dealer in hardware) of London.

Donne, Lucy. Daughter of Donne. Born and baptized in 1608, with the COUNTESS OF BEDFORD as her godmother. Died in 1627.

Donne, Margaret. Daughter of Donne. Born and baptized in 1615, with SIR ROBERT KER as her godfather. Became Lady Bowles upon her marriage in 1633 to Sir William Bowles. Died in 1679.

Donne, Mary. Daughter of Donne. Born in 1611. Died in 1614.

Donne, Nicholas. Son of Donne. Born in 1613 and apparently died as an infant.

Dorset, Countess of. See CLIFFORD, LADY ANNE.

Dorset, Earl of. See SACKVILLE, RICHARD.

Doubt. *Verb*: (1) to be undecided, (2) to mistrust, (3) to fear, (4) to suspect.

Dough-baked. *Adjective*: (1) doughy; (2) unfinished, imperfect.

"Dream, The." One of the *SONGS AND SONNETS*. Donne was aware of classical writers such as OVID and of various Renaissance poets who wrote about men dreaming of their ladies, especially dreaming of the sexual fulfillment denied them by their ladies in their waking lives.

The man addresses the woman, the "love," who literally has awakened him from this dream that seemed too real, having too much of the rational, waking world to be mere fantasy. But seeing her as so true, as the very embodiment of his vision in the dream, she seems to be the continuation of herself in his dream. He implies that her awaking of him occurred at the height of his sexual excitation regarding her in the dream, and, therefore, she should allow him to physically embrace her ("Enter these arms") in order to carry out in this waking world the sexual intercourse that he was on the verge of experiencing in his dream. The dream is seized upon, then, as a means by which to try to seduce her. He compliments her beauty (in stanza 2) by comparing her eyes to both lightning and candles (tapers). As a further seductive ploy, he pictures her as an angel that he thought was in front of him as his eyes opened; yet, she actually is superior to an angel, since she is goddess-like and could read his thoughts. (According to AQUINAS, angels are not able to read thoughts, but God can.) Another seductive flattery appears when he says that his calling her anything but herself is "PROFANE": i.e., he is insulting and desecrating her goddess-like nature by comparing her to anything so lowly and inferior as an angel.

In the last stanza he says that her arrival and the fact that she did not disappear as just a figment of his imagination or dreamlike fantasy (her "coming and staying") reveal that she is indeed herself, the woman in reality to his waking eyes. But her "rising" from his bed to leave him (before they have "acted out" the completion of his dream) makes him "DOUBT" (both "suspect" and "fear") that she actually is not the "real" woman (or, at least, the one he wanted to believe in, the one who would sexually complete his dream). He wonders if their love is, in fact, "weak" and not "PURE," since it seems to be composed of several elements—"fear," "shame," and "HONOR" (each of which can apply to both the man and the woman). Or, to be more optimistic about succeeding in his seduction, he speculates (or proposes?) that the woman is enkindling his passion and preparing him sexually with her presence and brief departure while actually planning to return (to "come" back) shortly to consume him with sexual consummation. In a METAPHYSICAL CONCEIT this hope is made analogous to the way men briefly light and extinguish torches so that next time these torches will light more rapidly and burn more brilliantly. So, he will return to his dream that promises sexual fulfillment, but would rather "DIE" sexually with the real woman when she returns to him: ironically, the question of whether or not the "dream" of her returning is "only a dream" or will turn out to be "real" still remains at the end of the poem.

Donne deliberately suffuses this last stanza with words of sexual import, beyond their apparently literal, straightforward, or innocent meanings. This is most obvious with the common play on "DIE." "Kindle" here is a metaphor for sexual arousal. Related to "kindle," "torch" (both in shape and function) and "rising" suggest the penis and its physical erection. "Coming," "COME," and "cam'st" suggest both coming to bed for a sexual purpose and experiencing sexual orgasm. "GO" suggests being an effective sexual partner, one who can both experience and cause orgasm (Shakespeare, for example, [in *Antony and Cleopatra*] has Charmian hope that Alexas will marry a woman who cannot "go").

So, as we proceed through the poem, its "dream" as sexual wish-fulfillment becomes increasingly emphatic and apparent.

Drummond, William, of Hawthornden (1585–1649). Born near Edinburgh, Scotland, at the family estate of Hawthornden. Studied law before inheriting his father's estate and title as laird of Hawthornden. He then spent much time reading and collecting many volumes of books for his library before he began writing poems himself. After a poem in 1617 celebrating a visit to Scotland by King JAMES, Drummond became better known among English poets and readers, including Michael Drayton. In 1618 BEN JONSON walked from London to Edinburgh, met Drummond, and stayed with him for two weeks. Drummond invented several military and other mechanical devices, including types of pistols, pikes, telescopes, and measuring instruments. He supported the Royalists and CHARLES I and wrote some political prose and poetry in their support.

Drummond's own poems and prose pieces are minor, and his renown rests mainly on his recording of Jonson's comments during the latter's visit to Scotland. This prose account usually is referred to as Jonson's *Conversations with Drummond* (or simply *Conversations*). Some of the most famous and influential comments about Donne (as well as about other writers) are those attributed to Jonson by Drummond in this work. For example, Drummond records Jonson saying the following (among other remarks on Donne): "that Donne, for not keeping of accent, deserved hanging," "that Donne said to him he wrote that epitaph on Prince Henry . . . to match Sir Edward Herbert in obscureness," "he esteemeth John Donne the first poet in the world in some things," "affirmeth Donne to have written all his best pieces ere he was 25 years old," and "that Donne himself for not being understood would perish."

Drury, Elizabeth (1596–1610). Daughter of SIR ROBERT DRURY, one of Donne's patrons. As tributes after her death, even though he had never seen her, Donne wrote THE FIRST ANNIVERSARY (*An Anatomy of the World*) and THE SECOND ANNIVERSARY (*Of the Progress of the Soul*). Her elaborate tomb is at Hawstead Church in Suffolk, near Bury St. Edmunds.

Drury, Sir Robert (1577–1615). Soldier and courtier who was Gentleman of the Chamber under King JAMES. Enjoyed income from several properties. After the death of Sir Robert's daughter, ELIZABETH DRURY, Donne wrote an elegy to console the parents.

Shortly thereafter Drury became a patron of Donne, even inviting him to accompany the family on a trip to the continent during 1611–1612. Donne wrote other tributes to the daughter in *THE FIRST ANNIVERSARY (An Anatomy of the World)* and *THE SECOND ANNIVERSARY (Of the Progress of the Soul)*. Sir Robert provided Donne with a house (for minimal rent) on property he owned next to his own home in London.

Drury Lane. In the early seventeenth century, site of the property and London home of SIR ROBERT DRURY. Donne lived in a house next to Sir Robert's (provided by the Drurys to Donne at only a small rent) from 1612 to 1621 or 1622.

Dryden, John. See METAPHYSICAL.

Dull. *Adjective*: (1) slow of understanding; (2) lacking keenness in senses and feelings, unresponsive; (3) sluggish or stagnant; (4) depressed, gloomy, melancholy; (5) tedious or uninteresting.

Dunkirkers. Pirates whose haven was Dunkirk.

Dürer, Albrecht (1471–1528). German artist and engraver who wrote *Of Human Proportion*, containing numerous diagrams illustrating proportions of parts of the body. Donne refers to him in line 204 of "Satire 4."

E

E. of D. See SACKVILLE, Richard. Earl of Dorset.

Earth. *Noun*: (1) one of the four ELEMENTS; (2) the world on which humanity dwells, envisioned in the PTOLEMAIC concept as the center of the universe; (3) the land on this world, as opposed to the seas; (4) the ground and soil; (5) place for burial; (6) the body; (7) anything mortal; (8) personified "Mother Earth," fertile and bringing forth life.

Eccentric. *Adjective*: (1) elliptical or non-circular, (2) deviating.

Eclipse. *Noun*: (1) darkening or obliterating of the light of the sun or moon by an intervening body; (2) absence or cessation of light; (3) darkness or shadow; (4) dimness, loss of brilliance. *Verb*: (1) to cause darkening or obliterating of the light of the sun or moon; (2) to cause absence or cessation of light; (3) to cast a shadow upon, to darken, to obscure; (4) to cause loss of brilliance; (5) to hide or screen from; (6) to extinguish life.

"Ecstasy, The." One of the *SONGS AND SONNETS*. The title, as well as the word occurring in line 29 of the poem, refers to a mystical experience in which the soul is able to separate from the body and contemplate a divine truth not accessible to the soul while trammeled by the body. This is one of the most extensively-discussed and heatedly-debated of all of Donne's poems. Following the goal of this present volume, only an introduction to and an aid in grasping some of the fundamentals of the poem can be attempted here. For many other details and interpretations, the reader is urged to consult the extensive discussions found in the critical books, essays, and articles (as well as in some of the editions) listed in the "Selected Bibliography."

The first few lines present a man (the speaker) and his lover in a setting that establishes a sensual atmosphere of physical attraction. In a miniature METAPHYSICAL CONCEIT, the bank is "pregnant," this image enforced by its being "swelled up" in appearance, but it in turn is also compared to a pillow on a bed—a pillow supporting the head of the personified violet. This description suggests an aura of anticipated sexual union and the fruit of this union. Thus far the emphasis is on "we two," rather than on "we" as one. They are now merely "one another's best,"

with no identification or unity implied.   But physical contact is
portrayed in "cemented" hands, conveying the sense of touch.   The
"balm," a metaphor for perspiration here, binds their hands
strongly together and suggests perspiration in response to sexual
stimulation.   Each lover is looking into the eyes of the other so
intensely that their gazes, their "eye-beams," seem wrapped,
"twisted" together into a "double string" that "threads," sews,
connects their eyes: so, the contact of both hands and eyes is the
only physical union that foreshadows their eventually combining
completely through sexual consummation.   The "pictures" in their
eyes (i.e., the reflections of his face on her eye and hers on his) as
they look at each other are referred to as "propagation" (offspring,
children) that they "get" (beget, reproduce): such reflections were
traditionally referred to as "babies."   Thus, the imagery of
pregnancy, pillow, bed, and implied sexual union is made more
explicit here by anticipating their sexual union and the children
that will result.   The speaker still is conscious at this point,
however, of the essential separateness of the two lovers, since he
says that these means (through hands and eyes) are "as yet" the
only ways that the two people are "one."   But "as yet" implies that
eventually they will become one.   The fact that they only
"intergraft" (attach, like grafting a plant essentially different from
another into it) their hands at this point suggest a superficial,
mere attachment.   But later, in line 42, love will "interinanimate"
their "souls," implying that each soul gives vital life and is indeed
a part of the life of the other's soul: this connotes a vital
interdependence lacking in "intergraft."

The first twelve lines, then, imply a yearning for union by
the two lovers, and the union seems to be primarily bodily.   But
line 13 marks a sharp ascent into further dimensions of a perfect,
mutual love.   Suddenly the role of their souls enters.   In a
METAPHYSICAL CONCEIT, the two souls are like two armies that
seek "victory," that "advance" their causes, and that "negotiate."
This begins the awareness of and analysis of the spiritual element
of their love: the two individuals can find their mutual concerns
and arrive at peace, at agreement.   The vision of the two souls
"gone out" reflects precisely the poem's title: they have gone out
of their bodies to communicate on a non-bodily level, another
dimension of their love not fully apparent until now.   During this
time their bodies are lifeless, unmoving, dead—like "sepulchral
statues," like those statues of persons commonly placed on the
tombs, sepulchers of noble and royal personages in the Middle
Ages and Renaissance.   The speaker proposes that if "any" (i.e.,
any person) who has himself been refined, purified by love (so

that he is aware of the higher value of spiritual love) and can understand spiritual communication between lovers and can exist in the realm of intellect ("mind") were to overhear this negotiation occurring, then this person would be made even purer (implying the very high degree of spiritual love between these two lovers). Such a person imagined here is one who understands the principles of PLATONIC love.   The speaker says that this witness would not be able to distinguish the voice of the man's soul from that of the woman's soul in this negotiation, implying that in spirit they are truly one: this is particularly enforced by "both meant, both spake, the same."   The parallel structure of this clause makes "same" the object of each verb: "both" lovers have become the "same" in every respect.   Another METAPHYSICAL CONCEIT is employed, actually, in lines 21–28 to enforce the idea: the refining process is like that in ALCHEMY in which the alchemist attempts to transform baser metals into gold.   The new "concoction" is the purified result of this process: it is the now-apparent absolutely pure gold of a spiritual union that has been distilled out of what originally were only physical elements mixed, grafted together.

Significantly, the speaker does not refer to himself or the lady as "her" and "me" after line 16 of the poem.   Rather, he employs "we," "us," and "our" from that point on to embody their unity as opposed to their separateness.   For example, at one point "we" occurs five times in the course of three lines (lines 30–32). From line 29 on, the speaker is actually the one voice of the two lovers' souls.   By the end of the poem this voice makes a paradoxical statement in referring to "some lover, such as we," implying that they are now one lover, rather than two.   And the further paradoxical assertion is made that this is a "dialogue of one," of two that speak as one.   Their own awareness of this spiritual unity appears most explicitly for the first time in lines 29–48.   The "ecstasy" has revealed to them that their love in its essence and fundamental principle is not physical or bodily ("was not sex").   They understand now what they did not know before— i.e., that they were not moved or attracted to each other by the physical, but by the spiritual.   The idea that the individual soul which is combined with another soul is thereby improved is conveyed by another METAPHYSICAL CONCEIT developed by the reintroduction of the violet.   Here the violet transplanted into other soil improves in strength, color, and size.   The violet is equally symbolic of the soul of the man and the soul of the woman.   One is transplanted into the soil of the other, resulting in a reinvigorated flower (their two souls as one) in which one soul "interinanimates," gives life and is part of the life of the other.

Two souls together remedy the state of loneliness (or separateness) that exists for one soul to itself. Since they are two souls as one and are made up of spiritual roots, then, their spiritual unity and spiritual love are infinite ("no change can invade" [line 48]): their spiritual flower is not subject to the ravages of heat, cold, age, disease, and decay as is the ordinary physical flower.

Line 49 marks the next significant turn in the poem's development, leading to the climactic definition of this mutual love and its constituent elements. The physical and spiritual are merged, and the merging is justified by various images and analogies showing how body and spirit are related throughout the universe and how soul communicates with soul through physical means. The souls are like INTELLIGENCES: both souls and intelligences are spiritual in essence. The bodies and SPHERES, then, are both physical entities moved by spiritual ones. The speaker says that the bodies of the two lovers were first moved toward each other by their souls' inclinations toward each other: this is analogous to the way that the universal spheres were believed to be moved by intelligences, according to the PTOLEMAIC astronomy. So, the speaking voice argues, the two lovers should be grateful to the bodies for providing the means (such as the senses) by which their souls can communicate and know each other. The bodies are not contemptible, useless "dross" (worthless waste from processing metals) but are useful "allay" (i.e., alloy, an inferior metal mixed with another more valuable one to improve the latter's strength, durability, and appearance). The two lovers should not "forbear" (exclude) their bodies in this love relationship. Donne then employs another analogy (METAPHYSICAL CONCEIT) to reinforce the idea that the spiritual effectively can express itself through the physical. Lines 57–60 present a conceit that can be interpreted in two ways: (1) astrological influences affect man by coming down to earth from the celestial bodies, but they rely on the intervening element of AIR as a body through which to travel; (2) the angels of heaven (spiritual) must take on a body of air (physical) in order to speak to and communicate with the spiritual element in man (compare "AIR AND ANGELS"). Both analogies insist on the important role of the bodies in allowing lovers' souls fully to mingle and to experience each other.

Lines 61–68 create another extended analogy. Medieval and Renaissance physiology assumed that human blood creates "vapors" or "spirits" that are the links between body and soul: the feeling was that man's real nature does not reside in either sheer

body or sheer soul but partakes of both. These "spirits" tie the
two facets of man's nature together. They tie the "subtle knot"
joining body and soul. The speaker says that "pure lovers' souls"
(such as those of the two lovers speaking) must similarly link
themselves through intermediary emotions and powers of
physical action that are created by their bodies. If they do not
rely on their bodies to express both their souls and their love to
each other, then a "great prince in prison lies": i.e., the "prince" can
be interpreted either as the soul imprisoned within the body and
not being able to act through it or as love being imprisoned in the
realm of pure spirit without being able to express itself in action
through the physical agency of the body.

The concluding argument in lines 69–76 completes the
merging both of soul and body in each partner and of soul and
soul regarding the two lovers together. Their bodies express
physically the love inherent in their souls. Love is defined as a
spiritual "mystery" that can only be visualized through the
physical appearance of it expressed in the body: the body is like
the Bible in revealing to men's eyes the mysteries of the spiritual
realm that is unseen. The bodily expression of this love will be a
revelation to those "weak men" (the "doubting Thomases" who
have to see to believe) that have not been schooled in and cannot
immediately conceive the perfection of spiritual love, but, to
someone schooled in this perfection ("some lover, such as we"),
there will be little difference in this unified love, whether
expressed spiritually or physically: spiritual love and physical
love ideally are the same manifestation of the same love in a
perfect relationship in which two are one (spiritually and
physically).

Edith, Saint. Founder of a Benedictine Convent at Polesworth.
The Convent was dissolved under Henry VIII, and the land was
sold to the grandfather of Sir Henry GOODYER. See lines 28–30 of
"A Letter Written by Sir H. G. and J. D.," one of the *VERSE LETTERS*.

Egerton, Sir Thomas (1540?–1617). Served Queen ELIZABETH
capably in several governmental capacities, becoming Lord Keeper
of the Great Seal in 1596. Donne began serving as a secretary to
him in 1597. During this period of service Donne probably wrote
several (if not all) of his *SATIRES*, and in line 31 of "Satire 5"
apparently directly addresses Egerton as "Sir, whose righteousness
she [Queen Elizabeth] loves." Donne says also in this work that he
[Donne] is richly paid for his service. Egerton was at this time
investigating legal abuses, and Donne apparently was helping in

this regard. Such abuses are the concern of "Satire 5." But Donne secretly married Egerton's niece, ANN MORE, in late 1601. With the urging of Ann's father, Egerton dismissed Donne from his position in early 1602. Egerton became Baron Ellesmere and served as Lord Chancellor under King JAMES I, giving cordial and unhesitating support for Donne's gaining of positions in the church.

Eight and forty shares. The forty-eight constellations designated by PTOLEMY as divisions in the heavens. See line 258 of *THE FIRST ANNIVERSARY*.

Election. A special theological meaning pertains to God's choice of an individual to receive salvation.

Elector. See FREDERICK.

Electrum. *Noun*: an alloy of gold and silver and thus not as pure or as valuable as gold itself.

Elegies. In Donne's time the term "elegy" could refer both to poems mourning death and to poems concerning love. It is the latter topic that is treated in those grouped under *Elegies* in the canon of Donne's work. (For those poems that specifically honor and memorialize individuals who have died, see *EPICEDES AND OBSEQUIES, THE ANNIVERSARIES*, and "A NOCTURNAL UPON ST. LUCY'S DAY.") Donne's *Elegies* particularly are influenced by OVID's *Amores*. They tend to be bawdy, colloquial and realistic in language, anti-PLATONIC, anti-PETRARCHAN, harsh in sounds, irregular in many metrical stresses, and paradoxical (see METAPHYSICAL).

The *Elegies* cannot be precisely dated, but scholars generally believe that most of them were written in the 1590's, probably in the mid-1590's, although a few could have been written in the 1600–1610 period. Arguments among editors, scholars, and critics still prevail concerning exactly which poems belong in the group (also see *EPICEDES AND OBSEQUIES*). Disagreements also concern the order, the numbering, and the titles of the *Elegies*. Most scholars, however, follow the canon, order, numbers, and titles given in Grierson's edition (see "Selected Bibliography: Works") who, in turn, follows the edition of 1635, with some additions. Following is a listing essentially reflecting Grierson's order, numbers, and titles (I use these for all references in this "Dictionary"): "Elegy 1: Jealousy," "Elegy 2: The Anagram," "Elegy 3:

Change," "Elegy 4: The Perfume," "Elegy 5: His Picture," "Elegy 6: Oh, let me not," "Elegy 7: Nature's lay idiot," "Elegy 8: The Comparison," "Elegy 9: The Autumnal," "Elegy 10: The Dream," "Elegy 11: The Bracelet," "Elegy 12: His Parting from Her," "Elegy 13: Julia," "Elegy 14: A Tale of a Citizen and His Wife," "Elegy 15: The Expostulation," "Elegy 16: On His Mistress," "Elegy 17: Variety," "Elegy 18: Love's Progress," "Elegy 19: Going to Bed," and "Elegy 20: Love's War."

In this "Dictionary" the famous and frequently anthologized "Elegy 9: The Autumnal" and "Elegy 16: On His Mistress" are discussed fully in separate entries. The content of the remainder of the *Elegies* has been examined for elements to be included as other entries.

"Elegy 9: The Autumnal." See also *ELEGIES*. WALTON claims that this poem was written by Donne to one of Donne's patronesses, MAGDALEN HERBERT. Some manuscripts refer to her in the titles assigned this poem, thus adding some credence to Walton's assertion. Without definitive proof, however, all scholars have not been willing to endorse the theory of its association. The poem does playfully compliment a middle-aged woman (or, at least, one no longer in her late teens or early twenties!), and it is possible that there is autobiographical importance in that Donne has someone specific in mind and that she is more than an imaginary creation. The tradition, in sum, still is to project this woman as Magdalen Herbert.

The speaker begins (lines 1–12) by contrasting the "autumnal face" of the lady he describes to the beauty of "spring" and "summer" beauties: the younger women, the spring and summer beauties, do not equal in "grace" this lady in her autumnal season of life. Her beauty is like gold that has long been admired and experienced but retains its fresh, brilliant appearance. She is superior to younger women, also, since she is now in her "tolerable tropic clime," as opposed to the "torrid" heat of excess passion making up the environment around young, passionate beauties: that hot stage in her own life is over, and she now is in the ideal temperate stage of life. Lines 11–12 assert that anyone who would wish for more "heat" to come from her beautiful eyes is as ridiculous and suicidal as one who is ill with a fever and wishes the fever to become "pestilence," the plague (plague thrived in times of heat).

Lines 13–18 compliment her beauty in a very strange manner—by calling attention to her "wrinkles"! He says that it does not do justice to her to call her wrinkles "graves" (playing on the senses of "GRAVE" as both a burial place and a trench). If they are indeed "graves," they are "Love's graves"—i.e., Cupid's burial place or the trench in which he is hidden. Another meaning possible (noted by Shawcross in his edition: see "Selected Bibliography: Works") is a pun implying "engravings" created by Cupid (and thus lovely ornamentations and works of art). He compliments the lady very highly in saying that if Love cannot be found in this lady's face, then it or he (Love or Cupid) does not even exist. And if Love is here in these "graves," these wrinkles, he really is not dead but is quite alive and is residing there like an "ANCHORIT," a religious person vowed to this spiritual residence. This lady is the shrine or idol at which Cupid himself worships. Love is "here till hers . . . come": he is residing in her face until her death comes. And her death must also be "his death," since she is the embodiment of Love itself. With her passing, Love itself will pass from the world. Love creates in her face a "tomb," a beautiful memorial to Love, rather than a mere "grave."

Lines 19–24 picture Love as a king who travels around his realm to various places in his royal progresses but who has his permanent, most impressive dwelling ("standing-house") in this lady's face. Here is found all the pleasant variety and qualities of the royal retreat, such as life in the evening, entertainment, and council: such variety comes from this lady's well-rounded character.

In lines 29–32 Donne cites XERXES as one who illustrates the wisdom of choosing the qualities of the older woman, the older beauty. He loved a platan (plane) tree found in LYDIA, ornamented it, and had it guarded. Donne interprets Xerxes's attitude as one resulting from either the tree's age (since it was so large) or its barrenness (the tree would not bear fruit) while it was still young (a glorious quality of age is such barrenness, Donne implies, since pregnancy from love is then no worry?).

After briefly mentioning the "spring" and "summer" women early in the poem and then dwelling on the ideal of the "autumnal" woman through most of the poem, Donne turns at last to those of the "winter" period of life in lines 37–44, thus completing the four seasons surveyed in the life of women. Even the "winter" women are introduced, of course, to highlight the ideal of the "autumnal" stage just preceding. If his portrayal of the specifics of the "autumnal face" is surprising or shocking, then the strange outrageousness of his picture of old women is much more so. He says, in fact, not even to mention "winter faces": the thought is too disgusting, we assume, since he sees floppy skin hanging down without anything firm inside it, like the purse of some wastrel who has spent all of his money. These faces desperately need facelifts, but, alas, such cosmetology was not known in Donne's time. Such a "lank" face is so insubstantial that it best resembles a loose sack that only contains the soul, without any flesh to lend support. The eyes of such faces are sunken deeply into their sockets, and the mouths are just holes. Through their long lives these old women have lost their teeth in separate ("SEVERAL") locales, making it annoying to their souls on Resurrection Day, since each soul will have to zip around the earth to pick up every tooth in order to re-form the body with which it is to be reunited. The speaker reiterates that one should "name not" (i.e., do not even mention) such women: significantly, he now loathes them so much that he regards them as "living death's-heads" (line 43)—such a face is a MEMENTO MORI. The speaker even distinguishes between "ancient" and "antique": as noted by Gardner in her edition (see "Selected Bibliography: Works"), "antique" (or "antic") here plays on the Italian origin for the word (rather than the Latin) and means "grotesque" (Italian *antico* refers to grotesque designs on Roman artifacts). The skull-like "death's-head," then, has a grotesque grin.

Lines 45-50 emphasize the logical conclusion that he indeed hates "extremes" (such as "spring" and "winter" women, the very young and the very old). The implication is that the happy medium as ideal is in the "autumnal" one, of course. However, he seems to have put himself in an awkward position when he realizes that the "autumnal" lady he describes will herself necessarily pass into the "winter" stage eventually. Thus, lines 45–46 present him diplomatically trying to back out of his own trap ("yet I had rather stay / With tombs than cradles, to wear out a day"): if he had to choose between the very young and the very old as a companion, naturally he would choose the very old! Love's natural motion ("LATION") is to "descend" (playing on the sexual image of "descending" upon the woman's body for the sexual act and the "descending" or lessening of virility [sexual potency] with age). His own earlier sexual passion has abated to the extent that he no longer "pants" like an animal in sexual heat after young, physically-developing women ("growing beauties"). So, he shall "ebb out" with "them" ("autumnal" beauties who are aging and will eventually approach death in their journey "homeward" to heaven). The image of ebbing suggests a sea image in which he will ride the ship out on the ebbing tide with others in the latter stages of life, but also "ebb" plays on the sexual change from "panting" to a time of diminution of the sexual drive.

Whoever the "autumnal" beauty of the poem is, Donne compliments her highly in saying that she possesses superior beauty in an ideal stage of life, but he does so with quite a bit of wit, humor, and even comedy mixed, so that he and the lady can laugh and so that she can better accept the flattery without blushing and embarrassment about it.

"Elegy 16: On His Mistress." See also *ELEGIES*. Many readers have been tempted to see some autobiographical implications in this poem by interpreting the speaker as Donne and the lady addressed as ANN MORE. (Also see the section "Donne's Life.") Of interest are the references to some secrecy in the love ("spies" in line 6), an angry father ("thy father's wrath" in line 7), pains of "divorcement" (line 8), lovers' "oaths" of "joint constancy" (line 10), and the "long hid love" (line 48). However, there has been no specific evidence discovered to show that the lady is Ann More or any other particular individual, and she could well be only a character created for the poem. At any rate, the speaker is urging the woman he loves not to disguise herself as his page and accompany him on a trip to the Continent. He says that for her to do so is "dangerous" (line 12). Some of the reasons advanced that she not do so are a bit shocking, or at least unusual, but the man conveys strong feeling for the woman.

Lines 13–26 argue that she should not be his "feigned page," but rather she should remain behind. His desire to return will be increased by the prospect of coming back to her. Her beauty, however powerful, will not be able to remove the power of the seas and the north wind ("BOREAS") who even killed the beautiful nymph he supposedly loved ("ORITHEA"). To console or convince herself that it is best to stay, the speaker urges her to accept the FLATTERY that lovers physically absent from each other are actually united, are together (spiritually).

Lines 27–41 present specific arguments why her disguise as a page would be fruitless. He says that she will not be able to hide her womanly qualities under boy's clothing: all others will recognize her as a woman. Just as a "richly clothed ape" (either the animal or human kind!) is recognized as an ape under the surface, so will she be seen for what she is. Just as the moon is still the moon, whether in eclipse or not, so is she still a woman, whether or not her brilliant beauty is darkened by male clothing. One example of her certain recognition as they travel would be in France. Frenchmen are "changeable chameleons" (changing both clothes and women frequently), and they are "spitals (hospitals) of diseases," apparently the receptacles of venereal diseases. They also continually energize and regenerate themselves sexually ("Love's fuelers"), and they are also the nation of men that are truest "PLAYERS," implying that they are like actors in dressing up in so many costumes to play parts, but also that they are true participants in the sexual game. The speaker's lengthy characterization of Frenchmen, of course, is to show how adept they are in searching out and recognizing women, even under odd clothing: they will "KNOW" (recognize and sexually possess) her and no less than that (line 37). His supposedly bemoaning "alas" also can be read as a pun on "a lass": they will know her as no less than a lass. Not only would her disguise be useless in France, but also it would accomplish nothing in Italy. The "INDIFFERENT" Italian does not care if she is male or female: the Italian would be content, in his bisexual nature, to take either a man or woman, being as perverted as those men of Sodom who wanted the guests of LOT to satisfy their lusts.

Lines 41–56 conclude these observations with renewed insistence that the lady "stay" in England, the only worthy "gallery" (waiting room) on earth in which to anticipate entering the room of the "greatest King" (God) in the next life (i.e., England is the best place on earth, and the lady should have no desire to travel elsewhere). The speaker also appeals to fear and superstition in urging her not to dream or imagine bad things, even death, occurring to him while he is abroad: she should "augur" him "better chance." But he recognizes (in a final compliment to the lady) that Jove (i.e., God) might decide that the man already has lived long enough because he has had sufficient joy in life through possession of this lady's love.

Element. *Noun:* (1) in Ancient, Medieval, and ⸱ Renaissance thought, one of the four simple substances [from lightest to heaviest: fire, air, water, and earth] out of which all material bodies are made: anything composed of any one or more of the four elements is mortal and therefore subject to decay and death (see also HUMOR, COMPLEXION, and GALEN); (2) more generally, any constituent substance out of which a more complex substance is made; (3) the bread or wine of the Eucharist. *Verb:* (1) to compose or make up something out of a combination of some or all of the four elements (fire, air, water, and earth); (2) to constitute or compose.

Element of fire is quite put out, The. Line 206 of *THE FIRST ANNIVERSARY.* See NEW PHILOSOPHY.

Eliot, T.S. See DISSOCIATION OF SENSIBILITY.

Elixir. See ALCHEMY.

Elizabeth I (1533–1603). Queen of England, 1558–1603. Daughter of Henry VIII and Anne Boleyn, she was the last of the Tudor rulers. She was learned, witty, and a supporter of the arts. Upon her accession she attempted to reconcile the deep conflicts between Protestants and Roman Catholics by forging a compromise, a settlement dictating a middle-of-the-road Church of England. Some Roman Catholic threats continued through her reign, however, in the form of assassination plots against her and the Spanish Armada sent against England. Roman Catholics in England were severely penalized for not attending Anglican services and were not eligible for university degrees and offices in state and church, conditions applying to Donne until he decided to give up his Roman Catholic faith and embrace Anglicanism.
     In "Satire 5" (line 28) Donne addresses Elizabeth as "Greatest and fairest Empress." In *IGNATIUS HIS CONCLAVE* (1610) she is praised by Donne's device of having IGNATIUS say that she was one who deceived the hope of the JESUITS and escaped their cunning. Donne's first sermon at PAUL'S CROSS (1617) was on the occasion of an anniversary of Elizabeth's death, and a man present wrote later that Donne "did Queen Elizabeth great right."

Ellesmere, Baron. See EGERTON, SIR THOMAS.

Empale. See IMPALE.

Emperor's loved snake. Phrase in line 36 of "The Calm." See TIBERIUS.

Empery. Empire.

Empress. See ELIZABETH I.

Enchase. *Verb*: to ornament.

Engine. *Noun*: (1) a plot or snare, (2) a mechanical apparatus or tool, (3) an instrument of warfare, (4) an instrument or means.

Enoch. See CAIN.

Enow. Enough (also spelled "inow").

Epicedes and Obsequies. A group of several poems by Donne specifically honoring and memorializing individuals who have died. "Epicede" is an English word adapted from Latin *epicedium*, a funeral ode. "Obsequy" comes from Latin *obsequium*, a funeral rite or ceremony. Today we commonly regard these as elegies, and, indeed, most of those in the group have "elegy" in their titles. It is convenient, however, to distinguish these from the quite different group of poems entitled *ELEGIES*. Some editors disagree on which groups two or three poems should be included in— whether in the *Epicedes and Obsequies* or in the *VERSE LETTERS* or in the *ELEGIES*. For the purpose of categorizing and in order to follow the grouping of more than one editor, I consider the following seven poems to belong to this group: "Elegy on the L. C.," "Elegy on the Lady Markham," "Elegy on Mistress Boulstred," "An Elegy Upon the Death of Mistress Boulstred," "Elegy Upon the Untimely Death of the Incomparable Prince Henry," "An Hymn to the Saints, and to Marquis Hamilton," and "Obsequies to the Lord Harrington, Brother to the Lady Lucy, Countess of Bedford." From the dates of deaths, one can determine that most of these poems were written between 1609 and 1625 (although some speculation about the identity of "L. C." suggests that one poem could have been written as early as 1595).

The content of these seven *Epicedes and Obsequies* has been examined for important elements to be included as entries in this "Dictionary."

Epigrams. A group of compact poems written by Donne over a span of many years. In ancient times an epigram was an inscription, but through the centuries it became simply a very short poem written as concisely as an inscription, especially to memorialize something or someone. An epigram is expected to have conciseness, polish, and clarity. By Donne's time an epigram also might employ humor, wit, and satire.

Donne's hyperbolic, but serious, praise of one of the commanders at CADIZ in "Sir John Wingfield" (in which Donne says that no man dares go farther than WINGFIELD, making him comparable to the pillars of the Strait of Gibraltar that warned of and set the western limits of the Old World) shows his serious, memorializing use of the epigram. On the other hand, "A Licentious Person" ("Thy sins and hairs may no man equal call, / For, as thy sins increase, thy hairs do fall") reveals a bawdy and satirical use: the more the person sins sexually, the fewer hairs he has (because syphilis causes the hair to fall out).

In another two-line epigram entitled "Antiquary" ("If in his study he hath so much care / To hang all old strange things, let his wife beware") Donne creates two levels of pointed implication, one of straight humor, but another of bawdy humor. Both levels depend on wordplay involving "hang" and "things." It is funny on one level because it seems to say that if this ANTIQUARY, this collector of old items of the past, carefully hangs all old strange things on the wall of his study, then his old wife should be careful that she does not become one of the things that her husband either "hangs" on his wall or "hangs" as a means of executing. But the bawdy level appears by the fact that it could also be saying that if the antiquary so carefully hangs old things in his study, then the wife should beware because he also might wish to "hang" another "old strange thing" (his penis) in a different place (in her vagina). The bawdy play on "thing" as either the male or female sexual organ is common in Donne's time (see, for example, Donne's "FAREWELL TO LOVE" and other poems by him, as well as many places in Shakespeare [e.g., *King Lear*, I.v.51–52: "She that's a maid now, and laughed at my departure, / Shall not be a maid long, unless things be cut shorter"]). "Hang" also is bawdily played upon by writers of the time (e.g., Shakespeare, *Othello*, III.i.8–10: "O, thereby hangs a tail. / Whereby hangs a tale, sir? / Marry, sir, by many a wind instrument that I know").

In "An Obscure Writer" ("Philo, with twelve years' study, hath been grieved / To be understood; when will he be believed?") Donne presents the character Philo as a writer who is disappointed when readers understand his writing (apparently since he wants to feel superior to his readers). He is (or desires to be) "obscure" in the sense that his writing is (1) not clear or (2) not clearly expressed. Of course, such a writer also suffers the fate of being "obscure" in the sense of being undistinguished, unnoticed. Such a writer, in sum, can never be "believed."

The content of the remainder of the *Epigrams* has been examined for elements to make up other entries in this "Dictionary."

Epithalamions. A group of three poems by Donne celebrating weddings. The term "epithalamion" means "marriage song." The earliest of the three is "Epithalamion Made at Lincoln's Inn," apparently written during the 1592–1595 period when Donne studied at LINCOLN'S INN. No specific occasion or wedding has yet been identified for it, and it might be imaginary. The poem, in fact, seems influenced by (and possibly a parody of) SPENSER's "Epithalamion" that was published in 1595: Donne's poem echoes it in phrases. "An Epithalamion, or Marriage Song on the Lady Elizabeth and Count Palatine being Married on St. Valentine's Day" was written for the marriage of ELIZABETH STUART (daughter of King JAMES) and FREDERICK, ELECTOR PALATINE, on February 14, 1613. Through the marriage England hoped to improve its ties with Protestants in Germany. This important and lavish occasion was celebrated with many poems and masques by several writers. "Epithalamion at the Marriage of the Earl of Somerset" (or simply "Epithalamion" and "Eclogue") was written to celebrate the marriage of Somerset [see KER, ROBERT (2)] and Frances Howard, Countess of Essex, on December 26, 1613. The poem obviously was a means by which Donne hoped to strengthen his chances for advancement at Court through a favorite of King JAMES. (Especially see the entries for ALLOPHANES and IDIOS.)

The content of the *Epithalamions* has been examined for important elements included as entries in this "Dictionary."

Escape. *Noun*: (1) the action of fleeing or freeing oneself from something or someone, (2) a transgression, including a sexual transgression or adventure.

Escorial. See ESCURIAL.

Escurial (**Escorial**).   Grand palace and center of Roman Catholicism in Spain that was built in the 1580's by King Philip II.

Essays in Divinity.   Book (first published in 1651) containing discussions of Biblical passages, with commentary drawn from Donne's consideration of church Fathers and other writers through the centuries. A few prayers are also included. Donne seems to have written these during several years before he was ordained in 1615, perhaps writing part while still at MITCHAM and completing the work while living in DRURY LANE. Donne himself in the *Essays* refers to them as "these sermons," and they are precursors of some matter and techniques that he later does include in his *SERMONS*. So, in some ways they served as exercises that prepared Donne for writing sermons later, as well as private helps to him in sorting out some spiritual issues before he took the step to enter into a calling in the church, rather than to continue to pursue a secular career.

The first large division in the work begins by quoting the opening verse of Genesis ("In the beginning God created Heaven and Earth"). Included in this large consideration of creation are opening subdivisions titled "Of the Bible," "Of Moses," and "Of

Genesis." These are followed by Parts 1–4, with the following subdivisions occurring within them: "Of God," "Of the Name of God," and "Elohim." The first division concludes with a prayer. The second large division begins by quoting the opening verse of Exodus ("Now these are the names of the children of Israel which came into Egypt"). Included in the opening discussion is a subdivision titled "Exodus." This is followed by Part 1 with the subdivisions "Diversity in Names," "Of Number," and "Variety in the Number." The lengthy Part 2 is not subdivided. Following it are four prayers that complete the volume.

The work treats some topics that recur in Donne's writing, especially the concept of the BOOKS OF GOD, man's use of both reason and faith ("Reason is our Sword, Faith our Target [i.e., shield]"), the older concepts of the universe compared to the findings of the NEW PHILOSOPHY, unity and disunity in the Church, the centrality of Christ in the Church, and the various forms of worship (including what he and others elsewhere refer to as "THINGS INDIFFERENT") in different churches and sects. Among the many sources used and cited by Donne in the *Essays*, perhaps the most frequent and important are AQUINAS and AUGUSTINE. (The best beginnings for one who wishes to examine this prose work more fully and specifically are Evelyn M. Simpson's chapter on it in her *A Study of the Prose Works of John Donne* and her edition of *Essays in Divinity*: see citations in my "Selected Bibliography.")

Essex, Countess of. See KER, ROBERT (2).

Essex, 2nd Earl of. See DEVEREUX, ROBERT.

Etna. Volcanic mountain in Sicily.

Except. *Conjunction*: (1) unless [a frequent meaning in Donne's works]; (2) other than; (3) if it were not for the fact that. *Preposition*: with the exclusion of. *Verb*: to leave out, to exclude.

Exhalation. *Noun*: (1) action of breathing forth; (2) evaporation; (3) that which is exhaled, breath, vapor; (4) meteor or comet.

"Expiration, The." One of the *SONGS AND SONNETS*. The poem was first published, however, with a musical setting in Ferrabosco's *First Book of Airs* (1609). It was the first of Donne's English poems ever published. The title plays on both breathing and death as "expiration." The idea of a kiss as both a "coupling" of souls and a separation of the soul from the body is expressed memorably by Castiglione in *THE COURTIER.* The soul also was thought to be exhaled and life to be lost with breathing and sighing. A famous dramatic expression of the kiss as a sucking out of the soul is in *DR. FAUSTUS* by MARLOWE, in which Dr. Faustus (in Act 5) says of Helen's kiss, "Her lips suck forth my soul."

The man speaking urges the lady he is parting from to cease the final mournful kiss between them. The kiss is regarded as sucking out, breathing out, and evaporating their souls. Since they are "dead" through this "expiration," they are envisioned as spirits that should turn away from each other. The deadness conveys the melancholy, dark ("BENIGHTED") feeling as they have to part. Rather than allowing anyone else to part them, they freely choose to do so themselves. Rather than letting another say "Go" to them, they will so command each other.

The second stanza begins with the man saying "Go" to the woman and urging her to say the same to him. Here another point is added to the METAPHYSICAL CONCEIT of "expiration" as death: their parting is death (see DIE). And, paradoxically, the speaker will be "eased" by this death through the medium of her bidding him go away. It will put him out of his present misery. If his command to her already has killed her and thus she can no longer speak to say "Go" to him, then he wants his own command to turn back on him and deal out deserved death to himself, a murderer who has killed the lady (lines 9–10). He, then, wants to "turn the gun" on himself, so to speak. But he finally poses the possibility that it might be too late for her word to kill him: he already may be "double dead" from both his parting (as death) and the injury suffered to himself by telling her to part.

Through the poem the title comes to mean also a termination of the lovers' relationship, of the lovers' contract. And ultimately it is this that causes their individual deaths as they part: their sorrow means a rather lifeless existence without their relationship.

"Expostulation." See *DEVOTIONS UPON EMERGENT OCCASIONS.*

"Extasie, The." See "ECSTASY, THE."

F

Fable of King Log and King Stork. Fable originating with AESOP in which the frogs, tired of the log (Donne's "BLOCK") that Zeus had given them to be their king, demanded another king. He sent them a stork that ate them all. See "The Calm," lines 3–4.

Faculty. *Noun*: (1) power of or ability for an action, (2) a capability of the body or of a part of the body for a particular function, (3) body of persons in a department of learning.

Fain (faine, fained). *Verb*: (1) to be glad, (2) to make glad, (3) to rejoice in, (4) to pretend (FEIGN). *Adjective*: (1) glad or content, (2) obliged or necessitated, (3) willing or eager, (4) wished for, (5) pretended. *Adverb*: (1) gladly, (2) willingly. The word in various forms and senses occurs in Donne and is punned upon.

Fair. *Adjective*: (1) beautiful; (2) having light complexion or having light or blonde hair; (3) free from blemish, clean; (4) impartial, equitable.

Falling sickness. Epilepsy.

Fame. *Noun*: (1) public talk, report, rumor; (2) reputation or character; (3) celebrity, renown.

Fancy. *Noun*: (1) imagination, (2) things imagined or unreal or illusory, (3) a whim or mood, (4) individual taste or liking, (5) amorous inclination.

Fane. *Noun*: temple. Also see JOVE'S FANE and DIAN'S FANE.

Fantastic. *Adjective*: (1) imaginary, unreal; (2) impulsive, capricious, odd; (3) grotesque.

"Farewell to Love." One of the *SONGS AND SONNETS*. The speaker is either indeed disillusioned with "love" and is giving it up or he is assuming (with some humor and irony) the pose of one who feels and does so. "Love" might first seem to be romantic love in general, but it more explicitly plays on Cupid as Love—and finally becomes most explicitly sexual intercourse, physical love only.

In the first stanza the speaker presents himself as originally rather naive and inexperienced in love and life ("yet to PROVE"), because he once thought that there was a god, a deity "in love" (that there was a Cupid? that there was a holy state or nature inherent in love?). In this inexperienced period he revered and worshipped "love" (Cupid? romantic love? women? a particular woman? sexual desire without being able to name it as such?). He, in fact, sounds suspiciously like a PETRARCHAN man in this stage of being a novice in love. In a METAPHYSICAL CONCEIT he compares himself to an atheist dying and calling on an unknown power in his hour of despair. He also craved experience of an unknown power. "Things not yet known" suggests wordplay on KNOW: the "god" or "love" is not yet revealed or recognized or experienced. But, with the cynical hindsight of this particular speaker who is relating his naive past, the "things" are imagined instances of sexual intercourse and also (denigratingly) women not yet "known" sexually. Also, "things" are the female sexual organs not yet "known" by the man. It is the "craving" (i.e., the sexual "desire") of a man that forms his vision of "things" (instances of sexual intercourse, women, female organs). The multiple meanings and bawdy innuendoes persist in the last line of this stanza: just as "they" (the "desires") either lessen or grow greater ("size"), so do the imagined images (of sexual intercourse, women, female organs) fall or grow, but one must note also the bawdy undercurrent here that the male sexual organ also grows greater with erection or lesser with flaccidity, according to the dictates of his "desires" and the "fashion" that these desires give to imagined "things."

The second stanza presents disillusionment with the sexual act (of the now-experienced speaker) through a METAPHYSICAL CONCEIT. Just as a child who purchases (at a fair) a longed-for colorful gingerbread representation of a king on a throne soon tires of it after it is possessed, so does a lover, once possessed of the "thing" (in all the bawdy connotations) that was so admired and craved, soon lose his enjoyment of it. The only sense (out of all five of them) that might still be pleased, however ineffectively, is touch (the physical sensation of the sexual act). But even that sense, the lover has discovered, demands a retribution on the male lover because the physical act causes emotional lethargy for a period after it.

In the third stanza the speaker bemoans the fact that men ("we") cannot be like cocks and lions, animals believed (by GALEN) to be still lively after intercourse. The speaker supposes that Nature ("wise" Mother Nature, "she") made a law that the human male not be allowed to be jovially energetic after the sexual act. Since the belief was that sexual intercourse subtracted some time off one's life (see DIE), the speaker supposes Nature to be protecting man by this means to discourage intercourse. He also says that Nature decreed this unpleasant period after intercourse because she wished man to despise to some degree the sport of making love in order to compensate for the fact that he is inclined to breed for its momentary physical pleasure. One way, then, to read the latter part of stanza three is that the physical sensation of climax is "short" and only lasts a "minute," thus making man frequently seek to reenact breeding; therefore, Nature has placed a moderating element in the period following the sexual act that serves to temper man's desires to repeat it often. However, I think that another valid bawdy level implied by Donne here is that man is "cursed" by usually being "short," having a short, flaccid penis in its usual state, but with erection that occurs at infrequent times it becomes "eager" and thus desirous of taking advantage of this eagerness as much as possible. Since this stanza is acknowledged by scholars, editors, and critics to be one of the most difficult and ambiguous in Donne's work, the reader should be aware of a third level of meaning possible here. Several interpreters see the "curse" being that placed on man with Adam's fall, the curse of mortality, "short" life. Thus, they contend, since man exists only for a "minute" on the spectrum of earthly time, man wants to raise posterity to perpetuate something of himself after his own physical death and therefore is inclined to try to breed frequently while he is in his "eager" (virile) period. Thus, any of these reasons serves to argue why Nature wants to temper man's sexual inclinations (that subtract time from his life) by making the after-effects unpleasant enough to discourage excessive repetition of the sexual act. (For fuller study of the problems raised by this stanza, one should consult the essays, articles, and portions of critical books in the "Critical Studies" division of my "Selected Bibliography." Also valuable are the several editions under "Works" in this same bibliography. Particularly important is the discussion of the poem itself and an appendix devoted to problematic lines in Theodore Redpath's edition.)

In the fourth stanza the speaker says that, since all of the foregoing is the existing condition, he will no longer desire the perfect and harmless pleasure he once thought could be found in love. He will no longer seek out that which actually, it turns out, does harm him. When he does see "moving beauties," attractive women that move his desires and move him toward the women, he will resist: he expresses this in an analogy of these beautiful women to the sun. As men admire the summer sun's great light, so he will admire the women's beauty. But as men avoid the sun's harmful "heat," he will avoid the women's harmful passion. He will find a cool shade, something else to occupy him and keep him away from the attraction to the sexual act. If all of these efforts to avoid the instinctual pull toward women fail him, a last resort will be to apply a medicinal treatment of "wormseed," a substance having the opposite effect to that of an aphrodisiac. This will counteract sexual desire and thus the erection of his "tail," his penis. That would be his ultimate means of bidding "farewell" to "love."

Fashion. *Noun:* (1) form or shape; (2) a particular shape or pattern; (3) a certain (and usually current) style of clothing, attire; (4) a prevailing custom or mode; (5) showy outward form.

Fast. *Adjective:* (1) firm, secure; (2) strong; (3) rapid.

Fat. *Adjective:* (1) well-fed, plump; (2) corpulent, obese; (3) affluent, wealthy; (4) self-satisfied, complacent.

Fatal. *Adjective:* (1) destined, decreed by fate; (2) doomed; (3) prophetic; (4) ominous; (5) deadly.

Father. *Noun:* (1) male parent; (2) ancestor, forefather; (3) one of the "Fathers of the Church": early Christian writers, usually those of the first five centuries; (4) title by which God is addressed or referred.

Faustus, Dr. See *DR. FAUSTUS.*

Favor. *Noun:* (1) friendly regard, (2) exceptional kindness, (3) something given out of kindness or regard, (4) aid, (5) beauty, (6) charm.

Feign, feigned. *Verb:* (1) to pretend (sometimes spelled as FAIN), (2) to form or fashion deceptively. *Adjective:* (1) pretended (sometimes spelled as FAINED); (2) done or said deceptively, dissimulated. The word in various forms and senses occurs in Donne and is punned upon.

"Fever, A." One of the *SONGS AND SONNETS.* The occasion for the poem is that a woman loved by the speaker is ill and has a fever. It is tempting to read the poem as one concerning an illness of ANN MORE or the COUNTESS OF BEDFORD or another friend or patroness. But there is no existing evidence to specify the occasion beyond the fact of the poem itself. It would seem to be a topic not usually conducive to a love poem, but it is to Donne: he expands the fever as a METAPHYSICAL CONCEIT, and he uses much paradox in creating a poem with several of those qualities traditionally regarded as METAPHYSICAL. Through wit and hyperbole the speaker successfully conveys deep feelings for the woman.

The first stanza implores the ill woman not to die, and the reason for the speaker's wish is quite paradoxical and shocking. He does not want her to die because, if she does, he will hate other women (since they are so inferior and living while this one is dead?). His hate will be so extreme and irrational that it will blind himself to the difference between her and other women: (1) he will hate all women; (2) she was a woman; (3) therefore, he will hate her also! The "logical illogic," paradox, exaggeration, and wit that both convey and moderate grief appear here and elsewhere in Donne. Although the statement seems a strange one to make to a possibly dying woman, it conveys the depth of emotion felt for her above all others.

In stanza two he suddenly changes direction in thought: he concludes that she cannot die because he defines death as leaving the world behind. But if she passes away physically, then the whole world departs with her. Her life is the life of this world. Thus, he establishes her as a MICROCOSM: she is the world itself (primarily conveying the fact that she is his whole world, and, if she dies, his world—the world itself—dies). So, if she takes the world with her, she is not leaving it behind. By his definition of death, then, she, paradoxically, cannot die.

In stanza three he extends further his concept of her as the life of the world, now calling her the soul of the world. He is, then, developing further the conceit of her as a microcosm. She is the spiritual life of the world, as opposed to the mere physical bulk. So, if she dies, she takes the world's spirit (and, indeed, the spirit of the world and of life itself, as far as this man is concerned) with her. The physical world left becomes a dead body—expressed powerfully as only a "carcass." Life will be dead, completely lifeless, for him if she dies. No beauty will be left in this world: the most beautiful ("fairest") woman will be only a ghost, a nothing, compared to the lady he is addressing. There will be no worth left either: the "worthiest" men will be unworthy and corrupt, compared to her worth.   In fact, men will be only "worms" (maggots feeding on the "carcass"), compared to the admirable aspect of human nature that this lady exemplifies.

Since he has established her as the world, in stanza four he poses the likelihood that the fever now raging in her body is the fire that will end the world.   He ridicules the ignorance of the "wrangling schools" that could not draw this conclusion themselves.   Generally the "SCHOOLS" here are different schools or groups of religious thinkers or speculators throughout history. More specifically the reference applies to the "SCHOOLMEN" who argued about the precise kind of fire, as well as its source, that the Bible refers to that will eventually destroy the world.

With stanza five the speaker again reverses himself as he thinks.   He becomes optimistic about her recovery, since he realizes that the fever cannot last.   Since he has made the fever equivalent to a fire, he knows it will burn itself out because (it was believed) a fire feeds on corrupt matter.   This lady, he implies, has no corrupt, useless matter to fuel the fire (i.e., the fever).   Thus he compliments her perfect nature.

After this turning point, his optimism that the fever cannot last increases as he thinks of other reasons (in stanza six) to support this diagnosis of her condition.   The spells of fever ("burning fits") now are seen as "meteors."   The conceit of her as the world now expands into a vision of her as the whole universe. What is real in her is the "unchangeable firmament," the region beyond the moon and particularly the SPHERE of fixed stars in the PTOLEMAIC concept of the universe.   She essentially is the permanent universe above the earth.   The fevers are "but meteors" (i.e., only meteors) that are ephemeral, changing, decaying matter of the SUBLUNARY realm.   Meteors were believed to be engendered in the area of fire just below the sphere of the moon.   Just as meteors burn only briefly, so does fire, and so will her fever.   Meteors are inferior and subject to change, while the lady is not.

In the last stanza the speaker wittily says, however, that the fever had the same feeling about the woman that he always had: it wished to SEIZE her (implying both "to take hold of" and "to take possession of" [the latter in a legal sense, enforced by "owner" two lines later]).   Even though the transitory fever could not last ("persever"—i.e., "persevere") long in the lady, it did enjoy residing in her briefly.   Just so, the speaker would rather own her for one hour than to possess the rest of all creation forever.   She is the universe he prefers.

Figure. *Verb*: (1) to form or shape, (2) to represent or symbolize, (3) to express in metaphor, (4) to imagine, (5) to prefigure or foreshadow. *Noun*: (1) form or shape, (2) image or symbol or emblem or representation.

Fillip. *Verb*: (1) to flip or toss, (2) to strike or tap with the finger, (3) to strike.

Fire. *Noun*: (1) one of the four ELEMENTS; (2) the operative principle in combustion; (3) a flame; (4) in some contexts, a reference to hell; (5) in some contexts, a reference to the fire believed to end the world; (6) the means of lighting a fire, such as a live coal; (7) glowing appearance resembling a fire; (8) burning heat, fever produced by a disease; (9) in some contexts, ardor or enthusiasm; (10) creative imagination or poetic inspiration; (11) in some contexts, passion or emotion.

Firmament. *Noun*: (1) generally, the realm of the created universe above the SPHERE of the moon, according to the PTOLEMAIC concept of the universe: firmament is regarded as immortal and unchanging, as opposed to the SUBLUNARY realm; (2) more specifically, the SPHERE of the fixed stars in the PTOLEMAIC concept, also regarded as permanent and unchanging until the discoveries of GALILEO began to prove otherwise.

First Anniversary, The. The first poem seen through the press by Donne. Published in 1611 as *An Anatomy of the World*, it was printed again in 1612 with the title *The First Anniversary*, the original title becoming the subtitle. This 1612 printing was in conjunction with another poem titled *THE SECOND ANNIVERSARY*: *Of the Progress of the Soul*. Both of these together were referred to by Donne (in letters) as *The Anniversaries*. Editors and critics, therefore, refer to each poem either by its title or subtitle or by both. One should not confuse these two poems, however, with "THE ANNIVERSARY," one of the *SONGS AND SONNETS*. Also, one should not confuse the second poem with *METEMPSYCHOSIS*, alternatively titled *The Progress of the Soul*. Following the title(s) of the first poem in both 1611 and 1612 is this: "Wherein, By Occasion Of the untimely death of Mistress Elizabeth Drury, the frailty and the decay of this whole World is represented." Following the titles of the second poem in 1612 is this: "Wherein: By Occasion Of The Religious Death of Mistress Elizabeth Drury, the incommodities of the Soul in this life and her exaltation in the next, are Contemplated." The literal subject of both poems, then, is ELIZABETH DRURY, daughter of Sir ROBERT DRURY, but she, her death, and her new life in heaven are made symbolic of many other feelings and ideas. She died in 1610, without Donne having ever met her. After presenting a short elegy to her parents, he then wrote the first long poem for her, travelled to the Continent with the Drurys, and wrote the second long poem (see above, pages 17–18 in "Donne's Life"). "Anniversary" in the title of each poem implies a yearly remembrance of the death of someone, but, significantly, it also corresponds to a yearly church remembrance of specific saints and martyrs. Donne, in fact, says (in lines 443–51 of *The First Anniversary*) that he plans to celebrate the girl's death with a poem each year on the date of her death, a plan not carried out beyond *The Second Anniversary*.

Donne felt the sting from some contemporary criticism of the *Anniversaries* because of their lavish praise of a young girl and even found himself defending them as early as 1612. He wrote a letter to GEORGE GARRARD from Paris (while there with the Drurys) in April, 1612, expressing regret for having "descended to print anything in verse," yet he also says, " . . . my purpose was to say as well as I could: for since I never saw the Gentlewoman, I cannot be understood to have bound my self to have spoken just truth: but I would not be thought to have gone about to praise anybody in rime, except I took such a person, as might be capable of all that I could say. If any of those Ladies [whose criticisms have been relayed to Donne] think that Mistress Drury was not so, let that Lady make herself fit for all those praises in the book, and it shall be hers" (see *Letters to Several Persons of Honour*, 1651, p. 255). Also, WILLIAM DRUMMOND, reporting BEN JONSON's comments and opinions, says, "That Donne's *Anniversary* [i.e., *The Anniversaries*] was profane and full of blasphemies; that he told Mr. Donne, if it had been written of the Virgin Mary, it had been something. To which he [i.e., Donne] answered that he described the Idea [i.e., the ideal] of a Woman and not as she was."

The general structure of *The First Anniversary* has been variously analyzed by modern critics. Probably most influential is the scheme proposed by Louis L. Martz in *The Poetry of Meditation* (see "Selected Bibliography: Critical Studies, Poetry"). He sees Donne using a structure comparable to Roman Catholic meditations (especially of the JESUITS). He divides the poem into an introduction, then five sections, and a conclusion. Each of the five sections contains a meditation, a eulogy, and a refrain with a moral. Specifically, lines 1–90 are the Introduction and argue that the world is sick, dead, and rotten because Elizabeth Drury's death has removed the world's virtue and principle of life.   Section I (lines 91–190) concerns man as a trifle: the Meditation (lines 91–170) notes man's decay from original sin, exemplified in his shortened life, size, and intellect; the Eulogy (lines 171–82) exalts the girl's purity; the Refrain and Moral (lines 183–90) offer religion as the only hope.   Section II (lines 191–246) concerns the world as lame: the Meditation (lines 191–218) notes that all coherence in the universe, state, and family is gone; the Eulogy (lines 219–36) proposes that only Elizabeth Drury could have granted unity; the Refrain and Moral (lines 237–46) propose that one must condemn and avoid this sick world.   Section III (lines 247–338) presents the world as an ugly monster: the Meditation (lines 247–304) analyzes lack of proportion in the universe as the cause of its ugliness; the Eulogy (lines 305–24) points to the young lady as the ideal of symmetry, harmony; the Refrain and Moral (lines 325–38) say that human acts must be done in proportion. Section IV (lines 339–76) concerns the world as a pale ghost: the Meditation (lines 339–58) bemoans the lack of color and luster in the world; the Eulogy (lines 359–68) praises the girl's perfect color and her ability to give color to the world; the Refrain and Moral (lines 369–76) argue the absence of pleasure in an ugly world and the wickedness of using false colors.   Section V (lines 377–434) presents the world as a dry cinder: the Meditation (lines 377–98) sees the influence of the heavens upon earth as having weakened; the Eulogy (lines 399–426) argues that, because of this weakened correspondence between the heavens and earth, Elizabeth Drury's virtue can have little effect upon earth since her death; the Refrain and Moral (lines 427–34) propose that only the joys of religious virtue are worth our labor, grief, and death in this world. Lines 435–74 are the Conclusion.

An alternative view of the structure is proposed by O.B, Hardison, Jr., in *The Enduring Monument* (see "Selected Bibliography: Critical Studies, Poetry").   He sees the poem as composed of five major sections.   Section I (lines 1–60) is the Introduction, presenting Elizabeth Drury's death as a shock that makes us realize the defects of the world.   Section II (lines 61–248) emphasizes the physical decay of the world: included in this section are subdivisions lamenting the mortality of both man (the MICROCOSM) and the world (the MACROCOSM), considerations of Elizabeth Drury as the departed principle of both health and stability, and arguments that she teaches how to escape the world and its infection.   Section III (lines 249–376) concerns the qualitative (or aesthetic) decay of the world: included in this section are subdivisions lamenting the losses of proportion (or rational order) and color (or aesthetic order), considerations of the young lady as the departed principles of both proportion and perfect beauty, and arguments that she teaches the need to act fitly and to avoid using illusory colors. Section IV (lines 377–434) concerns the spiritual decay of the world: included in this section are subdivisions lamenting the loss of the heavenly regenerative influence, consideration of the dead girl as a spiritual force, and an argument that she teaches contempt for the world and love for her own rich joys. Section V (lines 435–474) is the Conclusion, arguing that it is best to speak of Elizabeth Drury in verse, since it is preserved in the memory.

Various themes and points for emphasis have been proposed by critics. Elizabeth Drury has been seen as symbolic of or like God, Christ, humanity before the Fall, the regenerate Soul, the Church, Harmony, Order, Wisdom, Virtue, Justice, Beauty, Life, Motherhood, ST. LUCY, Queen ELIZABETH, the Virgin MARY, and other dimensions. The poem has been interpreted as reflecting the Fall and all of its consequent losses to man, accompanied by corruption, decay, and death for all humanity, the earth, and the universe. The young girl's death reenacts the the Fall of Man and Christ's Crucifixion. The disruption of order is reflected in the NEW PHILOSOPHY and other elements presented by Donne as evidence through the poem.

Donne's exaggeration (see METAPHYSICAL) permeates the work. Elizabeth Drury is called a "Queen" (line 7), and her death is like an "earthquake" (line 11), recalling, of course, the earthquake at Christ's Crucifixion. With Elizabeth's death, man became "nothing," losing his very "heart" (lines 171–74). She gave the West Indies gold and the East Indies spice and perfume (lines 230–33), and she is the "measure of all symmetry" (line 310). Finally, she "gilded every state" (line 418). This exaggerated praise, of course, is what drew much of the criticism (referred to above) in Donne's day and which he defended. But it is a matter still assessed and argued (both in its literal and symbolic dimensions) by critics today.

Donne's love of paradox (see METAPHYSICAL) is quite evident in this poem. For instance, the world is "corrupt and mortal" in its "purest part" (line 62), and the "marriage" of Adam and Eve was our "funeral" (line 105): i.e., the marriage led to the Fall which introduced death to all succeeding humans. This paradox becomes part of the larger paradox that Eve "killed us all" (line 106), yet it is the lady Elizabeth Drury that represents regeneration for all. Donne also uses the common play on KILL and DIE (sexually) in the paradoxes that each woman kills "us" (i.e., men) now (line 107) and that "we" allow ourselves to die in that manner and even "kill ourselves" to propagate ourselves (lines 108–10)! In referring to the possible effect of his own poem, Donne says that a report of their own illness does not "smell well" to "hearers" who would like to think that they actually are well (lines 441–42). Finally, he designates the young lady's "death" as her "second birth" (lines 450–51).

One can see in the poem Donne's use of METAPHYSICAL CONCEITs and apt imagery in general. In the first fifty lines he creates the analogy of Elizabeth Drury, particularly her soul, as a queen, a ruler who was on a "PROGRESS" in this world but who now has gone to her "STANDING HOUSE" in heaven, a doubly interesting comparison since she bears the same name as Queen ELIZABETH who died seven years earlier. In the part of the poem concerning the lack of proportion and color in the earth (lines 285–376), Donne pictures mountains as "warts" and seas as "pock-holes" (line 300) on the face of the earth, vivid images of the disproportion and ugliness of the personified earth. Then line 342 states, "Were it [i.e., the earth] a ring still, yet the stone is gone": even if the earth were circular like a ring one wears, then the stone is out of the ring. The ring symbolizes proportion, and the stone symbolizes color: the color is lacking, with the added implication that the earth really is not that perfectly proportioned ring anyway.

One can also approach this poem as a serious, at times caustic, satire on human nature. Even at the beginning (lines 1–6) the speaker implies that many humans seem almost without a soul—those who do not "see," "judge," follow worthiness, and "praise it" by actions have at best a soul not really attached to the individual it dwells within. Man's presumption, his continuing fall into pride since Adam's Fall, is emphasized in lines 155–70: God made man out of nothing, but man tries to outdo God by undoing God's work and turning himself back into nothing. Examples are man's self-destructive tendencies in spreading diseases such as syphilis and in using medicine (PHYSIC) even worse than the diseases. Man's self-centered individualism evidences itself in the fact that each man wants to be a PHOENIX—i.e., to be unique, set apart from everyone else (lines 213–19). All sense of social, communal, and familial obligations and interrelationships has been lost. Scientists (especially astronomers) exemplify man's pride: in lines 278–84 humans are portrayed as fishers of the stars, throwing out a "net" on the heavens and presumptuously bringing heaven itself down to our earthly level to dissect and study according to our wishes. Human hypocrisy and deception (covering over both internal and external ugliness and evil) appear in lines 374–76. Admirable qualities in humanity seem woefully lacking: if Elizabeth Drury could give "some temperance" to Princes, "some purpose to advance" the common good to Counsellors, "some taciturnity" to women, and "some grains of chastity" to nunneries, then with her death there must be little or none of any of these. "Nunneries" lacking chastity seems doubly satirical, since Donne could mean literally religious nunneries but also could be referring to houses of prostitution, colloquially called nunneries in Donne's time.

(For other possible approaches in interpreting this much-discussed poem [and its relationships to *The Second Anniversary*], see both the general critical studies covering Donne's poetry and the specific ones on *The Anniversaries* cited in my "Selected Bibliography.")

First Mover. According to the PTOLEMAIC view of the universe, the outermost SPHERE is the one called the "First Mover" or "Prime Mover" or "*Primum Mobile*." Its function is to give the initial motion to all of the spheres and to keep all of them revolving in perfect harmony. As they thus revolve, they create a perfect music called the music of the spheres (see discussion under SPHERE).

Flattery. *Noun*: (1) pleasing praise; (2) insincere or false praise; (3) self-pleasing, consoling deception or accepted idea.

Flavia. Character personifying an ugly mistress in "Elegy 2: The Anagram." Probably playing on Latin *flavus*, meaning "yellow": "her cheeks be yellow" (line 7).

"Flea, The." One of the *SONGS AND SONNETS*. This poem presents a little drama with three "characters" (the man speaking, the lady spoken to, and the flea). Actions are described and implied in the course of this poem that divides into three stanzas of nine lines each. The dominating METAPHYSICAL CONCEIT is the flea itself: it is wittily and ingeniously compared to farfetched things and ideas.

The opening is emphatic with some irregularly-placed metrical stresses on the repeated "mark" to secure the lady's attention. The reader immediately perceives that the character speaking is one of the courtly seducers appearing in several of Donne's poems. The man and woman are looking at a flea that has just sucked blood from the man and has hopped over to the woman and now is sucking blood from her. The speaker will use the flea to illustrate to her, he says, "how little that which thou deny'st me is": i.e., he will show her how unimportant and undamaging that act of sexual intercourse is that she keeps preventing him from enjoying. He implies that the chastity she is guarding is not really something that should be of concern. With line 4 the speaker states the first analogy that begins to develop the overall conceit: the bloods of both the man and the woman are combined within the flea, and he implies that this is parallel to the bloods combining during sexual consummation (a combining that ARISTOTLE argued). So, the flea represents the sexual combining he would like to enjoy with her. Furthermore, he remarks that one cannot say that their combining of bloods in the flea is a sin or a shame or a loss of maidenhead (implying, with a twisting of words and logic, that human sexual intercourse also is not any of these). Lines 7–9 add the next extension to his conceit: the flea swollen with their blood now represents the appearance of a pregnant woman, the result of the sexual intercourse that the speaker already has made the flea symbolize. He moans an "alas," since he and the lady (because of her reluctance) have not reached the stage of the woman's pregnancy (when, in fact, they have not even experienced the preliminary intercourse).

The beginning of the second stanza implies action occurring just before the man's first statement: the woman has raised her hand and is threatening to crush the flea while it is sucking blood from her, since the man has to urge her to "stay," to stop her action. Literally she wants to kill the flea bothering her, but even more important is the implication that she wants to crush the man's argument early. To prevent her, the speaker says that she should spare the three lives in the flea—the flea's life, the man's life (since his blood is in it), and the woman's life (since her blood is in it). Secondarily, the three lives also suggest the man, the woman, and the unborn child (recalling the preceding analogy of pregnancy). The speaker then argues that he and the lady are "almost married" in the flea, but on second thought he says that they are "more than married," since they have symbolically not only joined in the flea but have reached the stages of both consummation and conception. One notices here Donne's METAPHYSICAL shifting of thoughts and changes of direction. So, at this point, the flea already represents marriage, intercourse, pregnancy, and three lives, but Donne still adds further dimensions to the conceit. After summarizing that the flea represents "you and I," he also calls it their "marriage bed" (the place in which their consummation, their mingling of bloods, has occurred) and their "marriage temple" (the holy place in which they have been united in matrimony). The temple analogy is fostered further by referring to the black body of the flea as "living walls of JET," black marble such as material that might be used in constructing temples. The man gloats over the fact that, despite parental opposition and the lady's own resistance, they are "met" within the flea, as if they have had a secret rendezvous for sexual purposes or a secret marriage. Being "CLOISTERED" ironically enforces the sense of meeting in a holy place, the "temple." The speaker sarcastically tells the lady (last three lines of the second stanza) that, although her habit or custom ("USE") is to "KILL" him (i.e., to reject him) and makes it likely that she is overjoyed to have another chance to kill him by crushing the flea (with his blood in it), she, nevertheless, should not kill the flea. If she does, she will be committing suicide ("self-murder"), since her blood is also in the flea. In addition, she will commit the sin of "sacrilege" (destroying or desecrating a holy place), since crushing the flea is crushing a "temple" (referring to his analogy in line 13). He makes her planned action supposedly an atrocious one of committing "three sins" (murder, suicide, and sacrilege) if she kills "three" (man, woman, and flea—all contained in the flea itself).

With the third stanza the reader discovers that more action has occurred: she has killed the flea in spite of the man's arguments against it. For her doing so, the man characterizes her as "cruel and SUDDEN." Her fingernail is purple with the blood from the flea, and the speaker says that the flea is "innocent." So, the flea has become a sacrifice, an innocent martyr for a cause. The implication is that the cause is the lady's preservation of her chastity: she feels that crushing the flea means crushing the man's whole argument and that it is a terminating of the real loss of her chastity before this threatened loss has a chance to develop further. The question asked by the man in lines 21–22 enforces this implication: from the woman's point of view the flea is guilty because of the man's making the flea's sucking of blood from her symbolize her giving in sexually—the loss of her blood represents a loss of chastity, a loss of her honor. In lines 23–24 the reader sees the lady gloating now: she feels that she has disproved all that the man has said. She says that she has killed the flea and that neither she nor the man are even any weaker (much less dead, as the man had claimed they would be). But in the last three lines the reader discovers that the man has spun a clever trap for this lady and is ready to capture her with it. He turns her argument against her by agreeing that what she says is true, but this should teach her how false all fears are. His fears about the flea's death were all wrong. So, similarly, she should perceive that her fears about loss of chastity and honor are wrong. The flea's death took no life from her, just as her yielding sexually to him will take no honor away from her. "Just so much honor [i.e., none] will waste," if she submits sexually. Crucial and witty is the play on "DEATH" in its sexual sense in the last line, enforcing his ultimate analogy that the literal death of the flea is equated with sexual consummation.

Flora. Roman goddess of flowers.

Fly. *Noun*: (1) any winged insect, such as a moth; (2) in fishing, [a] an insect attached to a hook as a lure or [b] an artificial insect or lure made with silk or feathers and placed on a hook; (3) a portion of the apparatus in a clock that regulates the speed of its striking.

Fond(ling). *Adjective*: foolish.

Footstool. Common metaphor for the earth, in Donne and other writers, following such Biblical uses as in Lamentations 2:1, Isaiah 66:1, and Matthew 5:35.

Forbear. *Verb*: (1) to endure, submit to; (2) to dispense with, spare; (3) to give up, part with; (4) to avoid, shun; (5) to abstain or refrain from.

Forswear. *Verb*: (1) to deny or repudiate on oath, (2) to swear falsely or break an oath or forsake previously sworn allegiance.

Forward. *Adjective*: (1) early or well-advanced, (2) ready or prompt or eager, (3) presumptuous, (4) extreme.

Four Ages. The four ages of the history of mankind were believed to be Gold, Silver, Bronze (Brass), and Iron, the movement from Gold to Iron suggesting progressive deterioration.

Frame. *Verb*: (1) to shape, form, create; (2) to direct something to a certain purpose; (3) to attempt; (4) to adapt oneself or conform; (5) to form in the mind, conceive, imagine; (6) to cause or produce. *Noun*: (1) a structure consisting of parts put together, (2) heaven or earth regarded as a structure, (3) a structure that provides support.

Frederick, Elector Palatine (1596–1632).   Count, Elector Palatine, and eventually King Frederick V of Bohemia.   Succeeded his father in 1610.   Married ELIZABETH STUART, daughter of King JAMES, in England on February 14, 1613.   Their marriage is celebrated in one of Donne's *EPITHALAMIONS* ("An Epithalamion, or Marriage Song on the Lady Elizabeth and Count Palatine being Married on St. Valentine's Day").   As Rhineland Elector, he was one of the rulers in Germany and vicinity who could vote for the Holy Roman Emperor.   His rule was assertive of Protestantism.   Accepted the election as King of Bohemia in 1619.   He was crowned in November, 1619, but he ruled only until November, 1620, when his army was defeated by the Catholic League.   He was nicknamed "the Winter King."   He and his family fled.   Eventually the League and the Spanish occupied the Palatinate.   Frederick became financially dependent upon the Dutch States General and Gustavus Adolphus of Sweden and died in exile in November, 1632.

During Frederick's reign as King, Donne preached before him and the Queen in Heidelberg during Donne's continental journey with JAMES HAY, Viscount Doncaster (see Potter and Simpson edition of *Sermons*, II, Sermon 12).

Frippery. *Noun*: (1) old, used, discarded clothes; (2) a place or shop where used clothes are sold.

Front. *Noun*: (1) forehead, (2) face.

Froward. *Adjective*: perverse, hard-to-please, bad, malicious.

Fruits of worms and dust.   Phrase used by Donne in line 154 of "Epithalamion at the Marriage of the Earl of Somerset" to refer to silk (fruit of worms) and gold (fruit of dust): the phrase parallels his mention of "silk and gold" previously in line 151.

Fruit-trencher.   See TRENCHER.

"Funeral, The."   One of the *SONGS AND SONNETS*.   The title suggests a death, but, as the poem progresses, one sees that the DEATH is the PETRARCHAN kind from the lady's rejection of the speaker.   He imagines people coming to wrap him in a death shroud and bury him (after he has been killed by the lady's refusal to yield to him physically, we later learn).   He urges these people not to bother the wreath of hair tied around his arm.   It is some of the lady's hair, apparently given or sent to him as a consolation when she would not submit to him. The wreath is "SUBTLE," both in being fine and in being hard to interpret: he calls it a "mystery" and a "sign" (symbol), one that seems to have religious significance. It has an aura of the holy of holies, not to be touched. Significantly, he says that it "crowns" his arm, anticipating his specifying of it as the "viceroy," the substitute ruler for his soul. His soul, he imagines, has gone on to heaven but has left the hair to control the bodily domain it used to rule. Supposedly the hair has a spiritual power to prevent the dissolution of the body. One notices a METAPHYSICAL CONCEIT here of the body as a kingdom ruled first by the soul and then by its viceroy (the hair), the analogy arising especially from the uses of "crown," "viceroy," "control," "provinces," and "dissolution." A double meaning of "dissolution" operates, applying both to the body's decay and to a state's collapse. Obviously, Donne wants "her" in the last line of stanza one to suggest not only the soul (always referred to as feminine) but also the lady. Both his soul and the lady governed him. Interestingly, from the first stanza his opinion of the lady seems to be one entirely of admiration, affection, and compliment: it is in the second half of the poem that we see other feelings he has toward her. Similarly, the death seems to be a projection of his own actual death in the first half of the poem, and we have to reorient ourselves to the real situation in the second half.

In the second stanza the man asserts that his spinal cord and nerves ("sinewy thread") from his brain was able to unite all parts of his body during life but that this hair wrapped around his arm can better hold his parts together because these hairs originated from a "better brain" than his own. Also, they should have an advantage because they grew "upward" toward heaven, rather than downward toward earth (as do the spinal cord and nerves). As A.J. Smith argues (see his edition in "Selected Bibliography: Works"), this direction implies a purer condition. To this point, the man seems only flattering toward the lady. But abruptly he attributes darker motives to her in giving him this circle of hair: she possibly wanted him to be like a prisoner wearing a manacle to remind him of his pain and to inflict more "pain" just before he dies. "Pain" gives the first clue that, despite her good qualities, the lady has treated him with the PETRARCHAN pain of rejection. We begin to see that he is a bit embittered because of her sadistic nature.

In the last stanza the speaker says, whether her intentions were good or ill in giving him this token of her hair, he wants it buried with him. Since he is a martyr in this religion of Love (he has been sacrificed, has "died" from it), he does not want either the hair or his bones (both can be taken as "RELICS") to be worshipped idolatrously by other lovers in this religion (here the religion of Love is made analogous to Roman Catholicism). The last four lines are, in a sense, the speaker's own acknowledgment of the poem's dichotomy: he grants that it was humility on his own part to so elevate the lady's character, action, and intention as to give to her hair the status of a substitute soul, but now he is justified in being "BRAVE" (being proud, bragging, and surlily daring) and seeking his revenge on her baser nature and on her possible ulterior motive in giving him the hair. In exchange for her painful rejection of him, for reminding him of his pain, and ultimately for "killing" him, he will also kill her by burying part of her with him. Secondarily, he may be gloating that he ultimately will enjoy "DEATH" with her in a sexual sense, because he will have part of her with him physically, after all. The speaker's bitterness is made more evident in the surprising shift to addressing the woman directly ("you") in the last line. It is as if his emotion has conquered his attempt at objectivity while addressing in most of the poem those who would come to bury him. In the final line he turns savagely to the lady herself, rather than simply talking about her.

Funeral bell. Bell tolled at a person's funeral. Compare DEATH BELL and PASSING BELL.

G

G., E. See GUILPIN, EVERARD.

Gabriel. Archangel who appeared to Daniel and explained to him the vision of the ram and goat (Daniel 8) and who appeared to MARY to announce that she was chosen by God to be the mother of Christ, this latter event commonly referred to as the ANNUNCIATION (Luke 1).

Galaxy. The Milky Way.

Galen (about 130–200). Greek physician and writer who eventually lived, lectured, and wrote in Rome. His experience in anatomy contributed significantly to knowledge of the circulatory and nervous systems. In the Middle Ages and Renaissance his writings were most influential in proposing a theory of HUMORS and COMPLEXIONS, all related to the four ELEMENTS. His work was particularly popularized and made available in English by Sir Thomas Elyot in the early 16th century, most notably in *The Castle of Health*, which undoubtedly influenced Shakespeare, Donne, BEN JONSON, and others. See also GALENIST and contrast to PARACELSUS.

Galenist. *Adjective*: one subscribing to the teachings, theories, or medicine proposed by GALEN, particularly the idea that to combat an imbalance in HUMOR and COMPLEXION, one ingests food and substances of opposite qualities. See also GALEN and ELEMENT. Contrast to PARACELSUS.

Galileo [Galileo Galilei] (1564–1642). Italian mathematician, astronomer, and physicist. Studied and made fundamental discoveries about gravitation and laws of motion. One of the major proponents of the basic truths of the theory of COPERNICUS and thus (with KEPLER, BRAHE, CARDAN, and others) one of the developers of the NEW PHILOSOPHY, as opposed to the older cosmology of PTOLEMY.

Galileo developed the first telescope that could be used for astronomical observation. In 1609 and 1610 he announced some discoveries and published *Sidereus Nuncius* (1610). He noted that the surface of the moon is irregular, that the Milky Way is a galaxy of distant stars, that the planet Jupiter has satellites, that there are spots on the sun, and that the planet Venus has certain phases. In 1613 Galileo asserted that Copernicus was right and Ptolemy wrong. Opposition to him from universities and the Roman Catholic Church began to develop from the fact that his arguments appeared to contradict the Bible. In 1616 the Church declared Copernicanism "false and erroneous." Galileo and others were told that the Copernican theory could only be debated noncommittally as a mathematical supposition. For many years Galileo studied and wrote a book published eventually in 1632 as a "Dialogue." Individuals and groups of the Church, notably the JESUITS, convinced the Pope that the work was not in fact an objective appraisal of the Ptolemaic and Copernican theories, but a dangerous, destructive argument for Copernicanism. The Church developed a case to prosecute Galileo for "suspicion of heresy," and he was tried. He was found guilty of holding and teaching the Copernican theory and was ordered to recant. He did so, and the Pope ordered house arrest (rather than imprisonment) for him. He made further discoveries with the telescope until he became blind a few years before his death, and he continued his studies of the laws of motion until his death.

Donne alludes to many ideas and discoveries of Galileo and the other developers of the NEW PHILOSOPHY, but he also refers to Galileo by name and to his *Sidereus Nuncius* by title in *IGNATIUS HIS CONCLAVE.*

Gall. *Noun:* (1) secretion of the liver, bile; (2) bitter bile; (3) bitterness of spirit; (4) poison, venom.

Gallo-Belgicus. See *MERCURIUS GALLO-BELGICUS.*

Gam(e)ster. *Noun:* (1) gambler; (2) lewd person, one who likes sexual games.

Garrard, George. A close friend of Donne with whom he corresponded frequently from 1609 to the end of Donne's life: see *LETTERS.* For Donne's comments to Garrard about criticism of the *Anniversaries,* see *THE FIRST ANNIVERSARY.*

Geneva. City in Switzerland situated by a lake. John CALVIN took refuge there after leaving France. It soon became the center and symbol of Protestantism, especially of the Calvinistic variety. Many individuals fled Roman Catholic persecutions in their own countries and chose Geneva as a temporary or permanent residence. In lines 50–54 of "SATIRE 3" Donne personifies the Calvinistic Protestant religion "at Geneva" as a "plain, simple, sullen, young, contemptuous, yet unhandsome" woman.

Genius. Attendant or protective spirit given everyone at birth to govern his fortune, determine his character, and conduct him out of the world (from classical, pagan belief).

Gesner, Konrad von (1516–65). Wrote *The Library of the Universe* (1545), admired by CORYAT. Donne refers to him in line 22 of "Upon Mr. Thomas Coryat's Crudities."

Get. *Verb*: (1) to obtain or receive or acquire or earn; (2) to capture or win; (3) to beget, propagate; (4) to make a sexual conquest, to succeed in having sexual intercourse with.

Gibraltar. Used by Donne in "HYMN TO GOD MY GOD, IN MY SICKNESS" to refer to a STRAIT, the Strait of Gibraltar that connects the Mediterranean Sea and the Atlantic Ocean between Spain and Africa.

Giddy. *Adjective*: (1) dizzy; (2) whirling rapidly; (3) easily excited, frivolous, inconstant.

Gilbert, William (1540–1603). Physician to Queen ELIZABETH. Wrote *De Magnete* (1600), a study of the magnet, magnetic forces, and the magnetic poles of the earth. Donne refers to this work both in line 221 of *THE FIRST ANNIVERSARY* and in Book 1, Part 4 of *ESSAYS IN DIVINITY*.

Glass. *Noun*: (1) substance made by fusing sand and used for windows, vessels, containers; (2) a mirror; (3) a telescope; (4) a magnifying glass ("crystal glass").

Glaze. Character in "Satire 4" who is portrayed as going to a Roman Catholic Mass, thus disobeying the Elizabethan statute against doing so and having to pay a fine.

Glorius. Character in "Satire 4" representing a repulsive, ill-mannered, disgustingly-dressed, and violent courtier (see lines 219–28).

Go. *Verb*: (1) to move or travel; (2) to walk; (3) to be in a certain condition habitually; (4) to pass or happen; (5) to issue or result;

(6) to depart, move away, leave; (7) to be a constituent element of something; (8) to turn [to] or be transformed [to]; (9) to die; (10) to proceed through the process of sexual intercourse, including orgasm.

Goat. One of the twelve signs of the ZODIAC. Also called Capricorn. Refers in some contexts to the winter solstice.

Gold, Age of. See FOUR AGES.

Golgotha. Hill near Jerusalem where Christ was crucified. CALVARY.

Good Friday. The Friday before Easter, a day recalling the Crucifixion or PASSION of Christ.

"Good Friday, 1613. Riding Westward." One of the *DIVINE POEMS*. The specific occasion of this poem has been identified as Donne's riding toward the home of Sir EDWARD HERBERT in Wales to visit him there in April, 1613. A portion of his journey indeed occurred on GOOD FRIDAY. Although the poem primarily is one that ponders Christ's crucifixion and resurrection with universal, Christian feelings and implications (done in a METAPHYSICAL way), it also seems very much a personal meditation by Donne on this specific occasion at this precise time in his own life. In fact, Donne might well have been aware of his entering the 42nd year of his life in April, 1613 (having been born at some date between January 24 and June 19 of 1572). This personal recognition, in fact, might explain the structure of the poem, since there are 42 lines, and these are not divided into stanzas. (See the argument along these lines in Severance's 1987 essay in "Selected Bibliography: Critical Studies, Divine Poems.") Donne here is concerned with time's passage and the uses of time in his own life. Line 6 evinces his awareness of the cycle of years in the heavens and in his own life. In this poem also, as in others such as "HYMN TO GOD MY GOD, IN MY SICKNESS," a westward journey signifies progression toward physical death, the end of earthly time, and the end of one's chance to be confident in spiritual aims and values in earthly life to assure spiritual salvation. At this stage in his life when "pleasure" and "business" have not reaped the advancement and rewards he has expected, Donne might well be assessing his own direction and destination. It is interesting, of course, that two years later he is ordained.

The central terms of the primary METAPHYSICAL CONCEIT in the poem are stated as an argumentative proposition in lines 1–8. The first assumption, the basis of the analogy, is that man's soul is like one of the Ptolemaic SPHERES. Just as an angel or INTELLIGENCE was believed to be assigned to govern each sphere's movement, Donne sees "devotion" as the intelligence that governs man's soul's motion. This is the ideal situation. However, just as "foreign" influences from other spheres or from other external forces seem to affect the movement of all of the Ptolemaic spheres, so is man's soul affected by foreign motions and forces other than devotion. Man allows "pleasure" or "business" to override the direction given by devotion when he allows "pleasure" or "business" to become his soul's "FIRST MOVER." Just as the Ptolemaic First Mover revolves the spheres, so are men's souls "whirled" by "pleasure" or "business": the choice of "whirled" here suggests a frantic, dizzying movement away from the proper direction that "devotion" should be giving the soul.

Beginning in line 9 Donne applies the conceit to his own activity on this Good Friday. He is being "carried to the West" (literally toward the home he is to visit, but also connoting the setting sun and death) on this day that he should be feeling only devotion to Christ and contemplating his crucifixion: his own "soul's form" (its natural guiding force) bends to the East (associated with Jerusalem and the place of Christ's crucifixion, but also with the rising sun and the rising of Christ the Son in his resurrection on Easter and its associations of life). Lines 11–14 use Christian puns and paradoxes: the "Sun" is also the "Son," and this "Son" rose up on the Cross in order to "set" (to die) and through that "setting" (death of the Light of the world) make possible the birth (begetting) of "endless day," endless light, eternal life. And if Christ had not both risen and fallen (been lifted on the Cross and crucified), Sin would have given mankind eternal darkness and damnation ("had eternally benighted all") rather than "endless day." Donne implies that looking (going) toward the East to meditate on all of this is his proper action, then, on this Good Friday, rather than being drawn in the opposite direction.

With the word "Yet" opening line 15, however, Donne reveals some reservations about this ideal focus on the East: in lines 15–32 he catalogs the unbearable sights that he would have to witness. The crucifixion and surrounding actions might be a "spectacle of too much weight" for him to see. First, he recalls that God told Moses (Exodus 33:20) that no man can see the face of God

and live (even though, paradoxically, God is life). So, it must be an
even more terrible "death" to see God die (line 18). Nature itself,
God's "lieutenant" (officer that carries out and embodies God's
being and will), did "shrink" (recoiled with abhorrence) in reaction
to the crucifixion of God (Christ), as seen in the earthquake (God's
"FOOTSTOOL" cracking) and in the eclipse (the sun made to
"WINK") at the time of Christ's crucifixion (see Matthew 27:45–51).
Donne is not sure he could bear to see "those hands" (i.e., Christ's)
pierced with the holes of the nails on the cross: Christ's hands are
ones that "span the poles" (double meaning of the horizontal poles
of the cross but also the poles [North and South] of the earth). His
hands also "tune all spheres at once": Christ tunes "SPHERES" both
in the sense of the various domains in which mankind lives and
acts (all life thus harmonized by Christ in all human hearts and
lives) and in the sense of the Ptolemaic spheres (thus making
Christ comparable to the FIRST MOVER that creates the harmony
that allows the music of the spheres). But early in the poem
Donne calls man's soul a sphere, and Christ tunes men's souls as he
does spheres. Donne does not know if he could see God humbled
below man—that God who is at such an eternal, unfathomable
height to be the ZENITH to both sides of the world ("to us, and to
our ANTIPODES"). He does not think he can look at Christ's blood
(the center or "seat" of all men's souls) spilled out to make dirt out
of dust or his body (his flesh as visible clothes over God's spiritual
being in this world) "ragged and torn." In addition to not being
able to view Christ in this lowly state, he does not think that he
can stand by to see MARY in the miserable condition of having to
witness the death of the son (for which she provided the half of
Christ's nature to be sacrificed) that redeems all mankind.

Lines 33–42 conclude Donne's meditation on his sense of
unworthiness to look at Christ. Even though his "eye" is turned
away from the East and all of the associated "things" on Good
Friday that he has listed, he does have them in his mind: his mind
("memory") "looks towards them," even though his body moves
toward the West, both spatially in his journey and temporally in
his yearly aging (now into his 42nd year?). He envisions Christ
looking toward him as Christ hangs on his "TREE." Now Donne says
that his own back is turned to Christ in the East only ("but") to
receive "corrections," punishments (like lashings with a rod or
whip) from Christ: these would be merely little crucifixions, little
crosses, that he as man would bear in order to participate in
Christ's much larger suffering. He knows that Christ's "mercy" will
soon spare him further punishment: Christ will "LEAVE" (cease)
his blows. Christ's anger will burn off Donne's "rusts" (i.e., sins)

and will eventually polish him to shine with the light of Christ's image again. This will make Donne again recognizable as a child of God, with a soul devoted to God: this "devotion" will again rightfully be the "intelligence" that "moves" him to turn both his soul and his face around and ultimately to look toward the East, rather than the West as at present. Donne indeed does that most fully with the change in direction of his entire life within two years. His ordination in 1615 marks his final decision to face the East, even as he rides West (to death). And, even as he was dying, he had the sketch of himself drawn in his shroud (the basis for his monument in ST. PAUL'S CATHEDRAL), as if arising out of an urn and facing the East toward Christ's Second Coming (see above, "Donne's Life").

"Good-Morrow, The." One of the *SONGS AND SONNETS*. This poem, as several others in the group, attempts to define a completely satisfactory, mutual love. The man speaking is addressing the lady he loves. Their love is not the old PETRARCHAN type, in which the man complains of the woman's unresponsiveness.

The opening stanza begins in the first line and a half with colloquial choices of words, irregular metrics conveying conversational tone with natural speech rhythm, and unconventional variance in ending the statement in the middle of a line: these qualities typify some of the traditional METAPHYSICAL characteristics, as practiced by Donne. The heavy stress on "Did" violates the normal iambic pattern, helps convey the sense of speculation, and emphasizes an important word with double meaning in the context. In one sense "did" (see DO) simply refers to what actions occupied their lives before they met each other, but another sense is doing sexually, having intercourse, as distinguished from truly loving—i.e., physical love alone is not the same as truly loving. There is more to love than simply the act of physical love: the contrast is enforced by the heavy stresses placed on "Did" and "loved." Then he raises the question of whether or not they were only like unweaned children, mere babies in love that knew only physical pleasures that met immediate needs: they were not mature in love until they met each other and experienced love involving more than the physical. They were childish, immature in only "sucking on country pleasures," like babies nursing for physical sustenance and warmth—but the suggestion is that of primitive sexual pleasures that they indulged themselves in with others before they met one another and experienced love beyond a sexual dimension.

Another analogy he proposes for their state of imperceptivity about love is that they were like the SEVEN SLEEPERS who slept so many years. The use of "snorted" (i.e., "snored") conveys a vividly realistic self-scorn for his own lack of awareness. (This colloquial word choice [seen also in "weaned" and "sucked"] further enforces the metaphysical characteristics of the poem.) But the Seven Sleepers awoke to a new world, with Christianity dominant: this METAPHYSICAL CONCEIT implies that they too awakened to a transformed life through a spiritual awakening in love (the title suggesting this awakening and greeting by their souls, made even more explicit with the beginning of the second stanza). Line 5 acknowledges that their past, before their love for one another, was like a sleep in which they were dead to the world, dead to real love, dead to the dimension of the spirit in love. They only physically existed in this past. Now he can say that except for ("BUT") this love (or this spiritual pleasure in love) that we have, all other pleasures (i.e., physical, worldly ones) are "FANCIES," unreal. In terms of the large conceit, these physical pleasures are like dreams in this past sleep, contrasted to the spiritual reality he is now awake to. A specific example follows: any "beauty" (i.e., any physical beauty, any beautiful woman) that he saw, "desired" (sexually), and "got" (conquered sexually) in his past (before meeting .the one he is addressing) was only a "dream" (unreal, a "fancy") in that past sleep that foreshadowed this present real woman, real beauty. (One notes here the emphasis on physical senses and responses, seeing and touching.) Any physical, sexual experience in the past was a mere hint of the spiritual experience of the present. In the midst of untraditional, anti-romantic colloquial language (furthered in "got") and metaphysical conceits, Donne actually is embodying PLATONIC ideas and feelings: Plato contends that the physical is unreal (like a dream, a fancy) and is a mere hint or shadow of the true reality residing in the spiritual.

The second stanza makes explicit that the awaking of their souls is most important, after this long past that was like a sleep. Their bodies were awake in that past, but they were spiritually and intellectually hibernating. The souls of the man and the woman say "good morning" to each other. And in this perfect love these souls have no "fear" (no fear of infidelity, jealousy)—rather, they watch each other out of love in its truest and fullest sense (which physical love alone does not define). In line 10 the man explains that they have no fear because ("for") "love" (in its fullest sense that primarily is spiritual) controls any "love" (mere liking or desire) to see other "sights" beyond the true love relationship: i.e., neither partner in such a perfect love relationship desires even to "see" (much less sexually conquer) any other person beyond the relationship, and, therefore, unfaithfulness is impossible and not to be feared. Line 11 begins another important METAPHYSICAL CONCEIT to express the idea and feeling of such a self-sufficient, essentially spiritual relationship that he and the lady have. This analogy employs the concept of the MICROCOSM, in that the "one little room" containing these two partners becomes (as far as these two are concerned) an "everywhere," an entire world or universe. Their whole existence is in each other, and they have no need or desire to go outside of themselves for any purpose. In their immature past they flitted from one lover to another—to other "worlds," in a sense. But not now. So, the man contemptuously says that "sea-discoverers" can go find and explore new lands, new "worlds": the implication is that the speaker could not care less. He already has been through his period of exploration and discovery (in his physical love affairs with several "beauties," "worlds" in the past). But now he has discovered the only world that matters in the lady he is talking to. Pursuing further the conceit of geography, discovery, and exploration, the speaker also says that other people (i.e., "others"—"other" was an accepted plural as well as singular) can be shown on maps (having to be redrawn with new discoveries on the earth) these countless, fascinating (to them) worlds: again, the clear implication is that the speaker cares not a bit because he has in the room a world that no mere physical world outside on earth can ever equal. And this is especially true if the best that other people can experience is second-hand: i.e., only to be "shown" a world certainly is not on the same exhilarating level of experience as to "POSSESS" (both spiritually and physically) a world. To own a world is far better than just seeing a world. Map-readers are at best superficial and vicarious in their experiences. He tells the lady that each of them, however, has one world and each of them is a world: i.e., each person is a MICROCOSM and, in possessing the other person, each lover has a world. The implication logically extends to the two united into one world, the perfect microcosm of spiritually-united lovers.

In the last stanza this perfect union is expressed in images that develop even further the geographical conceit of the microcosm. As each lover looks into the eyes of the other, each sees his/her face reflected on the other's eye. The "true plain hearts" seen in these faces imply again the idea of themselves and their love having no deception, no desire or attempt to hide treacherous, unfaithful hearts (motives, feelings, actions). A love based on complete fidelity and trust has no deceit, and the truth plainly shows in the partners' faces. Implying that there are no "two better hemispheres" again continues the analogy of the unified microcosm: two hemispheres make one world. But what are these two hemispheres? Donne seems deliberately to make the reference multiple: primarily they seem to be the "eyes" looking into and blending each lover, since the eye has the shape of a hemisphere or half of a world or half of a globe. The face "laid on" the eye is comparable to a land mass on the earth or to a map on the globe. But the reference could also be read to refer to their two "faces" (each a hemisphere) or to their two "hearts." Of course, ultimately, the eyes, faces, and hearts are all parts symbolizing the wholes, the two persons. The two persons, the man and the lady, are the most important hemispheres combined into one world. And the man suggests that their world is "better," is indeed superior to any other world, including the earth itself (a conclusion that has been prepared for by his denigrating attitude toward mere earthly discoveries and discoverers earlier). Their world is superior because it does not have the "sharp" (i.e., cold) North as the earth does: symbolically, their perfect world of love does not have any coldness of feeling in it. Also, their world has no "declining West": unlike in the ordinary world, there is no setting sun in theirs. The day does not fade and darken in the west in their world: the sun of their love is spiritual and thus undying, immortal. The speaker then picks up on this note of decay and death inherent in the image of the setting sun and formulates the powerful assertions in the last three lines. Drawing on classical philosophy and medicine as it was developed in the Middle Ages, Donne has the man assert the assumed truth that any two basic elements or substances that are not mixed in equal proportions will break down and decay. Any basic substance or any perfect compound of two substances was thought to be indestructible, immune from further reduction into elements. So, the speaker implies a conceit in which the love that he and the lady have is either a unified entity ("two loves be one") that cannot be decayed or a perfect compound made of perfectly mixed elements ("love so alike") that also cannot be decayed. In either case, their love cannot "die." Their world of love, inherently mutual and spiritual, is immortal.

For detailed explications of this poem, see "Selected Bibliography: Critical Studies, Poetry," Daiches under section 10 and Hunt under section 12.

Goodyer(e), Sir Henry (1571?–1627). A gentleman of the privy chamber to King JAMES and a very close friend to Donne. To him

Donne wrote many prose *LETTERS*, as well as one of the *VERSE LETTERS* ("To Sir Henry Goodyer," written when Donne lived at MITCHAM). Donne relied to some extent on Goodyer's commendations of him to people of influence: e.g., Goodyer probably introduced Donne to the COUNTESS OF BEDFORD and others. Goodyer's estate was at Polesworth in Warwickshire, where Donne apparently visited at times. He was generous, making some loans to Donne. Donne alludes to Goodyer's "indulgent" living in the verse letter. When Goodyer himself faced financial problems with creditors for many of the last years of his life, Donne (while he was Dean of ST. PAUL'S CATHEDRAL) gave a sum of money to help him.

Goth. *Noun*: any individual of a Germanic tribe that overran the Roman Empire in its latter stages and destroyed many marks of its civilization, art, culture, and history. The word variously connotes anyone or anything barbaric, rude, uncivilized, lacking culture or taste, ignorant, passionate, violent, or destructive. Usually associated with VANDAL.

Gracchus (Graccus). Personified character in "SATIRE 3" who represents the belief that all religions are essentially alike and equally true, an attitude that suggests blindness in failing to distinguish differences and falsenesses in them.

Graius. Personified character in "SATIRE 3" who represents an adherent of the Church of England, blandly accepting the church that his countrymen, preachers, and state laws designate as the true one.

Grave. *Noun*: (1) a burial place, (2) a trench, (3) [possibly in punning context] engraving: see, for example, lines 13–18 of "ELEGY 9: THE AUTUMNAL."

Great Carrack. Common reference to a large Spanish ship named *Madre de Dios* that was captured by the English in 1592. It had a huge cargo of pepper.

Greediness. *Noun*: (1) excessive longing for food or drink, (2) excessive longing for wealth or material possessions, (3) excessive longing or desire in general.

Gregory. Reference by Donne in line 96 of "SATIRE 3" to Pope Gregory of the Roman Catholic Church (probably Pope Gregory XIII or Pope Gregory XIV).

Groat. A small English coin, a silver piece valued at four pence.

Grudge. *Verb*: (1) to complain, to grumble; (2) to be unwilling to give or allow, to begrudge; (3) to envy; (4) to trouble mentally; (5) to be seized with an illness.

Grudging. *Noun*: (1) a complaint or grumbling, (2) a slight symptom of an approaching disease.

Guiana. Spanish territory in South America. Some of the English (including Robert DEVEREUX, Earl of Essex) wanted to take the Spanish silver being transported from Guiana to Spain after the English had successfully sacked CADIZ (also known as Cales). This plan is referred to in one of the *EPIGRAMS* ("Cales and Guiana"). But the English fleet was ordered not to pursue this course. See also one of the *VERSE LETTERS*—the one titled "To Mr. R. W." (beginning "If, as mine is").

Guilpin, Everard. The likely recipient of "To Mr. E. G.," one of the *VERSE LETTERS*. He was at Gray's Inn in 1591, was related to Guilpins in Suffolk, and was a minor poet. In the verse letter, Donne speaks of staying in London when almost everyone else has deserted it ("lank and thin is every street"), including Guilpin. The theaters apparently are closed ("filled with emptiness"), implying that it might be during the epidemic of plague in the summer of 1593. He suggests that Guilpin store up "Suffolk's sweets" to have in London during winter.

Gull. *Verb*: to deceive or cheat.

Gummy blood. Donne's phrase for the sticky sap of the holly plant that was used to make BIRD-LIME (see lines 212–13 of *METEMPSYCHOSIS*).

H

H., M., Mrs. See HERBERT, MAGDALEN.

"H. W. in Hibernia Belligeranti." See WOTTON, HENRY.

Halcyon. *Noun*: the kingfisher, a crested, brilliantly-colored bird supposed to be able to calm the sea.

Hall, Edward (?–1547). Historian and chronicler in the early sixteenth century. Wrote *The Union of the Two Noble and Illustrious Families of Lancaster and York* which justifies the Tudor family's claim to the throne and especially portrays the reign of Henry VIII. In lines 97–98 of "Satire 4" Donne groups him with those chroniclers who include trivialities ("trash") in their accounts.

Hall, Joseph (1574–1656). Educated at Emmanuel College, Cambridge. Wrote satirical poetry early in his career. About 1600 Hall took holy orders and in 1601 became rector of All Saints in Hawstead, the living provided by Sir ROBERT DRURY and his wife. In 1608 he was made a chaplain to PRINCE HENRY. Later he was elevated to a bishop (in 1627 at Exeter and in 1641 at Norwich). He enjoyed great favor under both King JAMES and King CHARLES. As did Donne later, he accompanied JAMES HAY on a diplomatic mission. Hall published *Meditations and Vows* (1605, 1606), *Epistles* (1608), *Characters of Virtues and Vices* (1608) [the first in English of the form termed the "character"], and many volumes of prose essays, treatises, tracts, and devotional writings. His prolific writing is known for its influential Senecan style. Hall defended the Anglican liturgy and government against CALVINIST attack, action leading eventually to his ouster from the cathedral in 1643 by the PURITANS.

    Hall contributed the prefatory poems to Donne's *THE FIRST ANNIVERSARY* and *THE SECOND ANNIVERSARY*. He knew ELIZABETH DRURY as a girl in his church at Hawstead and as the daughter of his patrons. His poems are "To the Praise of the Dead, and the Anatomy" and "The Harbinger to the Progress," the latter one particularly praising Donne's "aspiring thoughts."

Haman. (1) In the Bible (Esther) he is the minister to King Ahasuerus who plotted to exterminate the Jews, failed to do so, and was hanged; (2) in lines 86–87 of "Satire 5" he is a character who "sold his antiquities": this probably does not refer to the Haman of the Bible and may refer to some (as yet unidentified) person known to Donne and his time.

Hamilton, James (1589–1625). Man memorialized in one of the *EPICEDES AND OBSEQUIES* ("An Hymn to the Saints, and to Marquis Hamilton"). Donne's friend Sir ROBERT KER [see KER, ROBERT (1)] requested that Donne write this memorial for Ker's friend who had died on March 2, 1625. Apparently Donne had some reservations about writing an essentially secular tribute after he was Dean of ST. PAUL'S CATHEDRAL, but he did not refuse his old friend. He carefully called the poem a "hymn." Some scholars believe that this poem quite likely is the last one written by Donne.

Hamilton became Marquis of Hamilton in 1604 and later accumulated other titles. He served KING JAMES in Scotland and accompanied him to England. He was quite highly regarded, one man even writing in 1617 that the Marquis of Hamilton is held to be the "gallantest gentleman" in both Scotland and England.

Harmless. *Adjective*: (1) free from guilt, innocent; (2) causing no harm, inoffensive; (3) free from harm, unhurt.

Harrington, Bridget. See LADY MARKHAM.

Harrington, John (1592–1614). Man memorialized in one of the *EPICEDES AND OBSEQUIES* ("Obsequies to the Lord Harrington, Brother to the Lady Lucy, Countess of Bedford"). As the title (from a manuscript) indicates, he was the brother of Donne's patroness, the COUNTESS OF BEDFORD. He was 2nd Baron of Exton and died (at TWICKENHAM Park) of smallpox on February 27, 1614. Contemporary comments universally praise his handsome features, utmost courtesy, great learning, and devout religion. He was educated at Cambridge and was a close friend of Prince Henry (see STUART, HENRY). Donne apparently felt the loss as a close friend of the young man, having an affection for him beyond that of mere regard for his patroness's brother. In the poem Donne emphasizes the learning and spiritual depth of Harrington.

Harrington, Lucy. See BEDFORD, COUNTESS OF.

Harry. Reference by Donne in line 97 of "SATIRE 3" to King Henry VIII of England, especially to his role in establishing the Church of England.

Hart Hall, Oxford. Traditionally Roman Catholic hall where Donne studied from 1584 to 1587, leaving without taking a degree.

Hastings, Elizabeth. See HUNTINGDON, COUNTESS OF.

Hay, Sir James (died in 1636). Came to England from Scotland with JAMES I. Was made a gentleman of the bedchamber and later Master of the Wardrobe. Created 1st Viscount Doncaster and 1st Earl of Carlisle. Regarded by contemporaries as calm, even-tempered, and without envy or enemies. Went to France on several diplomatic missions for England, under both James I and CHARLES I. He was known throughout his life as one who lived and entertained lavishly and magnificently and, indeed, as a spendthrift, dying heavily in debt.

    Donne, as he relates in a letter to Sir ROBERT KER, was introduced to Hay by Sir FRANCIS BACON, and Hay became one of the most faithful of Donne's patrons and friends. Hay urged that King James appoint Donne as Secretary to Ireland in 1608, but the King remembered the unpleasant circumstances surrounding the secret marriage to ANN MORE seven years earlier and refused to honor Hay's request. Hay was later instrumental in securing support and patronage of Donne by ROBERT KER, Viscount Rochester and Earl of Somerset. After Donne had entered the church and was serving at LINCOLN'S INN, King James appointed him as chaplain to accompany Hay (Viscount Doncaster) on a mediating diplomatic mission to Germany in 1619. This journey became the occasion for "A HYMN TO CHRIST, AT THE AUTHOR'S LAST GOING INTO GERMANY." Donne preached some of his *Sermons* at the invitation of Hay and before his circle of family and friends.

Heavenly hierarchy. See HIERARCHY, THE HEAVENLY.

Hectic (Hectique). *Adjective*: consumptive.

Heliconian spring. In mythology, Hippocrene, the fountain sacred to the nine Muses on Mount Helicon, the mountain of the Muses. The stream originated where the hoof of Pegasus, the winged horse, had struck the ground. Hippocrene is reputed to be the source of poetic inspiration.

Hellespont. Strait connecting the Aegean Sea with the Sea of Marmara. Now called "Dardanelles." Also see HERO.

Henry, Prince. See STUART, HENRY.

Hephaestion. See "ALEXANDER'S GREAT EXCESS."

Heraclitus (about 500 B.C.). Philosopher of Ephesus who emphasized the impermanence of all things and thus was commonly called "the weeping philosopher."

Herbert, Sir Edward (1583–1648). Son of MAGDALEN HERBERT. Knighted in 1603. Created 1st Baron of Cherbury in 1629. Soldier, diplomat, poet, and philosopher. JONSON (to DRUMMOND) reported Donne as saying that he wrote the "Elegy on the Untimely Death of the Incomparable Prince, Henry" to equal Sir Edward Herbert in "obscureness." Donne wrote him the *VERSE LETTER* "To Sr. Edward Herbert At Juliers" (see JULIERS), and a journey to Sir Edward's home occasioned "GOODFRIDAY, 1613, RIDING WESTWARD." Served as ambassador to France for some years and wrote *De Veritate*, a philosophical work with rationalistic assumptions and usually seen as a precursor of deism in the next century. His poetry does not equal that of his younger brother, GEORGE HERBERT, but he is regarded as one of the minor METAPHYSICAL poets, and one quite influenced by Donne in the secular vein, especially in his intellectual complexity, compactness in style and language, and anti-Petrarchan love themes.

Herbert, George (1593–1633). Son of MAGDALEN HERBERT and brother of EDWARD HERBERT. Attended Westminster School. Took B.A. and M.A. degrees at Trinity College, Cambridge. Held post as University Orator at Cambridge from 1620 to 1628. In 1625 Herbert was at his mother's home in CHELSEA at the same time Donne was, during a time of plague in London. He served in Parliament briefly but was ordained as deacon in 1624 and later made canon of Lincoln Cathedral and prebendary of Leighton Bromswold. He married Jane Danvers in 1629, became rector of Bemerton in 1630, and was ordained as priest later in the same year. He served in St. Andrew's Church at Bemerton conscientiously and with a reputation for piety, humility, and charity until his early death from (apparently) tuberculosis.

Since Herbert's mother was an important patroness and close friend of Donne, Herbert likely grew up reading Donne's works. Although Herbert was much younger than Donne, they obviously would see one another at times and would converse. Donne wrote the Latin poem "To Mr. George Herbert" that comments on Donne's adoption of a cross and anchor for Donne's seal, and Herbert responded with Latin verses. Donne's writing is also linked to Herbert's by the fact that Herbert's Latin and Greek poetry to the memory of his mother was published with Donne's commemorative sermon for her (1627). Herbert had indicated, as early as 1610 in two sonnets sent to his mother, that he wished to dedicate his poetic talent to the service of God and to the celebration of God's love, rather than to secular loves. This dedication resulted in his major work, a book of Christian poems published (a few months after his death) as *The Temple*. He also wrote a prose work called *The Country Parson* (or *A Priest to the Temple*) that finally was published in 1652. He collected and translated proverbs from other countries that also were published posthumously.

Herbert today is regarded as the most important follower of Donne in poetry, the best of the METAPHYSICAL poets after Donne. He does employ many of the qualities regarded as typical of Donne and the metaphysicals (e.g., colloquial language, irregular metrics, and metaphysical conceits) in certain poems (such as "The Collar" and "The Pulley") and in parts of poems; however, debts to JONSON and the CLASSICAL strain appear strongly in Herbert's work, as well. Fusion of the influences from these two major poets is integral to understanding and appreciating the work of Herbert and others after Donne. The balanced mixing of characteristics may be seen in such poems as Herbert's "Virtue" and "The Windows."

Herbert, Magdalen (died in 1627). Mother of EDWARD and GEORGE HERBERT. Married Richard Herbert about 1581 and bore ten children by him. Shortly after his death she moved her household to Oxford (in 1599). It is at this time that Donne perhaps was first introduced to her, but the friendship between them did not fully develop until some years later. In 1601 she again moved her household, this time to London, specifically to Charing Cross. By 1607 Donne had renewed his friendship with Magdalen Herbert and had become one of the many guests received in her large household. He wrote letters to her during this period, and she became, in essence, a patroness, giving him gifts and financial support. A letter to her in July, 1607, thanks her profusely and accompanies some sonnets (referred to by Donne as "Holy Hymns and Sonnets"): these undoubtedly are the sonnets known as *LA CORONA*, and sent with them was another one addressed "To the Lady Magdalen Herbert, of St. Mary Magdalen." (See MARY MAGDALENE and BETHINA.) WALTON argues that "ELEGY 9: THE AUTUMNAL" was written to her: this may be true, but full evidence for the assumption does not exist.

Mrs. Herbert remarried in 1609, to Sir John Danvers, a man many years younger. In anticipation of the marriage, Donne sent her the *VERSE LETTER* "To Mrs. M. H." He wittily and graciously compliments her as being the epitome of goodness and worthy of both love and reverence, as he endorses her choice of Sir John Danvers. He wants to love "him" (Sir John Danvers) who shall be loved of "her" (Lady Danvers). And Donne indeed became a friend to Sir John, even as his friendship for Lady Danvers became deeper. The household spent much time, especially in summers, in Sir John's beautiful home and gardens in CHELSEA, where Donne frequently visited. Danvers was almost universally respected as a wise, generous, and kind individual. It was at this home that Donne spent several months in the latter part of 1625 in order to stay away from the plague in London. In June, 1627, Lady Danvers died, and Donne delivered a commemorative sermon for her on July 1 that was printed shortly after.

Hercules. In mythology, Roman name for Greek hero Heracles. A son of Zeus. Known for his courage, strength, and destruction of various animals and monsters. As an infant he squeezed two serpents to death. His Twelve Labors included such feats as killing the Nemean lion and the nine-headed Lernean Hydra. Among other weapons and armor, he carried a club of bronze.

Hermaphrodite. *Noun:* (1) a human or animal in which elements of both sexes are combined, (2) a person or thing in which two opposite qualities are combined.

Hermes. See MERCURY.

Hero. In Greek mythology, priestess of Aphrodite (see VENUS) at the city of Sestos. Leander fell in love with her at first sight. He would swim to her from his home in the city of Abydos across the Hellespont, using the light of a torch placed by Hero in a tower to guide him. One night the torch was blown out by the wind. Leander drowned. His body washed ashore the next day at Sestos where Hero found it. She then drowned herself out of grief. They are the subject of "Hero and Leander," one of Donne's *EPIGRAMS*.

Herod. Herod the Great (73?–4 B.C.), King of Judea from 40 to 4 B.C. He ruled at the time of Christ's birth and tried to frustrate the fulfillment of the prophecy of the birth of a "King of the Jews" by ordering the killing of the children of Bethlehem. JOSEPH and MARY, having been warned by an angel, took Jesus and fled into Egypt before Herod's order was given. See Matthew 2.

Hesper (Hesperus). The planet Venus as the evening star. Also called "Vesper." However, Donne uses "Hesper" to indicate Venus as the morning star in *THE SECOND ANNIVERSARY* (lines 197–98) and in *PARADOXES AND PROBLEMS*. MARLOWE, in *Hero and Leander*, also refers to Hesperus as the morning star. Both writers may have confused "Hesper" with "Phosphor," one of the names for Venus as the morning star. (See the article by Gill cited in the "Selected Bibliography" under *The Anniversaries*.)

Heterogeneous ideas are yoked by violence together. See METAPHYSICAL CONCEIT.

Hierarchy, the heavenly. The supposed nine ranks or levels or orders of angels, especially as proposed by Dionysius the Areopagite, a Christian Platonist (more strictly, Neo-Platonist: see PLATONIC) in the 5th century. His work *On the Heavenly Hierarchy* designated the highest division to be composed of Seraphs, Cherubs, and Thrones. The second division contains Dominations, Virtues, and Powers. The third has Principalities, Archangels, and Angels. The highest are the most contemplative, and the lowest are the most active. Those in the third division mediate between man and the realm of God and the angels by delivering messages to man and carrying out God's bidding. The nine orders are also analogous to the nine SPHERES, and, in fact, these orders were believed to be the INTELLIGENCES that were assigned to the spheres, enabling the creation of the music of the spheres. Most of the angels that fell with Lucifer were of the Seraphs (Seraphim).

Hierome. See JEROME, SAINT.

Hieronymous. See JEROME, SAINT.

Hilary term. The first legal session of the year held by the English High Court of Justice, usually January 23 to February 12. So named because the festival day of Hilarius, Bishop of Poitiers, is January 13.

Hilliard, Nicholas (1547–1619). English artist, goldsmith, and jeweler, particularly famous for his miniature portraits. Donne alludes to him with praise in lines 4–5 of "The Storm."

His. In many contexts, possessive pronoun for "its."

Holinshed, Raphael (?–1580?). Historian and chronicler during the sixteenth century. Wrote, with the help of others, the *Chronicles of England, Scotland, and Ireland* (1st ed. in 1577 and 2nd ed. in 1587). His tendency to include minor matters scattered with great events is ridiculed by Donne in lines 97–98 of "Satire 4."

Hollenshead. See HOLINSHED, RAPHAEL.

Holy Sonnets. A subdivision of *DIVINE POEMS.* In the first edition of Donne's poems in 1633, a large section is designated *Holy Sonnets* and includes the seven sonnets of *LA CORONA* and a subsection also called *Holy Sonnets* which contains twelve of the nineteen sonnets that editors now consider strictly to be the *Holy Sonnets.* (Some manuscripts refer to these latter ones as "Divine Meditations.") Thus, the modern tendency is to distinguish between *LA CORONA* and *Holy Sonnets,* the latter title being reserved for the nineteen most famous Christian sonnets by Donne.

Major problems in editions of these famous nineteen (and in selections of them in anthologies) have been determining their proper arrangement and deciding their numbering. Editors faced with confusing and exasperating differences in the early editions and manuscripts have developed various arrangements and numberings that they propose. Therefore, the reader today will find the same sonnet at different places and with different numbers assigned, if he compares several modern editions and anthologies. For simplicity, I use the first line of each of these sonnets as a title and make an individual entry in this "Dictionary" according to that first line for ten of the most famous and most frequently anthologized ones. Those chosen for separate entries are the following: "As due by many titles I resign," "At the round earth's imagined corners, blow," "Batter my heart, three-personed

God; for, you," "Death be not proud, though some have called thee,"
"I am a little world made cunningly," "Show me dear Christ, thy
spouse, so bright and clear," "Since she whom I loved hath paid
her last debt," "This is my play's last scene, here heavens appoint,"
"Thou hast made me, and shall thy work decay," and "What if this
present were the world's last night." The content of all of the
remaining poems of *Holy Sonnets* has been examined for elements
to make up other entries.

Home-meats. Homely, domestic gossip.

Homer (8th century B.C.?). Regarded as the greatest Greek poet.
Traditionally assumed to be the author of both *The Iliad* and *The
Odyssey*, even though various individuals may have contributed
to the epic poems as they were passed down through the
centuries. In "A VALEDICTION: OF THE BOOK" Donne refers to an
old story that Homer used a mythical woman's (Phantasia's) story
of the Trojan War and Odysseus as the source for *The Iliad* and
The Odyssey.

Honor. *Noun:* (1) high respect or admiration; (2) high reputation;
(3) chastity, purity [of a woman]; (4) exalted rank or position; (5)
title of respect given to a person of rank or quality [i.e., "your
honor"]; (6) a source of or cause of high respect.

Howard, Catherine. See SALISBURY, COUNTESS OF.

Howard, Frances. See KER, ROBERT (2).

Humor (Humour). *Noun:* (1) any fluid or juice of an animal or
plant; (2) one of the four major fluids of the body, according to
ancient and medieval physiology (primarily from GALEN): blood,
phlegm, choler (red choler), and melancholy (black choler). The
predominance of one humor over the others or the proportions in
which the humors were mixed in the body were believed to
determine a person's COMPLEXION—i.e., physical appearance,
personality, and disposition (e.g., a dominance of choler causes
anger). The healthy, well-balanced individual supposedly has all
humors mixed equally. The four humors correspond to the four
ELEMENTS (choler determines a choleric complexion and
corresponds to fire with its hot and dry qualities; blood
determines a sanguine complexion and corresponds to air with its
hot and moist qualities; phlegm determines a phlegmatic
complexion and corresponds to water with its cold and moist

qualities; melancholy determines a melancholic complexion and corresponds to earth with its cold and dry qualities). To correct imbalance, one would take food or substances of the opposite quality or decrease the humor in excess; (3) the temperament or disposition exemplified by a person as a result of the proportion of the fluid humors within the body; (4) the particular style, tone, or spirit of a piece of writing or other artistic composition; (5) temporary mood or whim; (6) a disposition toward a certain action; (7) odd or quaint trait. (The common modern sense of the word as the quality of being, or ability to be, comical or amusing or funny, or to perceive such comedy, does not occur in Donne's writing.)

Humorist. *Noun*: (1) a person subject to changes induced by the HUMORS; (2) whimsical, faddish person.

Humorous. *Adjective*: (1) pertaining to a bodily HUMOR and its result; (2) fanciful, capricious, subject to whim. (The common modern sense of something or someone being comical or amusing or funny does not occur in Donne's writing.)

Huntingdon, Elizabeth Stanley (Hastings), Countess of (1587–1633). Daughter of the Earl and Countess of Derby. After the Earl's death his widow married SIR THOMAS EGERTON (in 1600 while Donne was serving as his secretary). Elizabeth Stanley was, then, a part of the Egerton household and knew Donne from her youth. She married Henry Hastings and became a Countess when her husband became Earl of Huntingdon in 1605. Donne refers to her with admiration in several of his prose *LETTERS*, speaking of her "noble favors" to him and expressing in one to GOODYER (pp. 100–105 in *Letters to Several Persons of Honor*, 1651) his trepidation at writing a verse letter to the Countess of Huntingdon when his primary allegiance is to his patroness the COUNTESS OF BEDFORD. Two of his *VERSE LETTERS* titled "To the Countess of Huntingdon" survive: in the one beginning "Man to God's image" he says that "long ago" he prophesied her great virtue.

Husband. *Noun*: (1) farmer, worker of the land; (2) married man.

Hydroptic. *Adjective*: (1) dropsical, having dropsy; (2) being insatiably thirsty.

"Hymn to Christ, at the Author's Last Going into Germany, A." One of the *DIVINE POEMS*. The occasion, dating, and autobiographical importance of this poem are quite specific. Donne served as chaplain to accompany JAMES HAY, Viscount Doncaster, on a diplomatic mission to Germany from May, 1619, to January, 1620. Donne initially had reservations about the journey, since he was leaving all of his children in England and felt rather weak and ill at the time. He also wrote and said some things before embarking that suggest his realization that he might indeed die during the journey (see above, page 19, in "Donne's Life"). This prospect is faced and ultimately resolved spiritually in this hymn.

In the first stanza Donne says that whatever old, battered ("torn") ship on which he travels will be symbolic to him of the ark that God told Noah to build ("Thy Ark") to save himself from the coming flood in the Old Testament. The implication is that the literal sea between England and the Continent will be comparable to the Old Testament Flood with God's force evident in it. Donne feels that God saved Noah and that God also will save Donne; however, it becomes evident that Donne is thinking of himself being saved spiritually, whereas Noah was saved physically. Then lines 3–4 develop his comparison further and make it more complex: the literal sea that might drown him physically if the ship sinks becomes not just the Old Testament "flood" but also an emblem of "Thy blood" (i.e., God's blood as exemplified in Christ's blood shed to save humanity spiritually). So, he has alluded to the Old Testament God of power in the "flood," but now has brought in the New Testament God of love and mercy in Christ's "blood." The Old Testament "flood" cleansed the world of sin, saving man through the righteous Noah. The New Testament "blood" cleanses the world of sin for all who accept it and provides salvation for any individual submitting himself to its saving power. (It is interesting that in Donne's last sermon at LINCOLN'S INN before his departure on this journey he said that we sail to Christ's kingdom through "the sea of his blood, where no soul suffers shipwreck.") Lines 5–8 continue the implication of God's two sides: Old Testament wrathful power is evident in "clouds of anger" on the surface that might be perceived in threatening storm clouds at sea on his journey, but behind this surface "mask" is the more important loving face of God in Christ that Donne recognizes and ultimately has faith in. Even though he might die bodily from power on this earth, he is confident that Christ will not "despise" him, giving his soul eternal salvation. The first stanza, then, begins the METAPHYSICAL CONCEIT of this mundane trip from

England to Germany as ultimately a spiritual journey from this world to the next. In addition, with the final image of Christ's loving face behind the mask, there is the beginning of another conceit that continues through the poem: Christ is like a lover in a festival or party or entertainment at which participants wear masks, and Donne is a lover of Christ who recognizes Christ's identity behind the disguise. This motif of a love relationship with God occurs also in some of the *HOLY SONNETS*.

In the second stanza Donne sacrifices "this island" (England) and "all whom I loved there, and who loved me" (all children, other family members, friends) to Christ: Donne is prepared to face death and leave all worldly loves behind. He symbolically cuts himself off from them as the literal sea between England and the Continent ("our [earthly] seas") intervenes between the ship and England. In an implied exchange of sacrifices, he wants assurance that Christ's sea of blood ("Thy sea," picking up the image from the first stanza) will intervene between Donne's sins and Christ, allowing his spiritual salvation. The conceit of the journey expands to imply that leaving England is like leaving both the world and his sins behind. Going to Germany is like a journey to God's presence in heaven. This also acknowledges his turn toward the greater love of Christ and away from the lesser love of the world. In a small conceit within the two larger conceits of the poem, lines 13–16 compare Donne to the sap of a tree that retreats to the root of the tree in winter: Donne's "winter" is this latter period of his life during which he faces what seems to be a real possibility of death on the journey, but it also may reflect the sad, melancholy period he is in less than two years after the death of his wife (ANN MORE). This is particularly suggested since he says that he is now turning only to the love of Christ ("Thee") who is the "eternal root of true love": all lesser, worldly love comes from the true spiritual love of God as its source. The conceit of Christ as his true lover persists, and a serious play on "KNOW" seems suggested: the sexual "knowing" of love applies to his worldly love of Ann, and now it applies to the love relationship with Christ. (The feelings and ideas expressed in this stanza especially parallel those in "SINCE SHE WHOM I LOVED HATH PAID HER LAST DEBT," the one of the *HOLY SONNETS* that concerns the death of Donne's wife.)

In the third stanza Donne tells Christ that neither Christ nor the Christian religion (see "NOR . . . NOR") ordinarily tries to "control" (i.e., exercise restraint or to inhibit) the "amorousness" (the lovingness or capacity for love) that a soul in harmony with Christ and the Christian faith possesses: i.e., each human has free will to love what and how much the person wishes. Donne proposes, though, that if Christ wants all of a person's love to be directed only to Christ ("BUT" in line 19 means "unless"), then Christ will exert some control to bring this about. Playing, in lines 19-20, on God's own comment in the Old Testament that he is a jealous God (Exodus 20:5), Donne applies this to the love conceit in the poem. Donne tells Christ that Donne is also jealous. In lines 21-24 Donne explains why he is jealous: he thinks that Christ does not really love him (or, at least, is not showing it) because Christ is not preventing Donne from loving "more" (i.e., others): in a Christian paradox, for Christ to restrain Donne from loving worldly loves gives Donne's soul perfect freedom (true freedom comes only to the soul that is dedicated completely to Christ). He jealously accuses Christ of having other lovers: "whoever gives, takes liberty," meaning "whoever gives liberty also takes liberty." Donne here is implying that if Christ allows Donne to have other loves, then Christ also must have other loves, and ends the stanza with the jealous imputation that, if this is indeed the case, then Christ does not really love him (parallel to the kind of challenge presented a partner in a secular love relationship to protest and assure the one who says, "You don't really love me.").

The last stanza presents Donne giving the ultimate opportunity for Christ to prove His love for Donne. The stanza brings to fruition both the conceit of the journey and the conceit of the love relationship. He tells Christ to "SEAL" Donne's "divorce" (with wordplay implying both a legal document severing a marriage and a separation from previous attachments). Donne wishes Christ to divorce Donne from "all" on whom he earlier shed "fainter beams of love" (all worldly loves never having the strength of love at the source of all love which is Christ, the "eternal root of true love"). The "all" at first suggests specific people from his past life, such as Ann (who is now dead) and/or children, family, and friends left in England. But more specifically the "all" refers to personified values such as "Fame," "Wit" (in multiple senses—see WIT), and "Hopes" (worldly ambitions). These are now recognized as "false mistresses" in contrast to his true lover now seen in Christ. Donne urges Christ to take all of this misdirected love and redirect it to Christ, making a marriage between Donne and Christ. This command to Christ expresses Donne's wish to turn away completely from worldly values in favor of those of the spirit, and the transformation is thus expressed in a love conceit. But the journey conceit also expresses change: he has made a spiritual journey from worldly values to spiritual ones, as symbolized by travel from England to Germany.

He has journeyed to see "God only": all else has been left behind him. He has left behind the storms of the worldly life (and of the world itself, if he faces physical death) in favor of a much-desired new environment, "everlasting night." Paradoxically, it is also a journey from "day" to "night," and night is preferable: one is accustomed to and ordinarily expects to hear of a metaphorical journey from night to day, but, to Donne, "night" is like: (1) the atmosphere of a dark church in which prayer can concentrate undistractedly on God, (2) a place in which one can truly "see" in darkness [by seeing God], (3) death, and (4) eternity. These are all preferred destinations, and Donne reaches them by going "out of sight" of England, of this worldly life, and of the world itself.

"Hymn to God My God, in My Sickness."   One of the *DIVINE POEMS*. Despite the fact that WALTON assigns this poem to a period just prior to Donne's death, many scholars feel that it was composed shortly after Donne's serious illness late in 1623 (the same period of *DEVOTIONS UPON EMERGENT OCCASIONS*). It is written as a meditation on suffering and death and their acceptance, in order to prepare spiritually for salvation.

The first stanza relies heavily on a musical METAPHYSICAL CONCEIT. Donne ("I") prepares to enter heaven, with its "choir of saints" and music around God's throne (as described in Revelation 14). He will be both a part of the music in heaven's divine harmony and a musician joining in the playing of that music. Music, metaphorically, is divine harmony. Donne is like a musician standing outside the "door" (of death and heaven), in his sickness. He is tuning his "instrument"—metaphorically his own soul being tuned to harmonize with the saints and angels already inside heaven. But on a secondary level the "instrument" also might be interpreted as this hymn, this poem: "tuning" is, then, writing the poem that prepares him for death and the afterlife. In the context, "before" in line 5 is both spatial and temporal: standing in front of the door of heaven actually is temporally preceding his entrance into the final realm of existence for his soul, paradoxically a realm where neither space nor time matters.

Stanzas two, three, and four develop an extraordinarily detailed and complex conceit centered on maps and geography. As Donne is on his sickbed, he portrays himself as laid out like a map with his physicians being "cosmographers," readers and studiers of the map. The physicians are dedicated ones who love their patient, and Donne believes in the transforming power of love (see, for example, "TWICKNAM GARDEN"). Therefore, the physicians "by their love are grown" into these intent examiners of him. They see that Donne is making a "southwest" journey of discovery, implying one comparable to that of MAGELLAN through the strait south of South America (later named the Strait of Magellan) and on west into the Pacific Ocean where later Magellan died in the Philippines. "*Per fretum febris*" in line 10 means "through the strait of fever" and "through the raging of fever": Donne puns on "*fretum*" which means both "strait" and "raging heat." Ingeniously, therefore, he associates the southern Strait of Magellan with the hot area of the world and thus with his own raging fever in his sickness that he foresees as being followed by his own death, just as Magellan's death followed his own passage through this southern strait. And "west" connotes the setting sun and thus death. Significantly, though, Donne regards his journey as a "discovery," one of excitement comparable to Magellan's at seeing, in essence, a new world: in Donne's case, it is a vision of heaven beyond the suffering and death endured in the "strait" of fever. Adding even more layers of meaning here are Donne's punning on and allusiveness in "STRAITS" (lines 10 and 11): the three senses relevant are (1) a narrow passageway of water connecting two large bodies of water; (2) a distressing situation; and (3) an allusion to Biblical uses of the word, such as in Matthew 7:13–14 ("Enter ye in at the strait gate: for wide is the gate, and broad is the way, that leadeth to destruction, and many there be which go in thereat: Because strait is the gate, and narrow is the way, which leadeth unto life, and few there be that find it.") Donne says that he feels joy that through these "straits" he sees his "west" (i.e., his death). Even though, like the currents of the Strait of Magellan flowing west, the "currents" of his fever propelling him to death allow no turning back. Nevertheless, he is not afraid of death (his "west," line 13), since he already has called himself a flat map, and on such a map the point at extreme left ("west") corresponds to the point at extreme right ("east"): Donne makes these two points of "west" and "east" symbolize "death" and "resurrection," and they "touch" just as do west and east in a flat map. So, Donne's death becomes also his resurrection. Secondarily, "east" suggests the rising sun (and the rising Son, Christ, who enables Donne to rise too). The questions in the fourth stanza pursue the matter of where the passageway, the "strait," takes one: to the Pacific? to the riches of the East, the Orient? to Jerusalem? But Donne is alluding to the location of both the earthly Paradise and Heaven and its spiritual "riches." Death is the passage by which he will reach this ultimate destination of Heaven (or, in a sense, return to man's original "home" Paradise). The last three lines of the fourth stanza emphasize that, regardless of where Adam's earthly Paradise is found, the straits on earth (such as those named ANYAN, MAGELLAN, and GIBRALTAR) are the ways to this larger end. Thus, his own death will be a means to a larger end, a more important destination at the end of a spiritual journey. He does not have to worry about whether the earthly Paradise is located in Europe ("where JAPHET dwelt") or in Africa (where CHAM dwelt) or in Asia (where SHEM dwelt). The important fact is that the strait of death will take him to the ultimate Paradise, Heaven.

Stanza five develops from the previous questioning of the location of Paradise. Donne expresses the belief surviving from medieval writings and art that Paradise (the Garden of Eden) and CALVARY were located at the same spot and that "Christ's cross" on Calvary stood where "Adam's tree" (the Tree of Knowledge) grew. So, Christ redeemed man on the same spot where Adam (and thus man) fell. Suffering and death were imposed on man with Adam's fall, and Donne accepts his own suffering and death through his current sickness as his participation in the ordained state of man from Adam. But his suffering and death also reflect those of Christ (called the "last Adam" by St. Paul). And, just as east meets west and the setting sun meets the rising sun at that point, so does Donne here see Adam's fall meeting Christ's resurrection. Indeed, Christ's own death meets Christ's resurrection. So, Donne contains both fallen man (Adam) and risen man (Christ) within his own nature—i.e., "both Adams" meet in Donne. And Christ is the last and victorious Adam within Donne. The "sweat of thy face" (Genesis 3:19) ordained for Adam and man in general at Adam's fall is symbolic of suffering, which Donne, in turn, exemplifies as his "face" (representing the body) sweats with fever on his sickbed (see SURROUND). But, again, the more important fact is that Christ's "blood" overcomes suffering and death by embracing and giving salvation to Donne's soul. Deliberately echoed by Donne and of primary importance in this stanza are the following Biblical passages from St. Paul in I Corinthians 15:21–22 ("For since by man came death, by man came also the resurrection of the dead. For as in Adam all die, even so in Christ shall all be made alive.") and 15:44–47 ("It is sown a natural body; it is raised a spiritual body. There is a natural body, and there is a spiritual body. And so it is written, The first man Adam was made a living soul; the last Adam was made a quickening spirit. Howbeit that was not first which is spiritual, but that which is natural; and afterward that which is spiritual. The first man is of the earth, earthy: the second man is the Lord from heaven.").

In stanza 6 Donne emphasizes his own hope to rise above the old Adam in himself and above his own suffering and death into the salvation attainable through Christ. He wants God to receive him in Christ's "purple," meaning both Christ's blood and the kingly robe of royal purple worn by Christ the King (also recalling the mocking robe of purple in which Christ was dressed before he was crucified—see Mark 15:17–20). Donne's asking the "lord" to "receive" him recalls the opening of the hymn where he is outside the "door" to "that holy room." He wants God to grant him, through the agency of Christ's suffering crown of thorns (also in Mark 15:17–20), Christ's "other crown," the "crown of glory that fadeth not away" (I Peter 5:4). Lines 28–29 quite personally voice Donne's perception of his own role as a clergyman who has preached God's word to others' souls, but now this very hymn is his "text" and "sermon" to his own soul to prepare for death of the body and salvation of the soul. The last line of the hymn summarizes in a paradox what his soul has learned: the Lord "throws down" (into a sickbed, but ultimately into a grave) in order that the Lord "may raise" the soul out of the grave and into heaven, that "holy room."

For a detailed and quite influential explication of this poem, see "Selected Bibliography: Critical Studies, Poetry," Hunt under section 12.

"Hymn to God the Father, A." One of the *DIVINE POEMS*. Donne apparently wrote this hymn during or shortly after his serious illness in 1623 (the same time of *DEVOTIONS UPON EMERGENT OCCASIONS*): WALTON assigns it to this period. Puns and ambiguous pronoun references create some of the richness of the poem.

Donne first asks God to forgive "that sin where I begun," apparently original sin: Donne, as all humanity, begins with original sin in Adam, but also he begins with it from its inheritance in his own conception and birth. He acknowledges it as his sin, even though "done before"—i.e., committed ("done") before him by Adam and Eve but also reenacted ("done") and carried by the "Donne" family: line 2 begins a recurring play on his own name and that of his family through the poem. Some ambiguity in reference appears in "it" in line 2, referring primarily to the sin but also secondarily to the act of forgiveness— i.e., Christ already has granted the forgiveness through crucifixion. He still needs personal assurance that original sin (through which he continually runs or participates in or commits) in himself is forgiven. In line 5 "When Thou hast done" means "When You are through with forgiving [this one sin]"; however, "Thou hast not done" means both "You are not through with forgiving" and "You do not [yet] have [John] Donne [until all of his sins have been forgiven]." The reason is in line 6: Donne has both "more" sins and "more" forgiveness to ask of God.

In the second stanza Donne asks forgiveness for "that sin which I have won / Others to sin," apparently any sin of any type during his life. These sins provided bad examples for others to follow or tempted others into sin (his sin became their "door" into sin). He might have avoided a particular sin for a year or two but (typical of corrupt human nature) would fall back into the sin for twenty years ("a score"): he, like a hog in muddy filth, "wallowed" in it, displaying his animalistic, fallen side of man. The refrain (lines 11–12) contains the same puns and double meanings as lines 5–6.

In the third stanza Donne asks God to forgive his "sin of fear," the fear of death without having complete faith in his salvation in the next life: he fears perishing "on the shore" (the image for this earthly life). By implication, he will not sail on the sea of eternity, into the heavenly sea of the next life. The image of spinning his "last thread" refers generally and figuratively to spinning the last thread of his life. But more specifically it alludes to the three Fates of classical mythology and their respective functions regarding the thread of life. Clotho spins the thread, Lachesis determines its length, and Atropos cuts it. The use of such a classical, pagan allusion suggests a non-Christian view of death, with no vision of heaven beyond—i.e., the very consideration for which Donne needs forgiveness. But the fear will be overcome and forgiveness of it assured if God will swear that at Donne's death "Thy Son [Christ the Son and sun]" will "shine [with the light of grace]" as he does now and always has. Christ's light can overcome the darkness Donne contemplates at death. God "having done that" (i.e., given this assurance that Christ's grace will apply to him at his death) now "hast done" (meaning that God is now through with forgiving, but also that God has John Donne as His saved creature). The last line ("I fear no more") also has multiple meaning. It means "I fear no longer" or "I fear death no longer." But also suggested are "I fear no more sins" and "I fear no more need of forgiveness."

The structure of the hymn is simple but quite effective. The first stanza pictures a sin at the beginning of life, the second stanza presents any sin during all of his life, and the last stanza portrays a sin at the very end of his life. Forgiveness for all of these assures complete coverage for Donne from birth to death.

(For similar punning on his name, see "Expostulation 19" of *DEVOTIONS UPON EMERGENT OCCASIONS*.)

I

"I am a little world made cunningly." First line of one of the *HOLY SONNETS*. This opening states the central analogy of the sonnet, the belief that man is a MICROCOSM. The speaker proceeds to portray himself as a "world" with correspondences to both the earth and the universe within the context of their histories from a Biblical and Christian perspective.
He is made of the ELEMENTS (i.e., his body) and a SPRITE (i.e., his soul). But sin means the death of both body and soul: "endless night" is the everlasting damnation in hell that dark sin will condemn both body and soul to at the Last Judgment, unless corrective steps can be taken to cleanse his world (himself) of sin. For help in this task the speaker calls on both astronomers who (in the early 17th century) are discovering new SPHERES in the heavens (or more vastness in the heavens than previously thought to exist) and discoverers who journey to new parts of the earth and find new lands. Donne is drawing here on contemporary activities of interest. Since the astronomers and explorers are able to find new facets of creation that before seemed nonexistent, the speaker hopes that the same can be done by them in the parallel universe/earth of himself. If so, they might discover new "seas" of tears within him to allow himself to weep even more earnestly to repent of his "black sin": this would be a flooding ("drowning") of his little world that is comparable to the Old Testament flood that cleansed sin from the earth. But then the speaker remembers that God (in Genesis) promised that such a flood over the world would not again occur; therefore, he says that at least it can be a "washing" of his own world to cleanse the sin. Then he remembers something else (line 10): II Peter 3: 5–10 notes that the world will be destroyed by fire. So, he feels that this must also apply to his own correspondent world if he too wants to burn away the old earth and anticipate "new heavens and a new earth" (II Peter 3:13). The speaker feels that up to this time the "fires," the burning passions, of "lust and envy" have caused the "black sin" covering his earth. But he is determined to dispense with those sinful fires and to call on God to use a paradoxically cleansing fire by causing the fire of zeal, of zealousness in the speaker, to serve God (echoing Psalms 69:9). This spiritual fire will burn up the old charred world of his sinful

self: paradoxically, it is an "eating" up that will "heal" him spiritually by making him a "new earth," a new world.

Ide. Mount Ida, where Eris (Greek goddess of discord) threw the apple of discord into the midst of the guests at the wedding of Peleus and Thetis. APHRODITE, Athena, and Hera all claimed it, since it was designated "for the fairest." This necessitated Paris's judgment which, in turn, led to the Trojan War.

Idios. Character speaking in one of Donne's *EPITHALAMIONS*, the "Epithalamion at the Marriage of the Earl of Somerset" (in the "Eclogue" and at the closing of the poem). The Greek name means "own" or "private" and seems to refer to Donne himself, as the person who has not yet succeeded in securing the position or favor at Court that he desires. He feels isolated from its life-giving qualities and instead feels "dead, and buried." Also, the "nuptial song" itself is written by Idios (i.e., Donne), and he sees this "poor song" as a means that might "advance his fame" (lines 99–104). See also ALLOPHANES, ROBERT KER (1), and ROBERT KER (2). (For another view of Idios, however, see the essay by Dubrow listed under "Epithalamions" in "Selected Bibliography.")

Idolatry. A special use of the word by Donne is to refer to his (or his speaker's) past false worship of women and love in their secular, PROFANE senses (with an implied contrast to his true devotion and worship of God in the present). See, for example, the *HOLY SONNETS*, that begin "O might those sighs and tears return again" and "WHAT IF THIS PRESENT WERE THE WORLD'S LAST NIGHT."

Ignatius His Conclave. Prose work by Donne published in 1611, first in Latin as *Conclave Ignati* and then in Donne's own English translation. The volumes were published anonymously, but most readers at the time knew that it had been written by Donne. The work primarily is a witty satire attacking the JESUITS and IGNATIUS OF LOYOLA. It apparently was written in part to appeal to the anti-Catholic sentiment in England at the time and to King JAMES himself, especially since the Jesuits were regarded as promoting the assassination of Protestant rulers. [See *PSEUDO-MARTYR*.] It also reflects Donne's continuing interest in the NEW PHILOSOPHY, containing references to the work of COPERNICUS, BRAHE, GALILEO, and KEPLER.

    The narrator of the work claims to have a vision of the universe that becomes mainly a vision of Hell that opens to his sight. With Lucifer there in a special room are individuals who "attempted any innovation in this life, that they gave an affront to all antiquity, and induced doubts, and anxieties, and scruples. . . ." He sees Copernicus desiring entrance. Ignatius Loyola is there, "a subtle fellow" who is "indued with the Devil." PARACELSUS wants to enter, promoting his own innovations in medicine ("PHYSIC"). MACHIAVELLI seeks to enter, addressing both Lucifer and Ignatius (considering them as two persons in an unholy TRINITY, the other person being the Pope), building up himself in their eyes because he "went always that way of blood" and preferred "sacrifices of the Gentiles, and of the Jews." He also pictures himself as having the same virtue as the Jesuits in teaching "perfidiousness and dissembling of religion." Ignatius, however, successfully persuades Lucifer not to allow these three into the privileged room and position enjoyed by Ignatius himself. ARETINE and Columbus are also denied the room by Lucifer. Finally, perceiving the dangerous ambition of Ignatius, Lucifer pretends to want to promote him. He proposes having the Pope call on GALILEO for aid (because of Galileo's discoveries about the moon with the telescope) and then to send Ignatius and the Jesuits to the moon to have a new world and a new Hell to preside over. A soul arrives in Hell at this point, bringing word that the Church plans to canonize Ignatius. Ignatius then considers the nature of the Pope (Boniface) who is sitting in the principal place in Hell next to Lucifer's own throne, decides that he is not an innovator, and convinces Lucifer (who wishes to protect his own position) to expel Boniface from his place in order for Ignatius to move into it. The narrator awakes from his vision and concludes that seeing a "Jesuit turn the Pope out of his chair in Hell" makes him suspect that the Jesuits will "attempt as much at Rome."

The satire particularly directs itself to serious concerns with human presumption, pride, and disturbances of order and beliefs. But Donne's senses of humor and paradox very much pervade the work to make it an entertaining mode of criticism. (The best beginning for a fuller examination of this work is T.S. Healy's edition, with its valuable introduction and commentary: see "Selected Bibliography: Works.")

Ignatius of Loyola (Ignatius Loyola) [1491–1556]. Founder of the Society of Jesus: see JESUITS. Born in Spain to a noble and wealthy family. Served as a soldier. Founded the Society of Jesus in Paris, the members taking vows of poverty, chastity, and obedience. Was canonized by the Roman Catholic Church in 1622, thus becoming Saint Ignatius of Loyola. He wrote a volume entitled *Spiritual Exercises*, a book of devotion, meditation, and prayer that may have influenced Donne to some extent as far as meditative techniques in *THE FIRST ANNIVERSARY, THE SECOND ANNIVERSARY,* and *DEVOTIONS UPON EMERGENT OCCASIONS.* For the most part, however, Donne's writing conveys loathing for Ignatius and the Jesuits, particularly in *PSEUDO-MARTYR, IGNATIUS HIS CONCLAVE,* and in many *SERMONS.*

Illude. *Verb*: to trick or deceive.

Immure. *Verb*: to confine or enclose.

Impale. *Verb*: to enclose with pales or posts, to fence in.

Impertinent. *Adjective*: (1) not to the point or inappropriate or irrelevant; (2) presumptuous or intrusive; (3) insolent.

Impute(d). In a theological sense and according to CALVIN, one may be "imputed" to be righteous or may secure "imputed grace" only as freely attributed and given by Christ to his chosen ones from his store of grace, since no one can gain salvation by good works or merit.

In ordinary. Regular.

Inde. INDIA.

India. In Donne's time the term referred to the countries of the East generally and was associated with an area or symbol of great wealth. The "Indias of Spice and Mine," however, refer to, respectively, the East Indies and the West Indies: see stanza 2 of "THE SUN RISING."

Indifferent. *Adjective*: (1) impartial or unbiased; (2) unconcerned or apathetic; (3) of neutral quality, neither good nor bad; (4) unimportant or immaterial; (5) nonessential.

"Indifferent, The." One of the *SONGS AND SONNETS.* This is one of those poems in which Donne is being anti-conventional, anti-romantic, and anti-PETRARCHAN. He presents a cynical, flippant, bawdy man speaking. The man is INDIFFERENT, particularly in seeing himself as impartial about most characteristics in women and about most women in general, except for his demand that they should have one quality that he desires in them.

From the first line we see the speaker as unbiased about characteristics that were assumed as ideal in a woman, according to the Renaissance (and particularly PETRARCHAN) view: he does not care if the lady is blonde ("fair") or brunette ("BROWN"), but the Renaissance, Petrarchan ideal was the blonde. He goes on in the first stanza to catalog other characteristics he could care less about, as far as preference in a female: plump (fat abundantly melting over in layers) or slender (who is revealed to have a "want," a lack, of flesh); the homely (loving loneliness) or the socialite (wears "masks" to festivals, parties and generally likes the social world and fun); country girl or city girl; a bit gullible and tends to believe what the man might tell her or more intellectually testing, trying before accepting matters; weepy and continually ("still") crying with eyes dropping tears like sponges dripping water or the restrained, unemotional, dry-eyed one whose eyes are like corks in their lack of moisture. Donne's rebellion here against traditional poetic and Petrarchan images can be seen in the vivid, realistic, colloquial "spongy" and "cork" for the lady's eyes, rather than the more common views of the lady's eyes as stars or suns or diamonds. So, some of his METAPHYSICAL characteristics appear in word choices. His statements convey his nature as indifferent, but the feeling is reinforced by using a style and structure with opposites balanced in lines, half-lines, and phrases. This technique of balance and parallel places equal weight on the two opposites (i.e., "who believes" or "who tries") and truly implies his impartiality. The summation of his indifference is in lines 8–9 ("her, and her"; "you, and you"; "any"). But suddenly he thrusts to the fore at the very end of the stanza the one quality about which he is not indifferent: for him to love her, she must "be not true." This type of paradoxical statement also typifies METAPHYSICAL poetry: a man ordinarily would wish his lady indeed to be "TRUE," to be faithful, to him in a love relationship. But this particular man is revealed to be one who wishes a rather loose woman, one who is satisfied with a brief, ephemeral physical love without trying to limit their love to each other only. This man likes a variety of lovers and wishes a lady who desires the same, then. The inconstancy wanted here opposes the ideal constancy assumed in a Petrarchan relationship.

The second stanza gathers an increasing tone of anger and frustration on the part of the speaker. He begins to ask sarcastic questions of and to throw caustic accusations toward "you" (i.e., any woman who tries to be "true" to him or to any man in a love relationship). In fact, he even calls such a trait of being faithful a "vice." He sneers at these women who feel that they are better than their own mothers, implying that their mothers did not hesitate to "DO" sexually, without strings attached to the man that they "did" it with. So, he asks why these modern women are not satisfied to act both generally and sexually as their mothers did. Line 12 implies again that faithfulness is a "vice," one newly-discovered by these modern women. He assures her that she need have no concern that men are true: men are not, so women should not be. In fact, he and the lady should both "KNOW" twenty lovers, obviously not just to be socially acquainted with, but to have sexual affairs with. Line 16 suddenly portrays the woman who is true, paradoxically and in a miniature METAPHYSICAL CONCEIT, as a thief, as a female robber of sorts. The man wants her, however, only to rob him of sexual love and not to tie him up. He wants to be left free to "travel" on down the road of love and life to other adventures: the pun on "TRAVAIL/TRAVEL" has several possible meanings but at least implies "travel" (passing on beyond her to other affairs, but also literally moving through her vagina), and it implies "travail" as an arduous, grievous experience (i.e., her attempt to constrain him). He does not want to be bound, tied up by one woman and thus become her "fixed subject," belonging only to her and subject to her whims—i.e., he does not want to be in the ridiculous position of the PETRARCHAN man who continually worships and stays subservient to his lady.

The third stanza presents VENUS (here as the sensual goddess of love) having heard the man's complaint about women. Ironically, the man refers to his "sighing" (it has been a bit more vociferous than the traditional Petrarchan or romantic sighing, however!) and to the complaint as a "song" (it is not one of the traditional ones with regular and smooth lines, as far as length and metrics). The reader sees immediately that Venus is on the man's side, since she refers to "variety" in love as "love's sweetest part." Venus says that she was not aware that there were women trying to overthrow variety by being true to men, and she plans to correct the situation. After investigating matters, she returns. Then she states [all of the poem after "said" in line 23 are the words of Venus] that she did find two or three women who are attempting to be constant in their love to men. Ironically, she calls these women "heretics" in love: this plays off on the notion that PETRARCHAN love is a kind of religion with rituals of worship and faithfulness. The god and goddess of love (as well as the lady beloved as a goddess) are to be faithfully idolized, and constancy is the true doctrine. Here that is reversed because Venus calls constancy the false doctrine, the heresy. She has told these women who try to be constant in love that they will be true to "them" (i.e., men) who will be false (unfaithful, fickle, inconstant) to the woman. So, the women will be punished with infidelity in return for their fidelity. Venus, therefore, endorses the opinions and feelings of the "indifferent" man.

Indifferent, things; indifferent things. See THINGS INDIFFERENT.

Infanta. *Noun*: (1) in its strict meaning, a daughter of the king and queen of Spain or Portugal, especially the oldest daughter who is not heir to the throne; (2) in analogous usage, the term is applied to similar daughters of other countries and even cities, especially those from wealthy families who are excellent prospects for marriage that will bring much wealth to the husband: see line 58 of "Satire 1."

Ingenuity. *Noun*: (1) ingenuousness, honesty, freedom from dissimulation; (2) nobility of character or quality.

Ingle. *Verb*: to fondle or caress.

Ingress. *Verb*: (1) to enter; (2) to invade; (3) to enter or invade sexually, to copulate with.

Inhere. *Verb*: (1) to be fixed in or to lodge in something, (2) to abide in something immaterial, (3) to remain in mystical union with a divine being.

Inmate. *Noun*: a person living in a dwelling but who is not really of the household. To Donne and others of his time the term was negative, in that it connoted someone foreign, nonvital, and unimportant. See, for example, line 18 of "THE ANNIVERSARY" and line 6 of *THE FIRST ANNIVERSARY*.

Innocent. *Adjective*: (1) harmless, doing no harm; (2) free from moral wrong, sin, or guilt; (3) simple, unsuspecting, without guile, naive.

Inns of Court. The English "law schools," actually legal societies that confer the right to practice law upon their students. Donne studied at LINCOLN'S INN. The Benchers of each Inn are its senior members that administer the society: those of Lincoln's Inn chose

Donne as Reader in Divinity, made him an honorary Bencher, and made up a significant portion of the hearers at many of his sermons.

Inow. Enough (also spelled "enow").

Intellectual Soul. See discussion of stanza 5 in "A VALEDICTION: OF MY NAME IN THE WINDOW."

Intelligence. *Noun*: an angel assigned to move one of the SPHERES, according to the PTOLEMAIC concept of the universe. See also HIERARCHY, THE HEAVENLY.

Invest. *Verb*: (1) to dress or adorn; (2) to endow with attributes or qualities; (3) to install in an office or rank; (4) to endow with property, power, or authority; (5) to purchase something for the sake of interest or profits.

Iron, Age of. See FOUR AGES.

J

Jack Donne, and not by D[octor] Donne. Phrase in a letter by Donne: see KER, ROBERT (1).

Jacob. Son of Isaac and Rebekah who unfairly and cheaply bought the birthright of his older brother Esau and duped his blind father into giving him the patriarchal blessing that also should have been Esau's. His trick was to dress in animal skins (Donne's "vile harsh attire" in the *HOLY SONNET* beginning "Spit in my face you Jews") to make Isaac think he was blessing Esau. "Jacob" means "supplanter." On a journey seeking a wife, Jacob had a dream at Bethel of a ladder extending from earth to heaven with angels ascending and descending on it. He eventually acquired Rachel as a wife by bargaining with her father Laban and then returned to Canaan. On his return trip he wrestled with an angel at Peniel and was renamed "Israel." Of his sons, JOSEPH was sold into slavery and then rose to high position in Egypt, where eventually Jacob was reunited with Joseph, and Jacob died in the land of Goshen. See Genesis 25–50.

James I (1566–1625). King of England, 1603–1625. The son of Mary Queen of Scots of the Stuart family, he was James VI of Scotland prior to succeeding his cousin ELIZABETH on the English throne. Well-educated and a lover of the arts, James himself wrote on religion, government, witchcraft, and demonology. He commissioned a group of English theologians and scholars to produce a new translation of the Bible that was published in 1611 as the Authorized Version, now more commonly called the "King James Bible." James argued for the divine right of kings and insisted on absolute power and abuse of privilege in some matters that increasingly alienated factions in Parliament. His dependence upon and granting of rewards and power to such favorites as ROBERT KER, EARL OF SOMERSET, and GEORGE VILLIERS, DUKE OF BUCKINGHAM, further alienated many of his subjects.

Donne initially sought favor from King James through such friends at court as Sir HENRY GOODYER and JAMES HAY. Later he approached both Somerset and Buckingham for help in securing desired positions. King James played the major role, eventually, in determining Donne's course in life. *PSEUDO-MARTYR* (1610) convinced the King that Donne's advancement should lie in serving the Church. After Donne's ordination in 1615 the King saw to it that Donne was one of his chaplains, that he was granted an honorary Doctor of Divinity degree, and that eventually he was made Dean of ST. PAUL'S CATHEDRAL. Donne preached one of his *SERMONS* by the body of King James in April, 1625, and walked a few days later in the procession to Westminster Abbey for the burial.

Janus. Roman god with two faces looking in opposite directions. God of doorways, beginnings and endings, before and after, past and future. In *METEMPSYCHOSIS* Donne refers to Noah as "holy Janus," since others before Donne already had established Noah as analogous to Janus because Noah, like Janus, saw the world before [the Flood] and after [the Flood]. In a *SERMON* of 1627 (see Potter and Simpson edition, VIII, Sermon 4, p. 112) Donne explains this about Noah, and here he calls David a Janus also, since he looked backward [at what God had done] and forward [to what God would do].

Japhet. One of Noah's three sons who repopulated the world after the Flood. The others were CHAM and SHEM. (See Genesis 9 and 10.) Japhet's descendants were believed to dwell in Europe. See "HYMN TO GOD MY GOD, IN MY SICKNESS."

Jelly, A. A type of algae (of the genus *Nostoc*) formed in a jelly-like mass on soil after rain: the popular belief was that it was the remains of a meteor (a "star" or "falling star"). See lines 204–205 of "Epithalamion at the Marriage of the Earl of Somerset."

Jeremy. The Old Testament prophet Jeremiah. A poetic paraphrase of Lamentations is presented by Donne in "The Lamentations of Jeremy, for the Most Part According to Tremellius."

Jerkin. *Noun:* a short coat, usually sleeved, with a collar.

Jerome, Saint (about 342–about 420). Studied in Rome and then travelled for many years. On a pilgrimage to Jerusalem, he stayed in Antioch where he suffered an illness that almost killed him. During his sickness he had a dream of being taken before a tribunal of God and being accused of not being Christian. He saw himself being whipped and vowing never again to read pagan literature. For years after the dream he would not read classical literature. He was ordained in 378. He then spent three years in

Constantinople and was a disciple there of NAZIENZEN. He returned to Rome and served as secretary to Pope Damasus, concentrating on Biblical scholarship and the ascetic life. Eventually his criticism of clergy and monks led to such condemnation of Jerome that he left Rome in 385 and returned to the Holy Land, spending time in all of Palestine and part of Egypt. Finally he lived in Bethlehem directing a monastery until his death.

Jerome wrote commentaries, argumentative works, homilies, and letters. His Latin translation of the Bible (the Vulgate) basically is the Roman Catholic authorized version: formed from Jerome's examination of the original texts under the eye of his own linguistic and scholarly abilities, the Vulgate set many precedents and has been of great influence on later Biblical scholars and translators. He is one of the four traditional "DOCTORS" of the western church. Donne refers to Jerome numerous times in his prose, especially in the *SERMONS*.

Jesuits. Members of the Society of Jesus, an order founded by IGNATIUS OF LOYOLA in 1533 to support and defend the Roman Catholic Church in the Reformation of the sixteenth century and to spread Roman Catholicism. The aggressive and secret nature of the order led to plots and schemes to undermine Protestant governments and to assassinate Protestant rulers, particularly known to Donne during the time of ELIZABETH I and JAMES I.

Jet (Jeat). *Noun*: (1) black marble; (2) a hard black form of lignite that can be polished and used to make cheap rings, ornaments, buttons, etc.; (3) extremely black color. *Verb*: to throw.

"Jet Ring Sent, A." One of the *SONGS AND SONNETS*. The man speaking is addressing a ring made of JET (the cheap material commonly used for rings and other ornaments). The reader learns in the last stanza that a lady who has worn the ring on her thumb (a common practice at the time) has sent the black ring to him. Ironically, such rings were many times tokens of love in the Renaissance, but this speaker is rather disillusioned about this love and this lady.

In the first stanza the man says that, despite the extremely black material of the ring, it is not so black as his own heart. "Black" here has more than one connotation. It may reflect the gloominess of his heart or the anger he feels: his resentment at the lady's treatment of him (that is revealed later) justifies these senses. But black also suggests constancy: as several editors note (see "Selected Bibliography: Works"), black was proverbially regarded as an unvarying color. So, through this color of the ring, the man speaking conveys his own gloomy, angry condition, especially since the lady has not rewarded his faithfulness to her. He pointedly contrasts (in line two) his own constancy to the lady's inconstancy by designating her heart as "brittle" (easily changed in form, not stable or firm). The alliteration in "black" and "brittle" underlines the contrast he is drawing. The placement of "thou [i.e., the ring] art" at the end of the second line implies wordplay: "art" can be taken simply as a verb (i.e., "you are"), but just as validly it can be taken as a noun (i.e., "you art"—calling the ring a piece of art). In this latter sense the artifice of the ring expresses the artifice, the artificiality and cheap superficiality of the lady. In fact, he says that hers exceeds that of the ring by far. Line three acknowledges the ring as an oxymoron, a paradox in little, since it symbolizes (it says and speaks) both the man's and woman's characteristics. The ring's paradoxical nature is summarized in the last line of the opening stanza: the ring as a circle is "endless" (symbolizing the infinite constancy of the man), but its cheap material is easily "broke[n]" (symbolizing the flighty fickleness of the woman).

The second stanza contrasts the destructible material ("stuff" as he contemptuously calls it) of this ring with the permanence of gold used for wedding rings. He poses the question of why the same valuable and permanent kind of ring would not be sent by her to him, if it is a symbol of their supposedly permanent love. His conclusion is that the lady's message to him (arrived at by interpreting the ring's symbolism) is that the man (like the ring) is cheap, a mere "FASHION" (showy outer form for the woman to use and display temporarily?), and ultimately only to be thrown away. A play on "JET" as the cheap black material and as the verb "to throw" is implicit in this final assertion. There seems to be deliberate ambiguity in the second stanza about just whom or what is being addressed. Clearly it is the ring itself in the first and third stanzas, but "Except in thy name thou have bid it say" (line 7) might be interpreted as said either to the ring or to the lady. He could be stating that the ring itself has caused the name of the ring (i.e., "jet") to say what he quotes it as saying in line 8. Yet, even more plausibly, the speaker's emotions have caused him momentarily to talk directly to the lady, without the more objective intermediary approach through the ring. He seems to be accusing the lady ("thou") directly of having told the ring ("it") to say in the lady's name ("thy name") what he quotes the ring as saying in line 8. Thus, he sees the lady as deliberately appointing the ring as her viceroy and spokesman to the man. In line 8 the "I," depending on the way the previous lines are read, can be interpreted as (1) the ring, (2) the name of the ring, (3) the man, (4) the love between the man and the woman, or (5) the woman. In the third stanza the speaker tells the ring to remain with him and be on his finger as it previously was on the lady's thumb. He implies that the ring is lucky to be with him now, since the lady that could so easily break her faith to her lover would surely also break the ring itself that symbolizes that love. The mournful, painful exclamation "oh" in the last line also seems ambiguously placed by Donne, perhaps suggesting a pun on its alternate spelling "o": the speaker has concluded, in fact, that the lady is an "o" or zero or cipher, a nothing in the realm of love. The ring as a circle, on another level, represents ultimately that "o" which is the woman who sent it.

Circles and *o*'s become increasingly important as the poem progresses and seem to constitute a framework for its meaning, development, and unity. The ring itself is circular on its face, and, in its encircling of the finger, it has the traditional connotation of something unending, such as "endless" faith (first stanza) or the ideally infinite love in "marriage" (second stanza). But the immortal turns out to be indeed "nothing" in this love and lady: the word "oh" actually occurs twice in the poem (lines 6 and 12), and in stanza two "ought" and "nought" reinforce the speaker's bitter awareness of nothing beneath the surface of this lady, her "love," and her ring. The word "Circle" itself occurs in the final stanza as a climax to the dominating image, with its paradoxical symbolism of both infinity and nothingness.

John Donne, Anne Donne, Undone. Phrase said by WALTON to have been written by Donne in a letter to ANN MORE after their secret marriage was revealed and after Donne was removed from his job. The authenticity of the phrase is seriously questioned by scholars today: see especially (in my "Selected Bibliography: Life") Bald, p. 139.

Johnson, Samuel. See METAPHYSICAL.

Jointure. *Noun*: (1) joining or union, (2) a junction or joint, (3) holding of an estate by two or more persons, (4) holding of property by both husband and wife, (5) estate settled upon a widow as her rights.

Jolly. *Adjective*: (1) gay, joyous; (2) lively, sprightly; (3) presumptuous, arrogant; (4) wanton, lustful.

Jonah. See JONAS.

Jonas (Jonah). Man called upon by God to go to Ninevah and rail against its wickedness. He tried to escape this duty by sailing away, but God sent a storm that threatened to destroy the ship. The sailors woke up the sleeping Jonah to question him and then threw him into the sea (as Jonah said they should), since he was the cause of the storm from God. Jonah was swallowed by a "great fish" and was kept in it until he was vomited out on land. He preached against the evil in Ninevah, and the people repented. God spared them, making Jonah angry. God then provided an object lesson by withering a gourd, for which Jonah had pity: God said that He could show the same pity for a city of many thousands. See the Old Testament book of Jonah.

Jones, Inigo (1573–1652). Architect, artist, and designer. Served as Surveyor-General of the Works under King JAMES and King CHARLES. Formulated the plans for the rebuilding of the chapel at LINCOLN'S INN and the banqueting house at Whitehall Palace, both of which exist today. Carried out the restoration of ST. PAUL'S CATHEDRAL before its later destruction in the Great Fire. Designed and built many other buildings and homes of the time, as well as scenery and mechanical devices for plays and masques. BEN JONSON collaborated with him on some masques, but they eventually quarrelled and became bitter enemies. Jones was especially influential in his use of classical styles in building and design.

 Jones, along with Donne, belonged to the circle of friends and wits that met at the MERMAID TAVERN. Donne refers to Jones and others of this group in a letter to SIR HENRY GOODYER, written in 1612.

Jonson, Ben (1572–1637). Dramatist, actor, and poet. Jonson's turbulent life included some time as a soldier, imprisonment, and killing a man in a duel. After many years as a Roman Catholic, Jonson reverted to Anglicanism about 1610, draining the whole cup of wine at communion to signify his embracing of the state religion. Some of his best plays are *The Alchemist* and *Volpone*, satiric comedies. He published his plays, masques, and poetry in a volume of *Works* in 1616, containing his "Epigrams" (including epitaphs on some of his children and friends) and another group of poems in a section entitled "The Forest" (with the poem "To Penshurst" included). Jonson is the primary exemplar of CLASSICAL ideals in Renaissance drama and poetry, both in content and style, and he influenced younger dramatists and poets (the "sons of Ben" and, later, "cavaliers") to follow his examples. King James granted Jonson a pension for life in 1616. Two years later Jonson spent some time in Scotland with WILLIAM DRUMMOND of Hawthornden, who recorded many of Jonson's comments on himself and others. In 1623 Jonson's tribute to the memory of his friend and fellow actor, dramatist, and poet William Shakespeare was published in the opening pages of the *First Folio* (Shakespeare's *Works*, his plays, collected and published seven years after his death). Jonson suffered a paralytic stroke in 1628, with subsequent decline physically and artistically. He is buried in Westminster Abbey.

Donne's relationships with Jonson encompass friendship, artistic assessment and criticism, support by a common patroness, and influences from both of them that are married in the younger generation of poets after them. Donne contributed a commendatory Latin poem to Jonson's *Volpone* in 1605. Jonson's "Epigram XCVI: To John Donne" straightforwardly testifies to Jonson's faith in Donne as a reader and critic of Jonson's poems, and his "Epigram XXIII: To John Donne" with a tongue-in-cheek manner employs some of Donne's own style, compactness, and wit to make some ambiguous comments that can be interpreted as either praise or satire, ultimately a nice joke between the two poets. Both wrote poems to their patroness, the COUNTESS OF BEDFORD, one of Jonson's entitled "To Lucy, Countess of Bedford, with Mr. Donne's Satires": Jonson compliments both the Countess and Donne by saying, "Rare poems ask rare friends." In a letter that Jonson writes to Donne he calls him "my true friend."

Some of Jonson's remarks made in his commonplace-book *Timber* and some of those reported by Drummond reflect the friendship and respect but also some differences in poetic principles between the CLASSICAL Jonson and the METAPHYSICAL Donne. Jonson writes denigratingly of a "rough and broken" style, of farfetched metaphors that "hinder to be understood," and of "obscurity." It is, then, interesting that Drummond reports Jonson saying that Donne, in one poem, wanted to match SIR EDWARD HERBERT in "obscureness" and that Donne's work would not last because of not being "understood." Jonson also told Drummond that "Donne, for not keeping of accent, deserved hanging," the classicist's criticism of the metaphysical's irregular metrics. Ironically, some of the characteristics of these

two become fused in such younger and later poets as GEORGE
HERBERT, THOMAS CAREW, HENRY VAUGHAN, and ANDREW
MARVELL.

Joseph. (1) In the New Testament, husband of MARY [Christ's
mother]. See accounts early in Matthew and Luke; (2) In the New
Testament, a wealthy man, secretly a follower of Christ, who took
the body of Jesus after the crucifixion and placed it in his own
new tomb. See Matthew 27:57–60 and John 19:38–42; (3) In the
Old Testament, son of Rachel and JACOB who was sold into slavery
in Egypt but rose to high position under Pharaoh. Refused to
touch Potiphar's wife. See Genesis 37–50.

Jove's fane. Jove's temple. In line 14 of "To the Countess of
Bedford" (beginning "To have written then"), one of the *VERSE
LETTERS*, Donne refers to the belief that St. Peter's Basilica in
Rome was built on the site of a temple to Jove.

Jove's urns. Jove possessed two urns, one holding evil gifts and
the other good gifts. Through these he could dispense evil or good
fortune or a mixture of evil and good.

Jovius, Paulus (1483–1522). Paolo Giovio, Italian historian and
Bishop of Nocera. His account of the religious history of the early
sixteenth century was regarded by Protestants as extremely
unreliable and prejudiced toward Catholicism. Donne refers to
him in line 48 of "Satire 4."

Judith. Young widow in the apocryphal Book of Judith who is
described as beautiful, wise, and faithful to both God and her
husband. See one of the *SERMONS* (Potter and Simpson edition,
VI, Sermon 11, pp. 230–31) and line 44 of "To the Lady Bedford,"
one of the *VERSE LETTERS*. In the poem Donne consoles the
COUNTESS OF BEDFORD after the death of someone very close to
her (assumed by most scholars to be either LADY MARKHAM or
MISTRESS BOULSTRED) and compares the dead companion to
Judith.

Julia. Lady described as a living she-devil in "Elegy 13: Julia," a
work that many scholars contend is not really by Donne.

Juliers. City in the Low Countries where Catholics were under
siege by the Protestant forces led by the Prince of Orange in the
summer of 1610. SIR EDWARD HERBERT participated in the

English force that joined Dutch and French forces there and, indeed, claims in his *Autobiography* to have been the first man to break into the city. Donne's *VERSE LETTER* "To Sir Edward Herbert at Juliers" alludes to Herbert's active participation.

Julip (julep). A medical syrup used to lower fever.

Juvenal (60–140?). Roman satirist. In his sixteen surviving satires the corruption, decay, immorality, and greed of Roman society are portrayed harshly with vivid indignation and savagery. Was one of the influences on Donne's *SATIRES*.

Juvenilia: or Certain Paradoxes and Problems. Book (first published in 1633) containing some pieces of prose by Donne. Although they are supposedly of Donne's youthful period, Bald (see *John Donne: A Life*, p. 200) argues that most of the *Paradoxes* probably were written before Donne's marriage in 1601 and that the *Problems* were written after King JAMES came to the throne in 1603, citing evidence from some of the *LETTERS* to GOODYER that indicate 1607 as the year for some of the *Problems*. (For information on the history of these two literary forms, see Peters's introduction in her edition: see "Selected Bibliography: Works.")

The *Paradoxes* generally have much in common with Donne's poetry, especially with the *SATIRES, ELEGIES*, and some of the *SONGS AND SONNETS*. The deliberately audacious, witty, flippant, paradoxical, punning, and colloquial Donne clearly appears in them. The eleven paradoxes are as follows in the 1633 edition: (1) A Defense of Women's Inconstancy, (2) That Women Ought to Paint, (3) That by Discord Things Increase, (4) That Good is More Common Than Evil, (5) That All Things Kill Themselves, (6) That it is Possible to Find Some Virtue in Some Women, (7) That Old Men are More Fantastic Than Young, (8) That Nature is Our Worst Guide, (9) That Only Cowards Dare Die, (10) That a Wise Man is Known by Much Laughing, and (11) That the Gifts of the Body are Better Than Those of the Mind. Just judging by the titles, one can see that the central device is to argue against the common opinion or accepted truth—to create indeed a "paradox." Perhaps the paradoxical, punning, and bawdy Donne is epitomized in the following from "A Defense of Women's Inconstancy": "For as philosophy [see PHILOSOPHY] teaches us that light things do always tend upwards and heavy things decline downwards, experience teaches us otherwise, that the disposition of a light woman is to fall down, the nature of women being contrary to all art and nature." The joke depends, of course, upon the double meaning of "light," its second use here referrring to a woman's moral laxity which causes her to fall down readily into bed with a man.   In a similarly bawdy and punning vein is the following in "That it is Possible to Find Some Virtue in Some Women": "Or who can deny them [women] a good measure of fortitude, if he consider how many valiant men they have overthrown, and being themselves overthrown, how much and how patiently they bear?" Women have "overthrown" many men sexually (as if in battle) and have been "overthrown" sexually by men: the cynical, flippant jibe is the fact that the women do not at all seem to mind being overthrown ("how much and how patiently they bear").   Subjects in the *Paradoxes* such as the inconstancy, appearances, and uses of women; the relation of body and soul; the true natures of the MICROCOSM and MACROCOSM; the decay of the world; the Fall of mankind; good and evil; discord and harmony; and death all in fact reveal a spectrum of those topics Donne handles with more breadth and depth in his other secular and Christian works through his career.   And perhaps a hint of the ease with which Donne at this early stage already can mold, twist, and invert both language and tone to create difficult ambiguities for his reader appears in the conclusion of "That a Wise Man is Known by Much Laughing": "Which promptness of laughing is so great in wise men, that I think all wise men (if any wise men do read this paradox) will laugh both at it and me."   Do wise or foolish men read his paradox?   Do they laugh because they are wise to see the funny truth in it?   Or to see the ridiculous nonsense in it?   Do they laugh at Donne because of his entertaining presentation of truth?   Or because his paradox is a foolish creation?

The *Problems* actually are posed as questions (and many are "answered" simply by a series of questions).   Most scholars and critics see them as having some of the same qualities of wordplay, colloquialism, paradox, flippancy, etc., as the *Paradoxes*; however, the *Problems* generally are regarded as a bit more cynical, melancholy, and disillusioned.   Some scholars argue that they seem to be a logical outgrowth of Donne's own bitterness and stagnation in the 1603–1610 period when his aspirations for a grand secular career seemed futile.   The "problems" are usually pseudo-problems, false issues, and largely unexplainable.   Even if they are explainable, the writer puts forth the most outrageous, illogical, and unexpected "reasons" for the sake of entertainment and satire.   The 1633 edition prints ten problems as follows: (1) Why have Bastards best Fortunes? (2) Why Puritans make long Sermons? (3) Why did the Devil reserve Jesuits till these latter Days? (4) Why is there more Variety of Green, than of any other

Color? (5) Why do young Laymen so much study Divinity? (6) Why hath the Common Opinion afforded Women Souls? (7) Why are the Fairest falsest? (8) Why Venus Star only doth cast a shadow? (9) Why is Venus Star Multinominous, called both Hesperus and Vesper? (10) Why are new officers least oppressing? The 1652 edition extends the number of problems to seventeen as follows: (11) Why doth the Pox so much affect to undermine the Nose? (12) Why die none for love now? (13) Why do women delight much in Feathers? (14) Why doth not Gold soil the Fingers? (15) Why do Great men of all dependents, choose to preserve their little Pimps? (16) Why are Courtiers sooner Atheists, than men of other conditions? (17) Why are Statesmen most incredulous? Since these printed editions the number of problems has been increased to a total of nineteen by the addition of two found in manuscripts as follows: (18) Why doth Sir Walter Raleigh write the History of these times? (19) Why doth Johannis Salisburiensis writing de Nugis Curialium handle the Providence and Omnipotency of God? A cynical attitude toward women prevails in the speaker of the *Problems* in such ones as "Why hath the Common Opinion afforded Women Souls?" and "Why do women delight much in feathers?" But even more apparent is a cynicism expressed with overt or implied moral condemnation of many elements of the Court and the powerful and privileged individuals there. For example, the conclusion of "Why have Bastards best Fortunes?" poses as one possible answer to the question the fact that bastards "abound most at Court, which is the forge where fortunes are made, or at least the shop where they are sold." And some possible answers to "Why are Courtiers sooner Atheists, than men of other conditions?" are implied to be the following: courtiers (1) see men's destinies determined at court (and thus strive for no higher source of destiny), (2) see vice prosper best at court, and (3) feel burdened with sin and then avoid fear and knowledge of God as added burdens. Such ethical, social, and political concerns relate some of the *Problems* to the *SATIRES*.

K

Katherine. A representative queen or ruler (or an as-yet-unidentified real person) who is referred to in "Raderus," one of the *EPIGRAMS*. She is said to "for the Court's sake, put down STEWS." The joke is that she either suppressed brothels for governmental morality or suppressed brothels so that women of the Court could enjoy all of the sexual activity that men otherwise might exercise in the brothels.

Kennel. *Noun*: (1) a gutter or drain of a street, (2) shelter for dogs.

Kepler, Johannes (1571–1630). German astronomer. Studied and extended the ideas of COPERNICUS. Corresponded with GALILEO and BRAHE, joining the latter in Prague for the last year of Brahe's life. Developed many of Brahe's observations more fully. Kepler argued that the planets revolve around the sun in elliptical orbits (thus contradicting the perfect, circular universe hitherto envisioned). Studied the planets, their moons, and comets with a telescope. Discovered some "new stars" in the heavens and published works significantly discrediting the older cosmology of PTOLEMY and developing the "NEW PHILOSOPHY."

Donne alludes to Kepler's *De Stella Nova* (1606) in *BIATHANATOS* (in a criticism of Aristotle's followers) and in the "new stars" of "To the Countess of Huntingdon" (line 6 of the poem beginning "Man to God's image"), *THE FIRST ANNIVERSARY* (line 260), and "To the Countess of Bedford" (line 68 of the poem beginning "To have written then"). In the last poem Donne seems to use the "new stars" to symbolize the departed souls of MISTRESS BOULSTRED and LADY MARKHAM. Donne refers to Kepler in *IGNATIUS HIS CONCLAVE*, and he actually met him during Donne's journey to Germany in 1619 (see Applebaum in "Selected Bibliography: Life").

Ker (Kerr, Karr, Karre, Carr), Robert. (1) [1578–1654]. Appointed groom of the bedchamber in the household of Prince Henry, 1603, and knighted. In 1623, gentleman of the bedchamber to Prince CHARLES, and promoted to lord of the bedchamber when Charles succeeded to the throne in 1625. Served later as master of the privy purse. Created first Earl of

Ancrum in 1633. On the death of Charles, he went to Amsterdam and died there in a state of poverty. Until Donne's death Ker was still a knight, and Sir Robert Ker was one of Donne's closest friends and one to whom he wrote many of his *LETTERS*: these are very important in reconstructing the chronology of Donne's life and works and are revealing about some of Donne's private attitudes. Ker was the godfather for one of Donne's daughters (MARGARET) in 1615. In 1619, when preparing to leave for Germany with Doncaster (JAMES HAY), Donne sent Ker his manuscript of *BIATHANATOS* with a famous letter in which Donne says that the work was written many years ago, before he was ordained, and says that it is a book written by "Jack Donne, and not by D[octor] Donne." After his serious illness at the end of 1623 and shortly before the publication of *DEVOTIONS UPON EMERGENT OCCASIONS* in 1624, Donne described this account of his sickness in a letter to Ker as "meditations" that "may minister some holy delight." In his will Donne refers to Sir Robert as his "honorable and faithful friend" and leaves him "that picture of mine which is taken in shadows and was made very many years before I was of this profession [i.e., a clergyman]." This portrait referred to is a famous one of Donne: it shows him as a courtier and melancholy lover with a dark hat and dark clothing. During the 17th century this portrait was "lost" and remained a mystery until it was discovered in 1959, in the home of a descendant of Ker, having long been misidentified as "John Duns" and thus interpreted as a portrait of Duns Scotus.

(2) [1587?–1645]. Knighted in 1607. A favorite of King JAMES. The King gave Ker the manor of Sherborne, an estate formerly belonging to Sir Walter Raleigh. Created Viscount Rochester in 1611 and Earl of Somerset in 1613. Married Frances Howard, Countess of Essex, after she had secured an annulment from Robert, 3rd Earl of Essex. Before the marriage in late 1613 SIR THOMAS OVERBURY opposed it, was imprisoned in the Tower of London, and apparently poisoned by the Countess through some means unclear to this day. Before the discovery of this apparent murder, Somerset's fortunes and power continued to rise, until his jealousy toward a new potential favorite for the King, GEORGE VILLIERS, began to alienate James. Charges concerning the murder were brought, and an investigation into it was begun in 1615. In 1616 both the Earl and Countess of Somerset were tried and convicted, but remained in the Tower until 1622, by which time James had issued pardons for both. They lived obscure lives afterward, with the Countess dying in 1632 and the Earl in 1645. Donne approached Viscount Rochester in 1613 through both a

letter written by Donne and delivered to Rochester by JAMES HAY and a later formal introduction of the men by Hay. Rochester regarded Donne favorably and apparently employed him and supported him financially during 1613–1615. In letters to Rochester Donne refers to his "buying me" and to having "lived upon your bread." After their marriage Lord and Lady Somerset were honored by Donne with an "Epithalamion" and accompanying "Eclogue" (together sometimes referred to as "Epithalamion at the Marriage of the Earl of Somerset"—see *EPITHALAMIONS*). For a time, then, Somerset became another patron, causing Donne to postpone taking holy orders in light of his renewed prospects for secular advancement. He was relying on Somerset's help to secure some substantial position, but the King preferred that Donne enter the Church to serve, despite the urging of the favorite.

Kill. *Verb*: in relation to secular love, see DIE and PETRARCHAN. One common use of "kill" and "murder" is in reference to the Petrarchan lady or any lady rejecting the man who is wooing or attempting to seduce her. Another common use refers to a woman indeed providing sexual intercourse, orgasm, for a man, thus subtracting some moments from his life and causing him to "die" a little.

Klockius. The name of the male character who is the subject of "Klockius," one of the *EPIGRAMS*. He has so deeply sworn nevermore to "COME in bawdy house" that he dares not "go home."

Knell. See DEATH BELL.

Knotty. *Adjective*: (1) tied in knots, (2) intertwined, (3) difficult to comprehend or to explain.

Know. *Verb*: (1) to recognize or distinguish; (2) to perceive; (3) to be acquainted with; (4) to have carnal experience with, be sexually intimate with, have sexual intercourse with. Donne frequently puns on the word in the last sense: see, for example, line 31 of "THE BLOSSOM," line 15 of "THE INDIFFERENT," and line 6 of "CONFINED LOVE."

L

L., I. "To Mr. I. L." is the title of two *VERSE LETTERS.* The identity of the recipient is unknown.

L. C. Person referred to in one of the *EPICEDES AND OBSEQUIES* (in "Elegy on the L. C."). There is disagreement on the title of the poem because of variations in manuscripts and printed editions (appearing in one manuscript simply as "To L. C."). The person has not been identified, although he seems to be one of the following three: (1) Lionel Cranfield [later Privy Councillor and Earl of Middlesex] whom Donne might have addressed regarding the death of Cranfield's father (Thomas) in 1595; (2) the Lord Chamberlain, Henry Cary [Baron Hunsdon], who died in 1596; or (3) the Lord Chancellor, Sir THOMAS EGERTON, whom Donne had served as secretary and who died in 1617. Whoever is honored in the poem is one, Donne says, who has his tomb in all of those friends and family members who have turned to "stone" through grief after his death.

La Corona. A series of seven Christian sonnets included as a part of the large division titled *HOLY SONNETS* in the first edition of Donne's poems (1633). Since the second edition of 1635 it generally has been considered a subdivision of *DIVINE POEMS.* These seven sonnets undoubtedly were sent by Donne to MAGDALEN HERBERT in 1607.

The title of this sequence means "The Crown." The seven Italian SONNETS are linked by the last line of each one carried over and repeated as the first line of the next. The last line of the seventh repeats the first line of the first, thus completing a circle, such as in a ringlet, a crown. The crown is at once Christ's crown of thorns and the crown of glory for the faithful rewarded by eternal life in heaven: the integral relationship between Christ's suffering and death symbolized by the crown of thorns and man's ability to achieve through it the crown of glory is in itself an infinite circle. Donne himself in the first poem of the seven suggests the importance of this relationship and also says that this crown of poems (including "prayer and praise") is weaved out of his own "low devout melancholy."

The sequence progresses through key events in Christ's life, death, and ascension (and, by implication, in man's life, death, and salvation). The second and third sonnets praise the Virgin Mary as the chosen mother of Christ and picture the Nativity. Such paradoxes of Mary as being her "Maker's maker," her "Father's mother," and having "immensity" contained in her womb are noted. Christ's speaking in the Temple, his crucifixion, his resurrection, and his ascension complete the progression in poems four through seven. Emphasis continues on Christian paradoxes: Christ in the Temple blew out the sparks of learning that he himself had bestowed on the learned men ("DOCTORS"), Christ's death killed death, and Christ's ascension lightens the dark clouds. Wordplay and brief METAPHYSICAL CONCEITS also appear through the series: Christ the "Son" is also the "Sun," and Christ is a "ram," a male sheep (paradoxically both a "strong ram" and a "meek lamb") and a battering ram to crash open the door of heaven for the faithful.

Lame. *Adjective*: (1) crippled in foot or leg; (2) lacking a part, imperfect, defective; (3) metrically defective (of verse).

Last Day. The Last Judgment, Judgment Day.

Lation. *Noun*: (in astrology) motion of a body from one place to another.

Laud, William (1573–1645). Made Dean of Gloucester Cathedral in 1616 by King JAMES. After the accession of CHARLES, Laud held the following positions (among others): Bishop of Bath and Wells (1626), Privy Councillor (1627), Bishop of London (1628), Chancellor of the University of Oxford (1629), and Archbishop of Canterbury (1633). Laud enforced strict uniformity, orthodoxy, tradition, and royal authority in matters of the Church of England, criticizing and punishing deviations that favored PURITANISM and CALVINISM, particularly alienating some factions in the House of Commons rapidly gaining strength before and during the English Civil War. Laud was impeached in 1640 and executed by beheading in 1645.

In 1627, after a sermon by Donne before King Charles on April 1, Laud ordered Donne to submit to him a copy of it to be examined for possible offense against the King. Donne visited Laud about the matter, provided the copy, protested his innocence in intending any offense, and subsequently was forgiven by the King in a special meeting with him arranged by Laud. There is no other record of any occasion on which Donne displeased (even inadvertently) Laud or the King in any matter of Church doctrine, ceremony, or the King's headship of the Church.

Laura. See PETRARCHAN.

Leander. See HERO.

Leave. *Verb*: (1) to cease, stop, abandon, forsake an action, habit, or practice; (2) to depart from a place or person; (3) to cause or allow to remain; (4) to bequeath or transmit to heirs at death.

Lechers, burnt venomed. Persons infected with, and bearing the poisonous sores of, syphilis.

"Lecture Upon the Shadow, A." One of the *SONGS AND SONNETS*. Although no independent evidence exists that this poem was either written to ANN MORE or concerned Donne's secret love and marriage, the autobiographical suggestions are quite strong indeed.

The speaker uses a literal walk with his loved one, the direction of walking, the sun, and the shadows cast to create a METAPHYSICAL CONCEIT embodying the past, present, and future of their love relationship. The first two single-syllable words ("Stand still") receive two heavy metrical stresses that violate the normal iambic pattern. The pronunciation is slowed and made emphatic, thus conveying the sense of the couple suddenly stopping in their walk as he tells her to do so. The poem is probably best understood by visualizing their walking in the morning, with the sun rising and the couple facing east. The man uses the action and situation to explain the nature of love in general and their love in particular ("love's philosophy"). They have walked for three hours (from 9:00 to 12:00). Their shadows were cast toward the west, then. At the instant they stop upon his command, it is noon ("now the sun is 'just' [precisely, exactly] above our head"). They now stand ("tread") on the shadows: i.e., they cast no shadows. All is brilliantly clear (line 8). With line 9 he begins the development of the extended analogy with the comparing word "so." The man tells the lady that their "infant loves" (their early, less mature, still-developing loves for each other) grew in this way: the sun here is a symbol of their love, and their love (like the sun in the morning) cast "disguises" and "shadows." The "shadows" cast in their early love refer to the deliberate darkening, hiding, of their secret love from others. This implication is verified in lines 12–13 (they were diligent that others could not perceive their love) and in line 16 particularly: the "first" or morning shadows were cast in order to "blind" others, to keep others in the dark about this couple's love for one another (again, especially suggestive of Donne's relationship with Ann More). But, like the sun reaching noon, their love has grown in intensity and clarity and beyond the necessity or desire for secrecy ("shadows" and "disguises"). Their love now has reached its noon, its zenith of perfection and brilliant beauty. It is at a stage of perfection that could not be claimed for it earlier when they had to hide it, since a perfect and confident love has nothing to hide.

The midpoint of the poem (line 13) occurs where he points out the noontime perfection they now enjoy in their love. In line 14 he introduces the paradox that their love, however, cannot be allowed to be completely analogous to the sun. Their love cannot be permitted to descend from the height of noon, as the sun inevitably does. If the sun of their love begins to decline toward the west, they will throw shadows toward the east: the shadows here symbolize their blinding of each other, as they this time see shadows as they face east, as opposed to those morning ones (i.e., their deception is practiced on each other, rather than on others: they both "falsely" disguise their actions). If this occurs, the bonds of trust and confidence in this perfect love begin to break and to form an imperfect love. Once this happens, their love is dying—as surely as the sun declines and its light dies with its setting. These shadows which come "BEHIND" (here a temporal word, meaning "later"—i.e., sequentially after the earlier morning shadows) are danger signals of a love in decline. So, the lovers miraculously have to stop both time and change to maintain this intense and perfect love at its noon. The "shadows" of the afternoon grow longer: the darkness in their love relationship increases as the love, like the sun, declines and dies in the west.

The final lesson of his "lecture" in love is made in the paradox of the last two lines of the poem: love is defined as only being love when it is in the process of developing and growing or when it is at its height (comparable to the sun in the morning or at noon). But the first bit of decline in love's intensity (the "first minute after noon") is already love dead ("night")—not love at all. Once love begins to decline, it might as well be dead. So, the speaker is aware of the precarious position that has to be maintained to continue an ideal, perfect love. He only postulates what can happen in order better to assure both the lady and himself that it will not happen. They must exert themselves to keep their sun of love at its noon and to prevent any "shadows" at all. (A helpful reading of the poem is given by Moody [see "Selected Bibliography: Critical Studies, Poetry"].)

Leese. *Verb*: to lose.

"Legacy, The." One of the *SONGS AND SONNETS*. The man speaking in this poem plays on meanings of "DIE" common in Donne's time, especially the parting of lovers as death. After "death" the lover leaves his strange "legacy," building a METAPHYSICAL CONCEIT around the idea.

The first phrase of the poem is paradoxical ("When I died last") since it is striking that someone can die more than once. But the speaker goes on to explain the paradox: he tells the lady that every parting from her is a death. He parted from her only an hour ago, but an hour apart seems an "eternity" to a lover. Already he has begun the conceit of his "death" followed by "eternity." He thinks back on his last words—as if he could remember murmuring something on his deathbed and leaving something ("something did bestow") as a legacy. Line 7 is ambiguous but may suggest that he was "dead" from her fickleness before he was "dead" again in parting from her: i.e., her inconstancy is what sent him away, thus causing him to die twice. So, he is the dead person, but at the end of the stanza he further complicates the conceit by saying that he also is his own "executor" (who will see that his last will is carried out) and his own "legacy" (what he is leaving to someone). This creates a thorough puzzle to be solved in the rest of the poem.

The second stanza gives his dying words. His dying self commands his executor self to tell the lady "ANON" that his self ("myself") killed himself—but parenthetically he tells the lady that she ("you") is the self ("myself") referred to (he has placed all of himself in her—i.e., they have exchanged hearts as lovers). So, she has "killed" him in the sense of being fickle, unfaithful, to him in their avowed love. As he died, then, he heard his dying self tell his executor self to send the lady his heart after he is gone (rejected? parted? both?). This "deathbed" statement reveals that the "legacy" is his own heart (which, in turn, explains how he could be his own legacy) that he is leaving to the lady. He looks into his bodily chest (a kind of treasure chest, metaphorically?) to pull out the legacy, the heart. But, surprisingly, his heart is not there. The implication is that, since they earlier exchanged hearts as lovers, she already has his heart. Donne likely is punning on "LIE" here, however, and a second meaning is conveyed: "searched where hearts did lie" also enforces the idea that the lady is one of those whose hearts tell falsehoods—he has discovered indeed that she has been unfaithful and false to him, to his love, and to his heart. Playing further on "KILL" and "DIE," he says that he is "killed" again by realizing that he has unwittingly been made to cheat ("cozen") her in his last will and testament by not producing the legacy, the heart, to give her: he always ("STILL") was true to her during life and is proud of that fact (implying a contrast to her being false to him in life), only to be disappointed that now he has cheated her after his "death."

In the third stanza the man says that, however, he did find in his chest "something like a heart"—it resembled a heart but had "colors" and "corners." In the Renaissance a square or something with corners was regarded as unnatural, artificial, imperfect, and not occurring in nature itself. Also, a circle was the symbol of perfection. In addition, since this heartlike object has more than one color, it is associated with variety, change, inconstancy, and fickleness. Since the man and the lady had exchanged hearts earlier, this must be her heart within him: the speaker sarcastically is pointing this out, with the implications that it is so unnatural as to be almost unrecognizable as a heart and that it reflects her own falseness and inconstancy. Line 19 also is a damning comment on her heart's mediocrity, the idea enforced by the precise parallelism of words and balance of stresses and syllables in the half-lines ("It was not good, it was not bad"). Her flighty fickleness is emphasized in line 20 by the statements that her heart was "entire to none" (she could not wholly devote herself to one man) and that "few had part" (few men could claim to really have a share of her or her love in the truest senses). Lines 21–22 enforce the earlier suggestion that this heart is not a natural one: it is not created by nature but by "art." Therefore, it is imperfect and in turn employs artful deviousness. The man tells the lady that he is sad for "our losses"—i.e., his loss of his heart (but also his loss of hers and of her?) and her loss of her heart (but also her loss of his and of him?). He planned, then, to replace his heart as a legacy with the one he found within him, but he was not successful, since he (as well as any other man) could not even hold it (enforcing its, and thus her, inconstant quality). The conclusion underlines these truths: it was indeed her heart that he found in him.

Lemnia. *Noun*: (1) clay found in Lemnos used as an antidote for venom and poison, (2) an ingredient used in ALCHEMY (in the elixir) to aid in changing base metal to gold. In line 58 of "An

Elegy upon the Death of Mistress Boulstred" (one of the *EPICEDES AND OBSEQUIES*) Donne seems to combine the two meanings.

Let. *Noun*: hindrance or obstruction.   *Verb*: (1) to hinder or obstruct, (2) to permit or allow, (3) to cause.

Lethargy. *Noun*: (1) condition or state in which a person sleeps in a prolonged and unnatural way because of illness or physical deterioration, such as in a coma before death; (2) a condition of apathy or torpor.

Lethe.   In Greek mythology, the river in Hades that gives forgetfulness of their past to those departed souls that drink of it.

Lethean. *Adjective*: pertaining to LETHE—i.e., forgetful of or oblivious to the past or causing such forgetfulness or oblivion.

Letters.   Over two hundred prose letters by Donne survive, most of them published by his son (John) in *Letters to Several Persons of Honour* (1651) and *A Collection of Letters, Made by Sir Tobie Matthews* (1660).   Additional ones appear in early editions of Donne's *Poems*, in WALTON's *Life of Mr. George Herbert*, and in other miscellaneous volumes.   A few have been discovered and published since the seventeenth century.   Donne wrote to over forty individuals: some of the most frequent and most important correspondents are the COUNTESS OF BEDFORD, GEORGE GARRARD, Sir HENRY GOODYER, MAGDALEN HERBERT, Sir ROBERT KER, and Sir HENRY WOTTON.   Significant letters have been surveyed for the most important persons, places, phrases, and other elements of content to constitute entries (or to be included within entries) in this "Dictionary."   (For further examination of the *Letters*, see the relevant studies cited under "Works," "Life," and "Critical Studies: Prose, Letters" in my "Selected Bibliography.")

Letters to Several Personages. See *VERSE LETTERS*.

Liberal. *Adjective*: (1) giving, bountiful, generous; (2) abundant, ample; (3) free from restraint.

"Licentious Person, A." See *EPIGRAMS*.

Lie. *Verb*: (1) to recline for rest or sleep, (2) to be positioned on a bier or in a coffin or in a grave at death, (3) to have sexual intercourse with, (4) to be or remain in a condition of captivity or illness or misery, (5) to be in an unmoving position or at anchor, (6) to await in order to entrap, (7) to dwell or lodge temporarily, (8) to remain unworked, unused, or untouched, (9) to be brought to bed in labor and to give birth, (10) to tell a falsehood.

Limbec(k). See ALCHEMY.

Lime-twig. See BIRD-LIME.

Lincoln's Inn. One of the INNS OF COURT. Donne studied law here but with no intention of pursuing it as a career. He spent more time reading in other areas, polishing his courtly demeanor, and writing some of his *SONGS AND SONNETS, ELEGIES, VERSE LETTERS*, and other early works (1592–1595 or 1596). Was later its Reader in Divinity (1616–1622) and was made an honorary Bencher upon his resignation from the position. Donne played a major role in securing funds for a new chapel for the Inn (one that still stands today), and he preached its dedicatory sermon.

Litany. A form of prayer in which supplications are made with the clergyman leading and the congregation responding.

Loadstone (lodestone). Magnet.

Lot. In the Bible, nephew of Abraham who was in Sodom when God sent two angels there appearing as men: God had told Abraham that He would not destroy the city if ten righteous men could be found there. Lot greeted the angels as they approached and invited them to stay as guests in his house. That night some men of the city came to Lot's house and told him to bring out his two guests so that they might "KNOW" them sexually. Lot refused, and the men threatened to break down his door. The two angels pulled Lot back into the house and blinded the men. The angels told Lot to gather his family and leave the city, for they planned to destroy it. The angels warned Lot and his family to flee to the mountain from this city in the plain and not to look back. God rained brimstone and fire upon both Sodom and Gomorrah, the cities of the plain, destroying them and their inhabitants. Lot's wife looked back as they were fleeing and was turned into a pillar of salt. Lot and his two daughters dwelled in a cave in the mountains. The two daughters decided that, since there were no other men that they could have sexual intercourse with and be impregnated by, they would have Lot drink wine and then lie with him in his drunken state. They both did so and became pregnant. The older daughter bore a son named Moab, and the younger had a son named Benammi (or Ammon). See Genesis 18 and 19.

"Lovers' Infiniteness." One of the *SONGS AND SONNETS.* Paradoxes and shifting thoughts and assumptions characterize this poem that pictures a lover's wish (in itself paradoxical) to have both all of the partner's love and the potential to secure more.

In the first stanza the speaker expresses almost mournfully that, if he does not already possess all of the other's love, he has little hope of ever gaining it all. He declares that he can put forth no more [PETRARCHAN] lover's sighs, tears, oaths, and letters to win any further love. Metaphorically, he has spent all of his "treasure" (the sighs, etc.) to "purchase" her—no more can be brought forth. Then he poses the possibility that, in their original agreement or contract (i.e., "bargain," a word furthering the economic/legal METAPHYSICAL CONCEIT), he was allotted only so much of the lady's love: she thus would retain the right to grant some of her love and herself to other men. In such a case, the speaker will not be able to have all of her.

The second stanza shifts to another hypothesis. If (instead of being "partial" at the bargain) the lady indeed granted him all of her love at that time, then "all" can be defined as only ("BUT") the sum total at that particular time. This means that new love possibly has sprouted forth in her heart (like new growth from the ground) that other men have stimulated in her. These men have unspent "stocks," stores of treasure (tears, sighs, oaths, letters), that allow them to "outbid" the speaker in purchasing this new crop of love in the lady. If such be the case, his fear is that this new love was never vowed to him by the lady and that he thus has no right to claim it. But lines 20–22 show the speaker's second (and better) thoughts: he concludes that she did indeed vow this love also to him, since her gift is a "general" one—i.e., without exception. He supports this conclusion with the legal principle that "ground" (i.e., her heart) purchased by someone yields all of its crops, as well, to the owner (i.e., the speaker).

After the speaker's lengthy pursuit in the first two stanzas of some hope that he does have all of the lady's love, he surprises us at the beginning of the third stanza by tossing it all away. He says, paradoxically, that he does not want to have all of her love now, after all. He wants hope for securing more love from her in the future, rather than to be essentially bound in a stagnant, unchanging relationship. He tells the lady that it is far better that both of them be able to hope for, and indeed expect, new love to

be both generated from and given to each other every day. These
infinite expectations and infinite grantings of infinite love through
infinite capacity truly constitute "lovers' infiniteness." Certainly
carrying double meaning in this regard is line 26 ("thou shouldst
have new rewards in store"): she has new rewards in store for
herself because of his continual generation and granting of new
love to her, but equally true is the fact that she has new rewards
in store for him because of her corresponding generation and
granting of new love to him. The last few lines of the poem are
filled with witty paradoxes and tongue-in-cheek statements, but
an underlying current of seriousness. He quibbles first that she
cannot be expected to re-bargain and re-contract every day to
give her heart to him (since, in a sense, it is a new heart with new
growth and dimensions). And, besides that (he further quibbles),
if she can give her heart now, then the earlier contract or gift
must not have been valid—she "never gavest it." Quite conscious
of all the paradoxes ("riddles") he can wring from the relationship,
the speaker next says that although her heart leaves her, it stays
at home (with him, where it belongs). Also, in "losing" her heart
she "saves" it (granting it to him assures its careful preservation
by him). Several editors have noted, as well, that the last
statement echoes Christ's words recorded in several Biblical
passages (Matthew 10:39 and 16:25, Mark 8:35, and Luke 9:24)
about losing one's life in order to save it. The emphasis on
spiritual life transfers sacredness and a sense of Christian
"infiniteness" to this secular love, thus reinforcing its depth and
immortal vitality from the speaker's perspective. But his final
solution is one more "LIBERAL" (more giving and generous) than
simply exchanging hearts, and that way is to "join" them, to unite
and fuse them into one. Their lives are infinitely identical, then:
there is no worry about giving, granting, taking, portions, etc., if
they become one forever.

"Love's Alchemy." One of the *SONGS AND SONNETS*. The
dominant METAPHYSICAL CONCEIT and one's understanding of
the poem depend upon a knowledge of ALCHEMY.
　　The first two lines immediately imply that "some" men
supposedly have probed more deeply into the nature of love than
the speaker has and that these men claim to know where love's
basic ("CENTRIC") happiness is. Later in the poem (especially in
lines 18–20) it is suggested that these men are those who
subscribe to the PLATONIC concept of love, those who claim that
love of the intellect and spirit is superior to that of the body. The
image of "love's mine," however, creates the analogy that these

Platonic men claim to have secured the true gold out of this mine of love, and further makes them comparable to alchemists who strive to create gold out of baser metals. This innuendo begins the unifying conceit of Platonists compared to alchemists. But the speaker also uses language quite conducive to sexual, bawdy interpretation that undercuts and ultimately sarcastically ridicules the means and claims of both Platonists and alchemists, implying that the two groups are both fraudulent and deceiving in their claims. For example, "love's MINE" in an ulterior fashion suggests the vagina and womb (in which man's sexual tool digs). And "CENTRIC" also suggests the centrally-located female sexual organs as the source of love's ("HIS," its) happiness. So, the lofty views of Platonic claims about the non-bodily nature of true love already are being in a sense "undermined" by the very bodily, sexual images of physical love. The explicitly sexual "GET" and "got" in lines 3–4 convey his experiences with physical love, but he is exasperated that he has found nothing beyond the physical experience. He has found no "hidden mystery," no spiritual revelation in it. He has followed every step of the experiment in proper sequence, like a chemist with a formula: (1) loved, (2) got, and (3) told [i.e., kept count or tabulated]. The metrical stresses on these words enforce his almost mechanically carrying out his tests. But nothing works for him; therefore, he concludes that the claim of the Platonists is pretended and falsified ("imposture").

The last half of the first stanza makes more explicit the conceit of the Platonists being like alchemists: just as no alchemist ever discovered the elixir (see ALCHEMY), so too does the Platonist never really discover that spiritual quintessence of love that he claims exists. The alchemist puts unjustified faith in and ridiculously lauds the importance of his "pregnant pot" (his alembic—see ALCHEMY), and so does the Platonist make more of the female womb than is really there. (The plosives and stresses in "pregnant pot" serve to convey the speaker's utter scorn and disgust as he spits the syllables out.) The alchemists and Platonists both "glorify," idealize, what are really only physical elements that remain physical. Similarly deluded lovers who try to find the "hidden mystery," he says, imagine a full, warm, and long ideal love relationship, but the reality turns out to be a cold one ("winter-seeming") and one as short as a "summer's night." So, this speaker, it is now apparent, not only cannot find the intellectual and spiritual nature in love, but he cannot find the supposed lasting pleasure available in even the physical aspect. He is disappointed to find no "centric happiness" in any part of love.

The second half of the poem (lines 13–24) begins with the idea that men are just wasting their life ("day") and are giving up on comforts and all other expected accumulations, amenities, and respect coming to them if they try to chase this nonexistent pleasure in love: its insubstantiality is well conveyed by calling it only the shadow of a bubble. The completeness of his disgust with the whole matter of trying to find any pleasure in love appears in lines 15–17: even his servant or valet ("my man") can have as much joy as he can just by playing the insipid role of a bridegroom for the brief period of a wedding ceremony, and the wedding is something one has to "endure." So, no man of higher social, educational, or spiritual nurture should expect pleasure any different from the common, animalistic one that any other man will have by just going through the wedding. But again one suspects Donne of also implying here another meaning of "play" used before and during Donne's time—i.e., "play" as amorous play or sexual foreplay. If he goes through the expected actions preliminary to intercourse, he will be rewarded with the "happy" result of sexual climax. In either sense the speaker implies that the vaunted pleasure claimed to exist in love fails to fulfill expectations. Then he most specifically turns to the particular type of man that most irks him, the "loving wretch that swears" that the bodies do not marry—rather, the minds (the intellects and spirits) marry, and the mind of the lady is angelic. Again, the "loving wretch" is the Platonic philosopher of love, the fraudulent "alchemist" of love. The speaker's ridicule of this Platonist is at its most vicious in lines 21–22: anyone who would swear that the minds marry and that a woman's mind is angelic would also swear with equal justice, equal truth (i.e., with absolutely none, in this speaker's opinion) that all the harsh, discordant sounds and shoutings at the celebration on the wedding day are as beautiful as the music of the SPHERES. Lines 18–22 also illustrate some of Donne's METAPHYSICAL "harshness" of sound and metrical irregularity, but they are quite fundamental to carry the speaker's feelings and emotions here. The harsh *s* and *ch* permeating these five lines convey his disgust, and the extreme number of heavy stresses in line 22 powerfully pound out his anger. In addition, the harsh sounds and irregular rhythms in themselves convey the very discordance of the wedding day's banging music and noise: it enforces the reader's aural sense of the event and his intellectual sense of how ridiculous anyone indeed must be (as the speaker says) to call this the "music of the spheres."

The final two lines epitomize the speaker's disgust and exasperation. He says that a man should not even hope to find a mind at all in women, to say nothing of an "angelic" mind! Even the sweetest and wittiest (both "most intelligent" and "most clever"—see WIT) of women are only ("BUT") "MUMMY POSSESSED" (see both of these words in this "Dictionary"). The last two words both have a multiplicity of meanings used here by Donne to create interesting, ambiguous meanings in combination (and the reader should consult all of the possible meanings for each of these terms). Is the speaker saying that even the most superior woman is like an Egyptian mummy walking around as if possessed by a demonic spirit, the body moving but not thinking? Or is the woman like a dead, lifeless Egyptian mummy when a man possesses her sexually? Or like the supposedly miraculous medicine (echoing the earlier "elixir" and "medicinal") made from the bodies of Egyptian mummies (or other bodies) but, when sexually possessed, are proved to be fraudulent and disgusting? Or vivacious before being possessed in marriage and dead after marriage? Or does the speaker imply all of these meanings at once? Any and all of them surely embody his feeling that there is no gold of love to be distilled or extracted out of these physical mines called women, regardless of the outrageous claims that are made by any of love's alchemists, especially the Platonists. (For a detailed explication, especially of the poem's anti-Platonic vein, see "Selected Bibliography: Critical Studies, Poetry," Hunt under section 12.)

"Love's Deity." One of the *SONGS AND SONNETS*. In his elegy on Donne, THOMAS CAREW notes that Donne abandoned the dependence on classical gods and goddesses as subjects for poetry. Here Donne uses the god of love (Cupid) but in a way different from most sixteenth-century poetry. The speaker here feels humiliated by loving a lady who does not reciprocate. So, he blames the god of love.

The speaker imagines talking to the ghost of some man who lived and loved before Cupid's reign: he implies that these were the "good old days" when love was natural and no man was forced into the unnatural, PETRARCHAN-like state of having to love a woman who would only scorn and reject his love. He speculates that any man of this golden time loved "most," apparently implying that he could experience love to the full, love in its fullest sense without limitations and barriers. But the speaker asserts that once Cupid took the throne and accumulated some power he became a tyrant who decreed a fate, a "destiny" that a man must love a woman who will not love him in return. This became the accepted "custom" and still persists: by calling custom a "vice-nature" he implies that it is an unnatural substitute or viceroy for nature, but the term also connotes that it is a vice or an evil or almost a sin against nature. Custom is nature in a depraved form.

The speaker in the second stanza assumes that the people who set up Cupid as a god did not intend that he eventually become this kind of unreasonable tyrant. And he does not feel that the youthful Cupid acted this way. He even speculates that originally Cupid recognized that an "even" (equal) "flame" of passion motivating male and female should naturally lead to a complementary, mutual love relationship of "actives" (men as active wooers) with "passives" (women as the accepting loved ones). In his early days Cupid endorsed "correspondency"—i.e., mutuality in love. The end of the stanza defines love as reciprocal love; if it is otherwise, it is not even love.

The third stanza pictures Cupid as becoming one of the modern gods with dangerous ideas and grasping for the power ("PREROGATIVE") of even Jove himself. He has taken on more power and territory: he has extended the boundaries of the realm into the outskirts of it ("purlieu"). The outskirts of love (and not at all a part of love as the speaker has defined it—i.e., mutual love) are such matters as "to rage," "to lust," "to write to," and "to commend": all of these are actions of a man (courtly and/or PETRARCHAN) who feels unsatisfied passion and is expected to write imploring messages of love and make endless flatteries of his lady without any hope of response. These are not properly part of love, but the speaker accuses Cupid of encroaching on these outer actions and bringing them into his domain. The speaker wishes that he and other men thus subjugated by Cupid would become alert to their condition, rebel against that dictator, and overthrow ("ungod") him. If this could occur, then he would not be loving a woman who does not love him. As readers at this point, of course, we suspect that this whole history of the life and reign of Cupid is the speaker's own clever, courtly way of suggesting to the lady herself that she could change the situation. In other words, the lover speaking is attempting to reach the real power behind the throne of Cupid, the lady, by blaming her actions and nature on that of her figurehead god, Cupid.

In the fourth stanza there is one of the sudden reversals or changes of direction found in many of Donne's poems. The speaker refers to himself as a "rebel" (justified by his previous accusations and threats against the ruler Cupid) and as an "atheist" (justified by his lack of belief in Cupid's Jove-like divinity). But now he implies that, on second thought, he should not be a rebel and atheist. He actually is better off under the present conditions of Cupid's kingdom and should accept them without "murmur," without complaint. He knows that Cupid ("love") could make things much worse for him in two ways: (1) Cupid might cause the man to stop ("leave") loving the lady or (2) Cupid might cause the lady to love the man back. In light of his earlier wishes that feelings should be mutual, these "bad" things seem paradoxical now. One would think that he would wish one of these very conditions to occur. We might suddenly feel at this point that he is turning into a very cynical, bitter, and sarcastic speaker (one such as we do find in many of Donne's poems) that is giving up on the lady and viciously seeks his revenge by these statements. But the last three lines of the poem make us reorient ourselves completely to see the final meaning and feeling of the poem. He reveals that the lady already ("before") loves another (and in fact might be married to another) and that he would thus "hate to see" her also love the speaker: i.e., it would besmirch her character by revealing her fickle, unfaithful nature. This is why he says that "falsehood is worse than hate" and that she would prove her falseness (both to another man and to her own integrity and character) if she returned the speaker's love. The speaker would prefer her "hate," rather than to have her "love" that would show her false nature.

So, the speaker here turns out not to be bitter and cynical after all. And actually the poem becomes high praise and a great compliment to the lady for whom it was intended (possibly one of Donne's married patronesses, such as the COUNTESS OF BEDFORD or MAGDALEN HERBERT). Ultimately the poem also speaks very well of the speaker himself: he is a man of integrity who willingly foregoes his own pleasure to see the integrity of the lady preserved. He is a man of principle, rather than one in the mold of the seductive courtier. Paradoxically, he is reconciled with Cupid, "Love's Deity," and is almost grateful to him by the end of the poem because Cupid could have treated him so much worse than he has. (This poem is interesting to compare to "TWICKNAM GARDEN," one with similar feelings and one definitely written for the Countess of Bedford.)

"Love's Diet." One of the *SONGS AND SONNETS*. The dominant METAPHYSICAL CONCEIT is the analogy between his "love" (i.e., his emotion of love) and an animal (primarily a "buzzard," a sluggish hawk that is inferior to those other types commonly trained by falconers). A few points in the conceit seem strange (the speaker becomes the animal's secretary in line 19, for example), and there are other subsidiary conceits along the way. It is quite conceivable that Donne deliberately sacrificed absolute consistency for the sake of injecting farcical scenes and images. This poem, in fact, seems to be like an extended cartoon.

The man speaking justifies placing his "love" on a diet by the fact that, if he had not done so, the love would have grown extremely fat and unmanageable. So, he forced it to avoid excesses (apparently normal in love, especially PETRARCHAN love) and rather to choose discretion: being discreet in love is what love hates most ("worst endures"). The first item in his plan to reduce his love was to permit it only one sigh a day, and even at that the sigh could not be only because of his feeling for a woman: it had to include any sadness about the speaker's fortune and faults. If his love tried to cheat on the diet by sneaking around to find other sustenance such as a sigh from the lady, then the speaker discouraged such action by pointing out that the lady's sigh is not "sound" (i.e., "wholesome" or "free from being spoiled" as nutritious food should be). And another discouragement told his love was that if the woman sighed, the sigh was not meant for the man speaking; therefore, that sigh will provide no nutrition for the "love" that is a part of that particular man.

The third stanza moves to the parallel impossibility of his "love" being nurtured by either the speaker's tear or the lady's tear. (The underlying irony is that a PETRARCHAN man always fed his love with sighs and tears—they were of the essence in that kind of love. And, of course, Petrarchan love was a kind of bloated, slow hawk: it never acquired its prey, the lady!) If the "love" caused a tear from the speaker, then the speaker "brined" (salted) it with repulsive grains of "scorn or shame" (which he apparently has received from the lady): such salty drink will not, then, nourish the "love." If the love tried, in turn, to suck one of the lady's tears, the man would point out that the love has mistaken a drop of her sweat for a tear, since this lady's eyes that roll toward (and thus flirt with) all men are incapable of weeping (apparently the sweat originates because the eyes work so hard that the exertion causes the skin around her eyes to perspire). So, he convinces his "love" that no sustenance comes from either the "drink" (the lady's tear-sweat) or the "MEAT," the food (the lady's sigh).

The fourth stanza pictures the "love" dictating letters—i.e., his feeling of love would prompt the speaker to write love letters to the lady, but the man would burn those pieces of "food" so that love could not really feed on them. If love began to increase by feeding on a letter from the lady, the speaker would squelch that by convincing love that no real favor will ever be received or inherited from her: he compares her letter to an "entail," a legal document specifying the order in which heirs will inherit (all of the men that the lady flirts with are metaphorically the heirs of her love). Since he is so far down on the list at number forty, there is no conceivable chance that he will inherit any affection from her.

In the last stanza the speaker asserts his final control over the "buzzard love" that he has tamed ("RECLAIMED") and trained through this strict diet. Now the man can determine what women to pursue with this love and when, where, and how to do it. At times ("now" in line 27) the man is negligent of "sport" (falconry as a metaphor for the sport of courtship), but at times ("now" in line 28) he participates in the "sport" just as other "falconers": if he decides to chase down a mistress, he will "spring" her (i.e., stir her out of hiding) as other hunters do their game. He will let his "buzzard love" then pursue her with protestations of love, writing letters, sighing, and weeping (as ordinary in the courtly game of love). After his "buzzard love" swoops on the prey in a final attack, he allows it to "KILL" the prey, the lady, in the sexual sense. But the speaker is nonchalant about it if this particular prey gets away (is "lost"): he simply will go on to other matters, such as conversation and sleep. He is not bothered, since there will always be other days to hunt again with greater success from his reduced "love." Love is not the be-all and end-all to him now: he can "take it or leave it."

"Love's Exchange." One of the *SONGS AND SONNETS*. The poem begins directly addressing "Love," i.e., the god of love, Cupid. But paradoxically the speaker calls this god a "devil." His treatment by Cupid seems devilish until later in the poem when he finally concludes that Love is indeed godlike. The first two lines berate Cupid for not striking a bargain with the speaker and granting him something in exchange for the speaker's soul (thus the basis for the poem's title). The speaker says that any other devil, like Lucifer and Mephistophilis in MARLOWE's *DR. FAUSTUS*, would willingly provide some benefit to the man who gives his soul to the devil. He further tries to make Love feel guilty for being so ungenerous by noting that fellow devils at Court give courtiers the ability to write poetry (or, at least, rhyming verses!), to go hunting, and to gamble ("PLAY"). And the injustice of this situation is heightened by the fact that these fellow devils did not even have to give anything, since these courtly characters were already damnable and damned: the courtiers already were "their" (i.e., the devils') own "before" the devils gave them anything. But Love has given the speaker nothing in exchange for a sacrifice far greater than any of these courtly ne'er-do-wells ever made.

In the second stanza the speaker says that he asks no favors, no special exclusions from truth and natural law (a "dispensation" sets aside political or ecclesiastical law in a particular case, and a "*non obstante*" licenses a person for an action despite any existing statute or law that forbids it). Since the speaker is truly in love, his tears, sighs, and vows are true. He, then, will remain true to nature's inclination for one to be true, rather than attempt to falsify and commit perjury ("FORSWEAR"). He will not infringe on the special privileges, the "PREROGATIVES," of Love and any special favorite ("minion") of Love: to be false and to swear falsely are actions inherent in the nature of Love and pertain mainly to the subservient disciples of Love. The speaker obviously sees Cupid's (Love's) realm as opposed to the realm of Nature and Truth to which he himself belongs.

After having said what he does not ask for, in the third stanza the speaker says what he does not want. He wants the traditional "weakness" of Love, blindness; therefore, he can never perceive his own love or its childishness. He also will not perceive that others are aware of both his pain and the lady's consciousness of his pain.

In the fourth stanza the speaker begins to turn from the idea of an exchange by recognizing that Love still might not give him anything. But now he sees that, after all, there might be justice in Cupid's refusal. Since he did not at first yield to the incitements of Love and recognize its superiority, he now must "pay the price" to a superior force. In a military analogy he portrays himself as a small town who resisted a superior warrior, not letting him enter until forced to by a military attack of large dimensions. The conquered cannot then propose conditions to the conqueror; the rights of war determine that the conqueror sets all terms, including whether or not the conquered receives anything at all. He has no right to "article," to stipulate treaty terms, at all, especially to stipulate that love grant him mercy ("grace"). The speaker realizes that he has brought this fate on himself by not yielding in the early stages, since it made necessary Cupid's displaying his warlike nature ("face"): wordplay creates "face" also as the lady's face which is the heavy artillery that finally conquered the speaker.

The fifth stanza continues the double meaning of "face" as both Cupid's and the lady's. Love or the lady has the power to change whatever any country values or idolizes or worships (any "idolatry"), can cause religious hermits to give up celibacy, and can raise the dead (making Love here certainly godlike and even Christlike, rather than a "devil" as described earlier). This image of raising Lazarus or Christ or all of the faithful at the end of time illustrates METAPHYSICAL exaggeration that is frequently audacious: here Donne makes a lady's power in the religion of love (to revitalize men sexually) comparable to God's power in the Christian religion. She (or he, Cupid) can melt both the North and South Poles with love's warmth, create life in barren deserts, and make rich mines outnumber sterile quarries. This Lady-Cupid has, then, the power of creating a new Genesis, a new Exodus, a new Israel, a new Jerusalem, and a new Heaven and Earth! She/He epitomizes fertility and vitality.

In the last stanza the speaker realizes that, not only will Love not give him anything, Love (Cupid and the lady?) is extremely angry because of the man's obstinate and foolish refusal to yield to such an obviously superior god. But Love has not killed him. So, the speaker proposes that Love proceed to "KILL" him: whether the "death" is one by sexual consummation or rejection, it will end his misery. He offers Love two reasons for killing him quickly: either as a lesson to teach potential rebels against love not to commit the speaker's error or to provide a cadaver for future generations of physicians to study. If Love continues to torture him as if on the rack, the instrument of torture that pulls a body apart (i.e., if the lady continues to dally with him and torment him to no end), he will be pulled apart and will not make a good object lesson for rebels or a good cadaver for medical students (i.e., the woman's torments are tearing him up physically and emotionally). Therefore, it is in the best interests of Love, so that He/She will achieve His/Her own end, to dispatch the man quickly (either by responding sexually or rejecting him outright).

"Love's Growth." One of the *SONGS AND SONNETS*. The man speaking seems surprised and almost disillusioned by his two discoveries (lines 1–6): (1) his love is not as "pure" as previously he had thought it was and (2) his love is not "infinite" as previously he had sworn it was. These at first seem to be flaws in love, but, in the particular ways that these qualities are defined and in the nature of his love delineated through the poem, they actually are virtues and strengths. "PURE" here means composed of only one substance or element (and thus not subject to change): he has discovered that his love is not a mixture of things, and does change like the grass through seasons, and, paradoxically, being "not pure" is admirable and optimistic for the growth, variety, and full development of his love relationship. "Infinite" means unchanging: he has discovered that his love does change, as the grass in spring accumulates and changes bulk and color. But, again, this capacity for change and variety is optimistic in his love relationship. Through periods of "vicissitude" or trials in love (its winter periods) flux occurs, and "spring" (the warmth of love after its trials) then adds to the love itself. Then, to elaborate, the speaker calls love a "medicine" that paradoxically cures all sorrow with more sorrow (as PARACELSUS argued for curing one pain with another): this conveys the speaker's awareness that a deep love involves deep sorrow and that lovers that live in the real world full of various experiences and emotions are not themselves immune to sorrows that may appear at times in their own relationship. But through the experiences of sorrow and the conquering of sorrow, even greater love and joy can result. As he says, love is "mixed of all stuffs," all kinds of qualities and experiences, even though they may be painful ones both to soul (including the mind) and body. Certainly the ambiguous phrasing also allows the reading that love "cures all sorrow with more" *love*. Related both to the view of love as a medicine and to the assertion that love is not pure, the man says that his love is not a "QUINTESSENCE," which was believed to be the pure, miraculous medicine or fifth essence (but *not* a medicine "mixed of all stuffs" that would cure "all sorrows with more," as the medicine "love" does). Also love invigorates itself under the sun, in this earthly life of time and change, and thus is not some supposedly intangible and celestial element found somewhere beyond the reaches of the four earthly ELEMENTS. Thus can the speaker say not only that love is not pure but also that it is not "abstract," not beyond the realm of the senses and normal human experience in some imagined ethereal realm. Those who are in the custom ("USE") of saying that love is abstract are those poets (PETRARCHAN ones?) who have no real flesh-and-blood lady but only their MUSE, symbolically their poetically-imagined lady. The speaker sees far more emotional complexities and varieties of experiences in love than that love only proposed as real by the imaginations of poets without experience in love. In lines 13–14 (concluding the first half of the poem) the man asserts that real love is like "all else" in the real world: it is "elemented," made up of several elements (i.e., again, it is not "pure"); therefore, love sometimes would "contemplate" (exist in passive forms of emotion, of thought, of spiritual and intellectual communication between the man and woman) and sometimes would "do" (exist in

active expressions of love, through actions that express love for
the other partner, but especially with the physical, sexual
connotation of "DO").

At the mid-point of the poem (and most editions indicate a
break between two stanzas of 14 lines each), the speaker seems to
pause, think, and then to sharpen distinctions and perceptions
based on all he has just said about love. He more closely defines
the nature of the "growth" that he finds in love. And he defines it
primarily through a series of METAPHYSICAL CONCEITS in the last
half of the poem. Lines 15–16 argue that now he sees that love
does not really increase simplistically in bulk but rather becomes
more "eminent," more prominently visible and more obviously
and more clearly seen in the whole and in parts. Facets of the
love relationship can be perceived more sharply in "spring" of
love after a "winter." The three conceits to illustrate this
phenomenon occur in lines 17–28, and actually each conceit is a
double analogy. Lines 17–20 compare "love deeds" to both "stars"
and "blossoms." Donne assumes that the light of the sun is
reflected by the stars and makes them visible (and the five
known planets of the time were referred to as the "five stars").
So, the stars are always the same size, whether illuminated by the
sun or not, but the light of the sun reveals them more clearly
(makes them more "eminent") than when they are not or are only
partially illuminated. The speaker says that in a similar way do
deeds of love appear more conspicuous, can be seen more clearly
at times: the springtime "sun" of energized love will reveal them,
even though (like the heavenly stars) they were already there,
potentially ready to be revealed by action. The love deeds are
also similarly like blossoms appearing on a bough: the blossoms
were potentially there already in the vegetative system, but in
spring they manifest themselves in new and more beautiful form.
By comparing love deeds to stars and blossoms Donne transfers
their beauty to the love relationship described. The second
conceit (lines 21–24) compares love (the love relationship between
the speaker and the lady who is addressed as "thee" in line 24) to
both a pond of water and "heaven" (the created universe,
according to the PTOLEMAIC vision of it). The love relationship is
a closed system like a pond of water, but within that system
accretions can occur such as circles emanating from the center
where the water is stirred—again illustrating "growth" as
paradoxical "additions" that really are flux, change, "eminence" of
matters within the bounds of what already was potentially there.
The pond is a MICROCOSM of the love relationship, but it and the
relationship are also analogous to an even larger MACROCOSM, the

universe itself.   The concentric circles of the SPHERES of the universe revolve around the center of the universe, earth: here the speaker makes the lady ("thee") the center of his universe, his earth at the center of their love relationship, a quite complimentary vision of her.   The final conceit (lines 25–28) compares the love relationship to both the winter-to-spring and spring-to-winter seasonal cycle (an image that in itself echoes the early lines of the poem and brings it full circle) and a political system.   The new heat of spring (deepened emotions, new experiences, new actions and manifestations of love) adds new growth that winter (any time of sorrow or trouble in love) will not lessen.   Similarly, just as a clever "prince" (i.e., any ruler of a country) can easily secure new taxes from the people to support war ("action") and will not do away with those taxes when peace is restored (retaining the added income), so the new dimensions to love will not be cut away but will be maintained.   Again, the "growth" occurs within the bounds of closed systems (seasonal and political): the potential for all change and addition is already there, as it is in a love relationship.   The "growth" occurs within the realm of the whole closed system, and the "growth" actually is change and varied manifestation.

Donne, then, uses seasonal, vegetative, liquid, cosmological, and political systems or microcosms to compare to the love relationship that is defined in the poem.   This great range and these disparate experiences combined and united in the work illustrate one of the characteristics of METAPHYSICAL poetry. Impressive also in the unity of this poem is the recurrence through it of the circle and the circular.   For example, the seasonal cycle introduced early is circular, but it is reintroduced at the end of the poem to bring the poem itself full circle.   The blossoms, pond, circles in the water, and spheres of the universe emphatically repeat the image of a circle.   Of course, the circle concretely implies that recurring closed system within the boundaries of which important change and manifestation occur. But also more subtly implied is the important symbolism of the circle in Donne's time—the symbol of the perfect and infinite. Thus, the poem that begins with the speaker's discovery that his love is not "pure" and "infinite" ends most paradoxically by implying that it is!   And love's "growth" that turns out to be change and varied appearances within both finite and infinite boundaries increases the sense of paradox permeating the poem.

"Love's Usury." One of the *SONGS AND SONNETS*. The man speaking is a flippant, cynical, bawdy type that recurs in Donne's secular poems. The title points to the METAPHYSICAL CONCEIT of moneylending at exorbitant interest (USURY). But the man is willing to bargain with the God of Love (Cupid) at a high rate of interest in return for early benefits. He says that for every hour that Cupid allows him to be free of restrictive ties of love to one woman now the speaker will repay him twenty hours later. While he is young, he wants to be free to love and love as loosely as he desires, but, when he is older (when half of his hair has turned gray), he will repay with the fact that Cupid can restrict his hours then to a love relationship with a particular woman. But until that point of age he wants Cupid to allow the speaker's body to rule ("reign") him and allow him to go anywhere and do anything to satisfy his physical, sexual desires with a multiplicity of women. He wants to be able to "travel" anywhere in his search for women, stay ("sojourn") for some time if he finds one that attracts him, and "snatch" both her and the sexual satisfaction she can provide. He then phrases his free actions another way: he will "plot" his seduction, "have" the woman sexually, and then "forget" her and move on to the next prospect. The words, syllables, and heavy metrical stresses in a series in line 6 enforce the sense of his continual movement and systematic progression through sexual partners. If he wishes, he will take up again with the "RELICT," the woman he previously enjoyed sexually and then dropped. He will go back to her as if he had never met her, in order to have another transitory physical experience.

In the second stanza he bargains further for Love to allow him to assume that any "rival's" (i.e., any rival for the affection of a lady) letter to be his own. Ambiguously, the letter could be from the lady to the rival or from the rival to the lady—Donne does not specify which. At any rate and regardless of which, the man will intercept the letter and will go at 9:00 p.m. to keep the sexual rendezvous for himself that the rival arranged for three hours later. Not only that—the libertine will supposedly "mistake" the lady's maid to be the lady and have sexual intercourse with the maid (punning on "mis-take") on the way to meet the lady. He also will have the audacity to tell the lady why he was late in arriving (since he has no true love for her and no obligation to be faithful to her). At the middle of the poem (line 13) he reiterates that Cupid, by the terms of the bargain, must be sure that the speaker at this early stage must not fall in love with any individual lady. He still wants to be free to hear reports of various kinds of women available to be enjoyed by him: he wants a variety of women to be able to "transport" his mind to them in sexual imaginings (and then soon he will transport his body to them). He visualizes the different kinds of women as different kinds of food: "country grass" represents plain country lasses that he, like an animal, will be able to feed on; "comfitures" are literally confections made of preserved fruit—thus the ladies of Court are a bit sweeter and more expensively decorated and colorful; and "quelque choses" are elegant, dainty (but insubstantial) dishes—i.e., fancy, pretentious women of the city.

Opening the third stanza the speaker tells Cupid that this is a good bargain and implies that Cupid should take advantage of the speaker's offer. When the speaker reaches the age of equal brown and gray hairs, then Cupid will be able to uphold his own honor (i.e., do what Love is expected to do and inflame a man to love a woman) or to cause shame for the man (especially since he will fall in love at an older age) or to cause love's pain for the man. Whatever Cupid "covets" most of these things he will surely "gain": one notes that these monetary images harmonize with the idea of Love as a usurer. He tells Cupid to do as he wishes at that future time when repayment is due: the man will submit himself to Love's decisions regarding (1) whom the speaker will love (i.e., whatever lady who will be the "subject" of his love), (2) to what "degree" he will love her, and (3) what the results ("fruit") of the love will be (including the idea of children as "fruit"). Even if the woman returns his love (the worst of fates to this cynical man), he will endure it for the sake of keeping his word given in this bargain to the "usurious God of Love."

Loyola, Ignatius. See IGNATIUS OF LOYOLA.

Lucan [Marcus Annaeus Lucanus] (39–65). Roman poet. Wrote an epic *On the Civil War*. Served Nero but eventually broke with him and joined a conspiracy against him. Was arrested and forced to commit suicide. Despite his narrative and descriptive strengths, Lucan tends toward an overly rhetorical, bombastic style. Donne implies in "A VALEDICTION: OF THE BOOK" that Lucan's wife (Polla Argentaria) helped Lucan in writing and strengthened what otherwise would have been even weaker poetry.

Lucy. See ST. LUCY and BEDFORD, LUCY.

Lunatic. *Noun:* (1) a person who is insane, mad; (2) a person influenced by and characterized by the moon in its association with change, inconstancy in the SUBLUNARY realm of the

PTOLEMAIC universe and in the changing of the moon itself in its various phases.

Lustre. *Noun*: (1) a lustrum, a period of five years; (2) quality of shining by reflected light; (3) brilliance or luminosity.

Luther, Martin (1483–1546). Initiated the Protestant Reformation in his native Germany, leading to its later spread throughout Europe. Was an Augustinian monk in the Roman Catholic Church. Wanted to raise questions for debate on papal indulgences by nailing his *Theses* on a church door at Wittenberg in 1517. Eventually he was excommunicated, but he refused to recant. He left his monastic order, married, translated the Bible into German, and published the Augsburg Confession that called for a separate church. Luther's writings and arguments emphasize the doctrine of "justification" (salvation) by faith alone for the individual, lessening the importance of salvation through works, sacraments, priests, indulgences, and other means emphasized in the Roman Catholic Church. To an Augustinian monk like Luther, the writings of ST. AUGUSTINE were crucial in their emphasis on the importance of faith to salvation. Luther also disagreed with the Roman Catholic Church's insistence that there are seven true sacraments: Luther instead emphasized the two that are directly sanctioned by Christ, Holy Baptism and Holy Communion. (Compare and contrast the doctrines of CALVIN and Calvinism.)

Ideas of faith and other doctrines of Luther are seen throughout Donne's Christian prose and poetry. Many mentions of Luther appear in Donne's *SERMONS*. In the poetry Luther is referred to as "Martin" in ""SATIRE 3" (line 97), and he is mentioned in *METEMPSYCHOSIS* (line 66). Also in lines 91–96 of "Satire 2" Donne slyly uses the contradiction between the young Luther who, as a monk, liked short prayers because he had to say so many each day and the older Luther, no longer a monk, who himself lengthened the "Our Father" (*Pater Noster* or Lord's Prayer) by adding a clause ("For thine is the kingdom and the power and the glory").

Lydian. *Adjective*: referring to an ancient country named Lydia (on the Aegean Sea).

M

Macaron (**Maccarone**, **Macaroon**, **Makeron**). *Noun*: (1) a buffoon, blockhead; (2) a fop.

Maccabees. Two apocryphal books, not admitted into the Biblical canon by Protestants. Donne refers to their humble ending (their "modesty") at the end of "Satire 4."

Machiavel. See MACHIAVELLI.

Machiavelli, Niccolò (1469–1527). Italian statesman, political thinker, and writer. Went on many diplomatic missions on behalf of Florence. After the Medici gained control of Florence in 1512, Machiavelli was dismissed from government service. His most famous and influential work is *The Prince* (1513), an analysis of the way power is gained and maintained by a strong ruler. In the 16th and 17th centuries Machiavelli's work was interpreted as admiration for tyrannical, deceptive, hypocritical cleverness and grabbing of power by any means, and one who was called "Machiavellian" and/or a "Machiavel" was seen as a most unscrupulous, realistic military and/or political opportunist who believes that the end justifies the means. This kind of opportunist formed many characters in the plays of Shakespeare, MARLOWE, and others. In *IGNATIUS HIS CONCLAVE* Donne portrays Machiavelli as one who seeks to enter the special room in hell for innovators, pointing to his "way of blood" and to the fact that he taught "perfidiousness and dissembling of religion." In a *SERMON* of 1626 Donne says of Roman Catholic controversial enemies, "in this political Divinity, Machiavel is their Pope" (see Potter and Simpson edition, Vol. VII, no. 4, p. 131).

Macrine. Character in "Satire 4" illustrating a ridiculously fastidious courtier (lines 197–218).

Macrocosm. The "great world" or "large world," as opposed to the "little world" or MICROCOSM. In most contexts the word refers to the universe, but in others it may refer to the earth or to any large whole or large world in itself (e.g., society or humanity). See MICROCOSM.

Magdalo. See BETHINA.

Magellan. For the strait so named and for the explorer after whom it was named, see MAGELLAN, FERDINAND.

Magellan, Ferdinand (1480–1521). Portuguese navigator. Early in his career he sailed in fleets and fought in battles that assured Portugal's power in the Indian Ocean. After not receiving the advancement he desired from King Manuel of Portugal, he and Portuguese cosmographer Rui Faleiro went to Spain. They renounced their nationality and offered to serve King Charles I of Spain, the future Emperor Charles V. They proposed to sail west in order to prove that, by decreed demarcation of longitude, the Spice Islands were within Spain's hemisphere of possession by discovery, and not within Portugal's. Approval for the expedition was granted in 1518. Magellan felt that he would discover a strait from the Atlantic to the "Sea of the South" (later named the Pacific Ocean). The ships sailed in September, 1519. After sailing and exploring down the coast of South America, Magellan finally reached the Cape of the Virgins, sailed around it, and entered the strait he sought in October, 1520. Upon sighting the Pacific at the west end of the strait, Magellan wept with joy. The strait was named the Strait of Magellan. After suffering from thirst and near-starvation in passing over the Pacific, the ships landed at Guam and secured fresh food. From there the group sailed to the Philippines where, in 1521, Magellan died in a fight with natives. One ship of the expedition finally returned to Spain in September, 1522, the first to circumnavigate the earth.

For Donne's use of Magellan, the Strait of Magellan, and the implications of Magellan's voyage, see the elaborate geographical and cosmological METAPHYSICAL CONCEIT in "HYMN TO GOD MY GOD, IN MY SICKNESS."

Magius, Hieronymus (about 1523–1572). A prisoner in Turkey who wrote *De Tintinnabulis*, a treatise on bells, while in captivity. It was published in 1608. Donne refers to him at the beginning of "Meditation 16" in *DEVOTIONS UPON EMERGENT OCCASIONS* as "a convenient author, who writ a discourse of bells when he was a prisoner in Turkey."

Mahomet's paradise. A paradise to be filled with beautiful women providing sensual pleasure. See "Elegy 19: Going to Bed," line 21.

Mandrake. *Noun*: a plant (the name is a shortened form of "mandragora") that has forked roots and is thought to resemble the human body. It was believed, according to fable, to groan or shriek when pulled from the ground. It also has been taken as a narcotic and has been believed by some to promote conception in women.

Manna. *Noun*: (1) the miraculous food given by God to the Israelites in the wilderness, according to Exodus 16; (2) spiritual nourishment; (3) in some contexts, symbolic of the bread (or host) of Eucharist (or Holy Communion); (4) sweet white or yellow substance exuded from and deposited on plants; (5) honeydew on plants (from aphids).

Mantuan. The Italian Johannes Baptista Spagnolo (1448–1516) whose fourth eclogue satirizes women. See "Elegy 13: Julia," line 13.

Markham, Lady. Woman memorialized in one of the *EPICEDES AND OBSEQUIES* ("Elegy on the Lady Markham"). She was Bridget Harrington, first cousin of Lucy Harrington, COUNTESS OF BEDFORD. She married Sir Anthony Markham in 1598, was later widowed, and then died at TWICKENHAM Park on May 4, 1609, at the age of 30. Donne compares death to an ocean that eats away the bodies of humans, but he asserts that this "sea of death" has made no breach in her: her flesh even is refined by death's hand, and her soul is freed by death. She is perhaps the dead companion of the Countess who is praised highly in the consolatory "To the Lady Bedford," one of the *VERSE LETTERS*. See JUDITH. Also see KEPLER for Donne's apparent use of "new star" to symbolize her departed soul.

Marlowe, Christopher (1564–1593). Dramatist and poet. Took his B.A. and M.A. at Cambridge. Wrote *DR. FAUSTUS* and other plays, the long poem *Hero and Leander*, and the song "The Passionate Shepherd to His Love." Influential especially in illustrating the power of blank verse in drama (in his poem to the memory of Shakespeare, JONSON refers to Marlowe's blank verse as "Marlowe's mighty line"). Marlowe lived a rather sensational and violent life, dying after a fight over the bill in a tavern.

Donne frequently refers to *DR. FAUSTUS*, especially in the *SERMONS*. Also, Donne's "THE BAIT" is a parody of Marlowe's "The Passionate Shepherd to His Love."

Martial (about 40–about 104). Marcus Valerius Martialis. Roman poet, writer of about 1,500 epigrams. Perfected the form of the epigram, writing a variety of them, including some coarse, satirical, and witty ones, tender ones concerning the deaths of children, and loving ones for friends. Especially influential on the CLASSICAL poets of the 17th century, particularly JONSON. In "Raderus" (one of Donne's *EPIGRAMS*) Donne refers to RADER's expurgated edition of Martial.

Martin. Reference by Donne in line 97 of "SATIRE 3" to MARTIN LUTHER.

Marvell, Andrew (1621–1678). One of the major METAPHYSICAL poets. Born in Yorkshire and educated at Cambridge. From 1650 to 1652 he served as tutor to Mary Fairfax, daughter of Lord Fairfax, a general for the parliamentary side in the English Civil War. During this time Marvell probably wrote "The Garden" and other major lyric poems. Was appointed Latin secretary to the Council of State. Later he was elected a Member of Parliament from Hull and served as such until his death. Marvell's influence early in the reign of Charles II secured John Milton's release from prison and probably saved him from execution.

Marvell's use of the METAPHYSICAL CONCEIT, his love of paradox, his sometimes shocking images, and his wordplay qualify him as a metaphysical poet very much under the influence of Donne; however, one must note that the CLASSICAL strain and influences from JONSON are also strongly present in much of Marvell's poetry. The combination of influences can be seen in such a poem as his famous "To His Coy Mistress." In a defense in 1613 of his own *The Rehearsal Transposed*, Marvell refers to Donne and *METEMPSYCHOSIS*.

Mary. Mother of Jesus (Christ) and wife to JOSEPH. Virgin Mary. Referred to as "faithful Virgin" and "kind mother" in *LA CORONA* and as "mother-maid" in *THE SECOND ANNIVERSARY* and "The Litany."

Mary Magdalene. A follower of Christ who was healed of demons by Christ (Luke 8:2), is commonly regarded as the repentant sinner or harlot who wept and washed Jesus's feet (Luke 7:37), and was once traditionally identified with Mary of BETHINA (Bethany) who was the sister of Martha and Lazarus

(Luke 10 and John 11, 12).   She was later canonized as a saint.
(Also see BETHINA.)

Measure. *Noun*: (1) size or quality determined by measuring, (2) an estimate or opinion, (3) that by which anything is computed or estimated, (4) an extent or limit not to be exceeded, (5) proportion or symmetry, (6) moderation, (7) meter in poetry.

Meat. *Noun*: (1) food in general or nourishment or solid food; (2) the edible part of fruits or nuts, the pulp or kernel distinguished from the peel or shell; (3) the flesh of animals as food.

Medal. *Noun*: (1) an old coin of antiquarian interest and use; (2) a metal disk with a figure or inscription and used as a charm or trinket; (3) a piece of metal with an inscription or figure to commemorate a person, action, or event.

"Meditation." See *DEVOTIONS UPON EMERGENT OCCASIONS*.

Meet. *Verb*: (1) to find, (2) to come face to face with, (3) to encounter or oppose in battle, (4) to unite or combine, (5) to know sexually, (6) to agree, (7) to experience or undergo. *Adjective*: appropriate, fitting, suitable.

Memento mori. Latin phrase literally translated as "remember that you must die." In Donne's time the phrase was used as a command to warn against death and was also used as an adjective. But most commonly the phrase was used as a *noun*: (1) a warning or reminder of death; (2) a "death's head," especially in the form of a skull or some representation of a skull, such as in a ring to be worn. See, for example, lines 21-22 of "A VALEDICTION: OF MY NAME IN THE WINDOW."

Mephibosheth. In the Bible, the son of Jonathan and grandson of Saul. He was lame. King David called for him (II Samuel 9) in order to do a kindness to the family of Saul. Mephibosheth fell on his face reverently before David and called himself a "dead dog." David gave him all of Saul's land and had him eat at David's own table from then on. Donne refers to him in "Expostulation 2" of *DEVOTIONS UPON EMERGENT OCCASIONS* and in a *SERMON* of 1627 (see Potter and Simpson edition, VIII, Sermon 5, p. 146).

Mercurius Gallo-Belgicus. An annual register of news and events (in some years semiannual) published in Latin at Cologne from 1588 to 1654. It was popular, but unreliable, reporting much gossip. The full title of it is used as the title of one of Donne's *EPIGRAMS*. Also, Donne refers to it as "Gallo-Belgicus" in line 112 of "Satire 4" and in line 23 of "Upon Mr. Thomas Coryat's Crudities." (See also MERCURY.)

Mercury. (1) Roman name for Hermes, a son of Zeus and the messenger of the gods. He was god and patron of many things and people, including wealth, commerce, travelers, athletes, oratory, eloquence, wind, and thieves. His major attribute was his speed. His son was Autolycus who became the world's greatest thief. Mercury invented winged sandals and the lyre. Zeus gave him a winged cap. Zeus also called on the shrewd Mercury to find a way to kill Argus, the hundred-eyed watchman Hera had guarding Io. Mercury dressed as a rustic and played on a pipe of reeds, the music attracting Argus. Mercury played and talked until Argus's hundred eyes finally all fell asleep. Mercury then killed him. Hera took the eyes and put them in the peacock's tail; (2) The element quicksilver; (3) The planet Mercury.

Donne refers to Mercury as the patron of thieves in one of his *EPIGRAMS* ("Mercurius Gallo-Belgicus"). His role in charming Argus is alluded to in "*THE SECOND ANNIVERSARY*," lines 199–200. In two sermons (see Potter and Simpson edition, III, Sermon 10, pp. 234–35, and IV, Sermon 3, p. 112) Donne mentions the fact that the Lystrians referred to St. Paul as "Mercury" because of his eloquence.

Mermaid Tavern. Inn at 29–30 Bread Street in London that was the meeting site (on the first Friday of each month) of a convivial group of friends, writers, and courtiers. This dining club included Donne, JONSON, CORYAT, CHRISTOPHER BROOKE, JONES, and others. The tavern was destroyed in the Great Fire of 1666.

Mermaids. See SIRENS.

Meshach. See "CHILDREN IN THE OVEN."

"Message, The." One of the *SONGS AND SONNETS*. The first two lines of this song (for which there is a contemporary musical setting by Giovanni Coperario) lull us into thinking that the speaker is complimenting the lady being addressed: his eyes have dwelled on her for such a long time. But suddenly line 3 reverses his request for the return of his eyes, and, more significantly, reveals the criticism and bitterness that have been under the surface. She is a lady of evil ("ill"), pretentious ways ("forced fashions"), and hypocritical emotions ("false passions"); therefore, his eyes have been spoiled by her company and are incapable now of even recognizing goodness. So, she should just keep them.

The second stanza, in a parallel manner and parallel phrasing, asks her to return his "HARMLESS" (guiltless, innocent) heart that, in loving her so deeply, he has given her. But, just as the eyes "learned" ill from the lady, he suspects that his heart has been "taught" by her heart to make light of protestations (possibly both his protestations of love to her which she ridiculed and her protestations which she herself made insincerely) and to speak hypocritically. In such a case, she has changed the nature of his heart, and he refuses to acknowledge it. So, she should also keep it.

But the third stanza reverses things yet again, after he thinks about matters. He does want his heart back after all (to know her lies) and also his eyes (to see her lies). He also wants to be able to gloat over and enjoy the lady's own eventual pain when she (like the speaker now) wants someone who does not want her (i.e., someone "that will [desire] none [of you]"). Or possibly she eventually will have someone that will prove as false to her as she is proving to be to the speaker now: he will enjoy immensely seeing this situation.

The literal "message" of the title is the sum total of the man's written or spoken requests or commands made to her through the poem/song. Yet the ultimate "message" seems to be the unflattering character sketch of the lady—a vivid message to both her and the reader or hearer of the poem/song.

Metaphysical. As used in this "Dictionary," "metaphysical" refers to the particular style and content of the poetry of Donne and of those poets influenced by and/or similar to him in the 17th century. "Metaphysical" was first applied to the poetry of Donne by the writer John Dryden quite late in the century, after all such poetry had been written: he said (in *A Discourse Concerning the Original and Progress of Satire*, 1693) that Donne "affects the metaphysics, not only in his satires, but in his amorous verses, where nature only should reign; and perplexes the minds of the fair sex with nice speculations of philosophy, when he should engage their hearts, and entertain them with the softnesses of love." He thus ridicules Donne and takes him to task for supposedly dwelling on philosophical speculations about the nature of reality and for pretentiously intellectualizing love, when he should be only emotional and romantic. Apparently taking his

cue from Dryden, Dr. Samuel Johnson in the 18th century first
called Donne and his followers in poetry the "metaphysical poets."
Johnson's comments appear in his life of "Cowley" in his series *The
Lives of the Poets* (1779). He describes with great hostility many
of the characteristics of such poetry. The irony is that he very
well describes the style and techniques of metaphysical poetry,
but only to denigrate what many in the 17th and 20th centuries
praise quite highly! What Johnson considers "bad," many consider
"good" in Donne and his followers.

Johnson's label for Donne and his followers has been
retained to the present time, and his comments serve as a way to
define much of what metaphysical poetry and the metaphysical
style indeed are. Johnson says that the metaphysical poets wrote
verses with the "modulation . . . so imperfect that they were only
found to be verses by counting the syllables." This does point to
the use of irregular, distorted metrical patterns in some lines and
poems, but in good metaphysical poetry such variation functions
to convey specific feelings and meanings and thus is not in itself a
flaw in poetry but can indeed be a virtue. Donne's contemporary,
BEN JONSON, holding much earlier some of the same CLASSICAL
assumptions as the later Dr. Johnson, comments to DRUMMOND
that "Donne, for not keeping of accent, deserved hanging," thus
also disagreeing with such irregular metrics. Similarly Ben Jonson
says that "Donne himself, for not being understood, would perish,"
and Dr. Johnson complains of the metaphysical poets only wanting
to "show their learning": it is a demanding, complex, intellectual
poetry that is said to be obscure in thought and syntax at times,
but it can be quite rewarding, despite the contrary view of its
detractors. Ben Jonson also says (in his commonplace book titled
Timber) that "metaphors far-fet hinder to be understood," and
this perhaps anticipates Dr. Johnson's remark that these poets'
"conceits were far-fetched": thus, another characteristic of
metaphysical poetry is the use of the METAPHYSICAL CONCEIT
(see the entry on it for fuller definition and for further comments
by Dr. Johnson about it). Dr. Johnson also notes the use of
"hyperbole": exaggeration indeed is a characteristic of the works
of Donne and his followers. Another characteristic of much
metaphysical poetry is implied by a comment of one of Donne's
admirers in the 17th century: THOMAS CAREW notes that Donne
exiled the "goodly train of gods and goddesses" from noble
poetry—i.e., Donne's work especially does not rely as much on
classical allusions, themes, and forms as earlier Elizabethan and
CLASSICAL poems do. T.S. Eliot, an admirer of metaphysical
poetry in the 20th century, points out its unified "sensibility," the

ability to fuse thought and feeling perfectly (see DISSOCIATION OF SENSIBILITY).

Although oversimplified, a working definition of "metaphysical" might be completed by the following characteristics (added to those six characteristics designated above as being extracted from the comments of Jonson, Johnson, Carew, and Eliot): (1) construction of many poems frequently irregular in style and structure—use of irregular divisions, stanzas, and lines; (2) use of the rhythms and pauses of natural speech; (3) use of informal, colloquial, everyday word choice and tone; (4) conveying a sense of unrestrained emotion in many lines and poems; (5) presentation of the poet and/or speaker primarily in a private, personal role writing to or speaking to a select, limited audience or hearer(s); (6) writing many poems in a deliberately anti-PETRARCHAN, anti-PLATONIC, anti-SPENSERian vein; (7) use of much paradox, other forms of irony, and wordplay; (8) reliance on argumentative form and content in many poems. (One should compare and contrast these characteristics with those designated as CLASSICAL.)

The "metaphysical poets" embrace a large number of poets, both secular and religious, in the 17th century. Scholars and critics have achieved no absolute agreement about the specific number, particular individuals, and even which are major and which are minor poets. Certainly four major ones are Donne, GEORGE HERBERT, ANDREW MARVELL, and HENRY VAUGHAN. Others that might be included as sharing "metaphysical" characteristics, however, are THOMAS CAREW, Henry King, Richard Crashaw, Thomas Traherne, Abraham Cowley, and perhaps other minor writers. In such a classification, however, one should be alert to how much both Donne (the "metaphysical") and Jonson (the "classical") influenced all of the younger and later poets after them: many combine "metaphysical" and "classical" characteristics in their poems.

Metaphysical conceit. One of the characteristics of METAPHYSICAL poetry is the frequent use of the metaphysical conceit, a lengthy, far-fetched, ingenious analogy developed in detail and relating unexpected or remote areas of experience or knowledge. Such a conceit many times is developed over several lines or over several stanzas or even through an entire poem. In a famous essay (actually in his comments on Abraham Cowley in *The Lives of the Poets*) Samuel Johnson, in the 18th century, refers (with hostility) to the metaphysical poets using a "combination of dissimilar images" and of their "discovery of occult resemblances in things apparently unlike." He also says that in their poetry "the most heterogeneous ideas are yoked by violence together," that they wasted their intelligence on "false conceits," and that their "conceits were far-fetched." All of these remarks describe the metaphysical conceit; however, in the 17th and 20th centuries many poets and critics admire Donne and his followers for their employment of such conceits, valuing precisely what Dr. Johnson denigrates (see, for example, DISSOCIATION OF SENSIBILITY for some of T.S. Eliot's praises).

Since Donne's poetry is so filled with metaphysical conceits, it is difficult to select only a few for examples. Many are precisely designated and discussed in the entries on individual works in this "Dictionary." However, one can say that some of Donne's most famous that quite clearly illustrate this characteristic of his verse are to be found in the following: (1) "A VALEDICTION: FORBIDDING MOURNING" [containing four metaphysical conceits, the last of which is the most famous in all poetry, the ".compass" conceit], (2) "THE CANONIZATION," (3) "THE GOOD-MORROW," (4) "A VALEDICTION: OF WEEPING," and (5) "THE FLEA."

Metempsychosis.   An unfinished poem published in the 1633 edition of Donne's *Poems* (i.e., in the first edition). The work also is titled *The Progress of the Soul* (not to be confused with Donne's *Of the Progress of the Soul*—see *THE SECOND ANNIVERSARY*). The poem has 52 stanzas of ten lines each (i.e., a total of 520 lines), designated as the "First Song." It is dated "16 August 1601." But it also has under the title the Latin phrase *Infinitati Sacrum*, meaning "sacred to infinity," an apparently ambiguous phrase referring to the soul but possibly to the poem (written in 1601 and extending infinitely, since its topic is the soul that exists infinitely). Judging from the "Epistle" to the poem, one assumes that Donne apparently planned to use the supposed doctrine of Pythagoras of the transmigration of the soul (i.e., metempsychosis) from a human or animal at death into a new body in order to trace the soul through various bodies from Creation up to some "he" of "this time" (up to Donne's time or possibly even specifically to "16 August 1601"). The poem also has after its title the phrase "Poema Satyricon" (a satiric poem).

JONSON put forth the opinion (as reported by DRUMMOND) that Donne traced the soul of Eve's apple, wishing eventually to bring in all the heretics from the soul of CAIN onward and finally to leave it in the body of CALVIN. However, Donne implies in line 60 of the poem that he planned for the soul eventually to reside in someone in England (on the banks of the Thames). In the poem as it exists the soul is traced from its beginning in the TREE OF KNOWLEDGE into the apple and subsequently through a MANDRAKE, a sparrow, a fish, a whale, a mouse, a wolf, the offspring of a wolf and a dog, an ape, and into THEMECH. Thus, the pattern is to follow it up the ladder of creation and types of beings, but ironically to show it more corrupt in the process.

The chosen form of the poem echoes an epic, especially in its beginning "I sing" and in its apparently planned divisions into "Songs" (like epic cantos, books, etc.). It is indeed like a mock-epic. Especially convincing is the argument by M. van Wyk Smith that the primary ridicule is in the political satire directed throughout the poem at ROBERT CECIL. Smith argues that he is the "great soul" that moves Queen ELIZABETH, the great and sinister power behind her throne that was to be the final recipient of the soul, had Donne finished the poem. But also in the poem such an incident as the mouse causing the destruction of the elephant can be interpreted in light of the fate earlier in 1601 of ROBERT DEVEREUX, Earl of Essex: the elephant is Devereux, and the mouse is Cecil. (For further observations and speculations on this puzzling fragment of a poem, see in the "Selected Bibliography" the introduction to Milgate's edition of the *Satires* and the various critical items cited under this poem.)

Methridate. See MITHRIDATE.

Methusalem. See METHUSELAH.

Methuselah. Son of ENOCH. He lived 969 years and is thus commonly taken as the epitome of long life and old age. See Genesis 5:21–27. Donne refers to him in line 128 of *THE FIRST ANNIVERSARY*, as well as in many *SERMONS*.

Mews. *Noun*: a set of stables that served as a riding school.

Microcosm. The "little world," as opposed to the "great world" or MACROCOSM. Donne and other writers of the Middle Ages and Renaissance usually employ the word and the concept to refer to man (i.e., the individual human), and they depend upon the ideas of ARISTOTLE in this regard. But the word can in some contexts refer to or imply any kind of smaller world in itself that reflects in little the MACROCOSM: e.g., the state as a microcosm of the universe (the King or Queen like God presiding over all, with various ranks and types of people down the scale of being to the lowest, a structure that reflects the NATURAL ORDER or chain of being). Donne uses a bedroom or two lovers or two lovers in a room as a self-sufficient microcosm, a universe or earth in itself, in many works (e.g., in "THE CANONIZATION," "THE GOOD-MORROW," and "THE SUN RISING"). A tear can be a microcosm (see "A VALEDICTION: OF WEEPING"). Or a flea (see "THE FLEA").

In its most frequent uses the microcosm or little world is believed to contain within it all of the elements and structural principles that are contained in the MACROCOSM that it reflects: for example, the individual human (the microcosm) was believed to have been created with elements and principles corresponding both to the earth (a MACROCOSM) and to the whole universe (a MACROCOSM). Man is composed, in his physical being, of the four ELEMENTS that make up everything on earth. His blood is analogous to the rivers of the earth, and his hair is like grass. Man's passions are like storms on earth (in Shakespeare's *King Lear*, Lear's raging in the storm illustrates the direct correspondence of microcosm and macrocosm). Man's spirit and intellect correspond to God in the universe. As discussed by writers of the time, the correspondences are seemingly endless. Donne's uses of the individual as a microcosm are numerous: see, only as a few examples, "I AM A LITTLE WORLD MADE CUNNINGLY," "Elegy on the Lady Markham" (beginning "Man is the world, and death the ocean, / To which God gives the lower parts of man"), and *DEVOTIONS UPON EMERGENT OCCASIONS* ("Meditation 1" relates the onset of Donne's illness to earthquakes and thunder; "Meditation 4" says, "It is too little to call man a little world"; "Meditation 11" calls one's heart the "King of man"; and in "Meditation 21" Donne contends that he is a "new argument of the NEW PHILOSOPHY" of the universe).

Midas. In mythology, a king of Phrygia who was given by the gods his wish that all he touched would turn to gold. After his food and daughter also were changed, he wanted to be rid of this ability and was granted this wish also.

Militant Church. See CHURCH, MILITANT.

Mine(s), myne(s). *Noun:* (1) place(s), excavation(s) in the earth from which metals and minerals are taken; (2) abundant source(s) of something; (3) mineral(s) or ore(s); (4) in military usage, [a] an underground passage to allow either movement beneath or undermining of a wall or [b] an underground excavation in which gunpowder is placed to explode an enemy's fortifications; (5) metaphor for the womb.

Mingle bloods. To experience sexual intercourse in which the bloods were believed to combine and result in conception.

Miriam. Sister of Moses and Aaron. She is referred to as a "prophetess" in Exodus. She sings and plays a timbrel to celebrate the crossing of the Red Sea (see Exodus 15). Donne refers to her and to her singing of praise in "Upon the Translation of the Psalms by Sir Philip Sidney, and the Countess of Pembroke His Sister."

Mirreus. Personified character in "SATIRE 3" who represents an adherent of the Roman Catholic Church, loving its tradition, history, ceremony, art, and other trappings.

Mis-devotion. Roman Catholicism, with its devotion to saints. See line 13 of "THE RELIC" and lines 511–13 of *THE SECOND ANNIVERSARY*: in the latter work, the "mis-devotion" is in Roman Catholic France where Donne was writing the poem.

Mistress. *Noun*: (1) a woman who employs, cares for, has authority over others; (2) a woman who is loved and courted by a man—i.e., a sweetheart or a lady love; (3) a concubine or a woman used by a man for sexual pleasure in addition to or in place of a wife; (4) as a title or prefix, a term of respect; (5) a title of courtesy for a married woman; (6) a title of courtesy for an unmarried woman or girl. *Verb*: to dally with a mistress.

Mistress of my youth, Poetry; wife of mine age, Divinity. Phrases written by Donne in a letter of 1623: see VILLIERS, GEORGE.

Mitcham. Village (in Surrey) near London where Donne and his family lived from 1606 to 1611. Donne read, studied, and wrote much here, even while responsible for a large family in a small cottage. In a letter Donne refers to his house (during a particularly depressing period of illness affecting many family members) as his "hospital at Mitcham." In one of the *VERSE LETTERS* ("To Sir Henry Goodyer") he tactfully expresses disappointment on one occasion when Goodyer did not visit here as he apparently had promised.

Mithridate (Methridate). *Noun*: (1) a compound of many substances that was believed to be a universal antidote against poisons, (2) any antidote against poison.

Moaba. Supposedly a daughter of Adam and Eve and wife to SETH: the idea and the name are non-scriptural, coming only from rabbinic tradition. See lines 439–40 of *METEMPSYCHOSIS.*

Monarchies, the four. Babylon, Persia, Greece, and Rome.

Moorfield Crosses. Walkways built across the marshy Moorfield after 1606.

More, Ann(e) (1584–1617). Donne's wife. Daughter of Sir George More. Lived in the household of her uncle, SIR THOMAS EGERTON, while Donne was employed by him. Secretly married Donne in late 1601. Because of pressure from Ann's father, Donne was dismissed from his position, and the ill feelings stirred by the marriage probably prevented Donne's advancement in a secular career. The couple lived at Pyrford, then MITCHAM, and finally in London on DRURY LANE. After twelve children (two of which were stillborn), Ann died August 15, 1617 (following a stillbirth) and was buried at ST. CLEMENT DANES Church where a monument for her (since destroyed) was commissioned by Donne from the sculptor NICHOLAS STONE.

Donne's grief was deep for the loss of the mainstay of his emotional life, the woman with whom he seemed to have forged near-perfect love and marriage. Some of his secular poems that describe perfect and mutual love relationships (both physical and spiritual) and that concern partings, reunitings, and partings that are not really separations (e.g., "A VALEDICTION: FORBIDDING MOURNING," "A VALEDICTION: OF WEEPING," and "THE ECSTASY") probably were written from his experience with Ann, and maybe even on specific occasions, but there exists no documented material to let us pass beyond probability and conjecture about dates and occasions in many cases. Perhaps more likely is the connection of "A FEVER" with one of the spells of illness that frequently affected Donne's family, and "A LECTURE UPON THE SHADOW" tantalizes in its autobiographical suggestions about their secret, hidden marriage. Most clearly autobiographical, however, is the poem beginning "SINCE SHE WHOM I LOVED" (from the *HOLY SONNETS*). It and "A NOCTURNAL UPON ST. LUCY'S DAY" likely refer to his wife's death and his response to it. (Also see the section "Donne's Life" above.)

Morea. Peloponnesus, joined to Greece by an isthmus.

Morpheus. God of dreams (or, less accurately, sleep) who can assume any human shape. His brother Icelus (or Icelos) can assume any animal shape. See line 3 of "To Mr. R. W." (beginning "If, as mine is"). (The father of Morpheus and Icelus is Somnus [or Hypnos], the actual god of sleep.)

Moschite. *Noun*: a mosque.

Moses' cherubins. The two gold cherubims depicted on the Ark of the Covenant, between which God would commune with Moses (Exodus 25:17–22). Referred to in line 49 of "Elegy on the Lady Markham" (see MARKHAM, LADY and *EPICEDES AND OBSEQUIES*).

Mother-in-law. *Noun*: (1) the mother of one's husband or wife, (2) stepmother [Donne uses the word in this sense in "Meditation 18" of *DEVOTIONS UPON EMERGENT OCCASIONS*, contrasting the word to "natural mother"].

Mother-maid. The Virgin MARY.

Motley. *Adjective*: (1) of many colors, (2) varied or varying, (3) changeable.

Move. *Verb*: (1) to change the position of something or someone; (2) to remove or shift; (3) to stir or disturb; (4) to put or keep in motion; (5) to excite, to stimulate, to stir up emotion or passion or anger; (6) to provoke some action or reaction; (7) to urge, exhort, incite, appeal, or propose.

Mucheron. Mushroom.

Mummy. *Noun*: (1) an Egyptian mummy, preserved corpse; (2) the flesh of an Egyptian mummy used as a medicine by some physicians; (3) the flesh of any corpse that had chemicals added, was baked, and then used as a medicine; (4) general term for dead flesh.

Munster, Sebastian (1489–1552). Wrote *The Cosmography of the Universe* (1541), a work used (and acknowledged) by CORYAT in writing his own travel accounts. Donne refers to him in line 22 of "Upon Mr. Thomas Coryat's Crudities."

Murder. *Verb*: For some common implications in relation to Donne's secular love poetry, see DIE, KILL, and PETRARCHAN.

Musco. Moscow.

Muse. *Noun*: (1) in Greek mythology, one of the nine goddesses who inspired learning and arts [including poetry and music] who frequently are called on (invoked) by a writer or artist for such inspiration; (2) loosely, a poet's inspiration or talent or particular style.

Music of the spheres. See SPHERE.

Musk cat. The musk deer is the source of musk used in perfume, but it was commonly confused with the civet cat, also the source of secretion used in perfume. See "Elegy 8: The Comparison," line 2.

Muskat. See MUSK CAT.

N

Natural order. The common concept of the Middle Ages and Renaissance that God created a perfect, ordered universe in which everything is placed in a particular position with an assigned function or purpose. As long as each entity's position and function are maintained, the universe operates smoothly and harmoniously. But if this God-given order, rank, or hierarchy is disrupted, chaos results and is destructive to each entity and to the whole universe. For example, God is at the top of order in the universe, followed by the ranks of angels, humans, animals, plants, and inanimate things. All elements in the cosmos (SPHERE, planet, sun, moon, etc.) have their specific places and functions that must be adhered to so that natural order is maintained.

The concept was easily extended to any MICROCOSM that reflects this MACROCOSM of the universe. For example, in each nation the proper king or queen is like God in the universe, and all subordinate ranks of people have their proper places and functions, being superior to some and inferior to others; therefore, political and social rebellion against proper authority could be viewed as rebellion against and sin against God, since God seemingly ordained natural order to be followed in every realm. The same reflection of natural order can be seen in the hierarchical structure of the church, family, and any group of humans. Indeed, within man as a MICROCOSM his own constituent elements ideally must adhere to natural order (e.g., controlled by his Godlike soul and reason, rather than the rebellious passions and senses), or chaos within the world or universe of himself will result.

Such ideas are used throughout Donne's work, and Donne (like his contemporaries) finds some of the discoveries of the NEW PHILOSOPHY profoundly disturbing to the concept of natural order.

Natural spirits. Vapors believed to be formed in the liver and carried with HUMORS in the veins. Associated with the lowest, VEGETATIVE part of man.

Nazienzen (Nazianzen or Nazianzus), Gregory of (about 329–388). Greek Christian (one of the Cappadocian Fathers of the Church). Reorganized the orthodox church at Constantinople (briefly serving as Bishop) but lived the remainder of his life at Nazianzus. Wrote discourses (including orations and sermons), letters, and poems. Known particularly for his defenses of the Nicene Creed and the humanity of Christ. In a funeral oration for his sister (Gorgonia), he says that she threatened God that she would not remove her head from the altar until her prayer for being cured was granted. JEROME was a disciple of his. Nazienzen is one of the four traditional "DOCTORS" of the eastern church. Donne frequently refers to Nazienzen in his prose, particularly in the *SERMONS*.

Nebuchadnezzar. Babylonian king who ruled for forty years. He marched on Jerusalem four times, taking many captives to Babylon and sacking the Temple of its riches. Erected an idol that was not worshipped by some of those still faithful to God (see CHILDREN IN THE OVEN). Daniel interpreted dreams for him. Daniel predicted from one of the dreams that God, because of Nebuchadnezzar's pride, would have him driven from men and cause him to dwell with animals, where he would have to eat grass. Daniel later told Nebuchadnezzar's son that this prediction had come true. See especially chapters 1–5 of Daniel.

Neck-verse. See BENEFIT OF CLERGY.

"Negative Love." One of the *SONGS AND SONNETS*. The speaker begins by contrasting himself to other men who love: some of them seem birds of "prey" who "STOOP" (swoop down) to feed on a lady's eye or cheek or lip (i.e., only concerned with the physical attributes of a lady and with bodily love through the senses), but the speaker never "STOOPS" (condescends) to be as lowly as these other men. He also seldom "stoops" to the level of those who do not "soar" (again, like a kind of limited bird) higher than an admiration limited to a lady's virtue or mind (i.e., like a PLATONIC lover). It is ironic that virtue and the mind are not high enough for the lover who is speaking! These two types of lovers, in addition to being metaphorically described as birds, seem to be worshippers of opposite extremes in love and the lady: the Platonist admires the virtue and mind, while the sensualist seems to "STOOP" down on bended knee to kneel and (punningly) "pray," as well as "prey," on the lady's eye, cheek, and lip. So, the speaker sees himself as superior to both of these other types of men who only have a limited love focused on particular attributes of a lady and of love in general. They are inflamed (on "fire") to love either "sense" or "understanding" (one is "fuel" for the "fire" of the lustful and the other is "fuel" for the "fire" of the Platonist). Anyone with these same qualities (i.e., any ordinary human) "knows" what causes this kind of love: so, it is a common love with no mystery in its makeup. This is precisely why the speaker feels superior—his love is not one of the common types: it is a mystery. It is more "BRAVE" (in several senses of the word!). Paradoxically, his love is both "SILLY" (primarily "ignorant" of its own nature, but also "simple") and wise, since it is finer to have a love that is not limited and simplistic in its object, one that maintains a mystery, a "nothing" (see line 16) that cannot be pinned down. He simply cannot formulate specifics about why and what he loves. To be able to define love is to limit it. So, the last two lines of the first stanza (lines 8–9) express the wish that, if he ever "craves" something specific in a woman (as do the two types of men delineated earlier), then he wants to "miss" (not achieve: but in terms of his earlier metaphor, not to hit his prey like one of the birds pictured earlier do). If he knows what he wants ("what I would have"), then his love loses its mystery and becomes as inferior as those of the run-of-the-mill lechers and Platonists.

In the second stanza this superior lover says that a perfect entity can only be expressed by negatives, by what it is not: behind this assertion is the quantity of medieval Christian writing, such as that of the SCHOOLMEN, including AQUINAS, that argues for humanity not being able to know what God is and therefore only being able to define Him by negatives. Examples of defining God by negatives would be abundantly known by Donne, not the least of which is in the Creed of Saint Athanasius, found in *The Book of Common Prayer*: the Father, Son, and Holy Ghost are called "uncreate" and "incomprehensible"; also stated is that "The Father is made of none: neither created, nor begotten." So, the speaker of the poem rather audaciously places his own perfect love on a level with God: both can only be expressed negatively, rather than with positive knowledge of any particular quality. In line 13 he forcefully expresses his endorsement of the negative in his "no," his refusal to take the usual in love. But the line is ambiguous, possibly deliberately by Donne: is it "I say 'no' to all of those ordinary men who love all the declarable attributes of women"? Or is it "I say 'no' to all of those declarable attributes of women that all ordinary men love"? Both meanings, in fact, are relevant, indirect negatives to try to characterize the speaker's love. And the line itself, the speaker, and his love are indeed mysteries that one has to "decipher," as he implies (again, *negatively*) in the next three lines (14–16). If anyone (a challenge to the reader?) is able to understand our "selves," let him reveal to the speaker just how to do so—but the speaker is being sarcastic: no man truly can understand himself and thus surely will have "nothing" to teach. How can anyone decipher either "nothing" or (its equivalent) "what we know not"? So, the mysteries of God, of the speaker's self, and of the speaker's love will remain mysteries, only to be commented on with negatives—with what they are not (just as the speaker began the poem telling what his love is not, rather than what it is). So, the last two lines of the poem state that he is comforted (paradoxically) by that fact, even though he does not progress or succeed ("SPEED"), he does progress and succeed: i.e., even though he does not move forward to a positive definition of his love, he cannot fail in this type of love because he has no stated goal. He can either (1) aim at nothing and secure nothing or (2) aim at nothing and secure something: whatever happens, this "negative love" allows him to win.

Neo-Platonic. See PLATONIC.

Nestle. *Verb*: (1) to make a nest, (2) to settle in a nest or comfortable place.

New ingredients. PARACELSUS and his followers argued that salt, sulphur, and mercury ("new ingredients") make up the body, rather than the [old] four ELEMENTS (earth, water, air, and fire) believed to do so by GALEN and the GALENISTS. See lines 263–66 of *THE SECOND ANNIVERSARY*.

New philosophy. The new science (or cosmology or astronomy) encompassing the theory of COPERNICUS that the earth is not the center of the universe (as the conception of PTOLEMY argued) but that the earth (as well as the rest of the solar system) revolves around the sun. The discoveries of BRAHE, KEPLER, GALILEO, and others verified and extended the arguments of Copernicus and became a part of the "new philosophy." This new science questioned the existence of the layers of ELEMENTS surrounding the earth, as envisioned in the Ptolemaic universe: the particular questioning of the "element of fire" (asserted as nonexistent especially by KEPLER and CARDAN) is alluded to in line 206 ("The element of fire is quite put out") of *THE FIRST ANNIVERSARY* and in the *SERMONS* (see Potter and Simpson edition, Volume VII, p. 184, and Volume IX, pp. 230–31). These astronomers argued for the existence of worlds other than earth in the universe, a proposal that (along with the contentions that earth is not the center and that the universe and solar systems are not in perfect circles) raised disturbing questions about whether humanity and earth were indeed formed and placed by God as central in his perfect, harmonious creation (see lines 207–12 of *THE FIRST ANNIVERSARY*).

Some other examples of Donne's great interest in (accompanied with some disturbance by) these radical concepts that seemed to disprove what had been assumed formerly to be a constant, perfect, unchanging universe are reflected in the following passages containing the phrase "new philosophy": line 205 of *THE FIRST ANNIVERSARY*, line 37 of "To the Countess of Bedford" (beginning "To have written then"), near the end of "Meditation 21" in *DEVOTIONS UPON EMERGENT OCCASIONS*, and in a *SERMON* of December 12, 1626 (see Potter and Simpson edition, VII, Sermon 10, p. 271). Concepts, ideas, and analogies based on both the old (i.e., Ptolemaic) and the new philosophies permeate Donne's works.

New stars. See BRAHE and KEPLER.

Nile. The Nile River in Egypt. In "To E. of D. with Six Holy Sonnets," "Satire 4," and a sermon on Psalms 32:5 (No. 58 in *LXXX Sermons*, No. 13 in Vol. IX of Potter and Simpson edition), Donne refers to the slime of the Nile and alludes to the belief (from Pliny) that the sun would father living creatures out of the mud of the Nile River.

Niobe. In Greek mythology, the daughter of Tantalus and wife to Amphion. She had (depending on the specific accounts) from 12 to 20 children (divided equally in sons and daughters: 6 and 6 or 7 and 7 or 10 and 10). She made the mistake of arrogantly pointing out the fact that her number of children far surpassed the two of Leto whose children were the god Apollo and the goddess Artemis. After they had heard Niobe brag, Apollo and Artemis killed her children. She was struck with grief and wept unceasingly. She was turned into stone, but the stone stayed wet with tears. Compare Donne's treatment of the myth in "Niobe," one of his *EPIGRAMS*.

"Nocturnal Upon St. Lucy's Day, Being the Shortest Day, A." One of the *SONGS AND SONNETS*. Crucial to the poem are the connotations of ST. LUCY and her particular day of the year. Apparently the poem is written about either the actual death or the anticipated death of some woman whom the poet is relating to St. Lucy and/or her day. The time of the writing is at midnight during this longest night of the year preceding the shortest day of the year. The word "Nocturnal" in the title suggests an artistic creation (i.e., the poem itself) centered on night, with its feelings and events. But also it echoes a "nocturn" or midnight church service or period of prayer. The connotations of darkness and the deadness of winter at the winter solstice reflect the emotions of the speaker surrounding the death that is his subject.

Editors, scholars, and critics have proposed various possibilities for reading the poem autobiographically. Some feel that Donne wrote it about the Countess of BEDFORD, one of his patronesses, either during her very serious illness or at her death. Especially tempting in this argument is the fact that her name was Lucy. Also, LUCY DONNE, one of his daughters, died young and thus is a possibility as the subject of the poem. However, many agree with John T. Shawcross (see Shawcross in "Selected Bibliography," both in "Works" and in an article of 1965 in "Critical Studies: Poetry") that the name "Lucy" is not as important as the feelings associated with the festival day and that the actual circumstance is the death of Donne's wife ANN MORE in August, 1617, thus leading to Donne's writing of the poem focusing on St. Lucy's Day a few months later.

In the opening stanza Donne (if we take it as autobiographical) notes that it is midnight, in the "dead of night" preceding St. Lucy's Day and that this night also is the midnight for the year itself—the longest period of darkness and the "dead of the year." It is a day that reveals ("unmasks") itself for hardly more than seven hours (i.e., of daylight). The stars are portrayed as "flasks" of gunpowder that are almost exhausted, sending forth only bare "squibs" (like flashes from firecrackers) of light. So, the darkness of the day and of the year is almost total, reflecting the darkness of death and despair that he feels with the absence of the light, vitality, and life itself of the woman whose death (or near-death) he is lamenting. The "sap" or "BALM" of the world has itself sunk and disappeared. The "BALM" here is the life-preserving fluid that was believed to exist in every living being, the disappearance of which would bring death (an idea from PARACELSUS). So, to Donne, the world itself seems dead, and, indeed, he compares the world to a body on its deathbed. This analogy implies a correspondence to the death of the person being elegized: the death of this woman means the death of the world and of life itself to Donne. Paradoxically he states that he is far more dead: all that he has designated as being dead or near-dead seem vibrant and laughing when compared to his own dead status as an epitaph for all else. The picture given suggests that this person's burial in the earth is equivalent to the life of the earth sinking and shrinking, leaving all humanity and life on the surface withered and dead, and Donne is the epitome of all this deadness, indeed the receptacle in which all the deadness is concentrated. Since he is the epitaph for all deadness, Donne urges (in the second stanza) all other lovers who still will be living in the spring (which he calls a "next world," a new world for them after the deadness of winter) to study him. They will see that love reversed all normal processes of ALCHEMY in him. Rather than taking ingredients to arrive at the life-giving QUINTESSENCE, love as an alchemist "expressed" (squeezed out) from "nothingness" a quintessence. Donne's quintessential nothingness came from other nothings: "privations" (deprivations of emotions? deprivations of the company of the loved one? deprivation of the loved one's life itself?), "lean emptiness" (dispiritedness and despair after her death that wasted him away physically, emotionally, and spiritually?), "absence," "darkness," and "death." All of the preceding are "things which are not" or "nothingness," and he is the greatest state of nothingness that can be formed from all of these conditions that love subjected him to. He was collapsed into ruins by nothings and paradoxically rebuilt into an utter state of nothingness.

The third stanza proceeds with further differences in love's alchemy: the "limbec" (see ALCHEMY) used by love makes Donne the burial place, the earthly repository, of all that is nothing, as opposed both to normal alchemy that tries to make concrete somethings of value out of inferior ingredients and to the normal process of life itself which allows humans to draw out of everything that exists the good qualities that generate and sustain life. Love's process caused him and the lady to be the whole world, but in weeping they drowned the world (like the Old Testament flood): a destroyed world is a "nothing" coming from something. Also, they became like "chaoses" (primordial states of disorder) if they had to divert themselves from their own world of each other: this chaos is a "nothing" coming from a previous something. Finally, being absent during physical separation from each other in this perfect love meant that he had her soul with him and she had his soul with her; therefore, his body was a dead one (a "carcass") without his soul in it, and hers was a "carcass" without her soul in it. Each body became a "nothing" that previously was a something.

The assertions in the third stanza present love's strange alchemy during their life together. But in the fourth stanza Donne says that this state of "first nothingness" cannot compare to the

end of love's alchemy, the appearance of the "elixir" itself (see
ALCHEMY) after the lady's "death" (the word "wrongs" her, since
he is assured of her eternal life, but he cannot yet enjoy this state
himself).   He is (as he mentioned earlier) himself the
"quintessence" or "elixir" of nothingness.   The death of the lady
was the final step needed in the process of love's alchemy to
create this elixir, then.   He is no longer even a man, he feels.   In
fact, he is not a man, not even an animal, not even a plant, not
even a stone.   He has no attributes of any of these levels of
creatures—no   choice,   desire,   instinct,   response,   movement,
attraction, repulsion.   He is not a something at all.   But, even
worse, he is not even an "ordinary nothing," such as an
insubstantial "shadow," which at least has a body that produces it.
So, he is more nothing than a nothing: he feels as if he is indeed
the elixir or quintessence of nothingness—he is in utterly hopeless
despair.

    In the last stanza Donne says that his "sun" (the lady) will
not renew, will not return.   This cleverly follows from the shadow
having a body and a sun to cast the shadow: Donne has neither a
body nor a sun (the lady).   Again, he is "none," nothing.   Then he
addresses again the "lovers" spoken of in the second stanza, those
who will be able to experience love again in the spring (in contrast
to Donne).   He tells them that the "lesser sun" (i.e., the literal sun
in the sky: it is "lesser" than the most important "sun" for Donne,
his lady) has now (at the winter solstice) entered the constellation
of Capricorn.   His personal "Lucy" as his sun reminds us of the
name itself suggesting light (from Latin *lux* and *lucere*).   The name
"Capricorn" signifies "Goat," and the goat is its zodiacal sign.   Since
a goat is a traditional symbol of lechery, Donne takes this as an
appropriate foreshadowing of the revitalized passion and love that
the sun will pluck out of Capricorn: he then will beam down this
fertility and energy into lovers in the spring.   He tells these lovers
to enjoy their coming "summer" of love, clearly underlining the
fact that he himself is excluded from such.   Donne seems to be
using "summer" here in one of its older senses that connotes the
warmer half of the year, specifically in contrast to the "winter"
half.   As for himself, Donne says that he can only "PREPARE"
towards his lady who has died.   "Prepare" here primarily has one
of the older meanings of the word, "to go" (arising from the sense
of preparing for a journey), but also suggests the spiritual
preparation he is making on this St. Lucy's festival that he also
equates with the dead lady's "long night's festival."   So, the long
night preceding St. Lucy's Day symbolizes also the long night of
death anticipating release through resurrection.   The speaker

himself will have to bear lingering a long "night" on earth before he eventually can join the lady in death and the festival of resurrection. The "deep midnight" of the winter solstice expresses the dark, cold, lonely, unending grief and isolation he must endure in his remaining earthly days until such release. The last line of the poem returns us full circle to its first line, suggesting perhaps the seemingly endless cycle of no progression in his earthly life. His life remains now at midnight of the longest night of the year.

This poem is one of Donne's most complex and debated, and for other arguments concerning it the reader should see the editions of poetry, the discussions of it in many of the critical books, and the articles and essays on it that are listed in the "Selected Bibliography." One particularly detailed reading is that by Richard Sleight (see "Selected Bibliography: Critical Studies, Poetry").

Noisome. *Adjective:* (1) harmful, noxious; (2) ill-smelling; (3) unpleasant.

Nor . . . nor. Correlative conjunctions used by Donne and other writers of the sixteenth and seventeenth centuries: equivalent to the modern "neither . . . nor." An example is in line 21 of "AIR AND ANGELS": "nor in nothing, nor in things."

O

Obnoxious. *Adjective*: liable or likely, (2) liable or exposed to harm or evil or injury.

"Obscure Writer, An." See *EPIGRAMS*.

Observe. *Verb*: (1) to notice, remark, perceive; (2) to treat with attention; (3) to treat with ceremonious respect or reverence.

Octave. See SONNET.

Of the Progress of the Soul. See *THE SECOND ANNIVERSARY*.

Officious. *Adjective*: (1) attentive, eager-to-please; (2) kind; (3) dutiful.

Offuscation. *Noun*: (1) obfuscation, obscuration, darkening; (2) bewilderment.

"On His Mistress." See "ELEGY 16: ON HIS MISTRESS."

One born blind. Reference to HOMER in line 76 of "To the Countess of Salisbury."

Optic. *Noun*: a telescope.

Or . . . or. Correlative conjunctions commonly used by Donne and other writers of the sixteenth and seventeenth centuries: equivalent to the modern "either . . . or." An example is in line 2 of "THE CANONIZATION": "Or chide my palsy, or my gout."

Orbity. *Noun*: condition of being bereaved of children.

Orcus. Roman name for PLUTO.

Order, idea of. See NATURAL ORDER.

Order(s). See HIERARCHY, THE HEAVENLY.

Ordinary, in. Regular.

Origen (about 185–about 254).   Born in Alexandria, Egypt. Taught grammar and philosophy and lived an ascetic life of chastity.   A wealthy Christian provided Origen with secretaries, and he began to write prolifically.   Travelled to Rome and Greece. Was ordained and established a school in Palestine where he taught and wrote.   Was tortured and imprisoned during the persecution of Christians by the Roman emperor Decius, treatment eventually leading to Origen's death from weakness after his release.

Origen wrote extensive commentaries, some versions of the Old Testament in different languages, and other philosophical and theological works.   Quite influential in developing allegorical interpretations of the Bible.   Many of his arguments (for example, about the TRINITY, preexisting souls, and resurrection of the body) were quite controversial and unorthodox, leading to many of them (a few centuries after his death) being pronounced heretical.   Donne refers to Origen frequently in the *SERMONS*.

Orithea. See BOREAS.

Outlandish. *Adjective*: foreign.

Outstreat. *Verb*: to exude.

Ovid (43 B.C.–A.D. 18).   Roman poet whose Latin name is Publius Ovidius Naso and who sometimes is referred to as "Naso."   Studied rhetoric, travelled, and eventually decided to be a poet.   His most famous and influential works are *Amores*, *Ars amatoria*, and *Metamorphoses*.   Ovid is regarded as an entertaining storyteller and writer of amorous and erotic verse.

Donne's more flippant and bawdy amorous poems (some of the *SONGS AND SONNETS* and *ELEGIES*) clearly reflect influences from and affinities with Ovid.   Donne's use of one of Ovid's stories from *Metamorphoses* is most clearly reflected in one of the *EPIGRAMS* entitled "Pyramus and Thisbe": see PYRAMUS.

Oxymoron. *Noun*: a form of paradox in which two apparently contradictory terms occur in conjunction—one example is "unkindly kind" in line 27 of "SONG (SWEETEST LOVE, I DO NOT GO)."

P

Page. *Noun*: (1) a boy employed as a servant or attendant; (2) a boy in training for knighthood, personally serving a knight but not yet a squire; (3) one side of a leaf of a book or manuscript or letter.

Pair. *Noun*: (1) a set of two; (2) two persons or animals of opposite sexes, an engaged or married couple; (3) a set of more than two—e.g., a "pair of beads" designating a string of beads (see the *VERSE LETTER* "To Sir Henry Goodyer," line 4).

Palatine. See FREDERICK.

Panes. *Noun*: strips of cloth joined in a garment.

Panurge. Character in Rabelais's *Gargantua and Pantagruel* who is skilled in twelve languages. Referred to in line 59 of "Satire 4."

Paracelsus. Physician whose full name was Philippus Aureolus Theophrastus Bombast von Hohenheim (1493–1541). Donne was aware of and influenced by some of his ideas and terms concerning ALCHEMY and medicine. Paracelsus attempted to discredit GALEN and the HUMORS. He saw God as the ultimate alchemist who derived the creation out of chemical processes, and he speculated on the nature of MUMMY. Paracelsus also popularized the terms MICROCOSM and MACROCOSM. His comments on such matters as the QUINTESSENCE and BALM seem directly echoed by Donne.
　　In medical treatment, Paracelsus and the chemics (or chemiques) disagreed with the methods of Galen and the GALENISTS. Instead of correcting imbalances of HUMORS with foods of opposite qualities, the chemics tried to purge from the body the essence of the disease by using an antagonistic medicine. See lines 59–62 of "To Sir Henry Wotton" (the *VERSE LETTER* beginning "Sir, more than kisses") and lines 25–30 of "The Cross." Paracelsus also is one of the "innovators" in Hell depicted in *IGNATIUS HIS CONCLAVE.*

"Paradox, The." One of the *SONGS AND SONNETS.* The poem seems to divide structurally into introduction (lines 1–6), illustration (lines 7–16), and conclusion (lines 17–20). The meanings and feelings of this poem depend on the common meanings (in Donne's time) of KILL and DIE as sexual consummation. In addition, "love" here largely is equated with sexual love, sexual intercourse. Therefore, the speaker says that no lover can utter the words "I love" (line 1) or "I loved" (line 6) because a dead person cannot speak: love "kills" at the moment it is experienced. Also, in lines 1–4 it is said that each lover, with his egotistical nature, feels that no one else can truly be in love and that no one else can understand another's account of love. So, even if the lover could speak of his love, he would not.

The speaker in lines 7–8 says that love kills more young people with excess of heat (i.e., passion—since it causes them to "die" in sexual intercourse) than death kills old people with excessive coldness. So, lines 9–10 play on the word "die" as the speaker implies that these young are already dead and thus cannot die of old age! Anyone who says a person dies twice is lying (and to this speaker the "once" comes with sexual intercourse, not with natural physical death). Such a person who has died once by love might appear to be moving around, but it is a deception to the senses: he is really already dead (lines 11–12). This seeming life is only like the bit of light that lingers after the sun ("light's life") already has set (lines 13–14) or it is like the bit of heat that lingers in the coals for two hours after the fire has been extinguished.

In the conclusion the speaker applies all of the preceding to his personal situation. In line 17 he says that once "I loved" (a statement he earlier noted [line 5] could not be made). So, he "died" as a young lover and is now his own epitaph and tomb (line 18) before he is physically dead of natural causes. Line 19 asserts that "Here" (in epitaphs on tombs) dead men present their last words; therefore, he presents his. Line 20 is his epitaph: he was slain by love (i.e., "killed") and "here" he does "lie." The epitaph is deliberately ambiguous and might be the final joke of the poem: is it simply in the vein of the traditional epitaph in saying that "here" (in this tomb) I "lie" (repose) buried? Or are there puns that suggest "here" (in this epitaph) I "lie" (am telling a falsehood)? He said earlier that no one can say he loved—does he indeed "lie" about this? Or does the pun imply that his assertion about being slain by love in this epitaph is a lie? If so, it removes his assertion about love's "killing" power all through the poem, and, if this prop is removed from the poem, the whole thing collapses like a clever house of cards erected by Donne: and this might be the ultimate "paradox."

The question of "paradox" in the poem and in the title is indeed crucial. The poem was not given a title in its first appearance in print in 1633, but it was called "The Paradox" in the edition of 1635. Some manuscripts upon which the printed versions depend do not provide a title for the poem. Some editors of the poem attempt to define "the paradox," the dominating one, in the poem. See, for example, in "Selected Bibliography: Works" such editions as the following: Redpath ("The paradox seems to be that no lover while alive can say that he loves or that he has loved") and Craik ("The paradox is that no lover can be said to be a lover"). The task to define "the paradox" is not a simple one. Donne, of course, might not have given the poem a title at all or might not have given it this particular title. Whether he titled it or not, it seems best perhaps to think of the poem as one that is paradoxical in nature and as one containing many paradoxes interwoven, rather than only one. I find the poem progressing through at least ten paradoxes: (1) lines 1–6: no lover can speak of his love because he "dies" when he loves; (2) lines 1–6: even if the lover were alive to speak of his love, he would not do so because he feels that no one else can love or understand love; (3) lines 7–8: love kills more young people with excessive heat than death kills old people with excessive cold; (4) lines 9–10: we die only once and that once is when we love, not when we die of old age or natural causes; (5) lines 11–12: even though the living lover moves, he is not really a living lover at all, because the lover already died when he loved; (6) lines 17–18: [even though "I" earlier said that no lover can say he loved,] I do say "I loved"; (7) lines 17–18: [before my natural death] I already am my own epitaph and tomb (because I "died" when I loved); (8) line 19: dead men speak; (9) line 20: through this epitaph I, the dead lover, can say what I earlier said could not be said—i.e., I loved [and thus was slain and lie buried here]; (10) line 20: I am lying, being untruthful, in this epitaph when I say that I was killed by love [and thus in the entire poem, paradoxically, I "lie," I am being untruthful, because every assertion in the poem depends upon the assumption that one "dies" when he loves].

Paradoxes. See *JUVENILIA: OR CERTAIN PARADOXES AND PROBLEMS.*

Paradoxes and Problems. See *JUVENILIA: OR CERTAIN PARADOXES AND PROBLEMS.*

Parasceve. *Noun*: the day of preparation for the Jewish Sabbath (i.e., the day before the Sabbath).

Parcel gilt. Partly gilded.

Parnassus. Mountain in Greece that was sacred to the Muses, Apollo, and Dionysius.

Parts. *Noun*: a special meaning, common in Donne and other writers of the time, refers to a person's natural or acquired attributes, qualities, talents, or abilities.

Passing Bell. Bell tolled softly and slowly as a person is dying (passing away) in order to secure prayers for the soul. Compare DEATH BELL and FUNERAL BELL.

Passion, the. The suffering of Christ on the cross. Also used to designate GOOD FRIDAY.

Pastoral. A pastoral work of literature strictly is one in which the major characters are shepherds (in Latin "pastor" means "shepherd"). The form introduced by Theocritus accrued from Vergil and others later certain conventional elements and ideals that were continued in the Renaissance. The work usually presents the country or non-urban life as ideal, natural, innocent, simple, and peaceful. The corruptions and vices of the court and city are imagined as lacking in the pastoral setting, many times referred to as the "golden world" or as a "garden" or like the Garden of Eden or Paradise. Shepherds usually are natural musicians playing on their "pipes" or "reeds," like wooden flutes.

Patriarch. *Noun*: (1) one of the twelve sons of JACOB, from whom the tribes of Israel descended; (2) one of the forefathers of the race from Adam through Abraham, Isaac, and Jacob.

Paul's Cross. A covered pulpit outdoors (within the precincts of ST. PAUL'S CATHEDRAL) where respected clergymen were asked to preach. Donne's first invitation to deliver a sermon there was in the spring of 1617. During the English civil war Parliament ordered it destroyed (1643). A cross now marks the approximate site.

Paul's Walk. See ST. PAUL'S CATHEDRAL.

Pembroke, Countess of. See SIDNEY, MARY, and CLIFFORD, LADY ANNE.

Perverse man that barrelled himself in a tub. Phrase in *DEVOTIONS UPON EMERGENT OCCASIONS*, "Meditation 3." See DIOGENES THE CYNIC.

Pervious. *Adjective*: (1) allowing passage, passable; (2) intelligible; (3) accessible.

Pestiduct. *Noun*: a channel or duct through which pestilence (plague) or another infection is conveyed (in *DEVOTIONS UPON EMERGENT OCCASIONS* ["Meditation 5"] Donne refers to a person who visits a sick individual as then being a possible "pestiduct").

Pestilence. *Noun*: plague.

Petrarch. See PETRARCHAN.

Petrarchan. Francesco Petrarca (1304–1374), better known as Petrarch, was an Italian poet most famous for his lyrics concerning his love for Laura, either a real or imagined lady. According to Petrarch, she was indeed a real lady who was married. By his account he met her in 1327, and she died in 1348. His lyrics portray his love for her, doomed to lack physical response and fulfillment. (JOSEPH HALL alludes to Laura in line 36 of his prefatory poem for Donne's *THE SECOND ANNIVERSARY*.) Among these lyrics those in the SONNET form give Petrarch his lasting fame and influence.

As an adjective "Petrarchan" can be found in reference to the particular sonnet form that Petrarch used (also called the "Italian") that was introduced into English by Sir Thomas Wyatt, eventually being employed and adapted by later Renaissance poets, including Donne. See SONNET.

But "Petrarchan" also refers to the content of these sonnets, particularly to the assumptions about love, women, and the relationship between men and women. The "Petrarchan love convention" is a particular set of literary assumptions, descriptions, and techniques that stem from Petrarch's sonnets to Laura that were continued and developed further by poets up to Donne's time. In a poem (or poems) employing this convention, the speaker typically is a man talking to or about the extremely beautiful woman he wishes to win as his love. This "Petrarchan lady" is beautiful, but she also is proud and disdainful. Usually she cruelly rejects the man's overtures to her. The man is her humble subject and worshipper in a kind of idealized and spiritualized love-religion, with the lady as a goddess (or, at least, presented as if on a pedestal above the lowly man). The lady ordinarily is blonde (the ideal) and is described with stereotypical characteristics and comparisons such as cheeks like roses, lips like cherries, teeth like pearls, eyes like suns or stars, breath like perfume, and hair like fine golden wire. With her goddesslike power, she has the ability to grant the man mercy ("pity") and life (by accepting him) or suffering and death (by rejecting him). She typically will not respond to the man, and this plunges the man into despondency and disillusionment. Despite his tears (like rain) and sighs (like winds), she cruelly rejects him: his passion causes him to "burn" with desire, but her rejection causes him to "freeze." The man sometimes must turn to other concerns and activities (going to war, reading philosophy, writing poetry, etc.) to purge him of his grief and to occupy his mind after this great disappointment in love. Many times the poet will use a "Petrarchan conceit," a lengthy, detailed analogy comparing the love or the lady or the man to something else (e.g., the love relationship to a journey at sea or a declaration of love to a military campaign). Cupid, with his "darts" (arrows), at times is portrayed as helping the lady to tempt, capture, tantalize, and torture her victims.

Phaëton (Phaëthon). Foolish son of the sun god PHOEBUS. He drove his father's chariot (the chariot of the sun) one day, but he could not guide the horses and almost burned up heaven and earth. Zeus killed him.

Phao (Phaon). See SAPPHO.

Philaenis. See SAPPHO.

Philip. Reference in line 96 of "SATIRE 3" to King Philip II of Spain, especially in his role as the leading secular ruler promulgating Roman Catholicism.

Philippus Aureolus Theophrastus Bombast von Hohenheim. See PARACELSUS.

Philo. See *EPIGRAMS*.

Philosopher, The. Called "Nature's secretary" in "Satire 1," "the Philosopher" (line 6) could refer to (1) ARISTOTLE or (2) any scientist or scientists in general. In some instances in the *SERMONS* Donne indeed refers to Aristotle simply by this phrase, rather than by his name.

Philosopher's Stone. See ALCHEMY.

Philosophy. *Noun*: (1) the love of wisdom; (2) advanced knowledge and study of natural, moral, and metaphysical matters; (3) science [natural philosophy]. Also see NEW PHILOSOPHY.

Phlegm. See HUMOR.

Phoebus. The god of the sun. Also referred to variously as Helios, Hyperion, and Apollo. Also see PHAETON.

Phoenix. Mythical bird that exists in only one representative of its species. It lives for five hundred years (one thousand years in some accounts), builds its own funeral pyre, consumes itself, and arises as a regenerated bird from the ashes. Commonly regarded as a symbol of resurrection, immortality, and the spirit rising from the body.

Phrygius. Personified character in "SATIRE 3" who represents a careless attitude toward searching for the true religion, since he assumes that they are all bad.

Phryne. Name of a famous courtesan of ancient Greece, used by Donne to represent any "painted" courtesan of any time: see "Phryne," one of the *EPIGRAMS*.

Physic. *Noun*: (1) medical science, medicine; (2) the medical profession; (3) medical treatment. *Adjective*: medical or medicinal.

Picture. *Noun*: (1) the art of painting, (2) portrait, (3) miniature portrait, (4) mental image or impression of something or someone.

Picture of mine which is taken in the shadows. Phrase in Donne's will referring to a famous portrait of himself. See KER, ROBERT (1).

Pillars. The "old Pillars" (or the "Pillars of Hercules") are the two mountains across from each other (in Spain and North Africa) at the western entrance to the Mediterranean Sea from the Atlantic Ocean. Between the two mountains is the Strait of Gibraltar, supposedly marking the western limit of the Old World.

Pillars, Seth's. See SETH.

Pindar (522–443 B.C.). Greek lyric poet, most admired and influential in the seventeenth and eighteenth centuries for his odes (especially by the poets that can generally be classified as CLASSICAL). Donne, however, mentions him in his own poetry once, only to emphasize the superiority of CORINNA over Pindar (see "A VALEDICTION: OF THE BOOK").

Pink. *Noun*: a decorative hole in a garment.

Pistolet. *Noun*: (1) a small firearm, an early name for a pistol; (2) a Spanish gold coin.

Pith. *Noun*: (1) spinal cord, (2) essential or central part.

Plaguy bill. A list of deaths caused by the plague during an epidemic. Posted weekly in each London parish.

Platan. *Noun*: the plane tree.

Plato (about 427–about 347 B.C.). Greek philosopher. Influenced by Socrates. Established a school (the Academy) in Athens about 387 B.C. and taught there until he died. His most famous and influential works are the dialogues, including the *Symposium*, the *Republic*, the *Timaeus*, and the *Laws*. For some of his and his followers' basic ideas, see PLATONIC.

Platonic. In its strict use, referring to the beliefs of PLATO, but, more generally and loosely, to the beliefs and later developments of his philosophy as pursued by followers such as Plotinus (3rd century A.D.) and Dionysius the Areopagite (the philosophy of these followers is more properly called "Neo-Platonic"). Donne himself generally does not make sharp distinctions between the doctrines of Plato himself and those of the Neo-Platonists. (Generally throughout this "Dictionary" the term "Platonic" is used in senses that embrace concepts from both Platonism and Neo-Platonism.)

Plato argues that each physical entity in this world is a mere shadow or imitation of the original or real Idea (or Form) of that kind or class of creature that exists in an eternal and unchanging realm beyond time and physical space. Since the soul knew these Ideas in its previous state of existence, human reason tries to recollect them. The ultimate Idea is the Idea of the Good. The greatest wisdom of man, as well as the greatest goal for man, is contemplation of and striving toward this Good. The soul and intellect, therefore, are valued as real, while the body and senses are comparatively unreal. From the value placed on the soul, it follows that true beauty is spiritual and that true love is spiritual. Union of spirits, then, is "Platonic love" and is a reality beyond mere physical union of lovers. A lover also is severely limited if he or she contemplates only the beauty of a single individual when one should ascend to beauty of the many in physical bodies and then higher to intellectual beauty and then higher to the beauty of the Idea.

Neo-Platonism suffused Plato's thought with mystical and/or Christian concepts, effecting a reconciliation of philosophies. Plotinus developed the precise argument that the "Absolute" or "One" (source of all beauty, truth, and goodness) generates everything material and spiritual in the world. Since God is easily identified as the "One," Plotinus's arguments fostered development of more specifically Christian Neo-Platonism by AUGUSTINE, medieval Christian philosophers, and such Renaissance Christian humanists as CASTIGLIONE. They saw God at the top of that stair of love ascended by one's soul through the help of reason. The beauty of the body gives only an external hint of the beauty and goodness of the soul within, and that soul in turn reflects its divine origin. In ideal love conventions (expressed most memorably for the writers of the Renaissance, including Donne, in Sir Thomas Hoby's translation of Castiglione's *THE COURTIER*) the ideal courtier (or lover) resists the temptations of the senses and physical attraction through passion by asserting his reason to overcome passion. His angelic and Godlike reason leads him up the ladder of love to a sense of spiritual beauty in the one woman, in all women, over everything beautiful in the world, and ultimately to a ravishment with heavenly beauty as the soul ascends the ladder into a union with God. See also HIERARCHY, THE HEAVENLY.

Play. *Noun*: (1) active, bodily exercise; (2) amusement or recreation; (3) sexual indulgence; (4) gambling; (5) drama, dramatic performance.

Player. *Noun*: (1) one who participates in a game, (2) a gambler, (3) an actor.

Pleas, the. The Court of Common Pleas.

Pleasure. *Noun*: (1) enjoyment, delight; (2) sensuous, physical enjoyment; (3) sensual, sexual enjoyment; (4) the source of or object that gives enjoyment.

Pliny the Elder (23–79). Roman historian, encyclopedist, biographer, soldier, and advisor to the Emperors Vespasian and Titus. His reputation rests on his surviving *Natural History*, a compendium that ranges over various fields of ancient science. When Mt. Vesuvius erupted in 79, he went there to help citizens in danger and to observe the event closely. He was killed by smoke at the base of the volcano, an event that Donne alludes to in "Meditation 12" of *DEVOTIONS UPON EMERGENT OCCASIONS* (but Donne incorrectly says that his death occurred at ETNA). Donne also refers many times to Pliny the Elder (as well as to his nephew and adopted son PLINY THE YOUNGER) in the *SERMONS*.

Pliny the Younger (62–112). Roman orator, statesman, and administrator. Served under the Emperors Domitian, Nerva, and Trajan. Nephew and adopted son of PLINY THE ELDER. His written orations (except for the "Panegyric on Trajan") have not survived, but his letters survive in ten books that make his literary reputation. They are to friends, relatives, and the Emperor Trajan and are interesting as history, biography, and character studies. Donne refers to him in several *SERMONS*.

Plotinus. See PLATONIC.

Plutarch (45?–125?). Greek biographer and essayist. Studied mathematics and philosophy at Athens. Held municipal posts at Chaeronea and directed a school there that emphasized philosophy. He also served as a priest at Delphi. His most famous and influential work is *Parallel Lives* that presents, in paired accounts, lives of Greek and Roman statesmen, orators, legislators, and soldiers. His *Moral Essays* treat philosophy, history, religion, education, literature, politics, love, PLATONIC subjects, and other topics. He employs many anecdotes in both the *Lives* and *Essays* that make his writing vivid and entertaining. Plutarch emphasizes moral and ethical lessons in his writing and was widely read by people of the Renaissance, including Shakespeare, BACON, and Donne. Donne's *SERMONS* frequently refer to and quote Plutarch.

Pluto. In Greek mythology, god of the underworld, of Hades. Also called "Hades."

Polesworth. See GOODYER and ST. EDITH.

Politic. *Adjective*: shrewd, cunning, diplomatic.

Polypus. A special use of the word describes a type of cancerous tumor on a mucous surface.

Pompey, Gnaeus (106–48 B.C.). Pompey the Great. Roman general and statesman whose impressive victories in Sicily and Africa served as the justification for his being given in 81 B.C. a Roman triumph (great triumphal procession), even though it was unlawful to grant such to one so young and unqualified to be a magistrate (a dictator, consul, or praetor).

Possess. *Verb*: (1) to reside in or occupy; (2) to hold as property, to own; (3) to have [as an attribute or quality]; (4) to seize or take; (5) [of a demon or spirit] to occupy, dominate, and control a body or other entity; (6) to have another person sexually, to have sexual intercourse.

Powder. *Noun*: (1) gunpowder; (2) cosmetic in the form of powder for face or skin or hair.

Powers. See HIERARCHY, THE HEAVENLY.

Pox. *Noun*: (1) reference to several diseases characterized by "pocks" or pustules on the skin; (2) most commonly used by Donne and others of his time to mean syphilis: Donne and others believed that syphilis came from and was prevalent in France and Italy, and they refer to these assumptions in their writing (see, for example, lines 101–104 in "Satire 1").

Practice (practise). *Noun*: (1) an action, (2) habitual action, (3) repeated action or exercise for learning something, (4) a scheme or plot. *Verb*: (1) to do or perform an action, (2) to do or perform habitually or constantly, (3) to perform repeatedly in order to study or to acquire skill or proficiency in something, (4) to scheme or plot or plan.

"Prayer." See *DEVOTIONS UPON EMERGENT OCCASIONS.*

Prefer. *Verb*: (1) to advance in status or promote; (2) to offer, present, recommend; (3) to hold one thing before others in esteem, to like better.

Prepare. *Verb*: (1) to make ready, set in order, equip; (2) to make ready mentally or spiritually; (3) to study for a lesson or speech or sermon, etc.; (4) to make ready for a journey; (5) to go.

Prerogative. *Noun*: (1) an exclusive right or privilege, (2) precedence or superiority.

Press. In some contexts, "oppress."

Prester Jack. Mythical "Priest John" who supposedly ruled in the Orient in the Middle Ages. Referred to in line 26 of "Upon Mr. Thomas Coryat's Crudities."

Pretend. *Verb*: (1) to stretch, extend, or put forward; (2) to profess or claim by right; (3) to put forward as a reason or excuse; (4) to allege; (5) to declare falsely in order to deceive; (6) to intend, design, or plan; (7) to attempt, to try; (8) to portend, to presage; (9) to aspire.

Prevent. *Verb*: (1) to anticipate or prepare for; (2) to arrive before, to precede, to outrun; (3) to outdo or surpass; (4) to forestall by precautionary measures; (5) to cut off or preclude someone or something from an action; (6) to stop or hinder; (7) to frustrate or defeat.

Prime Mover. See FIRST MOVER.

"Primrose, The." One of the *SONGS AND SONNETS.* Each stanza of the poem contains ten lines, and each half of each stanza is made up of five lines that are distributed as two short lines added to three longer lines: the form thus reflects the importance especially of the numbers "5" and "10" in the poem, but also of the numbers "2" and "3" that in sum make "5."
    In the first stanza the man speaking presents himself walking on a hill so full of primroses that they would equal the

number of drops in a shower of rain: each drop could conceivably fall on a primrose of its own.   There the drop might become "MANNA"—either simply honeydew or the miraculous food provided for the Israelites in Exodus.   This allusion actually seems a strange combination of both the Christian and the classical—the shower from heaven almost seems a multiplicity of Zeuses falling in a shower on their Danaes: just as Danae was impregnated by Zeus in the form of a shower, so do these drops beget fertility and growth in the primroses.   Significantly, in the poem the primrose symbolizes the female, and the speaker is searching for one to represent his "true love."   In Donne's time "HIS" was commonly used for the possessive "its," but in line 4 here the word strongly retains masculine connotations: each drop is like the male finding and claiming *his* own female (primrose), and the resultant fertility will "grow manna," possibly punning on the "man" within "manna." Zeus grew Perseus out of Danae, and this principle seems to be reflected by the drops, flowers, and fertility on the hill, in a foreshadowing symbol of the poem's subject—the matching and mating of males and females.   The starlike form and seemingly infinite number of flowers on the hill correspond to the Milky Way galaxy (lines 5–7).   The man walks to find a "true love"—i.e., a flower to symbolize a woman he wishes to love, but in Donne's time this flower would be an unusual four-petalled or six-petalled primrose (a five-petalled one being the ordinary), either of which was usually considered to be a sign of faithful love, and indeed such flowers were called "true loves."   (This background regarding symbolism of both flowers and numbers in this poem is probably best explained by Redpath—see "Selected Bibliography: Works.") In searching for an exceptional flower, the speaker concludes that he then must be yearning for an exceptional woman as his true love—one that is either more or less (see "OR . . . OR") than an ordinary woman (comparable to the five-petalled flower).

The second stanza presents the speaker facing the problem of whether to seek a six-petalled or a four-petalled primrose.   He realizes now that, if he seeks a "four," it implies that he is seeking a lady love that is less than the ideal potential in woman ("scarce any thing"): perhaps he implies that she would be only arms and legs—four members comparable to four petals—clinging to him only physically, sexually, animalistically.   In other words, she would lack the fifth projection from her center or trunk or body: she would lack a head (comparable to the fifth petal) and therefore would never think or even have a rational dimension to elevate her above the physical.   (Contrast this symbolism with the symbolism of five, given below.)   But, on the other hand, a six-

petalled primrose would symbolize a lady love more than a
normal woman—i.e., she might be elevated to the extreme of
intellect and spirit, completely ignoring the physical nature of
woman and "sex." (Cirlot [see "Selected Bibliography: General
Background"] notes that in number symbolism six represents both
the soul and virginity.) She might want a relationship that is pure
intellect, pure study, without normal human passion combined in
this "love." The man realizes that both of these types would be
"monsters"—freaks, unnatural creations. So, his implied solution is
that the happy medium, the ordinary "five," is better after all—in
primrose and woman. It symbolizes the woman who blends the
physical-emotional with the intellectual-spiritual in human nature
and love. (Cirlot [see "Selected Bibliography: General Background"]
notes that five represents the four limbs of the body and the head
that controls them.) The speaker, in joking cynicism, ends the
second stanza assuming that, however, some falseness will always
reside in women; therefore, he prefers the falseness that a real
and normal woman can artfully scheme herself, over the falseness
that Nature might give (i.e., in creating a "monster" of a woman
that is "more" or "less" than a normal woman).

   In stanza three the speaker endorses the ordinary primrose
(the five-petalled one) just as he subscribes to the ordinary
woman. The number "5" is "mysterious" in the sense that it is
symbolic and magical. Jokingly pursuing and adapting the
symbolism of numbers, the man speaking (lines 25–27) says that
"ten" is the highest number on the decimal scale: ten represents
unity, totality, and perfection, and the speaker makes the
assumption that this number represents man. Since he has
already said that "five" represents woman, he implies that woman
is half the value of man and deservedly can love or equal only
half of a man (5+5=10)! Then to twist his joke another way (and
to end the poem making a kind of peace with women), the man
says that, if this is not a pleasing representation of matters to
women, one can argue that all numbers are either odd or even
and that the first two numbers (not including "1") that make an
odd and even sequence are "2" and "3," the sum of which is "5."
So, in this sense of containing the first and thus all odd and even,
there is a unity, a wholeness also encompassed in "5," just as in
"10." Thus, that a woman can equal a man and can take all of a
man, the speaker is willing to grant. Again, the form of the poem
seems to express this ultimate equivalency in relating and
combining man and woman, since each stanza may be expressed
in lines as (2+3) + (2+3) = 10. Important as well is the fact that
there are three stanzas of ten lines each, since "three" symbolizes

spiritual synthesis, the solution of the conflict of dualism, and the harmonic product of the action of unity upon duality (see Cirlot, cited above).

Primum Mobile. See FIRST MOVER.

Prince Henry. See STUART, HENRY.

Principalities. See HIERARCHY, THE HEAVENLY.

Print. *Noun*: crimping of pleats in a garment.

Problems. See *JUVENILIA: OR CERTAIN PARADOXES AND PROBLEMS.*

Profane. *Adjective*: (1) secular, common, civil, not sacred; (2) unholy, desecrating something that is holy or sacred; (3) irreverent, blasphemous, impious.

Progress. *Noun*: (1) a journey, (2) a state journey made by a royal or noble person, (3) a state procession.

Progress of the Soul, The. See *METEMPSYCHOSIS*.

"Prohibition, The." One of the *SONGS AND SONNETS*. The man speaking tells the lady at first to beware of loving him. He explains that he is not telling her this because he plans to respond coldly to her (being scornful to her as she was to him) and thus to make up for ("REPAIR") all of his own wasted breath (his earlier sighs for her) and his own wasted blood (his own tears [each tear was believed to draw a drop of blood from the heart]) by drawing on hers. No, the reason he prohibits her from loving him, he says, is that such tremendous joy coming so suddenly can end anyone's life ("our"—i.e., the truth applies to all humans), and so it will happen to this man if he is struck by the sudden joy of the lady's love. And this would be self-defeating to the lady, since the object of her love (the speaker) would be dead and her love would be frustrated. So, he repeats his warning to her about loving him.

The second stanza suddenly shifts to the reverse: he tells her to beware of hating him (or of gloating that she has victoriously won him even while hating him). He explains (in a way parallel to the first stanza) what he is *not* trying to do by this warning—he is not planning to become a punishing "officer" that will carry out his revenge on her. Rather, he claims, she will lose the very name or title ("STYLE") of "conqueror" if she kills him, rather than letting him live in order to display him as the conquered: this is comparable, say, to Octavius Caesar in Shakespeare's *Antony and Cleopatra* being thwarted by Cleopatra's death, since he could not then take her to Rome and parade her triumphantly as his conquered. Paradoxically, then, the speaker argues that if the lady kills him with her hate and thus reduces him to a "nothing," she also is herself being reduced or lessened (she becomes less than a conqueror). In a way parallel to the first stanza, he ends by repeating his warning—this time about hating, rather than loving. This leaves a quandary: what should she do, if love and hate are equally bad and destructive?

The third stanza solves the problem, albeit quite paradoxically: in essence, it says that, since the lady should not either love or hate him, she should both love and hate him! The force of one will eliminate the effects of the other: if she loves him, he will not die by hate as described in the second stanza; and if she hates him, he will not die by love as described in the first stanza. If she loves him, he will die a "gentler way" (line 19) than through the way proposed through hate making him a "nothing." Dying through "great joy" (line 6) is preferable. Almost certainly he is punning on "DIE" as sexual intercourse that accompanies that great joy, as well. On the other hand, if she also hates (line 20), then this will moderate the "too great" love enough to let him live(?). Another possibility, he says in line 21, is to let both love and hate decay themselves but to leave him alive. In any of these proposed ways he will still live. Editors differ on whether he will be (in line 22) her "stay" or her "stage": readers will find editions choosing one or the other of these. The original 1633 edition uses "stay," and the 1635 and later editions use "stage." I agree with the 1633 version and those modern editors who follow it. The speaker will live to be her "STAY," in the sense of her "support"— the support for her own love that otherwise will not be supported, as he says in stanza one. Also in line 22 he says that, if he lives, he then will be her "triumph" (in stanza two he argues that this is appropriate for her as a conqueror). So, he drives home his point in the last two lines that this solution (posed in the third stanza) is best for both her and him: if she both loves and hates him, she keeps alive him, her love, and her hate. (The fullest explanations of, and best help with, many of the difficulties of the poem— especially in the third stanza—are found in Redpath: see "Selected Bibliography: Works.")

Promethean. *Adjective*: referring to Prometheus, who stole fire from heaven, gave it to mankind, and was punished for it by Zeus (who had Hermes [MERCURY] chain him on Mount Caucasus with a vulture feeding on his liver). Eventually he was freed by Heracles (Hercules).

Promontory, the hopeful. The Cape of Good Hope, as referred to in line 307 of *METEMPSYCHOSIS*.

Proserpine. In mythology, wife of Pluto and Queen of Hades. She put some of her beauty into a box that Psyche was to deliver to Venus. However, Psyche opened the box to take some of the beauty for herself, saw nothing, and fell into a deep sleep.

Prove. *Verb*: (1) to test or try, (2) to find out or learn, (3) to experience, (4) to establish something as true, (5) to show the existence or reality or validity of something.

Pseudo-Martyr. Prose work by Donne published in 1610. The work stems from a controversy between King JAMES and the Roman Catholics after James began requiring in 1606 an Oath of Allegiance: Catholics had to swear that James is a lawful King which the Pope cannot depose, that they will defend the King, that they will reveal any conspiracies directed at James, and that they regard as impious and heretical the idea that rulers excommunicated by the Pope may be deposed or murdered by their subjects. The Roman Catholic Church ordered Catholics in England not to take the oath. King James published his own *Apology for the Oath of Allegiance* (1607), and, after the Roman Catholics responded in 1608, King James published his *Premonition to All Most Mighty Monarchs, Kings, Free Princes, and States of Christendom* (1609). Some clergymen in England published books defending King James and the oath. Donne felt that published defenses had been inadequate and decided to write his own; however, it must be recognized that such a defense of King James and his policies could lead to attention and advancement from the King at a time when Donne greatly desired such. Upon its publication Donne personally presented a copy to the King.

Donne's primary purpose, as stated on the title page, is to argue "that those which are of the Roman religion in this kingdom may and ought to take the Oath of Allegiance." Donne had a unique claim to be listened to, since he formerly was a Catholic and had a history of those in his ancestry who had suffered for their faith, and he does not hesitate to use his own understanding of the Roman Catholic faith and references to himself and his family as he writes the book. He does not use impassioned, slurring methods but rather reasoned argumentation, logic, temperance, and objectivity far beyond similar controversial books and pamphlets of the time. He does, of course, ultimately criticize and point out the fallacies in assumptions and actions of the extreme Roman Catholics, especially the JESUITS. Donne, in effect, argues that those who do not submit to both the lawful oath and the lawful secular King are subjecting themselves to death that is a suicide, rather than a martyrdom. He argues that their allegiance to the King does not contradict their religious belief.

Pseudo-Martyr probably is Donne's prose work that is least read today (and, indeed, one of the least popular of all of his works). The political immediacy and interest for Donne's time and place are lacking for a modern reader, and the work is almost unrelieved somberness, allusiveness, and tight argumentation. Autobiographical hints, his wide-ranging intellect, and his wit break through too infrequently. If Donne had written nothing but this work, he and it would be virtually unknown today. The final irony of the work is perhaps twofold: by justifying so thoroughly King James's secular authority, Donne undoubtedly hoped to receive significant secular advancement for himself; however, the King's response was to regard Donne's contribution as primarily a theological achievement, and he ultimately would only advance him in the Church of England. (Useful beginnings for further study of this prose work are the following [cited in "Selected Bibliography"]: Sypher's facsimile reproduction of the edition of 1610, with an introduction; Simpson's discussion in *A Study of the Prose Works of John Donne*; and Bald's discussion in *John Donne: A Life*.)

Ptolemaic. Referring to Ptolemy and/or his concept of the universe. See PTOLEMY.

Ptolemy (Claudius Ptolemaeus). Greek astronomer, mathematician, and geographer in Alexandria, Egypt, during the 2nd century. Formulated (by building on earlier observations) the basic concept of the universe generally known as the "Ptolemaic" view, although many of its ideas were, in the Middle Ages, fused with some from ARISTOTLE. Ptolemy argued that the universe is geocentric—i.e., earth is its center. He argued that the earth itself does not move. The other created entities (moon, sun, planets, and stars) revolve around the earth in concentric, solid, transparent SPHERES. The FIRST MOVER is the outermost sphere that gives the first motion to all of the spheres and maintains their harmony, resulting in the MUSIC OF THE SPHERES. His view of the universe was accepted from his own century without serious question until the early 16th century when COPERNICUS proposed the heliocentric view. Ptolemy's ideas were increasingly challenged and discredited by other scientists of the NEW PHILOSOPHY. Terms, ideas, and metaphors from the Ptolemaic astronomy are numerous in Donne's works, and Donne also uses the conflicting views of the Ptolemaic and the new astronomical concepts of his own time.

Pule. *Verb*: to whine.

Pulling prime. Drawing a winning card or cards in the game of primero.

Pure. *Adjective*: (1) not mixed or adulterated with anything else; (2) unsullied, uncorrupted, clean; (3) visually clear, transparent; (4) perfect; (5) genuine, real; (6) free from moral defilement, untainted by evil; (7) chaste, sexually undefiled.

Puritan. *Noun*: (1) a type of Protestant under Queen ELIZABETH and later who wished to "purify" the Church of England by further ridding it of what were regarded as corrupt practices and forms of worship remaining from the Roman Catholic Church, such as some of the hierarchical organization, ceremonies, clerical vestments, etc. For example, in "The Cross" Donne criticizes (through implications) the attitudes of such Puritans toward using the Cross in worship (such as in baptism) and toward worshippers making the sign of the cross as part of their devotions. Also, a document survives (see pp. 403–4 of Bald, listed in "Selected Bibliography: Life") to show that, in his position as Dean of ST. PAUL'S CATHEDRAL, Donne reprimanded a Puritan for refusing to kneel when expected to during the Divine Service. Several of Donne's *SERMONS* criticize some of the extreme contentions of Puritans and argue for the ideal middle-of-the-road church in the Church of England. Also see THINGS INDIFFERENT; (2) later loosely applied to one who separated from the Church of England for worship; (3) one who is, or wishes to be seen as, extremely precise and scrupulous in morality, religion, and manners, etc. For example, in "Satire 1" (line 27) Donne uses the word in this sense.

Puritanism. The doctrines and practices of the Puritans. See PURITAN.

Pursuivant. *Noun*: an official who executes warrants, but especially to search out Roman Catholics, particularly disguised priests and JESUITS.

Pyramus. Young man who loved Thisbe in ancient Babylon. OVID includes their story in his *Metamorphoses*. They lived in homes next to each other but were forbidden by their parents to see one another. There was a wall with a chink in it, however, between the houses, and they would speak and vow their love through it. They ran away to meet at Ninus's tomb outside the city. Thisbe, frightened away by a lioness, dropped her cloak. The lioness smeared it with blood, and Pyramus found it when he arrived. Mistaking it for a sign that Thisbe had been killed and had been carried away by beasts, Pyramus killed himself with his sword. Thisbe returned, found the dead Pyramus, and killed herself with his sword. Their blood turned the white mulberry fruit to red from then on. Their ashes were put into a single urn. They are the subject of "Pyramus and Thisbe," one of Donne's *EPIGRAMS*.

Q

Quarters. The bodies of criminals were sometimes cut in quarter-portions and placed in open areas, such as above city gates, as examples.

Quintessence. See ALCHEMY.

Quotidian. *Adjective*: (1) everyday or common, (2) daily, (3) [of a fever] recurring daily.

R

Rader, Matthew (1561–1634). Subject of "Raderus," one of the *EPIGRAMS*, as well as a person criticized in *IGNATIUS HIS CONCLAVE*. He was a German editor (and JESUIT) who published an expurgated edition of MARTIAL. In both the epigram and in the prose work, Donne refers to Raderus and others of the Jesuits as taking the action of "gelding" poets and authors (by cutting out words from their works in their censoring zeal).

Raderus. See RADER, MATTHEW.

"Raderus." See RADER and KATHERINE.

Rags (Ragges). *Noun:* (1) small fragments, pieces, or shreds; (2) worthless or tattered clothes.

Ralphius. Name of a character in one of Donne's two-line *EPIGRAMS* entitled "Ralphius" ("Compassion in the world again is bred: / Ralphius is sick, the broker keeps his bed"). It is decidedly ambiguous. Is Ralphius the pawnbroker who is sick and staying in bed and thus sparing the world his own viciousness while he is there? Or is Ralphius a man who is in debt to the pawnbroker and is spared from being dunned by the broker while Ralphius is sick (with the broker retaining Ralphius's bed as security)?

Rational Soul. See discussion of stanza five in "A VALEDICTION: OF MY NAME IN THE WINDOW."

Ravish. *Verb:* (1) to seize and carry off with violence, (2) to rape [sexually violate] a woman, (3) to carry away from earth, (4) to carry away [mystically] in spirit and not in body, (5) to fill with ecstasy or delight.

Receipt. *Noun:* (1) a place for the reception of people or things, (2) a chamber, (3) accommodation or provided space, (4) a prescription or list of ingredients in a medicine, (5) a recipe.

Reclaim. *Verb:* (1) to take back a person or thing; (2) in hunting and falconry, to tame an animal; (3) in falconry, to call back a bird that has been turned loose to fly. For the last two senses, see especially line 25 of "LOVE'S DIET" and line 32 of "Elegy on Mistress Boulstred."

Recusant. *Noun*: (1) one who rejects or refuses to abide by a particular authority or law, (2) a Roman Catholic in England who refused to attend the Church of England.

Relic. *Noun*: in religious use (especially Roman Catholic), an object or clothing or part of the body remaining as a memorial after the death of a saint, martyr, etc., and preserved for veneration.

"Relic, The." One of the *SONGS AND SONNETS*. The man speaking assumes that at some future time his own grave will be destroyed in order to make a "room" in which to bury someone else (humorously referred to as a "second guest"). This was a common practice in crowded burial plots at the time (alluded to by Shakespeare, for example, in *Hamlet* when the gravediggers unearth and throw out the bones and skull of Yorick while digging a grave for Ophelia). He then satirically compares a grave to a woman: as the grave receives more than one person, so does a woman sexually receive more than one man; and both graves and women are like beds in which people lie ("woman-head" means "womanly nature"). The speaker imagines that the man digging up his grave will see the bone of his arm circled with a bracelet of "BRIGHT" (probably simply "beautiful," but the word could also imply "of vivid color" and "glorious") hair. Such bracelets of hair from a beloved were love tokens. He thinks that the gravedigger will recognize this as the couple's means of assuring that the souls of both the man (whose bone it is) and the woman (whose hair it is) will rejoin and meet here for a little while at Resurrection Day before completing the piecing together of bodies and then ascending to heaven. (Resurrection is the "last day," and it is a "busy" one because of all the souls of all bodies whizzing around the earth to pick up pieces and form again the bodies.)

In the second stanza the man, however, ponders what might happen if this disturbing of his grave occurs either in a time period or in a political entity controlled by "mis-devotion": Donne apparently satirizes Roman Catholic "mis-devotion" that venerates the wrong things, such as "RELICS" and saints. If the discovery in his grave occurs under such false devotion, then he envisions his bone and the lady's hair being made "RELICS." In the middle line of the poem (line 17) the speaker first addresses the lady he is speaking to, referring to her (with significant reverence) as "Thou." He tells her that she will be regarded as Saint MARY

MAGDALEN and that he will be regarded as "something else," possibly implying that whatever or whoever will be chosen to be represented by his bone does not matter, since it will be elevated ridiculously for adoration by the people. (Several editors and other interpreters raise the possibility that Donne's "something else" may imply Christ, in light of how people of "mis-devotion" might interpret Christ's relation with MARY MAGDALEN in a rather warped way.) He says (in line 19) that "all women" and "some men" then will adore the two: Theodore Redpath (see "Selected Bibliography: Works") quite correctly notes that Donne may be satirically implying the greater credulity of women and/or their greater receptivity to romantic situations. In order to satisfy the people's craving for miracles in these relics (AQUINAS said that miracles occur with relics), the man offers this "paper" (on which the poem is written) to illustrate all of the miracles that these two "HARMLESS" lovers carried out.

The third stanza catalogs these "miracles." These two had a faithful love that was primarily intellectual and spiritual—i.e., PLATONIC. They were as little concerned with sexual differences as sexless angels are. Even their kisses were only polite greetings and farewells, not for passionate purposes while they were together. He says that they never consummated their love sexually, even though Nature allows the freedom to do so: he implies that it is man's law that sets restrictions on this freedom (state and ecclesiastical laws against fornication, adultery, etc.), but it is not man's law that caused them to refrain—they "miraculously" chose to do so themselves, since their love was entirely between their souls. He ends saying that, beyond these miracles in their love, the woman was the greatest miracle. He cannot even describe her within "MEASURE" (as "meter" or "poetry," but also as known "size" or "limit") and within language: he cannot do justice to her in the limits of this poem.

So, ending with both this high compliment of the lady and the acknowledgment that their love is of the highest spiritual nature makes us see that his cynical and bawdy comments about women and love in the first stanza have nothing to do with the kind of woman his lady is and the kind of love that he and the lady possess. They are unique and indeed true "miracles" set against ordinary humanity and ordinary love.

Relict. *Noun*: (1) a deserted or discarded person [see especially Donne's "LOVE'S USURY," line 7], (2) a surviving part, (3) a widow.

Remora. *Noun*: a sucking fish believed to be able to stop ships by attaching itself to them.

Repair. *Verb*: (1) to go [to a place], (2) to restore to a sound condition, (3) to furnish or provide with, (4) to replace decayed or damaged parts, (5) to renew or restore by making up for previous decay or loss.

Residence. In Donne's time, a special meaning in some contexts is "residue" or "deposit" or "sediment."

Rest. *Verb*: (1) to take repose by lying down; (2) to take repose by refraining from activity or effort; (3) to take repose by sleeping; (4) to lie in death or the grave; (5) to remain or stay; (6) to stop or cease at a certain point; (7) to be at peace or to have quiet of mind; (8) to be supported by something; (9) to rely upon, trust to, or depend upon something or someone; (10) to remain confident or hopeful; (11) to remain to be done: (12) to reside in or exist in.

Rhodian. See COLOSSUS.

Rhubarb. *Noun*: a medicine to purge choler (one of the HUMORS) and to reduce fever.

Rich, Essex. See CAREY, LADY.

Rich, Lettice. See CAREY, LADY.

Ride post. Shortened version of "ride in post": to ride in haste (i.e., as a courier with important mail rides speedily on his horse). See line 14 of "To Mr. B. B."

Rise. *Verb*: (1) to get up from sitting, lying, resting, sleeping, or sexual activity in bed; (2) to recover from sin, from a spiritual fall; (3) to come back from death or the grave, to experience resurrection; (4) to take up arms for battle; (5) to move above the earth's horizon [said of the sun and other heavenly bodies]; (6) to ascend; (7) to be elated with joy or hope; (8) to appear, spring up, come into existence; (9) to move into an erect from a flaccid condition [said bawdily of the penis].

Rochester, Viscount. See KER, ROBERT (2).

Round. *Verb*: to encompass.

Russell, Lucy. See BEDFORD, COUNTESS OF.

S

Sackville, Richard, third Earl of Dorset (1589–1624). Young nobleman whom Donne looked toward for some favors, patronage, and possible help in clearing debts. Knole, the home of the Earl, was close to the parish of Sevenoaks held by Donne. The Earl and Countess (Lady ANNE CLIFFORD) regarded Donne and his works highly, and Donne stayed at Knole as their guest on occasions. He appointed Donne as vicar of ST.-DUNSTAN'S-IN-THE-WEST. The Earl of Dorset is the likely recipient of Donne's "To E. of D. with Six Holy Sonnets," although it is not known which particular sonnets were sent to him. In this poem Donne attributes his own composition of the sonnets to the engendering creativity and intelligence of the Earl and compares him to an ALCHEMIST who can bring good gold out of bad elements.

Sad. *Adjective*: (1) serious, somber; (2) sorrowful, mournful.

St. Albans, Viscount. See BACON, SIR FRANCIS.

St. Ambrose. See AMBROSE, SAINT.

St. Augustine. See AUGUSTINE, SAINT.

St. Bernard. See BERNARD, SAINT, OF CLAIRVAUX.

St. Clement Danes. Church on the Strand, London, where Donne and his family worshipped while residing on DRURY LANE. His wife ANN MORE was buried here in 1617. Only a portion of the original stone church (in the tower) remains since its rebuilding in 1679 and later: Ann's tomb was lost in the rebuilding.

St. Cyprian. See CYPRIAN, SAINT.

St. Dunstan's-in-the-West. Church on Fleet Street, London, where Donne was vicar from 1624 until his death. He preached there frequently while Dean of ST. PAUL'S CATHEDRAL, to a congregation including many lawyers and judges. IZAAK WALTON was also a parishioner. The churchyard was the site of the shops of many printers and booksellers of the time. Donne took an active role in parish business and in repairing the church. The services were well-attended, and overcrowding in the pews was a continual problem. The church escaped the Great Fire of 1666, but it was demolished with a widening of Fleet Street in 1830 and a new church built on the site. A bust of Donne is on the east side of its porch.

St. Edith. See EDITH, Saint.

St. Hierome. See JEROME, SAINT.

St. Jerome. See JEROME, SAINT.

St. John Chrysostom. See CHRYSOSTOM, SAINT JOHN.

St. Lucy (283–304). Virgin martyr of Syracuse in Sicily. She consecrated her virginity to God. Legend says that a powerful aristocrat was attracted by the beauty of her eyes and wished to marry her. She then plucked out her eyes, gave them to him, and stated that she wanted to live only for God. She was denounced for not marrying and would have been burned, but God saved her. Her eyes miraculously were restored. She was killed by sword. She is the patron saint of sight. St. Lucy's Day is December 13, regarded as the shortest day of the year in the Julian (or Old Style) calendar used in Donne's time. Her day is celebrated as a festival of light. The name *Lucy* originates from the Latin for *light*, and a folk saying about St. Lucy and her day is "Lucy light: shortest day, longest night." Donne particularly uses her and her day in "A NOCTURNAL UPON ST. LUCY'S DAY, BEING THE SHORTEST DAY," but he also refers to her in *THE SECOND ANNIVERSARY*, line 120.

St. Michael's [Islands]. Another name for the AZORES.

St. Paul's Cathedral. Cathedral in London where Donne was Dean from 1621 until his death. The building in Donne's time was the fourth one to be built on the site that originally had held a Roman temple dedicated to Diana. This fourth Cathedral was built in the late 11th century and existed until destroyed by the Great Fire in 1666: it was much larger than the present (fifth) Cathedral built by Christopher Wren. Its nave was known as "Paul's Walk" and had become, during the late 16th and early 17th centuries, an area in which merchants noisily carried on business, people and animals traveled through to reach one street from another, lawyers talked to clients, and the baptismal font and tombs were used as counters upon which merchandise was displayed, traded, and sold. It is in this area that the measurement of a foot was developed: it literally was the length of the carved foot of the statue of Algar in the Cathedral. Printers' shops and houses existed in the churchyard, in the precincts of St. Paul's. During Donne's tenure as Dean, with impetus from KING JAMES, KING CHARLES, WILLIAM LAUD, and INIGO JONES, some attempts at much-needed repairs began, but most were carried out after Donne's death.

Donne preached in the Cathedral, as well as at PAUL'S CROSS very near it. As Dean over the Chapter of a Cathedral with many clerical officers, employees, and much property, Donne's duties involved church appointments, financial affairs, administrative responsibilities, social obligations, numerous meetings, in addition to his spiritual duties and sermons both at St. Paul's and at his benefices (such as at ST. DUNSTAN'S-IN-THE-WEST and BLUNHAM). Donne's funeral and burial were in the Cathedral. A monument of Donne—a statue of him in a death shroud and standing on a burial urn—is the only piece from St. Paul's before the Great Fire to survive. Donne arose out of his sickbed to pose for it shortly before his death, and it was sculpted by NICHOLAS STONE after the death. It stands today in the south aisle of the choir.

St. Thomas Aquinas. See AQUINAS, SAINT THOMAS.

St. Valentine. See VALENTINE, SAINT.

Salisbury, Catherine Howard (Cecil), Countess of (died in 1672). Daughter of the Earl of Suffolk. Married William Cecil, 2nd Earl of Salisbury, in 1608. Sister to Frances Howard, Countess of Somerset (see KER, ROBERT [2]). Donne's friend and one of his correspondents in the *LETTERS*, GEORGE GARRARD, served the Earl and Countess of Salisbury and suggested that Donne write some verses to the Countess. The result is his *VERSE LETTER* (dated August, 1614) and titled "To the Countess of Salisbury," the "Noble Lady in whose presence you are," as Donne calls her in a letter to Garrard (*Letters to Several Persons of Honour*, 1651, pp. 259–61).

Salisbury, 1st Earl of. See CECIL, ROBERT.

Sallet. Salad.

Sam(p)son. Son of Manoah of the Danites who was so strong that he killed a lion with his hands. Married a Philistine woman who betrayed Samson: she talked him into revealing the solution to a riddle he had posed to the Philistines about the lion's carcass with honey in it, and she then told it to her people. After his father-in-law kept Samson from his wife and gave her to another man, Samson tied firebrands on the tails of three hundred foxes and let them run through the Philistines' fields of grain, thus burning their crops and vineyards. The Philistines later tried to hold Samson bound in cords, but he burst them and then killed one thousand of them with the jawbone of an ass. Eventually he loved a woman named Delilah who, for silver offered her by the Philistines, finally had Samson tell her that the secret of his strength lay in his uncut hair. She took the money from the Philistines and had Samson shaved while he slept. When he awoke, his strength was gone. The Philistines took him, blinded him, and put him in prison in Gaza. His hair grew while he was imprisoned; therefore, when thousands of Philistines gathered and brought Samson there in order to mock him, he was able to push apart the two pillars his hands were touching and to destroy the building, the Philistines, and himself. See Judges 13–16.

Sanserra. Sancerre, town in France where Protestants were under siege by Roman Catholics in 1573 for nine months. The residents were forced to use leather, books, belts, and anything else available for food to fight the terrible prospect of starvation.

Sappho (late 7th century B.C.). Greek female poet who was friend to many young girls living near her on the island of Lesbos. Many of her poems were written for them and express great affection and emotion. She was married and had a daughter. Her affection for women on Lesbos originated the meaning "female homosexual" for the word "lesbian."

Some editors still question whether "Sappho to Philaenis" actually was written by Donne, but it (in contrast to some other dubious ones) did appear in the first edition of Donne's poems in 1633. It presents Sappho addressing quite sensually "Philaenis," the name itself meaning "female friend." In the poem Sappho refers to her own love for "Phao" (Phaon), a young man: an apocryphal story says that when he rejected her Sappho jumped from a cliff into the sea (a purported action disregarded in the poem).

Sara(h). Half-sister and wife of Abram (Abraham). When a famine drove them into Egypt, they did not reveal that they were husband and wife. Pharaoh heard of her beauty, took her into his family, but God sent plagues on Pharaoh because he had Abram's wife. Therefore, he returned her to Abram with gifts of servants and cattle. When she was old and far past the normal childbearing stage, God promised her a son. She did become pregnant, and Isaac was born, to her great joy. See especially Genesis 12 and 16–21.

"Satire 3." One of the five *SATIRES*. One manuscript adds to the title "Of Religion" and another adds "Upon Religion." A recurring problem to Donne and others of his time was how one is to determine what religion, in the midst of many churches and factions, is indeed the true religion. The problem similarly appears in the one of the *HOLY SONNETS* beginning "SHOW ME, DEAR CHRIST, THY SPOUSE SO BRIGHT AND CLEAR."

.The speaker (Donne?) begins with conflicting emotions: "pity" prevents his "spleen" (considered to be the seat of scorn within one) from venting itself, while "scorn" prevents his tears (evidence of "pity") from flowing. He cannot, then, either laugh scornfully or weep pitifully: neither of these is the "wise" way. He will attempt to purge his emotions and convey his satire by "railing," bitterly and harshly scolding or criticizing the maladies he perceives ("worn" because of existing a long time). His railing then begins with the contrast made (in lines 5–16) between pagan virtue and Christian religion. His question in lines 5–7 implies that those of the "first blinded age," of pre-Christian times that did not have the light of Christian truth, were devoted to their ideal of virtue even more than Christians are to the Christian religion. Lines 8–9 point out (again by the implications of a question) that the pagan philosophers lived by a virtue that overcame lusts only for the sake of honor in this earthly life, without any hope of or attempt to gain a life after death; therefore, it is quite ironic that Christians, with their hope of gaining heavenly salvation and another life by the way they live on earth, do not seem to be overcoming lusts as well as the pagans did. Lines 10–15 imply that "we" (those with the advantage of divine revelation and the Christian faith) have far better "means" than the pagans did by which to live a virtuous life and achieve salvation but that we may find ourselves "damned" to hell because we did not use the means available to us to achieve salvation. The crowning irony is that some of those "blind philosophers" of ancient times lived such a morally and ethically strict life that they may be regarded as having faith that meets the requirements, through God's grace, to achieve salvation: Christ's grace can be imputed to such a one just as if he had faith in Christ. Line 16 insists that this fear of not gaining salvation, even though the means of doing so are easily at hand, is the greatest fear that takes the greatest courage to face and the one that the individual should consider above all others.

Lines 17–42 then speak of false courage and false foes, as opposed to true courage and true foes in order to define these true foes and then argue what is needed to do battle with them and ultimately conquer them. Lines 17–28 note that the courage men are ready to show in worldly adventures and values is false courage. It is false courage for Englishmen to go help the Dutch who were rebelling against the Spanish in the Low Countries (as the English had helped and were still doing at the time Donne was writing), for anyone to risk death in a ship at war on the sea, for anyone to dive deep into the sea or deep in caves of the earth, for anyone to risk his life on a ship trying to discover the Northwest Passage through frozen seas and earth, for anyone to try to be like a salamander (a lizard thought to be able to survive in fire) or to be like the divine "CHILDREN IN THE OVEN" (Shadrach, Meshach, and Abednego) and attempt to "bear" (i.e., to withstand) just for the sake of "gain" (making money) the "fires of Spain" (i.e., to risk receiving the punishment of burning heretics that was ordered by the Spanish Inquisition and/or to suffer the oppressive heat of Spain and its territories) and the "line" (to suffer the heat of the equator, the equatorial line). The countries of the tropics and equator are like "limbecks" (see ALCHEMY) to the bodies of Englishmen, heating them up and causing moisture (perspiration) to distill out of them. Also ranked with these acts of false courage is insulting with "poisonous words" or swordfighting with someone who does not show proper respect for a man's lady love (not addressing her as a goddess). All of these worldly actions, then, are labeled as worthless "courage of straw" (line 28). Such a one showing this so-called "courage" actually is a "coward" who only seems to be "bold" (line 29), because he actually has forsaken his true duty as a sentinel in God's garrison in this world: a person should guard against the "foes" of both God and himself, rather than flitting off, leaving his post to go fight extraneous, "forbidden wars" with the Spanish, other men, etc. So, true courage is being a true sentinel and soldier for God in the world (and not for a particular country or lady love or for making money only). The false foes, then, are other nations, countries, etc. Who are the true foes? Line 33 insists that one should know them to be able to recognize them, battle them, defeat them. The true foes for one who is on spiritual duty as a sentinel for God are, in essence, the three traditional Christian foes (the same ones mentioned by Donne in the *HOLY SONNET* beginning "SINCE SHE WHOM I LOVED HATH PAID HER LAST DEBT"), the world, the flesh, and the devil. The devil (lines 33–35) would gladly (FAIN) give you his whole realm (hell) to acquire you, doing it out of hate, though, not out of love. The world (lines 36–39) is becoming old and deteriorated (a common belief in Donne's time), and you are loving in her a worn-out prostitute (that grants only secular, sensual pleasure at a price and that pleasure itself is of poor quality). Flesh (lines 40–42) is itself death because (1) the original Fall of Adam and Eve, by the weakness of the flesh, introduced death [and death now destroys flesh] and (2) the joys of the flesh [its excesses and indulgences] destroy flesh. The "you" being addressed seems quite irrational to love flesh, then, especially since the soul (that gives the body its power to experience joy) is loathed by this person. All three of these "foes" are mistakenly being embraced as friends by the "you" of the poem.

To show one how to illustrate true courage and how to learn to defeat the true foes, Donne urges in line 43 to "seek true religion." But this raises the central problem he has been building toward: "O where" does one find this "true religion"? In lines 43–69 Donne presents several men (personified characters) who represent proponents of various religions or attitudes toward religion. Mirreus does not find true religion "here" (in England) but thinks it is found at Rome (in the Roman Catholic Church): Roman Catholicism was indeed "unhoused" in England when the Church of England replaced Roman Catholicism in its very buildings and church positions. Mirreus relies on tradition and history to indicate the true church: just because it existed "a thousand years ago," he assumes it is the true one. And he loves the "rags," the outer, showy clothing (the ceremonies, art, statuary, etc.) emphasized in Catholicism. The Roman Catholic Church is here described as "her" and "she," a beautifully-adorned woman. (One notes that Donne describes this church and the succeeding churches and types of religious beliefs as if they were kinds of women: this is very similar to the metaphorical pictures of Christ's bride in "SHOW ME, DEAR CHRIST, THY SPOUSE SO BRIGHT AND CLEAR.") The second type is Crants who is not attracted to such "brave loves" as in the showy beauty of the Roman Catholic Church. In fact, Crants chooses the opposite in the plain, simple, unadorned, drab church found in Protestant CALVINISM—in GENEVA, rather than in Rome. The third type is Graius who does find the true religion "here" in England: he simply accepts the

Church of England as it has been given to him by his English
forebears.   Donne suggests that he perhaps accepts it too easily
and too unquestioningly, since he seems just blandly to take the
word of Anglican "preachers" that it is the true church (when
these preachers themselves may be corrupt and selling their
church, as pimps ["bawds"] sell women, for their ambition to gain
lucrative and high positions within that church).   Also, Graius may
be choosing to live unthinkingly under all of the laws passed
during the reigns of Henry VIII, Edward VI, and ELIZABETH I that
regulate the state church and that punish those not abiding by
them.   So, Graius is like the ward who has to accept the woman
that his guardian proposes he marry: if he does not do so, he will
have to "pay values"—i.e., under the law he would have to pay his
guardian a fine designated as the "value of the marriage."   This is
analogous to the fact that someone who refuses to worship in the
state church must pay a fine (under the Act of Uniformity of
1559, this was indeed the law).   The fourth type is Phrygius who
is called "careless" because he naturally assumes that all religions
are bad and takes no pains or cares at all to ponder the serious
nature of finding the true religion and does not bother to search
for any good beneath the appearance of badness.   He carelessly
gives up the search for the good church, just as a cynical lover
might for a good wife.   His name may be based on the ancient
Phrygians who had various gods forced on them.   The fifth type is
represented by Gracchus, the opposite of Phrygius.   Gracchus
assumes that all religions are good, that one is as good as another.
To him, all churches are alike beneath their surface appearances
(as all women in various countries are alike beneath their
different clothing).   Paradoxically, Gracchus is blind because of too
much light—i.e., since he sees the light of truth everywhere he
turns, he fails to distinguish and perceive real and serious
differences and falsenesses.   Gracchus may be named by Donne
after the Roman family of that name that promoted the ideals of
democracy and equality.

   Beginning with line 69, Donne tells the "you" that, in contrast
to the five types just outlined, the individual must take the matter
of religion much more seriously.   One must not be influenced by
("unmoved") such insubstantial and ridiculous reasons and
pressures as the five types are in choosing something as
important as the true religion that will offer salvation for the soul.
"Of force" (i.e., by necessity) there is only one right one, and the
individual must use all possible means to search it out.   Lines 71–
75 argue that one must go back to the roots of the true church by
examining all the opinions of previous humans.   Even if one has to

go back to examine the truth existing before the Fall to achieve the "best" religion, one should do so, since falsehood began to corrupt truth even when Adam and Eve fell in disobeying God. The act of searching in itself is of great value, because it means that one is not an atheist ("of none," of no religion) and that one is not of the "worst" religion. One may discover through a close examination and discrimination of religions that to "adore" (like Roman Catholics) or to "scorn an image" (like the extreme anti-Catholic Protestants such as the Calvinists and Puritans) or simply to "protest" (like Protestants generally) may all be bad: i.e., one must search and examine to be sure, rather than simply to facilely accept any one way of worship as true and good (lines 76–77). Lines 77–79 use the analogy of someone on a strange road ("in strange way"): if he ponders the alternatives carefully, he is not straying; but, if he "sleeps" intellectually and acts without thinking and takes the wrong turn, then he is straying. The same is true on the road to truth. Lines 79–82 present personified Truth standing at the top of a large, high, and rough hill. The individual wishing to reach Truth must undergo an arduous, indirect journey requiring length in both time and space, and Donne effectively conveys the frustrating circularity with the repetition of "about must" in line 81. But it is an active struggle for truth that one must be willing to undertake before the night of death comes (alluding to a portion of John 9:4, "the night cometh, when no man can work"). The search requires both "hard deeds" achieved through bodily pains and "hard knowledge" gained through mental endeavors. One must both see the light of truth and attempt to penetrate it and understand it (made analogous to seeing the light of the sun).

Line 89 to the end of the poem concerns the contrast between the individual's own discovering and maintaining of the truth, as opposed to letting other human individuals of authority and power determine matters for one. Donne insists that one should "keep the truth" that one finds. He says that God has not given kings the absolute freedom to kill anyone they wish and that secular kings are not God's spiritual vicars: they are instead only the executioners carrying out the will of Fate (i.e., they are not Fate or God themselves). So, there is an important boundary between a secular ruler's worldly power and God's spiritual power. The person concerned with the salvation of his soul on Judgment Day (the "last day") must only obey God's laws and not man's laws in the spiritual realm: otherwise, he is both a "fool" and a "wretch" (lines 93–95). (The soul, referred to as "she" in line 94, typically is regarded as feminine in the Renaissance. See other examples of this concept and language in "SINCE SHE WHOM I LOVED HATH PAID HER LAST DEBT" and "BATTER MY HEART, THREE-PERSONED GOD, FOR YOU.") The speaker then sarcastically asks "you" what it will profit ("boot") you at the Last Judgment to tell Christ that you believed a certain way because a "Philip" (Roman Catholic King Philip II of Spain) or a "Gregory" (Roman Catholic Pope Gregory [most likely either Gregory XIII or Gregory XIV] or a "Harry" (Protestant, Anglican King Henry VIII of England) or a "Martin" (Protestant MARTIN LUTHER) told you to believe this? Innumerable people can use this excuse for their beliefs, but those beliefs are completely contradictory; therefore, how can they all be the true religion that will grant you salvation? The fate of your own soul is up to you, and you alone will be answerable to Christ for the belief you have chosen for yourself. Lines 100–103 explicitly summarize Donne's contention that one must indeed recognize the boundary between secular and spiritual power and just whom (a king or God) one must obey in each separate realm. The clear implication is that some secular powers and authorities have "passed," have crossed over, the boundary into God's territory and have encroached on God's power. One is committing "idolatry" to worship or obey a king or pope or any secular authority claiming to be God. Lines 103–110 then implicitly summarize, through a METAPHYSICAL CONCEIT, the entire argument about the relations between the individual, his own belief, the state of his soul, secular power, God's power, and eternal destiny. "Power" is like a stream that flows from its "head": the head of the stream is God, the source of all power. (Compare God as the head of the stream of love in "SINCE SHE WHOM I LOVED HATH PAID HER LAST DEBT.") The "blest flowers" that dwell at the head of the stream are symbolic of souls that remain rooted to God and his power and the spiritual domain of God: these "flowers" thrive, like souls will live and flourish eternally. But if the flower gives itself up to be carried by the stream of power that flows away from its source (the stream representing the power of kings, popes, and other claimants to authority in the world), then the flower is beaten on a violent journey to the "sea" where it is lost. The "flower," then, that leaves its source is a "soul" of one who mistakenly chooses to let itself be spiritually governed by the dictates of a "Philip" or "Harry," etc., in this world (those who *claim* power unjustly from God). Those souls who choose this stream of men's power, rather than choosing to trust in God himself for nurturing in spiritual truth, will indeed "perish" in the "sea" of eternity, through eternal damnation.

Satires. A group of five poems published in the first edition of Donne's poems in 1633. Although dating remains uncertain, most scholars feel that they were written during the 1590's. Donne's models were Roman satirists such as JUVENAL. The more modern assumption that satire is primarily humorous had not developed by Donne's time: in fact, satire could provoke laughter, but also it could properly be very severely critical, indignant, harsh, and biting toward types of people, occupations, morals, ethics, beliefs, and vices. And typical also are the harsh words, stresses, and sounds in the poetry that help to convey these feelings. The satirist could be a quite somber individual engaged in a most serious and deeply-felt criticism of wrongs and ignorances. These qualities are indeed found in Donne's *Satires.*

In "Satire 1" the speaker stabs at many types of individuals, including the contemplative person, the active person, a soldier, a courtier, a judge, a flatterer, the worldly person, the lecherous person, and the fop. "Satire 2" concerns bad poets and bad lawyers. "SATIRE 3" comments on religions and the search by the individual for truth in religion. "Satire 4" treats court corruption. "Satire 5" portrays the meanness of both legal suitors and figures in authority.

In this "Dictionary" the most famous and most frequently anthologized "SATIRE 3" is discussed fully in a separate entry. The content of the other four satires has been examined for elements to be included as other entries.

Schedule. *Noun*: a paper appended to a document to provide explanatory or supplementary information.

Schismatic. *Noun*: a person who breaks with a specific church or faith or who promotes any breach (schism) in unity.

School. *Noun*: (1) place for instruction; (2) a group of people holding similar beliefs and principles; (3) a body of teachers and scholars; (4) the SCHOOLMEN, scholastic philosophers of the Middle Ages.

Schoolmen. The scholastic philosophers—medieval European university teachers, philosophers, theologians, and writers who followed and developed the ideas of ARISTOTLE and early Christian writers in minute and profuse speculations: one of the Schoolmen was AQUINAS.

Science. *Noun:* (1) knowledge, (2) knowledge acquired through study. Compare PHILOSOPHY (especially "natural philosophy" and "NEW PHILOSOPHY").

Sea-gaols (i.e., sea-jails). Galleys (large vessels propelled by oars) that had chained prisoners manning the oars: a common punishment for convicted criminals was to be sent to the galleys for such labor. See line 37 of "The Calm."

Seal. *Noun:* (1) a design pressed into a piece of wax attached to a letter or other document to attest to its authenticity; (2) a piece of wax bearing the impression of a design or other symbol of authentication on a document; (3) a symbol of a covenant or confirmation, especially in a theological context; (4) the impression of a signet ring on something to claim ownership or to authenticate; (5) an impressed mark as a sign on anything; (6) a piece of wax that holds something closed; (7) a sign or symbol of a high office. *Verb:* to impress, affix, symbolize, authenticate, or close something with a seal (as defined above under uses as a noun).

Second Anniversary, The. See *THE FIRST ANNIVERSARY.* Donne repeats his intention in *The Second Anniversary* to produce a poem in Elizabeth Drury's memory each year (see lines 31–36), but this is, in fact, the last one he wrote for her.

Louis L. Martz in *The Poetry of Meditation* (see "Selected Bibliography" under "Critical Studies: Poetry") sees this poem as composed of an introduction, then seven sections, and finally a conclusion: as he sees in *The First Anniversary,* he perceives a correspondence to Roman Catholic meditations to a degree. The first section contains a meditation, a eulogy, and a refrain with a moral. The second section contains a meditation, a eulogy, and a moral. The remaining sections, however, contain only meditation and eulogy. Specifically, Martz analyzes the structure as follows: Introduction, lines 1–44; Section I, lines 45–84 (Meditation, lines 45–64; Eulogy, lines 65–80; Refrain and Moral, lines 81–84); Section II, lines 85–156 (Meditation, lines 85–120; Eulogy, lines 121–46; Moral, lines 147–56); Section III, lines 157–250 (Meditation, lines 157–219; Eulogy, lines 220–50); Section IV, lines 251–320 (Meditation, lines 251–300; Eulogy, lines 301–20); Section V, lines 321–82 (Meditation, lines 321–55; Eulogy, lines 356–82); Section VI, lines 383–470 (Meditation, lines 383–446; Eulogy, lines 447–70); Section VII, lines 471–510 (Meditation, lines 471–96; Eulogy, lines 497–510); Conclusion, lines 511–28. Martz feels that *The*

Second Anniversary is more unified and successful than *The First Anniversary* and that Donne consistently transforms Elizabeth Drury into a symbol of virtue to represent the image and likeness of God in man. He also argues that hyperbole is controlled in the second poem. The theme of grace, so lacking in the first poem, successfully pervades the second. The human soul can be released from the physical and mental bondage (such bondage as emphasized in the first poem) by thirsting after knowledge of God, not after worldly knowledge. Martz contends that, to Donne, God is both the object of knowledge and the means of knowing, a realization leading to the confidence reflected in the end of the poem. Martz also sees significance in Donne's use of seven sections in the second poem (as opposed to five in the first one): seven corresponds to the usual divisions of religious meditations and to those reflecting days of the week, but, even more important, seven expresses the infinite (as Donne himself says in the *ESSAYS IN DIVINITY*).

O.B. Hardison, Jr., in *The Enduring Monument* (see "Selected Bibliography" under "Critical Studies: Poetry") sees the poem composed of nine sections: these generally correspond to Martz's seven with added Introduction and Conclusion, but Hardison does not regard the subdivisions as Meditation, Eulogy, Refrain, or Moral. Specifically, Hardison analyzes the structure and related content as follows [I have somewhat abbreviated his designations of content]: I, lines 1–44, Introduction; II, lines 45–84, "Disestimation" of the world (a, lines 45–64, rotten world; b, lines 65–80, Elizabeth as pattern of perfection; c, considering Elizabeth teaches us to hate the world); III, lines 85–156, Death (a, lines 85–120, process of death; b, lines 121–46, Elizabeth seemed immortal; c, lines 147–56, considering Elizabeth's death teaches us that we all must die); IV, lines 157–250, Soul in and released from the body (a, lines 157–78, soul imprisoned in body; b, lines 179–219, soul released with marvelous powers; c, lines 220–46, Elizabeth as perfect soul in perfect body; d, lines 247–50, Elizabeth calls us to heaven); V, lines 251–320, Knowledge in and out of body (a, lines 251–94, here all things are dark; b, lines 295–300, after death all is known perfectly; c, lines 301–14, Elizabeth [knowing virtue] knew everything; d, lines 315–20, Elizabeth calls us); VI, lines 321–82, Society here and in heaven (a, lines 321–38, society on earth is corrupt; b, lines 339–55, society in heaven is perfect; c, lines 356–79, Elizabeth was a pattern for a perfect society; d, lines 380–82, desire to join her society leads us to heaven); VII, lines 383–470, Essential joy here and in heaven (a, lines 383–434, no permanent essential joys on earth; b, lines 435–46, sight of God is essential and lasting joy; c, lines 447–67, Elizabeth formed God's image in her heart; d, lines 468–70, Elizabeth was as close as man comes to essential joy on earth, and she is now in heaven); VIII, lines 471–510, Accidental joys in heaven (a, lines 471–86, on earth accidental joys are fleeting; b, lines 487–96, heaven's accidents are eternal and perfect; c, lines 497–510, Elizabeth has gone to heaven and her reward, where we may rejoin her); IX, lines 511–28, Conclusion. Hardison argues that Donne emphasizes a contrast between the miseries of earth and the joys of heaven, independent of Elizabeth herself, and that then he asserts that she was a pattern of virtue in life and encourages us by death to anticipate the perfection of each virtue in heaven. Hardison also notes that *The Second Anniversary* concerns a literal earth and heaven, rather than the metaphorical "old" and "new" worlds of *The First Anniversary*. He also contends that the second poem becomes a meditation on the soul's state in heaven, rather than a description of a journey.

METAPHYSICAL CONCEITS and striking imagery vividly convey the poet's arguments in the poem. For example, in lines 157–78 the soul is compared to a baby kept in the cell of the body in a condition more foul than an ANCHORIT "Bedded, and bathed in all his ordures" (line 171): the unpleasant analogy conveys the feeling of how loathsome to the soul is its entrapment in a sinful body. It can only "suck and cry" until released by death. After its escape from the world the soul becomes (in another conceit) like a string tying beads together: it links earth with heaven, including all of the spheres and stars united (lines 205–18).

The emphasis in *The First Anniversary* on caustic satirizing of human pride is dropped in the second poem to concentrate throughout on man's lowliness, ignorance, and necessary humility. The speaker tells his soul to give "Pride" up to one of "Satan's Sergeants" as death approaches (lines 102–104), thus allowing humility and grace to hold sway. He further tells his soul (lines 158–66) that it was made in a "SINK" (the cesspool of the body) and that the body is only "curded milk" and an "unlittered whelp." All of the presumptuous knowledge and futile speculations of either the old or NEW PHILOSOPHY emphasized in *The First Anniversary* are dismissed in *The Second Anniversary* as ultimately irrelevant to true knowledge and salvation: the soul goes from earth to heaven caring not a whit about the elements of air and fire, the moon, planets, or meteors (lines 189–98). The climax to the insistence on man's ignorance and humility occurs in lines 248–92: humans are crawling "snails" that know nothing. They do not know their own origin, makeup, history, environment, and destiny. The solution for all humanity is indicated, ultimately, by Elizabeth Drury: "She did high justice; for she crucified / Every first motion of rebellious pride" (lines 365–66).

(For other possible approaches in interpreting this much-discussed poem [and its relationships to *The First Anniversary*], see both the general works covering Donne's poetry and the specific ones on *The Anniversaries* in the "Selected Bibliography.")

Security. *Noun*: (1) condition of being protected from danger; (2) confidence and freedom from doubt or care; (3) something which makes secure; (4) property pledged to assure fulfillment of an obligation or payment of debt.

Seely. *Adjective*: (1) happy, lucky; (2) innocent, naive, harmless; (3) pitiable, helpless, defenseless; (4) insignificant, poor; (5) frail, worn-out; (6) foolish, simple.

Seize. *Verb*: (1) to take hold of, to grasp; (2) [in legal use] to take possession of (property).

Self Accuser. In one of the *EPIGRAMS* (entitled "A Self Accuser"), a woman who accuses her lover of following "whores," thus confessing herself to be one.

Sem. A version of the name SHEM.

Sensibility. See DISSOCIATION OF SENSIBILITY.

Sensitive (Sensible) Soul. See discussion of stanza five in "A VALEDICTION: OF MY NAME IN THE WINDOW."

Sequan. The River Seine in France.

Seraphim. See HIERARCHY, THE HEAVENLY.

Sere-bark. Encrustation of scabs, sores.

Sermons. Donne's surviving sermons are 160 in number, with only 6 of them published during his lifetime. Most of the sermons were first published in three large volumes extending through three decades after his death: *LXXX Sermons* in 1640, *Fifty Sermons* in 1649, and *XXVI Sermons* in 1660 (and/or 1661). These three volumes were seen through the press by Donne's son John. Donne, as typical of other clergymen of his time, preached from notes he had made of a sermon formulated and memorized before delivery. But for publication later the preacher would write out, revise, and polish the sermon from his notes. So, a printed version does not correspond in every detail to the oral one. The longest of Donne's sermons is the first one he gave at PAUL'S CROSS (on March 24, 1617: *XXVI Sermons*, no. 24 [see Potter and Simpson edition of the *Sermons*, Volume I, no. 3]). It would have taken about two and a half hours to deliver, quite long even in a time of sermons typically lasting from about an hour to an hour and a half. Most of Donne's apparently lasted about one hour. But people of the seventeenth century enjoyed hearing and reading sermons: the sources for entertainment at the time were much more limited than those available to us today. There were plays, of course, but one could see and hear the delivery of a lively sermon for free. For serious motivation, people were sincerely concerned with personal salvation and its achievement. Also, religion and politics were inextricably linked in Donne's time, providing additional interest in sermons.

Donne was one of the most popular and most famous preachers of his time, holding the interest of the hearers with many of those qualities we associate with his METAPHYSICAL poetry (paradox, conceits, wide-ranging experience and learning, vivid and colloquial language, striking metrical subtleties, audacious wordplay, personal feelings and tones, and a combination of humor and seriousness). His themes echo many of those in his poetry generally, but especially those of his Christian poems. The concerns are both personal and universal Christian ones of man's lowly and weak nature, man's guilt and need for God's grace and power, mortality and decay, the fear of death, death as the great leveller, the end of the world, the Resurrection, the Last Judgment, the fear of damnation, and the hope of salvation. In addition, some of his sermons touch on various controversies about worship, churches, and sects—especially some issues of disagreement among Roman Catholics, Anglicans, and PURITANS. Visions of the ELEMENTS, of MICROCOSMs and MACROCOSMs, of different CIRCLEs in the universe, and of the BOOKS OF GOD pervade Donne's *Sermons* as they do his other works, both poetry and prose.

Only a mere sample of the vast world of the *Sermons* can be attempted in this "Dictionary." I have chosen eight sermons to comment briefly on in this entry, emphasizing particular passages within them; however, they are indeed some of the most famous and most frequently anthologized portions of Donne's sermons. And I feel that they give one a taste of Donne's recurring themes and striking poetic artistry in prose. For full information on and further reading in the *Sermons*, one should use the standard 10-volume edition by Potter and Simpson cited in the "Selected Bibliography": its texts, notes, and introductions provide information and background with which to explore other scholarly and critical books, articles, and essays on the *Sermons*. The sermons I have selected are discussed below in chronological order by dates of their delivery: after each year is/are the sermon's important appearance(s) in print in the seventeenth century and its location in the Potter and Simpson edition.

1622[?] (*LXXX Sermons*, no. 76, 1640; Potter and Simpson edition, Vol. V, no. 13). This famous sermon (portions of which appear in many anthologies and other selections of Donne's works) was preached to the Earl of Carlisle (see HAY, JAMES) and others at "Sion," the home of the Earl of Northumberland, Carlisle's father-in-law. The text for the sermon is Mark 16:16 ("He that believeth not, shall be damned"). Donne expounds particularly on the articles of the Apostle's Creed and the Christian's profession of belief in the universal church, Father, Son, and Holy Ghost. He insists on the importance of Christ's injunction, his "commission" to his apostles, to go forth and preach the Gospel as the means of belief and salvation and the means to avoid "condemnation" (damnation). He also argues that Baptism and the Lord's Supper fall within this commission. Near the end of the sermon Donne concludes, "[one] must be saved by hearing the word preached, by receiving the sacraments, and by working according to both." Then he turns to the fact that "there is damnation, and why it is, and when it is, is clear enough" but that "what this damnation is" has not been made clear, despite speculations and descriptions. Donne proposes that "to fall out of the hands of the living God, is a horror beyond our expression, beyond our imagination." This leads to the last and extremely long paragraph of the sermon, its most famous and often-printed passage, in which Donne vividly portrays utter isolation from God as the true hell, the true damnation. The sentence opening the paragraph begins "That God should let my soul fall out of his hand, into a bottomless pit, and roll an unremovable stone upon it, and leave it to that which it finds there . . . .": this first sentence continues (through parallel clauses, connectives, and repeated words and phrases—especially through the repetition of "that") for an almost unbelievable number of lines, occupying 75% of the paragraph. Only two more sentences make up the remaining 25% of the paragraph. The sentence portraying damnation, then, *stylistically and structurally embodies* that very sense of eternal, unending damnation with a seemingly endless sentence. The conclusion of the sentence is as follows: ". . . that that God should frustrate all his own purposes and practices upon me and leave me and cast me away as though I had cost him nothing; that this God at last should let this soul go away as a smoke, as a vapor, as a bubble; and that then this soul cannot be a smoke, a vapor, nor a bubble but must lie in darkness as long as the Lord of light is light itself, and never spark of that light reach to my soul; what Tophet is not paradise, what brimstone is not amber, what gnashing is not a comfort, what gnawing of the worm is not a tickling, what torment is not a marriage-bed to this damnation, to be secluded eternally, eternally, eternally from the sight of God?" The repetition of "eternally" and its numerous syllables further enforce the senses of sameness and endlessness in this horrible isolation from God. Tophet (Hell) as it is ordinarily depicted as a place seems like paradise compared to this true damnation, exclusion from God's sight. A shocking, gruesome combination of opposed images and tones (gnawing of the worm in the grave and in hell versus a tickling) testifies to Donne's use of some of the same METAPHYSICAL qualities as in his poetry (compare, for example, "THE FUNERAL" and "THE RELIC").

1625 (*Fifty Sermons*, no. 33, 1649; Potter and Simpson edition, Vol. VI, no. 14). This sermon is the one that Donne preached by the body of King JAMES a few days before its burial (the sermon designated as "Preached at Denmark House, some few days before the body of King James was removed from thence to his burial, April 26, 1625"). The King had died on March 27 and lay in state in this home that James had given his Queen, Anne of Denmark, until a procession carried the body for burial in Westminster Abbey (a procession in which Donne participated). The text chosen for the sermon is Canticles 3:11 ("Go forth ye daughters of Sion, and behold King Solomon with the crown wherewith his mother crowned him, in the day of his espousals, and in the day of the gladness of his heart"). Donne implies a comparison of King James with King Solomon. He also assumes that Solomon is a TYPE of Christ, that the crowned Solomon prefigures Christ as the head of the Church. King James was God's viceroy and thus was Godlike and Christlike. However, the climax of the sermon, the long last paragraph, turns from Christ as a mirror of part of our nature to James as a quite human mirror ("GLASS") in which we see ourselves, and this passage is the most famous and memorable portion of the sermon, reflecting death as the great leveller of classes and ranks. This passage also illustrates Donne's powerful poetic techniques in prose that fuse style, structure, feeling, and meaning.   Donne describes James as "like thee in all things, subject to human infirmities, subject to sins" and yet "translated [see TRANSLATE (2)] by Death, to everlasting Joy, and Glory."   He then proposes for consideration the following: "And when you shall find that hand that had signed to one of you a Patent for Title, to another for Pension, to another for Pardon, to another for Dispensation, Dead: that hand that settled Possessions by his Seal, in the Keeper, and rectified Honors by the sword, in his Marshall, and distributed relief to the Poor, in his Almoner, and Health to the Diseased, by his immediate Touch, Dead: that Hand that balanced his own three Kingdoms so equally, as that none of them complained of one another, nor of him, and carried the Keys of all the Christian world, and locked up, and let out Armies in their due season, Dead; how poor, how faint, how pale, how momentary, how transitory, how empty, how frivolous, how Dead things, must you necessarily think Titles, and Possessions, and Favors, and all, when you see that Hand, which was the hand of Destiny, of Christian Destiny, of the Almighty God, lie dead?"   Donne repeats "dead" and arranges heavy stress to fall on each occurrence of it: these two techniques just in themselves convey the pervasiveness of death (the repetition) and its power (the stress).   But, in addition, each of the four major clauses impressively pictures and builds up the vitality and power of King James in life, only to undercut that vitality and power with the one word "dead" at the end of each clause: just as each clause ends with "dead", so does mortal life end with death.   Clause and sentence structures embody feeling and idea: the last word in the sentence, significantly, is "dead."

1625[?] (*LXXX Sermons*, no. 36, 1640; Potter and Simpson edition, Vol. VI, no. 16).   This sermon was preached on Whitsunday (i.e., Pentecost).   The text for the sermon is John 16:8–11, concerning the sending into the world of the Holy Ghost, the Comforter.   Yet Donne notes the paradox that "this Comforter reproves the world," and this comment leads into a passage about three-fourths of the way through the sermon (p. 323 in Vol. VI of Potter and Simpson) that is the most famous from this sermon and that reflects some important ideas of Donne and the early seventeenth century: "As the world is the whole frame of the world, God hath put into it a reproof, a rebuke, lest it should seem eternal, which is, a sensible decay and age in the whole frame of the world, and every piece thereof.   The seasons of the year irregular and distempered; the Sun fainter, and languishing; men less in stature, and shorter-lived.   No addition, but only every year, new sorts, new species of worms, and flies, and sicknesses, which argue more and more putrefaction of which they are engendered. And the Angels of heaven, which did so familiarly converse with men in the beginning of the world, though they may not be doubted to perform to us still their ministerial assistances, yet they seem so far to have deserted this world, as that they do not appear to us, as they did to those our Fathers." The first occurrence of "world" in the passage refers to the earth, and the second occurrence refers to the created universe. Since (in the PTOLEMAIC and traditional Christian conception) earth is the center of the universe and the central creation of God, earth is the mainstay and structural center for the whole universe. The third occurrence of "world" refers, then, to the earth. As man is a MICROCOSM of the earth as a MACROCOSM, so is the earth a MICROCOSM of the universe as a MACROCOSM. Donne argues that there is mortality in the earth that corresponds to mortality in the human: each is a body subject to aging, illness, physical decay, and death (especially compare *DEVOTIONS UPON EMERGENT OCCASIONS* and *THE FIRST ANNIVERSARY*). The transitory nature of the earth, then, reflects the ultimate destruction of the physical universe itself, in favor of the only eternal realm, the spiritual, in heaven. Donne's time was acutely aware of the impermanence and lack of stability in the universe that were increasingly implied by the discoveries of the NEW PHILOSOPHY. There is even a decline in the visitations by angels: they do not appear now to men as they were said to appear to many in the Bible. Donne and his time believed that the world was becoming older and weaker: it was only later in the seventeenth century that the ideas of progress and improvement began to seriously change men's perceptions of their "world."

   1626 (*LXXX Sermons*, no. 80, 1640; Potter and Simpson edition, Vol. VII, no. 10). This sermon was preached at the funeral of Sir WILLIAM COKAYNE on December 12, 1626. Its text is John 11:21 ("Then said Martha unto Jesus, Lord, if thou hadst been here, my brother had not died"). Early in the sermon Donne focuses on the many assurances of the Resurrection of both soul and body, relating the assurance to the concern of Martha for her brother Lazarus, as cited in the text for the sermon. The imperfection of Martha's faith leads to a consideration of many examples of imperfect faith and to Donne's oft-repeated note through the sermon that "even in spiritual things, nothing is perfect." As an example of this fact, Donne points even to prayer, and this example (about one-third of the way through the sermon—on pp. 264–65 in Volume VII of Potter and Simpson) is one of the most striking and famous passages from Donne's sermons: "But when we consider with a religious seriousness the manifold weaknesses of the strongest devotions in time of prayer, it is a sad consideration. I throw myself down in my chamber, and I call in and invite God and his Angels thither, and when they are there, I neglect God and his Angels for the noise of a fly, for the rattling of a coach, for the whining of a door; I talk on in the same posture of praying, eyes lifted up, knees bowed down, as though I prayed to God; and, if God or his angels should ask me when I thought last of God in that prayer, I cannot tell: sometimes I find that I had forgot what I was about, but when I began to forget it, I cannot tell. A memory of yesterday's pleasures, a fear of tomorrow's dangers, a straw under my knee, a noise in mine ear, a light in mine eye, an anything, a nothing, a fancy, a chimera in my brain troubles me in my prayer. So certainly is there nothing, nothing in spiritual things perfect in this world." The personal exploration and discoveries about his own mind are expanded to represent those of the typical human mind. Qualities found in his METAPHYSICAL poetry are also present in the passage—e.g., combining such heterogeneous images as angels and flies in his consciousness and the use of colloquialisms such as "whining." The style impressively conveys the content. Use of parallel short phrases in a series gives the sense of matters rushing in unceasingly ("for the noise of a fly, for the rattling of a coach, for the whining of a door"). And in the final sentence containing this type of series, a portion of the sentence steadily progresses from long phrases to short ones: "a memory of yesterday's pleasures" (10 syllables), "a fear of tomorrow's dangers" (8 syllables), "a straw under my knee" (6 syllables), "a noise in mine ear" (5 syllables), "a light in mine eye" (5 syllables), "an anything" (4 syllables), "a nothing" (3 syllables), and "a fancy" (3 syllables). This technique increases the speed in reading and hearing, conveying effectively the increasing and unstoppable rush of these multitudes of images that crowd into his consciousness, thus rushing in and crowding God out of it. Later in the sermon (p. 271, Potter and Simpson) Donne also argues that there is nothing "permanent" in temporal and earthly things (as there is nothing "perfect" in the spiritual). To prove this he says, "I need not call in new Philosophy, that denies a settledness, an acquiescence in the very body of the Earth, but makes the Earth to move in that place where we thought the Sun had moved; I need not that help that the Earth itself is in motion to prove this, that nothing upon Earth is Permanent." This is one of several references in Donne's prose and poetry to the new discoveries in astronomy during his time (see NEW PHILOSOPHY). Another of

Donne's favorite concepts applied metaphorically occurs in this sermon (p. 272, Potter and Simpson) in the following: "Even in the body of man, you may turn to the whole world; this body is an illustration of all Nature, God's recapitulation of all that he had said before . . ." (see MICROCOSM and MACROCOSM).

1628 (*LXXX Sermons*, no. 23, 1640; Potter and Simpson edition, Vol. VIII, no. 9). This sermon was preached in ST. PAUL'S CATHEDRAL on Easter, 1628. Its text is I Corinthians 13:12 ("For now we see through a glass darkly, but then face to face; now I know in part, but then I shall know even as also I am known"). Impressive in the sermon is its careful organization, making it easy for the congregation to follow. Donne develops four divisions based on his text: sight in this life, sight in the next life, knowledge in this life, and knowledge in the next life. He specifies these divisions early in his sermon. One "medium" or "glass" (mirror) by which we see God in this life is through the "Book of Creatures": the entire created universe reveals its creator (see BOOKS OF GOD). We study this "book" by the "light of reason," and there is "not so poor a creature but may be thy glass to see God in" (p. 224 in Volume VIII of Potter and Simpson)—i.e., anything in existence testifies of God the Creator. We "know" of God in this world in the Church, through Christ, with the "light of faith" (p. 226). The "most powerful means [of knowing] is . . . the Scripture in the Church" (p. 227). This is the other of the two BOOKS OF GOD, the Book of Scriptures, the Bible. It is interesting that Donne specifies "Scripture in the Church," to counteract the PURITAN contention of strictly individualistic study of the Bible outside of the Church. Donne goes on to say that certainly one is to "meditate at home" on the Scriptures after one "learn[s] at Church." So, Donne argues for study of the Bible both at Church and home, the middle-of-the-road Anglican position, as opposed to the extremes of Puritan (at home) and Roman Catholic (at Church). Further overt arguments by Donne for fundamental Anglican compromise positions appear in this sermon. For example, he says, "But the ear is the Holy Ghost's first door. He assists us with Ritual and Ceremonial things, which we see in the Church, but Ceremonies have their right use, when their right use hath first been taught by preaching" (p. 228). In his discussion of the sight of God in heaven, Donne says (p. 231) that our way to see him is by "God's laying himself open, his manifestation, his revelation, his evisceration, and embowelling of himself to us"—a rather shocking, grotesque image of a distinctly METAPHYSICAL nature! In knowing God in heaven, Donne concludes in his fourth division (p. 233), "God alone is all": He is place, means, and light, and our knowledge of Him will produce a love like His.

1628 [1629 under New Style, Gregorian, modern calendar] (*LXXX Sermons*, no. 48, 1640; Potter and Simpson edition, Vol. VIII, no. 14). This sermon was preached at ST. PAUL'S CATHEDRAL on the day commemorating St. Paul's Conversion (i.e., January 25, 1628 [1629 under New Style, Gregorian, modern calendar]). Its text is a portion of Acts 28:6 ("They changed their minds, and said that he was a god"). For this occasion Donne chooses the incident in which a viper attaches to St. Paul's hand, Paul shakes it off, is unharmed, and the people of Malta regard him as a god. The most interesting portion of the sermon is near the end. After considering the human tendency toward superstition and multiplication of gods, Donne comments on the Anglican ways regarding ceremonies and whether or not certain matters in the church are "superstitions" and then proceeds to a discussion of atheism (the most famous part of the sermon). Regarding ceremony and superstition, Donne again answers criticisms by the PURITANS, especially regarding THINGS INDIFFERENT: "And then, since man is also naturally apt to stray into a superstitious worship of God, let us be Christianly diligent, to preclude all ways, that may lead us into that temptation, or incline us towards superstition. In which, I do not intend, that we should decline all such things, as had been superstitiously abused, in a superstitious Church [i.e., the Roman Catholic Church]; But, in all such things, as being in their own nature indifferent, are, by a just commandment of lawful authority [see CHARLES I and LAUD, WILLIAM], become more than indifferent (necessary) to us. . . ." (p. 331 in Volume VIII of Potter and Simpson). He goes on to say that even though salvation does not consist of ceremonies, that obedience does and that "salvation consists much in obedience." He argues for the "right use of those things" and against their abuse in the "Roman Church," as opposed to the "good use which is made of them in ours [i.e., in our church, the Church of England]." Specifically against the Puritans' severe criticism of art and images, Donne says, "That because pictures have been adored [i.e., in the Roman Catholic Church], we [i.e., true Anglicans, true Christians] do not abhor a picture [i.e., as Puritans do]." Donne's endorsement of the middle way embodied in loyal Anglicanism is even more apparent as he says that the Lutheran Church retains more of Roman ceremonies than the Anglican Church does and that the Anglican retains more than the CALVINIST. But, he argues, both the Lutheran and Anglican do so "without danger," because both are "diligent to preach to the people the right use of these indifferent things." After this lengthy consideration of the natural inclination of man toward many gods and superstition, Donne turns to that "unnatural monster," the atheist who believes in no god. Donne imagines saying to the atheist the following: "I respite thee not till the day of Judgement, when I may see thee upon thy knees, upon thy face, begging of the hills, that they would fall down and cover thee from the fierce wrath of God, to ask thee then, Is there a God now? I respite thee not till the day of thine own death, when thou shalt have evidence enough, that there is a God, though no other evidence, but to find a Devil, and evidence enough, that there is a Heaven, though no other evidence, but to feel Hell; To ask thee then, Is there a God now? I respite thee but a few hours, but six hours, but till midnight" (pp. 332–33). Clearly Donne is recalling MARLOWE's play *DR. FAUSTUS*: Revelation 6:16 refers to mountains and rocks falling and hiding men from the wrath of the Lamb, and Faustus echoes this in his last speech of the play; however, Donne's allusion is closer to the version in the play. In addition, the respite until midnight and the finding of a "devil" specifically parallel the situation of the play. This passage, then, reinforces the validity of the statement made about Donne by Sir Richard Baker (*Chronicles*, 1643) that Donne in his younger days was a "great frequenter of Plays." And the memory of one of those plays appears even in a sermon near the end of his life.

    1630[?] (*LXXX Sermons*, no. 30, 1640; Potter and Simpson edition, Vol. IX, no. 10). This sermon was preached on Whitsunday (i.e., Pentecost). The text is John 14:20 ("At that day shall ye know, that I am in my Father, and you in me, and I in you"). Donne relates the Biblical text to what he calls "the mystery of the Trinity, of distinct persons in the Godhead" [see TRINITY]. As a part of his discussion of ways to know God, Donne elaborates on one of his favorite themes, the BOOKS OF GOD, in a well-known passage from this sermon: "Here God shows this inconsiderate man [i.e., one who does not observe and consider matters carefully] his book of creatures, which he may run and read; that is, he may go forward in his vocation and yet see that every creature calls him to a consideration of God. Every ant that he sees asks him, Where had I this providence and industry? Every flower that he sees asks him, Where had I this beauty, this fragrancy, this medicinal virtue in me? Every creature calls him to consider what great things God hath done in little subjects. But God opens to him also, here in his Church, his Book of Scriptures, and in that Book every word cries out to him, every merciful promise cries to him, Why am I here to meet thee, to wait upon

thee, to perform God's purpose towards thee, if thou never
consider me, never apply me to thyself?" (pp. 236–37 in Volume
IX of Potter and Simpson). The Book of Creatures (Nature) and the
Book of Scriptures (the Bible) point to God the Creator and Author.
Both are means by which humanity learns of God. To Donne, there
is no conflict between Nature and the Bible: they both lead to the
source of all Truth in God Himself.

   1631 (printed as *Death's Duel*, 1632 and 1633; *XXVI
Sermons*, no. 26, 1660/61; Potter and Simpson edition, Vol. X, no.
11). This sermon is famous as Donne's last one, delivered five
weeks before his death when he was quite ill. It was preached
before King CHARLES I and the Court at the beginning of Lent (on
February 25) and was designated as a preparation for Lent and
for pondering Christ's death. WALTON says that the people who
witnessed him in the pulpit for the last time regarded him as the
epitome of mortality and that they felt that Donne preached his
own funeral sermon in this one. The text for it is the conclusion of
Psalms 68:20 ("And unto God the Lord belong the issues of [i.e.,
from] death"), and Walton reports that people thought the text
was "prophetically chosen." When the sermon was first published
in 1632 as *Death's Duel*, it had an engraving of the portrait made
of Donne in his death shroud (see section above entitled "Donne's
Life"). The sermon begins with analogies and paradoxes centered
on the womb and birth as a grave and death. And even in birth,
Donne says, one is delivered into the "manifold deaths of this
world" (p. 233 in Volume X of Potter and Simpson). Vivid
repetition of "worms" and "dust" through the sermon insists on
physical mortality. Donne points out that man must "be mingled
in his dust, with the dust of every highway, and of every dunghill,
and swallowed in every puddle and pond" (p. 239). But Donne
ends the sermon pointing to Christ's crucifixion and resurrection
that enable man to "lie down in peace in his grave" (p. 248)
because of the assurance of resurrection to come.

Sestet. See SONNET.

Sestos. See HERO.

Seth. Third son of Adam and Eve. Eve said that God sent her this
son to replace ABEL who had been killed by CAIN (see Genesis
4:25–26 and 5:3–7). In *METEMPSYCHOSIS* (lines 9 and 517) Donne
follows Josephus's comment that Seth's descendants began the
study of astronomy, the order of the heavenly bodies. They were

said to have preserved their discoveries by inscribing them on two pillars (one brick and the other stone).

Seven Sleepers of Ephesus. Seven Christian youths who suffered from the persecution of the Emperor Decius were sealed in a cavern and slept for 187 years. Upon awaking, they found astonishing changes, including well-established Christianity. See "THE GOOD-MORROW."

Seventeen-headed Belgia. The seventeen Protestant provinces of the Netherlands. See "Elegy 11: The Bracelet," line 42.

Several. *Adjective*: (1) separate, distinct; (2) distinctive, particular; (3) various, diverse.

Shadow. *Noun*: (1) darkness produced by a body blocking the rays of the sun or of some other source of light; (2) a delusive or insubstantial object; (3) a representation of something or someone, such as a portrait; (4) a phantom or ghost or spirit.

Shadrach. See CHILDREN IN THE OVEN.

Shambles. *Noun*: slaughterhouse.

Sharp. *Adjective*: (1) having a keen cutting edge or fine point; (2) intellectually discerning, perceptive, clever; (3) [of climate or weather or wind] cold, especially bitterly or extremely or piercingly cold.

Shem. One of Noah's three sons who repopulated the world after the Flood. The others were JAPHET and CHAM. (See Genesis 9 and 10.) Shem's descendants were believed to dwell in Asia. See "HYMN TO GOD MY GOD, IN MY SICKNESS."

Shiver. *Verb*: (1) to break into pieces; (2) to tremble, especially from cold or emotion.

"Show me, dear Christ, Thy spouse so bright and clear." First line of one of the *HOLY SONNETS*. The sonnet begins emphatically with a heavy stress falling on the line's first syllable, reversing the normal iambic foot: this conveys the sense of urgency in the speaker's request to Christ that he reveal his true "spouse" (the bride of Christ, the true Church). "Bright and clear" connotes the church that shines with true light, the light of Christ's own truth. Also, the description of the true Church as Christ's bride echoes the description in Revelation 19, and Christ as the bridegroom is noted in Matthew 25. The problem of discerning which church is the true one, out of so many new churches and factions by Donne's time that were claiming to be the true church, was a very real one to Donne and others. (See the concern also expressed in "SATIRE 3.") He begins to look at the various churches claiming to be the bride of Christ: his major METAPHYSICAL CONCEIT through the entire sonnet, in fact, is the consideration of the church as various types of women. First he expresses a bit of surprise as he exclaims, "What!" The reversal of the iambic foot appropriately places heavy stress on the word. He is looking toward the "other shore" (i.e., on the European mainland, across the English Channel) and considers "she" (a church described as a woman) who goes "richly painted": as a woman the image suggests one who uses many cosmetics and adorns herself lavishly, but this is a metaphor for the Roman Catholic Church, with its ceremony, splendor, vestments, statuary, and art. Is this Christ's bride? Or is she the one "robbed and tore" who "Laments and mourns in Germany and here" (lines 3–4)? Is she the stripped, plain Protestant Church found in Germany and in England? (Some editors—see especially Gardner's edition of the *Divine Poems* cited in "Selected Bibliography: Works"—argue that "robbed and tore" refers to a military defeat suffered by a major Protestant leader in Germany in 1620, a defeat that meant failure for the Protestant cause in Bohemia and one that was quite lamented when news of it reached England.) The speaker then asks if the true Church is like a woman who sleeps for a thousand years and then suddenly "peeps up" [in three possible senses: (1) awaking and peering between eyelids, (2) to protrude the head from a place of hiding, and (3) sprouting up as a plant from a dormant seed]. This question reflects, with a bit of sarcasm, on the claim of some Protestants that the true Church had disappeared with Roman Catholic corruption of the early, primitive Church and has only reappeared with Protestantism. Line 6 raises the disturbing question of how the true Church, which is unchanging truth itself, can err and change. Lines 7–8 ask if the true Church is that on "one hill" (many editors speculate that this refers to Mount Moriah, where Solomon built his Temple) or the one on "seven" hills (undoubtedly the Roman Catholic Church, associated with the seven hills of Rome) or the one on "no hill" (most editors and scholars suggest the Calvinistic GENEVA, although others propose the center of the Anglican Church at Canterbury). Whether or not Donne has specific locales in mind for all three of these appearances of the "bride," he implies that they represent the many churches at many locations that have made, still are making, and shall make claims to be the true Church. And this is precisely the problem implied at the end of the octave: i.e., how is one to determine whether one of these is really Christ's bride or whether these are fragments of what is still to become the true, universal Church in the future.

The sestet of this Italian sonnet asks Christ if his bride already is present in our midst or do men, like medieval knights, have to "travel" (not just over space, but through time) on a quest to find the woman in order eventually to love her. Lines 11–14 present the shocking paradox, in erotic terms, that the true Church is like an unfaithful bride, and it is made additionally shocking by Christ (the "kind husband") actually wanting to "BETRAY" ("reveal," but another meaning of the word quite paradoxically relevant in the context is "to be false to") his bride so that men can make love to her: the Church is "most true and pleasing" when "embraced and open" to all men! What would be most untrue (i.e., unfaithful) of a wife in the literal sense becomes most "true" when applied as a symbol of the church. The last three lines, in fact, deliberately echo the Song of Solomon 5:2 ("Open to me, my sister, my love, my dove, my undefiled"). Donne emphasizes the erotic connotations present in the Biblical passage, beyond the opening of the door to the beloved. The opening in the erotic sense is the opening of the woman's legs and vagina to receive a lover. But Donne further plays on "open" to suggest the receptivity and inclusiveness of the true Church to all men, which is its ultimate mission and which Christ desires. Donne, then, amazingly and successfully uses a literal image of an action that would be sin in traditional Christian precepts to convey in symbolic terms what indeed offers spiritual salvation to humanity (i.e., the church's taking in of men). Christ provides his "bride" for all people's use in order to effect their salvation. It is this undoubted, true, united, universal Church that the speaker fervently wants to find with the help of Christ to reveal it to him.

Sibyl. *Noun*: the Cumaean Sibyl, a legendary prophetess who aided Aeneas and who sold three books of prophecy to Tarquinius Superbus. (Other women of antiquity also were prophetesses at various locations and were called Sibyls, but this particular one apparently is alluded to by Donne in both "A VALEDICTION: OF THE BOOK" and "Upon Mr. Thomas Coryat's Crudities.")

Sicil Isle. Sicily (with Mount Etna and its volcano on it).

Sidney, Mary (1561–1620).   Countess of Pembroke and sister of Sir PHILIP SIDNEY.   After her brother's death she published many of his works and completed the translation of the *Psalms* that her brother had begun: Donne's "Upon the Translation of the Psalms by Sir Philip Sidney, and the Countess of Pembroke His Sister" honors it.   She translated other works and was well known as a patroness of writers.   She was the third wife of Henry Herbert, 2nd Earl of Pembroke, and was the mother of both William Herbert, 3rd Earl of Pembroke (a patron of the theater company to which Shakespeare belonged and one of the candidates proposed as the "young man" to whom Shakespeare wrote his *Sonnets*) and Philip Herbert, 4th Earl of Pembroke, who married Lady ANNE CLIFFORD, the former wife of RICHARD SACKVILLE, Earl of Dorset.

Sidney, Sir Philip (1554–1586).   Poet, prose writer, translator, courtier, and literary patron during the reign of ELIZABETH I.   His *Arcadia* was written for his sister MARY [SIDNEY], COUNTESS OF PEMBROKE, while he stayed at Wilton, her home.   He began a translation of the *Psalms* that his sister completed after his death: Donne honors this work in "Upon the Translation of the Psalms by Sir Philip Sidney, and the Countess of Pembroke His Sister." Sidney's *Astrophil and Stella* sonnet sequence is the first important such cycle in English, influencing Spenser, Shakespeare, Donne, and all succeeding writers of sonnets.   He was regarded as the ideal of a courtier and died of a wound from battle in 1586. He was buried in ST. PAUL'S CATHEDRAL.

Silly. See SEELY.

Silver, Age of. See FOUR AGES.

Simple. *Noun*: (1) a medicine made from one herb or plant, (2) a plant or herb used to prepare a medicine.   *Adjective*: (1) innocent, harmless, honest, open; (2) humble; (3) plain, unadorned; (4) deficient in knowledge or learning or mental power; (5) pure; (6) composed of one substance or element.

"Since she whom I loved hath paid her last debt."   First line of one of the *HOLY SONNETS*.   This poem obviously is autobiographical in that it concerns the death of Donne's wife (ANN MORE) in August, 1617.   Death was commonly referred to as the last debt that any individual owes to nature (i.e., to one's physical, mortal nature): Ann has paid all debts to physically

creating Nature and to her own mortal nature received from it.
Ann's soul has been "into Heaven RAVISHED" (here, primarily
meaning "carried away from earth"): it has been taken "early,"
conveying Donne's sense of her young death at the age of thirty-
three. Her death seems to take all "good" from the earth, as far as
he is concerned; therefore, he turns his mind entirely to things of
heaven ("wholly" also seems to suggest a pun on "holy").

    Lines 5–8 (i.e., the latter half of the octave in this Italian
sonnet) argue that Donne's love for his wife "here" on earth caused
him to follow this love to its source (i.e., God is the source of all
love), like tracing a stream to its point of origin, its "head." (For
some interesting parallels, see the second stanza of "A HYMN TO
CHRIST, AT THE AUTHOR'S LAST GOING INTO GERMANY." Also
compare God as the head of the stream of power in "SATIRE 3.")
But even though he has found God as the source of his love for
Ann and even though God has given him water (love) to try to
quench Donne's thirst, he is still longing for more: he is still
thirsty, as if he has "dropsy," an unquenchable thirst. This
condition seems to be symbolic of his desire for some absolute
assurance of God's love and grace. To feel this assurance is the
problem acknowledged at the end of the octave.

    In the sestet his problem is resolved. He realizes that he
does not really need to beg for more love from God, because he
recognizes that God actively, masculinely courts Donne's soul.
When Donne says, "for hers offering all Thine," I think that it must
be read as "in exchange for my soul's love [the soul was commonly
referred to as feminine, thus the possessive "hers," meaning "her
(his soul's) love"] You, God, are offering all of your love." (I follow
the punctuation here as emended by Gardner's edition of the
Divine Poems—see "Selected Bibliography: Works, Poetry."
Gardner contends that "hers" refers to Ann's, but she cites Joan
Bennett's suggestion that the antecedent is "my soul": see Gardner,
p. 154.) The reference here is not to Ann's love or to any
replacement that God is providing for Ann's love: rather, it is a
one-for-one exchange of love with Donne's soul as the female
being courted. (The soul is referred to as feminine in Castiglione's
THE COURTIER and in countless other writers of the Renaissance.
Donne also refers specifically to the soul with "her" in "THIS IS MY
PLAY'S LAST SCENE," line 9, and in "Elegy 6," line 11.) And even if
this active wooing by God of Donne's soul were not enough
assurance, he also sees that God is "jealous" and that God fears
that Donne might give saints and angels some love that rightfully
should go to God and that, even worse, Donne might allow the
world, flesh, and devil (the three traditional Christian foes) to woo

his soul away from God.   This assurance in the sestet solves the
problem of the octave.

This sonnet, as some other Christian poems by Donne,
regards God as a lover and speaks of religion in terms of a love
relationship.   The sonnet also is interesting to consider in light of
Donne's life, particularly his decision to forego secular ambitions
for service in the Church and his rededications to his Christian
faith and God's service.

Sink. *Noun*: cesspool or sewer.

Siphatecia. Supposedly a daughter of Adam and Eve: the idea
and the name are non-scriptural, coming only from rabbinic
tradition.   See line 456 and following in *METEMPSYCHOSIS*.

"Sir John Wingfield." See *EPIGRAMS* and WINGFIELD.

Sirens. In mythology, sea nymphs who, with enchanting singing,
lured sailors to their death on the rocks.   CIRCE warned Odysseus
of them, so he closed the ears of his sailors with wax and had
himself tied to the mast of the ship.   When they failed with
Odysseus, the sirens killed themselves.   They were also referred
to as "mermaids."

Size. *Verb*: to increase in size or to swell.   *Noun*: (1) the bigness
or magnitude of anything; (2) shortened form of "assize," a judicial
session held for a given period in each county of England at which
traveling judges sit to hear and administer cases.

Skein. *Noun*: a specialized meaning (also spelled "skene") is an
Irish dagger or small sword.

Snuff. *Noun*: wick of a candle or portion of the wick that is
already burned and blackened and must be removed to again
light the candle effectively.

Sodom. See LOT.

Soldurii. Soldiers in France in ancient times who took vows to
share any fortune of a chosen friend, even death.

Solicitation. *Noun*: (1) the act of requesting earnestly, (2) the act
of begging favor of a woman, with immoral intentions: see, for

example, line 3 of "THE APPARITION" and (in verb form) line 459 of *THE SECOND ANNIVERSARY*.

Somerset, Countess of. See KER, ROBERT (2).

Somerset, Earl of. See KER, ROBERT (2).

"Song (Go and Catch a Falling Star)." One of the *SONGS AND SONNETS*. This poem is one of several in the group with a cynical speaker, concerned especially with women's inconstancy. The first stanza presents the speaker giving a series of commands to, we assume, another man. These seven commands are all impossible—at least the first five would be regarded as impossible by anyone, and the last two are regarded as equally impossible by this particular speaker (although others might disagree with him on these two). The first five, however, are outrageous. The "MANDRAKE" plant has a forked root that makes it resemble a human shape, but it certainly cannot be impregnated by a man. An old belief was that the devil has a cloven hoof, but, even if so, no one can tell who caused it. The "mermaids" are the SIRENS of classical mythology that no man but Odysseus heard and survived to tell of it. More revealing are the last two commands. He tells the person being addressed to teach him (the speaker) to keep off the stinging of envy. This man believes that everyone is envious, that no human is immune to envy. Then he tells the other man to find any wind (i.e., anything) that will "advance an honest mind": since this is grouped with the other impossible tasks, the speaker must feel that no honest person is rewarded or advanced (i.e., only dishonesty gets one ahead). These two comments especially characterize the speaker as extremely cynical about human nature, the world, and life in general. Grouping these last two with the first five implies, for example, that escaping from envy or seeing honesty rewarded is just as impossible as catching a falling star.

The relation of the random impossibilities of the first stanza to the central concern of the poem only becomes clear in the second stanza. He tells the person he is talking to that he should go see invisible things, if he is one that can perceive such strange sights. He can do this by riding around the world for "ten thousand days and nights": if we take this strictly, he tells him to go travel unceasingly for about twenty-seven years, but the intention must be to tell him to go spend just about all of his remaining years on earth—the rest of his life—on this quest. This sense especially is enforced by the fact that when he returns his hair will have turned white through the effects of aging. The feeling of this long ride is conveyed by the consecutive heavy stresses on the first three syllables of line 12. The speaker assures the other man that, when he returns with a report of all that he saw, the one thing he will not have found anywhere on earth is a woman who is both "TRUE" and "FAIR." In other words, no woman exists who is both faithful ("true") and beautiful ("fair"). The cynical assumption here by the speaker is that if there is a beautiful woman, she will be tempted into love relationships with many men and cannot remain constant to one. Finding such a woman is the greatest impossibility of all—the climactic impossibility that those of the first stanza prepared us for. The speaker assumes that a woman can be found who is both true and ugly or one who is both untrue and fair—but the woman with the magic combination, true and fair, is impossible.

After this definitive assertion, the speaker shifts his assumption in the third stanza by supposing for the sake of argument, "if thou find'st one [who is both true and fair]." He tells the person addressed to let the speaker know if there is such a miraculous woman in the world: if there is one, the speaker is willing to make a "pilgrimage" (said with some sarcasm!) like a religious pilgrim to the site of a shrine or to the site of a miraculous manifestation of the Virgin Mary. This kind of woman deserves a "pilgrimage," not a mere journey. Then, in line 21, the speaker suddenly shifts matters again. In fact, he reverses things with the word "yet": he tells the other man not even to mention it if he did succeed in discovering such a miraculous woman on this lifetime travel. The speaker would not even bother to go next door (much less make a pilgrimage!) to meet her. The reason he would not take the trouble to do so, he says, is that, before he could walk next door, she already would have had time to be false—not just to one man or to two men, but probably even to three men! (This kind of assertion illustrates, of course, some of Donne's METAPHYSICAL exaggeration.) So, to this cynical speaker, his finding of a true and fair woman remains a task equal to catching a falling star.

"Song (Sweetest Love, I Do Not Go)." One of the *SONGS AND SONNETS*. According to IZAAK WALTON, Donne wrote the poem to his wife (ANN MORE) on the occasion of Donne's journey in 1611 with SIR ROBERT DRURY to the continent. However, there is no other evidence supporting this argument, and it must be considered only as a possibility based on mere conjecture. It perhaps is simply Walton's reading of Donne's life into his works.

The speaker (or Donne) says in the first stanza that the reason he is leaving on this journey is not that he is tired of the lady he is addressing. He also says that he is not seeking any better love. His explanation is made with a bit of wit and humor that tempers the seriousness and sadness of the occasion: he says (lines 5–8) that actually he is practicing for death. He knows that he will die some day, and he now is practicing for it through a FEIGNED (pretended) DEATH (lovers' parting as death).

In the second stanza (lines 9–16) the man assures the lady of his rapid return through an analogy of his journey compared to that of the sun's daily course. He will return as surely as the sun does each day. Besides that, his own journey is much shorter than the sun's, and he has much more reason to return rapidly: the man has more "wings and spurs" (the previously-mentioned "desire and sense") to urge him back to her speedily.

The middle stanza (lines 17–24) makes a general statement about the feebleness of man (people in general) and the nature of human fears. If a person experiences good luck, he or she cannot lengthen this period of good luck (and its accompanying happiness) at all or call up and re-experience a period of good luck from the past: this inability illustrates the limitations of the human, the feebleness of "man's power." On the other hand, if people experience bad luck ("bad chance"), "we" (all people) make it stronger against us by worrying about it and letting it occupy our minds excessively. In this way we are teaching bad luck the art of being even worse and are allowing it to last longer than it ordinarily would. We make ourselves more miserable and for a longer period than the original situation of bad luck warrants. So, the speaker is making a generalization about human nature and human behavior, but he is clearly implying that the lady should not succumb to this human tendency in the present circumstance of their physical parting.

In the fourth stanza (lines 25–32) the speaker specifically requests that the lady not sigh or weep at their parting. He uses the belief that every sigh and every tear shortens a person's life: since he is assuming that they are two lovers unified into one, he says that her sighs and tears will shorten his life. This is why he can employ the OXYMORON "unkindly kind" for her: there is a type of kindness in her weeping, since it shows her concern for him; however, it is also unkind to weep away and thus shorten his life that is in hers. The larger suggestion is that their ideal love that is primarily spiritual should transcend this petty physical parting and the physical expressions of emotions at such parting. He can wittily and paradoxically, then, chide her for not really loving him as she says she does, if she is willing to sigh and weep his life away.

In the last stanza he urges her not to foresee or prophesy (i.e., with her "divining heart") any bad fortune for him because it might then happen. Rather, he proposes, she should regard their parting as if it were only ("but") the two lovers turning aside to sleep. His return later will be like their waking up after a sleep— i.e., their parting is the type in which they never were really apart in any essential way. Even though the journey physically parts them, they are still spiritually together. Lovers who keep each other alive (by being spiritually unified and by not weeping and sighing) are never "parted" in the most important way.

The speaker begins the poem by comparing parting to death, but he ends it by comparing parting to sleep. Since sleep itself is a common metaphor for death, the poem seems unified around death in a particular way: in parting and sleep and death of true, spiritual lovers, the separation is only physical and thus unimportant compared to the enduring spiritual togetherness.

Songs and Sonnets. Traditional title for the group of Donne's most famous secular love lyrics, although apparently Donne himself neither gave the title nor grouped his poems as such. This division first appears in the second edition of his *Poems* in 1635 (the first edition in 1633 has no such section, and it includes these poems with others of different types). Some of the lyrics are entitled "Song," but the remainder simply have individual titles: the term "sonnet" in the early seventeenth century could refer to a short lyric poem, rather than being restricted in definition to one of fourteen lines in iambic pentameter.

Also, Donne himself might not have given the titles to the individual lyrics: it is possible (and even likely) that the titles were given instead by one of the compilers of a manuscript that served as a source for the first edition of 1633. Dating the composition of the *Songs and Sonnets* as a whole or individually is quite uncertain and speculative. Probably Donne wrote most between 1592 and 1615, although he might have written a few a bit earlier and later than the limits of this span. Entries for individual poems in this "Dictionary" give some probabilities in determining dates to the extent that such probabilities exist.

Almost all of the poems now designated under *Songs and Sonnets* appeared in the 1633 edition, but later publications added a few. Fifty-three poems are now generally accepted as authentic in the group, while two others attributed to Donne probably are not his and are not included in this "Dictionary." All fifty-three authentic poems of the group are entered individually by title in this "Dictionary," and their content has been examined for elements to make up other entries.

Sonnet. In its strictest definition, a 14-line lyric poem in iambic pentameter meter. The two major forms of the sonnet in English are (1) the Italian or PETRARCHAN and (2) the English or Shakespearean. The Italian or Petrarchan form was used in Italian poetry by Petrarch and others before the English Renaissance, and Sir Thomas Wyatt introduced it into English verse with his translations of some of Petrarch's poems and in the writing of some of his own. Such a sonnet typically divides into two parts, the octave (lines 1–8) and the sestet (lines 9–14): usually there are changes of sorts between the two divisions (in imagery, tone, attitude, etc.). Most commonly the octave asks a question, poses a problem, or presents some situation or experience to which the sestet provides an answer, solution, or response. The rhyme scheme of the octave is *abbaabba*, but the scheme of the sestet varies. The English or Shakespearean form was developed by Wyatt's younger contemporary the Earl of Surrey (Henry Howard) and divides into three quatrains and a couplet with the rhyme scheme *abab cdcd efef gg*. Donne chose to write his *HOLY SONNETS* and *LA CORONA* in the Italian or Petrarchan form. This particular form hitherto had been used for poems primarily embodying the PETRARCHAN love convention, but Donne employed the form in poems of Christian love. Other variations in form of such 14-line sonnets have been developed with poets' experimentations in line length, meter, rhyme scheme, etc., but these two primary forms remain the bases for variations from the hands of such experimenters as Sir PHILIP SIDNEY, EDMUND SPENSER, and others.

One must realize, however, that by Donne's time the term "sonnet" was sometimes employed loosely simply to refer to a short lyric poem, not necessarily one of fourteen lines (see *SONGS AND SONNETS* and "THE CANONIZATION").

Soul, Feminine. See discussions of "SINCE SHE WHOM I LOVED HATH PAID HER LAST DEBT," "BATTER MY HEART, THREE-PERSONED GOD, FOR YOU," and line 94 of "SATIRE 3."

Soul(s), Tripartite or Three. See discussion of stanza five in "A VALEDICTION: OF MY NAME IN THE WINDOW."

Span. *Noun*: (1) distance from the tip of the thumb to the tip of the little finger or from the tip of the thumb to the tip of the forefinger of a fully-extended hand: this distance averaging nine inches was used as a measure of length; (2) a very small space or length; (3) a short space of time, frequently referring to the short time of a human's life. *Verb*: (1) to grasp or seize; (2) to measure by an outstretched hand; (3) to measure out or set a limit; (4) to form an arch across or over, to stretch or extend over in an arch, to cross from side to side; (5) to reach or extend over either space or time.

Spangled breastplate. Metaphor (picturing the lady as a warrior) for an ornamented or jewelled STOMACHER worn under her laced bodice. See "Elegy 19: Going to Bed," line 7.

Spanish journeys. The English privateers periodically raided Spanish ships carrying gold back to Spain from America. Donne refers to these forays as "our Spanish journeys" in line 17 of "Elegy 20: Love's War."

Spanish stamps. Spanish coins.

Specular stone. Donne believed that a particular transparent or translucent stone used for building and ornamental purposes, like marble in temples and churches, could no longer be found in his own time. Furthermore, he believed that when it had been used in the past, the persons who cut it had to be highly skilled to do so.

Speed. *Verb*: (1) to succeed or prosper; (2) to attain one's purpose or desire; (3) to make progress; (4) to hasten; (5) to make haste.

Spenser, Edmund (1552?–1599). English poet. Educated at Cambridge. Served in the Earl of Leicester's household in 1579 and thereby met Sir PHILIP SIDNEY. Wrote *The Shepherd's Calendar* and dedicated it to Sidney. Appointed secretary to Lord Grey of Wilton in 1580, serving him in Ireland. Spenser lived in Ireland until very near the end of his life. After he was forced to flee Ireland following an insurrection in 1598, he died the following year in London in near-poverty. ROBERT DEVEREUX, Earl of Essex, paid for his funeral. He was buried in Westminster Abbey, and Lady ANNE CLIFFORD erected a monument for him there about twenty years later.

Spenser's masterpiece is *The Faerie Queene*, dedicated to Queen ELIZABETH and portraying her as Gloriana, on one of the many allegorical levels in the long epic poem. Spenser also wrote *Four Hymns*, specifically reflecting the heavy influence from PLATONIC thought on Spenser. Among several other works, also important are his sonnet sequence entitled *Amoretti* that concerns his courtship of Elizabeth Boyle and *Epithalamion* that depicts his marriage to her. Christian Platonism suffuses all of Spenser's major works.

Donne was well aware of Spenser's poems, both using and parodying his Platonic and PETRARCHAN strains. Spenser's *Epithalamion* clearly is the seminal influence on Donne's *EPITHALAMIONS*, especially on the "Epithalamion Made at Lincoln's Inn."

Sphere(s). *Noun*: (1) very commonly in Donne's work, refers to one of the solid, transparent globes in which all of the known planets, the sun, the moon, and the stars are placed, according to the system envisioned largely by PTOLEMY. These Ptolemaic spheres were thought to number either 9, 10, or 11. Some contended that angels or INTELLIGENCES managed each separate sphere. It was believed that, as the spheres revolved, they created a perfect music known as the music of the spheres. Adam and Eve could hear the music before their fall, but no human after the fall can hear it. (See also HIERARCHY, THE HEAVENLY); (2) the circular, visible outer limit of space; (3) heaven; (4) the "sphere of forms" is a spiritual, heavenly region envisioned as the place where the ideal forms of earthly bodies wait for the Resurrection to be united with the soul; (5) domain in which one lives and acts; (6) a round body or ball.

Spirits. For specialized meanings in Donne's time, see NATURAL SPIRITS, VITAL SPIRITS, and ANIMAL SPIRITS.

Spital. A spelling of "hospital."

Spouse. Frequently used by Donne to refer to the Church (the Church as the bride of Christ).

Spright. See SPRITE.

Spring. *Verb*: (1) to rise out of or originate in or issue from; (2) to make an animal come out of hiding, the term especially used in hunting and falconry.

Sprite. *Noun:* spirit or soul.

Stablish. Alternate spelling of "establish."

Stand, standing. Used in some contexts by Donne and other writers with the bawdy implication of a male erection: see, for example, "Elegy 19: Going to Bed," line 4.

Standing house. Permanent residence.

Stanley, Elizabeth. See HUNTINGDON, COUNTESS OF.

Star, amorous evening. See "AMOROUS EVENING STAR."

Stay. *Verb:* (1) to stop or halt or stand still; (2) to cease carrying out some activity; (3) to remain in a place, rather than leaving; (4) to remain unmoving in position or unchanging in condition; (5) to tarry, linger, delay; (6) to reside in a place for a time; (7) to wait, to be inactive; (8) to detain or hold back or stop someone or something; (9) to support, sustain, hold up, comfort. *Noun:* (1) a delay; (2) a stop or pause; (3) a cessation; (4) a support.

Stew(s). *Noun:* brothel(s), house(s) of prostitution. So called because of their development from some heated public bathhouses.

Still. *Adverb:* ever or always or continually. *Adjective:* motionless or silent. *Verb:* to quiet or to calm. *Noun:* an apparatus for distilling.

Stock. *Noun:* (1) trunk of a tree or stem of a plant; (2) a fund, a sum of money; (3) a store, accumulated supply or wealth.

Stomacher. A vest, waistcoat, or similar covering for the chest.

Stone, Nicholas (1586–1647). Mason, sculptor, and architect. After working as a stonemason in Holland, he returned to his native England prior to 1614. Was employed by King JAMES and INIGO JONES to execute works at Whitehall Palace and elsewhere. Was made master-mason to James I in 1619 and received a patent from Charles I in 1626 to be master-mason and architect at Windsor Castle. Responsible for many of the monuments, statues, and tombs at Westminster Abbey and other locations. Stone carved a monument for Donne's wife (ANN MORE) after her death in 1617: it was erected in ST. CLEMENT DANES Church, but was later destroyed. He also made statues and a sundial for the garden of MAGDALEN HERBERT (Lady Danvers) in CHELSEA. One of his most famous creations, however, is the marble monument of Donne in his shroud (or winding-sheet) made from the sketch that Donne posed for shortly before his death, according to WALTON. The monument was placed in ST. PAUL'S CATHEDRAL, survived the Great Fire of 1666, and may be seen there today. Walton relates that Donne's surviving friends felt that the statue looks so much like him that it seems to breathe and that it is as close to a representation of a live individual as marble can be.

Stoop. *Verb*: (1) to bend or bow down; (2) to descend from a height; (3) to condescend to something unworthy; (4) [of a bird of prey] to descend swiftly on the prey, to swoop.

Store. *Noun*: (1) sufficient or abundant supply; (2) a person's accumulated goods or money; (3) a treasure; (4) a stock of anything laid up for future use.

"Storm, The." One of the *VERSE LETTERS* written to CHRISTOPHER BROOKE. Describes an incident when Donne served on the expedition proposed for the Azores Islands in 1597 under ROBERT DEVEREUX, Earl of Essex. See above, p. 14 (in "Donne's Life").

Stow, John (1525–1605). Historian and chronicler of the late sixteenth century. Wrote and published several historical accounts but is best known for *A Survey of London*, with its vivid descriptions of London's physical features, customs, and history. Stow examined original records and sites personally, walking around London and England for evidence. Donne, however, in lines 97–8 of "Satire 4" groups him with those chroniclers who include "trivial household trash" in writing (i.e., minor matters among the great).

Strait(s). *Noun*: (1) narrow passageway connecting two large bodies of water, (2) distressing situation or circumstance. *Adjective*: (1) tight or narrow, (2) confining or inadequate in space, (3) severe or rigorous.

Streight(s). See STRAIT(S).

Stuart. Family ruling England for most of the seventeenth century. See JAMES I and CHARLES I.

Stuart, Charles. See CHARLES I.

Stuart, Elizabeth (1596–1662). Daughter of King JAMES. Married FREDERICK, Elector Palatine, on February 14, 1613. Their marriage is celebrated in one of Donne's *EPITHALAMIONS* ("An Epithalamion, or Marriage Song on the Lady Elizabeth and Count Palatine being Married on St. Valentine's Day"). She became Queen of Bohemia in 1619 when Frederick accepted the election as King Frederick V. She was nicknamed "the Winter Queen" (in the role of Queen only from November, 1619, until November, 1620, when Frederick was defeated by the Catholic League). Driven out of their country, they lived in exile. Her husband died in 1632. She returned to England in 1661 and died there in 1662.

Donne's interest in Elizabeth probably was generated in part by the fact that the parents of Lucy, COUNTESS OF BEDFORD (one of Donne's patronesses), educated her. In addition to writing the epithalamion on her wedding, Donne preached before her and her husband in 1619 in Heidelberg during his trip to Germany as chaplain accompanying JAMES HAY, Viscount Doncaster (see Potter and Simpson edition of *SERMONS*, II, Sermon 12). He also sent her copies of his *DEVOTIONS UPON EMERGENT OCCASIONS* (1624) and his first sermon preached to her brother King CHARLES in 1625 (see Potter and Simpson edition, VI, Sermon 12). She responded in letters that speak of the "delight" she always had in hearing Donne deliver the messages of God to her and of her gratitude at the presentation of his "labors" to her.

Stuart, Henry (1594–1612). Son of King JAMES. Prince of Wales who was popular with the people and a future king of great hope. His death of typhoid fever stunned and greatly saddened the nation, and the death was followed by many written tributes, including Donne's "Elegy upon the Untimely Death of the Incomparable Prince Henry," one of the *EPICEDES AND OBSEQUIES*. One of the elegies for him was by Sir EDWARD HERBERT, and JONSON told DRUMMOND that Donne claimed to have written his own poem on Prince Henry "to match Sir Edward Herbert in obscureness." The death of Henry meant that CHARLES would succeed to the throne. Donne pictures Prince Henry as very Christlike.

Stuart, James. See JAMES I.

Stupid. *Adjective*: (1) stupefied or stunned, (2) lacking consciousness or thought or feeling.

Style. *Noun*: (1) a distinguishing title or designation or appellation, (2) a written work, (3) subject matter, (4) manner of expression of a particular writer or group or period, (5) an inscription or legend. *Verb*: (1) to give a name or style to, (2) to call by a name or style.

Sublunary. *Adjective*: below the moon—referring to the realm of the created universe below the SPHERE of the moon, according to the PTOLEMAIC concept of the universe; this area includes the earth and the layers of the other three ELEMENTS (water, air, and fire), and anything in the sublunary realm is associated with the worldly, earthly, and physical, and is subject to time, change, decay, and death (in contrast to the FIRMAMENT).

Substance. A special meaning (from ARISTOTLE) refers to the basic, essential nature of any material thing. Compare ACCIDENT.

Subtle (Subtile). *Adjective*: (1) impalpable, fine, or delicate; (2) [of ships] narrow or slender; (3) involving discrimination or fine points, abstruse, difficult; (4) clever or sly.

Sudden (Sodaine). *Adjective*: (1) happening without warning, (2) hasty or rash, (3) prompt or immediate, (4) brief or momentary.

"Sun Rising, The." One of the *SONGS AND SONNETS*. The situation portrayed in the poem is that of the speaker in bed with his lover in the early morning. The sun interrupts their privacy.

The first line contains irregular metrical stresses and colloquial language that convey the speaker's irritation and anger. He calls the sun "busy" in the sense of being occupied with prying and being meddlesome in others' concerns. The sun is "unruly," hard to control—the mixture of humor with seriousness in this statement appears in the pun on "sun" as if it were "son." So, the sun is pictured paradoxically as both an "old fool" and a young "unruly *son*," a juvenile delinquent of sorts. Donne is being deliberately anticonventional in this denigrating portrayal of the sun: the image is quite different from that of a god that many earlier writers call the sun. In lines 2 and 3 the sun is shown to be a kind of intruding spy, peeping both through windows and curtains into the lovers' room (the image developing further the idea that the sun is "busy"). Then his direct challenge to the sun in line 4 raises a question that will be central in the poem: "Must to thy motions lovers' seasons run?" introduces the relationship between love and time. This particular speaker argues that he and his lady do not have to obey the commands of the sun about when and what to do or not to do in life, but he expands this personal concern into the larger argument that lovers and love in general do not have to obey the time schemes measured by the sun. The rhetorical question of line 4, then, implies both the answer "no" and that love has its own time scheme independent of the sun's and the ordinary world's. Lines 5–8 proceed to catalog all those types of people that the sun should be concerned about, those that ordinarily do follow the dictates of the sun (declaring when night and rest turn to day and activity). The sun is now termed a "saucy" (impertinent, presumptuous) and "pedantic" (like a schoolmaster) creature of despicable qualities (i.e., a "wretch") that should concern himself with criticizing (1) "late schoolboys" that should get to school on time in the morning, (2) "sour" (ill-tempered) apprentices who have to report to their master's work on time, (3) "court-huntsmen" (courtiers accompanying the ruler on his hunt) that need to attend to their business of entertaining the King whenever he is ready, and (4) "country ants" (a belittling image for farm laborers who, like ants, regularly have to perform their duty when the crop is ready) that must carry out their "offices" (assigned tasks). (Many editors and critics feel that the reference to the King's wish to hunt alludes to King JAMES and his preference for hunting above all other recreations: he would indeed rise early and hunt on horseback for many hours. The poem, then, probably was written after he came to the throne in 1603.) One notes the scorn of the speaker as he looks down on all of these mundane types of people who are slaves to the sun and time—they are regulated by time and worldly duties that he and his lady are independent of and superior to. So, he and the lady and their love are outside of the ordinary world and its regulator, time (symbolized by the sun). He says in lines 9–10 that love is "all alike"—i.e., it does not change according to season or climate, and it does not have to proceed according to "hours, days, months" (the pounding three heavy stresses on these words conveying the sense of the regular, unceasing measurements of time that he and the lady are *not* subject to). The speaker condescendingly refers to "hours, days, months" as the "RAGS" of time, undoubtedly applying both meanings of the word to his denigration of time.

The second stanza opens with an increasing sense of superiority on the part of the speaker as he further belittles the sun and its supposed power. He even tells the sun itself that it should not regard its own beams as the respected and strong forces that people traditionally have seen them as. The speaker proves their weakness by saying that all he has to do is close his eyes ("WINK") to shut out those rays. He now (in line 14) compliments his lady by saying that he does not want to close his eyes, however, for he would then not be able to see her beauty for that period of time. In line 16 he goes so far as to imply that the lady's eyes are even brighter than the sun's beams: her eyes might have blinded the sun's! At this point (significantly at the poem's center, line 15) we realize that possibly the more important "sun rising" is the lady herself. Donne has taken the old PETRARCHAN image of the lady's eyes as suns and given it fresh life in the context of this poem. So, if the sun still has its sight, the speaker says that it should observe as it makes its journey around the earth to see if the two "Indias" are still in their usual places. The India "of spice" is the East Indies (source of spices and perfume), and the India "of mine" is the West Indies (source of precious metals and ores from mines, especially the source of gold). The sun might find that they are here in bed with the speaker—i.e., the lady has all of the qualities of the Indies, the sweetness and value. She is all the wealth of the world, as he begins to establish the bedroom as a MICROCOSM. In the midst of his serious complimenting of the lady, we note Donne's METAPHYSICAL exaggeration to make his point, and we note the humor in telling the sun to return tomorrow "late"—i.e., he tells him not to come around so early to interrupt the two lovers. He concludes the second stanza (lines 19–20) by saying also that the sun will find that all the "kings" (rulers) of the earth have disappeared and are now in the lovers' bed (epitomized by the speaker). So, the principle of power is in the bedroom in the form of the man, and the principle of wealth is there in the form of the lady.

The third stanza emphatically asserts the MICROCOSM in the bedroom that is more important than the entire MACROCOSM outside of it. The lady is "all states," and the man is "all princes": she is the territory of the whole earth, and he is the ruler of it. He goes so far as to say now that "nothing else is," that nothing else even exists. Their self-sufficient world or universe in the room is the only one that matters to them. Line 23 asserts that any rulers on earth are just imitating the two lovers as if the worldly rulers were acting in a play, implying that the two lovers are the true rulers of the true world or true universe. Compared to their relationship (to their world), all "honor" held by rulers on earth is mimicry and unreal, since the man is the true ruler, and all wealth of the world is fake gold and worthless fraudulence (see ALCHEMY), since the lady is the true gold, the true wealth. Addressing the sun in line 25, the man patronizingly talks as if he were giving advice to his "son"—at least he is assuming the tone of talking to an inferior, even to a dependent. The man and his lady and love definitely seem superior to the sun and time now. He tells the sun that it is half as fortunate ("happy") as the couple is, since the sun has such a large world (the earth itself) to encompass in its arduous journey each day. The lovers have only this "contracted," compact world (MICROCOSM) in the one room to be concerned with. So, even more patronizingly, the speaker tells the sun that they will offer to do him a favor: they will allow the sun to assume that this room is the earth (the man speaking already has made it so) and that the sun can carry out its ordained duty of circling the earth simply by revolving around this room with the two lovers. Condescendingly the speaker (in line 27) tells the sun that the sun is getting up in years and should relax a bit. If the sun simply will shine to them, it will shine "everywhere" (i.e., everywhere that matters to these lovers, at least—in their own microcosm of love). The bed is the "center"— i.e., the center of the universe which is the earth in the PTOLEMAIC concept assumed in this poem. The bed as the earth follows from the two lovers in the bed earlier being established as the epitome of rulers and countries on earth. Instead of the sun, then, taking the earth as "thy center," it can take the bed as a superior earth and as its new "center." The "walls" of the bedroom will be "thy sphere"—i.e., the sun can take on the walls as its SPHERE (in the PTOLEMAIC sense, with the sun set in its own universal sphere revolving around the earth).

This METAPHYSICAL CONCEIT of the MICROCOSM in the poem is thus completed with the sun in its new sphere, implying that the couple's love is at the center of all reality and that time (symbolized by the sun) is subservient to such a perfect love. So, the speaker's early contention (first stanza) that lovers' seasons do not run to the sun's motions proves true as he develops it—indeed, time's (the sun's) motions run in accord with love by the end of the poem!

Superficies. *Noun*: the surface of anything.

Surius, Laurentius (1522–1578).   CARTHUSIAN monk who wrote many volumes of ecclesiastical history that were regarded by Protestants as inaccurate and prejudiced toward Catholicism. Donne refers to him in line 48 of "Satire 4."

Surquedry. *Noun*: arrogance.

Surround. *Verb*: to flood or overflow.

Swage. Assuage.

Swan.   The bird traditionally is employed symbolically for its whiteness, purity, and grace.   The white swan is dedicated to Venus.   The swan also is dedicated to Apollo as the god of music, since it was thought to sing only at death and then to do so very beautifully.

T

Taper. *Noun*: candle.

Target. *Noun*: shield.

Tenarif(e). The high volcanic peak on the island of Tenarife in the Canary Islands (or the island itself). See line 286 of *THE FIRST ANNIVERSARY*.

Tenarus. Place in Laconia in Greece where a cavern was said to emit smoke and was thought to descend to Hades.

Tentation. Temptation.

Tertullian (Quintus Septimus Florens Tertullianus) [about 155–225]. Early Christian convert and writer in Carthage who defended Christianity against pagans, Jews, and heretical sects. Influential in his expression of the doctrine of the TRINITY; his arguments for the true birth, death, and resurrection of Christ; his arguments against pagan and heretical concepts of the soul; his writings on the history of baptism; his exposition of the Lord's Prayer; and his discussion of idolatry. One of the earliest and most important Christian writers in Latin, Tertullian is alluded to by Donne numerous times in his prose, especially in the *SERMONS*.

Tethlemite. Donne designates him as a son of Adam and Eve (in lines 487–8 of *METEMPSYCHOSIS*). The name comes from no known source.

Thames' right side. Southwark, the area south of the Thames River and across the river from London proper. The area rejected the claimed jurisdiction and authority of London and the Lord Mayor. See "Elegy 1: Jealousy," line 33.

Than. Common spelling of modern "then."

Themech. Supposedly a daughter of Adam and Eve and wife to CAIN; the idea and the name are non-scriptural, coming only from rabbinic tradition. Near the end of the unfinished *METEMPSYCHOSIS* (see line 505 and following), Donne designates her as "sister and wife to Cain," and at that point in the poem the soul that began in the TREE OF KNOWLEDGE is residing in her.

Then. Common spelling of modern "than."

Things indifferent. A phrase originating in the late sixteenth century and increasingly common during the seventeenth century to refer to such matters of worship as various ceremonies, clerical vestments, discipline, order, and trappings that are not essential to salvation. Donne, for example, refers to the Church as "a moveable pillar, for things indifferent, and arbitrary" (*SERMONS*, Potter and Simpson edition, Volume IX, p. 363). Variations of the phrase and idea occur—see, for example, in Donne's *SERMONS*, near the end of his sermon given on January 25, 1628 [1629 under New Style calendar] (Potter and Simpson edition, Volume VIII, p. 331): ". . . I do not intend, that we should decline all such things, as had been superstitiously abused, in a superstitious Church [i.e., the Roman Catholic]; But, in all such things, as being in their own nature indifferent. . . ." The PURITANS wished to rid the church of all such unnecessary "Roman" elements. Donne, as a staunch Anglican, especially under CHARLES I and the power of LAUD, argued for the value and necessity of "such things" in their "right use." He goes on to refer to them as "indifferent things."

"This is my play's last scene, here heavens appoint." First line of one of the *HOLY SONNETS*. Lines 1–4 convey the speaker's awareness of being at the very end of his life and facing imminent death by making this period of his life analogous to the very end of several things—the last scene of a play, the last mile of a pilgrimage, the last pace of a race, the last inch of a SPAN (primarily the measurement, but also a play on the span of life), and the last point (i.e., instant or moment) in the duration of a minute. His feeling, however, seems to be a complex combination of anticipation and fear. He seems to have reached a longed-for goal of his life, but, now that he is there, some fear rises in him as he anticipates death. The feeling of delay in trying to consummate his goal is felt especially in the repetition of and heavy stress on "last" in each of the four lines: it slows the reading and seems to keep the end from coming—it seems to remain just out of reach for both the speaker and the reader. A part of this feeling is created as well by having two or three consecutive heavy stresses at the end of each phrase or clause in which "last" appears: i.e., the syllables of "play's last scene," "last mile," "last pace," and "span's last inch" are heavily stressed and drag matters out, just as the speaker feels that the moment of death just seems never to arrive even as he is only a step away. But his fears of what he might face—the Christian fear of the Last Judgment—is implied in the image of death as "gluttonous," as a voracious and powerful animal of prey that will rip apart ("unjoint") body and soul (lines 5–6). So, despite looking forward to death and the peace, the "sleep," it will bring, the speaker "shakes" with fear at the prospect of seeing God's "face" when his soul (his "ever-waking part") is brought into God's presence (lines 7–8). So, at the end of the octave in this Italian SONNET, the speaker has the problem of fear and doubt regarding death, the Last Judgment, and his status in eternal life beyond death.

This problem is resolved in the sestet. He imagines his soul ascending to heaven, its original residence ("first seat"), while his earthly body of ELEMENTS will return to the dust from which it originated. He soothes himself with the assurance that his sins that came of the body will fall with the body and leave his repentant soul free. The sins stay with the body, and Christ now assigns ("imputes") righteousness to the repentant soul (a Protestant belief in the necessity of Christ's merit to apply to the individual soul—see CALVIN), just as at the beginning of all humanity Adam imputed guilt to every human born after him. So, the speaker has resolved his problem by the confidence that he can leave behind the old traditional Christian foes (the world, the flesh, and the devil) when his soul, imputed righteous by Christ himself, ascends to heaven to dwell with God.

One should compare and contrast this sonnet with the one beginning "AT THE ROUND EARTH'S IMAGINED CORNERS BLOW."

Thisbe. See PYRAMUS.

Thorough. Common spelling for modern "through."

"Thou hast made me, and shall thy work decay?" First line of one of the HOLY SONNETS. The speaker, a sinner, questions God in a challenging tone in the first line and establishes the major analogy (or METAPHYSICAL CONCEIT) of the poem: the speaker himself is a creation "made" by God, like an artistic creation or piece of sculpture or crafted work. He sarcastically implies that God, the artist or sculptor or artisan, is letting the work "decay," deteriorate and fall into ruin, neglecting the piece that He himself created! So, the sinner affected by sin is like a decaying piece of art that he expects God to cleanse and "repair" (i.e., to regenerate spiritually). The speaker conveys urgency because he feels that his death ("mine end") is rapidly coming. He is running toward death, while death (personified) is rushing toward him. All of his "pleasures" (of this world, of this life) are behind him. Death seems to be a threatening person "before" him (both in front of him and in his future), and "despair" is an equally threatening one "behind" him (both in back of him and in his past—i.e., he has not lived in a way that assures him of heaven and thus is in spiritual despair because his sinful past might exclude him from eternal salvation). He is in such "terror" that he does not dare to turn his eyes toward the front and back (or future and past): his "dim eyes" imply not only physical dimness from increasing age, but primarily spiritual dimness or blindness or lack of perception because of his entrapment by sin. This is one way that he is decaying and is needing repair. His "feeble flesh" (as a weak, sinful, easily-tempted human) is another flaw that needs repair, since it is wasted by accumulating sin in it that is making it heavy and is increasingly pulling him down toward hell: by implication he has ignored the spirit, in favor of the flesh, and the heavenly, in favor of the hellish. Line 8 ends the octave of this Italian SONNET with the speaker's emphasis on decay, the weight of sin, pulling down, and impending death. He also has acknowledged his spiritual problem and a needed solution through rescue by God.

The sestet, then, poses the solution for God's urgent consideration, and, with it, shifts the imagery from a dismal downward-looking motif to one involving looking up toward God and heaven. The speaker becomes optimistic as he is able to turn to God: "only" can mean "but," and it can also imply to see "only" Him (Him alone). The sinner feels himself "rise" with spiritual optimism and hope of heaven. Donne seems to play on "thou art above": "you are above" and "you, as the epitome of and source of all art, are above." The speaker as a creation acknowledges his allegiance to God as art and artist and looks for reclamation by God: this is particularly emphasized by the contrast made (in line 13) with the deceptive and inferior "art" of Satan, "our [God's and humanity's] old subtle foe" (line 11). God's superior artistry can "PREVENT" (in several senses) that of Satan, and the speaker trusts that God will apply this process to the speaker as a piece almost ruined by the art of Satan. The sinner speaking (as in many of Donne's Christian poems and prose works) cannot save himself after succumbing so entirely to sin; therefore, he must depend on God's grace to rescue him. Grace can add wings to this piece of art (the sinner) and allow it to fly out of the clutches of Satan. And in the final line God becomes like a magnet ("adamant") in another METAPHYSICAL CONCEIT: God is like a magnet that attracts the heavy iron (the sin) that is weighing the sinner down toward hell and can instead apply attractive force to pull the sinner up to heaven. This will not only completely repair the creation, but reunite it with its creator, God the Artist.

Three Souls. See discussion of stanza five in "A VALEDICTION: OF MY NAME IN THE WINDOW."

Thrones. See HIERARCHY, THE HEAVENLY.

Throughly. Common spelling for modern "thoroughly."

Through-shine. *Adjective*: transparent (i.e., through which light shines).

Tiberius (42 B.C.–A.D. 37). Roman emperor from A.D. 14 to A.D. 37. Succeeded Augustus. Largely continued policies of Augustus but was aloof, did not work well with the Senate, and alienated much of the aristocracy. Political intrigue and executions of traitors and suspected traitors marked his reign. He was "Caesar" during the time of the crucifixion of Christ.

Donne alludes (in lines 35–36 of "The Calm") to a story told by Suetonius that the pet snake of Tiberius was eaten by ants as he prepared to enter Rome on one occasion and that Tiberius saw this as a warning of the people's fury and thus turned away from the city. In a sermon of 1620 (see Potter and Simpson edition, III, Sermon 9, p. 220) Donne speaks of deception in Tiberius as a contrast to the truth of the one crucified (i.e., Christ) under Tiberius. In another sermon (see Potter and Simpson, VI, Sermon 5, pp. 121–22) Donne refers to both Tiberius and the Senate wishing to canonize Christ and thus admit him as a Roman God, but wishing to do so only for their own honor in proposing it, rather than for Christ's.

Tilman, Edward (died 1641). Took his B.A. in 1613 and M.A. in 1616 from Pembroke College, Cambridge. Ordained deacon in December, 1618, and priest the following March. He had wavered in his decision whether or not to enter the Church, his difficult choice reflected in a poem he wrote entitled (in a manuscript) "Mr. Tilman of Pembroke Hall in Cambridge his motives not to take orders." The poem dwells on his own sense of unworthiness to be ordained. It is not certain that Donne knew Tilman personally, but he apparently had read his poem. Donne himself wrote "To Mr. Tilman after He Had Taken Orders" as a kind of response, but

Donne seems more to justify his own reasons for ordination and the high calling of the clergy (despite the scorns of laymen), rather than to address Tilman's own earlier personal reservations. (Fuller information on Donne and Tilman is related in the Gardner edition of *Divine Poems* [see "Selected Bibliography: Works, Poetry"]. Also valuable is the discussion about Donne's poem in relation to GEORGE HERBERT in Novarr's *The Disinterred Muse* [see "Selected Bibliography: Critical Studies, General: Poetry and Prose"].)

Tincture. *Noun*: (1) color or dye; (2) stain or blemish; (3) in ALCHEMY, a spiritual principle or immaterial substance, the quality of which can be infused into things; (4) an active, physical principle that can be extracted from a substance; (5) an essence of a substance (such as gold) that supposedly can be extracted and used to change other substances.

Tires. *Noun*: (1) attires, attirings, apparel, clothes; (2) ornaments for the head.

"To Mr. B. B." See B., B.

"To Mr. C. B." See BROOKE, CHRISTOPHER.

"To Mr. E. G." See GUILPIN, EVERARD.

To Mr. I. L." Two of the *VERSE LETTERS* are so titled. The identity of the recipient is unknown.

"To Mr. R. W." See WOODWARD, ROWLAND.

"To Mr. S. B." See BROOKE, SAMUEL.

"To Mr. T. W." See WOODWARD, THOMAS.

"To Mrs. M. H." See HERBERT, MAGDALEN.

Tophet. Hell.

Torpedo. *Noun*: a flat fish with a circular body and tapering tail that gives off electric discharges or the electric ray or the numbfish.

Touchstone. *Noun*: (1) a black stone used to test the quality of gold or silver by the color each leaves when rubbed on this stone, (2) figuratively applied to anything that tests the value or authenticity of something else.

Translate. *Verb*: (1) to transfer or transport from one place to another; (2) to carry from earth to heaven [a sense used, at times punningly, by Donne in both prose and poetry]; (3) to render something in one language into another; (4) to express in other words, to paraphrase; (5) to change in form or appearance.

Transubstantiate. *Verb*: (1) to change from one substance into another, to transform; (2) theologically, to change miraculously the bread and wine of the Eucharist or Holy Communion into the body and blood of Christ.

Travail (Travel). *Verb*: (1) to afflict or trouble, (2) to labor or work hard, (3) [of women] to suffer pains of childbirth or to be in labor, (4) to journey. *Noun*: (1) exertion or hardship, (2) [of women] the labor and pain of childbirth, (3) a journey or journeying.

Travel. See TRAVAIL.

Tree. Donne frequently employs the noun in its special Christian senses: (1) the Tree of Knowledge (of good and evil) in Eden, the fruit from which Adam and Eve were forbidden to eat (also referred to as the "forbidden tree," "fruitful tree," and "Adam's tree") [see Genesis 2 and 3]; (2) the Tree of Life in Eden that held immortality for humanity [see Genesis 2 and Revelation 22]; (3) the cross on which Christ was crucified, Christ's cross (one of the three "trees") on CALVARY. Also referred to as "Christ's tree." An old Christian belief held that Christ's cross was made of the wood from the Tree of Knowledge and that Christ was crucified on the very site on which the Tree of Knowledge grew in Eden. Also, the Tree of Life has been interpreted as a symbolic foreshadowing of Christ and his granting of immortality again to humanity.

Tree, forbidden learned. See discussion of "Tree of Knowledge" in TREE.

Tree, fruitful. See discussion of "Tree of Knowledge" in TREE.

Tree of Knowledge. See TREE.

Tremellius, Immanuel (1510–1580). Biblical scholar who was born in a Jewish family but became a CALVINIST about 1530. Collaborated with Francis Junius on a Latin translation of the Old Testament that became the standard Latin version for Protestants in Europe. Referred to many times by Donne in sermons, as well as in his poem "The Lamentations of Jeremy, for the Most Part According to Tremellius."

Trencher. *Noun*: a plate on which food is served, frequently ornamented with moral sayings, lessons.

Trent. River in northern England.

Trent Council. See COUNCIL OF TRENT.

Trill. *Verb*: to trickle.

Trinity, the. The Christian concept that God or the Godhead is made up of three unified and indivisible divine figures or "persons": the Father (God the Creator), the Son (Jesus Christ), and the Holy Spirit (Holy Ghost). Frequently the Father is associated with wrath and power; the Son with love, mercy, and light (the "sun" and "son"); and the Holy Spirit with ever-present grace (Biblically, symbolically, and artistically represented as a dove, fire, and breath).

Tripartite Soul. See discussion of stanza five in "A VALEDICTION: OF MY NAME IN THE WINDOW."

"Triple Fool, The." One of the *SONGS AND SONNETS*. As Grierson (see "Selected Bibliography: Works") first noted, the man speaking is a triple fool because (1) he loves, (2) he says so in poetry, and (3) by writing in verse, he has made it possible for someone to set it to music that leads to song that reawakens the love and its emotions. Paradoxically, then, this is a poem arguing, in a particular way, against poetry!

The first stanza reveals how he is at least the first two types of fools. "Whining" poetry conveys an undignified picture of the poem (and the poet?) as a child venting his emotions. But, in sharp contrast, lines 4–5 say that all men would also write poems about their loves, if their ladies would respond favorably: this compliments his own lady for not being of the cold PETRARCHAN type. In lines 6–9 a METAPHYSICAL CONCEIT relates his original reason for writing about love, justifying his action on the basis of the psychological value of poetry. He thought that the discipline of writing would purge his emotion, the "grief" and "pains" of love: he wanted to lessen ("allay") his pains by expressing them in the difficult, demanding, vexing means of verse ("rhyme"). His analogy compares the lines of verse to "inward, narrow, crooked lanes" in the earth: a belief still popular in Donne's time was that underground channels filtered the salt out of sea water, allowing inland rivers to be fresh water, free of salt. (See especially Gardner's notes to this poem in her edition of the *Songs and Sonnets* in "Selected Bibliography: Works" for further details concerning this belief.) So, he hoped that, like the salt of the sea, his own pains (and "salt" tears of "grief"?) would be purged. The very image of hidden, inaccessible channels in the earth suggests that the lines of poetry are ideally just as hidden, secret, private. But his wish for the private expression and purging of emotion is doomed to be frustrated by the very act of writing it down. Lines 10–11 shift to an analogy of "grief" as a kind of animal to be tamed with verses (meter or "numbers") as the fetters to lock it in. An assumption here is a Renaissance one of "grief" being of the passionate side of the human, which is part of the human's animalistic or bestial nature. As an animal can be restrained by fetters, so can man's emotions be restrained by his reason: poetry written from man's rational self should control the emotion that he puts into it.

The effectiveness of the taming power of poetry, however, depends upon the poetry being kept personal and private. The second stanza reveals how the speaker sees this secrecy being violated and the animal (grief) being released. And then the speaker becomes a fool in the third way. Someone sets the poetry to music and sings it. It is done to the delight of those who hear it, but it releases the grief in the speaker again: grief is set free from the fetters of verse. Lines 17–22 note that both love and grief are proper subjects of verse, but only when the verse is kept personal. If the poet's private feelings are made public ("published," as in line 20) when performed for the entertainment of others, then both love and grief are increased (as if they were equally bad!). To reveal publicly the triumphs of love and grief over the poet defeats, and indeed reverses, his original motive of purging his emotions by putting them down in verse. This, then, causes him to "grow" into the third fool. The last line is the lesson he has learned, but the lesson seems to be quite conducive to an ironic, double interpretation. The reader wonders if "Who are a little wise, the best fools be" means (1) those [such as this poet himself] who are intelligent and creative enough to be able to write poetry make the biggest fools [triple ones, in fact] of themselves or (2) those [unlike this poet himself] who are not intelligent and creative enough to be able to write poetry make the most desired kind of fools to be [i.e., they will be only single fools for loving and are spared from being additional fools for writing poetry and having it set to music]. Does Donne mean one or both of these? He lets us decide.

For the importance of this poem and others to Donne's feelings about the privacy of verse, see Sackton in "Selected Bibliography: Critical Studies, Poetry."

Triumphant Church. See CHURCH, TRIUMPHANT.

True. *Adjective*: (1) steadfast, loyal, faithful; (2) consistent with fact, agreeing with reality; (3) exact, accurate, correct; (4) proper, legitimate; (5) real, genuine, not imaginary.

"True Character of a Dunce, The." A CHARACTER written by Donne and published in 1622 in a book titled *Sir Thomas Overbury His Wife. With Additions of New Characters, and Many Other Witty Conceits Never Before Printed.* This book contains 82 anonymous characters and miscellaneous pieces of prose and poetry written by various individuals, but they are known to include many by the dramatists John Webster and Thomas Dekker, as well as some by others such as Sir HENRY WOTTON. Donne's prose pieces "An Essay of Valor" and "News from the Very Country" are also contained in this volume.

A series of succinct, witty statements, Donne's characterization of a dunce includes (among many assertions) the following: he is one whose thoughts seldom reach an inch further than his eyes; one who eats, drinks, walks, and spits by imitation; and one who speaks only what he just read or heard without understanding it. Donne concludes by saying that one must take the dunce as he is, because there is no hope that he shall ever become better. Recurring in the sketch as a whole is the implication that the dunce is a nonentity or, at best, a kind of workhorse placed out of his element.

Try. *Verb*: (1) to separate, choose, select; (2) to extract; (3) to search by examination; (4) to determine; (5) to examine and determine judicially; (6) to test or prove the strength or goodness or truth of something; (7) to experience or undergo; (8) to attempt to do or perform; (9) to attempt to defeat.

Tudor, Elizabeth. See ELIZABETH I.

Tullia. The daughter of CICERO (Tully). An old story said that her body was discovered during the 16th century in a tomb with a lamp still burning beside her, after the passage of 1500 years. Immediately after the opening, however, her body crumbled to dust and the lamp was extinguished. Donne refers to the story in lines 215–16 of "Epithalamion at the Marriage of the Earl of Somerset."

Turtles. Turtledoves (symbolic of paired, faithful lovers).

Twickenham. Residential area (pronounced, and sometimes spelled, "Twicknam") on the banks of the Thames River about ten miles southwest of central London. Twickenham Park, an estate and primary home (from about 1607 to 1617) of the COUNTESS OF BEDFORD, was located here: Donne visited the estate and wrote "TWICKNAM GARDEN" based on it. He also refers to it by name in line 70 of "To the Countess of Bedford" (beginning "You have refined me"), one of the *VERSE LETTERS*.

Twicknam. See TWICKENHAM.

"Twicknam Garden" (also spelled "Twickenham Garden"). One of the *SONGS AND SONNETS*. Almost certainly this poem was written for and/or about the COUNTESS OF BEDFORD: her estate, Twickenham Park, was at TWICKNAM. During the time that she resided here, both she and Donne were married.

   The speaker assumes the pose of a PETRARCHAN man suffering from a lady who rejects him. In the first stanza he is "blasted" (blown upon as by a storm wind and/or withered) by the wind of his own "sighs," and he is "surrounded" (flooded) with his own "tears." "Hither" (in Twicknam Garden) he comes to seek the "spring," with double meaning including the spring season that should revitalize him and the water source for the flowing tears: the lady herself who resides here is the source of his tears and should be a force for new life. Lines 3–4 suggest that he would like to have hope of securing comfort and healing from the BALM here. But in lines 5–9 he designates himself as a traitor to himself: he prevents his own renewal by bringing with him a poisonous, killing spider called "love." Love can transform life-giving, sweet MANNA into poisonous, bitter GALL, just as (it was believed) spiders transform sweetness they feed on into poison.

Significantly, "TRANSUBSTANTIATE" is chosen to describe this process, making it the reverse of the Roman Catholic doctrine that sees the elements of the Eucharist miraculously become the body and blood of Christ, the ultimate in love's generative sweetness. To complete his picture of this garden as "true paradise" (the Garden of Eden), the speaker even brings in the "serpent" (i.e., Satan as the tempter in Eden)—but in doing so the speaker ironically has imported another element that is treasonous to himself: as the "spider" is "love," so the "serpent" is sin. His desire for this lady is a sinful one, as is revealed clearly later in the poem.

In the second stanza he acknowledges that winter (with its darkness, coldness, and deadness) would be more in harmony with his own situation and make him less miserable (because now he is so much in contrast to the spring all around him that it makes his own misery even more apparent and biting). (In line 10 "that winter did" can be read as "if winter were to.") Even the trees (bursting with life) seem to laugh and mock him: it would be better if a "grave" (in the senses of both "heavy" and "somber") frost prevented their doing so. The "winter" and "frost" wittily play on the lady's cold rejection of him that causes his "DEATH," in PETRARCHAN terms. The man, however, does not want to endure this "disgrace" of being mocked, but he also does not want to abandon his love and his suit of the lady in this garden: to solve the problem, he asks "Love" to let him be made into some unfeeling, insensible (i.e., "senseless," lacking the five senses) piece of the garden itself. In addressing this request to "Love," the man creates ambiguity in definition. Is "Love" the lady herself who owns the garden? Is "Love" Cupid, the god of love? Is "Love" the "spider love" that "transubstantiates all," including the speaker (thus transformed into a "piece" of the garden)? Or are all of these possibilities relevant? Concluding the second stanza, he even suggests some possibilities concerning what he can be changed into: a "MANDRAKE" would be expected to groan and a fountain to weep (i.e., flow with water); therefore, he could express his misery through the natural actions of these elements of the garden and yet not feel.

In the third stanza the speaker invites other men who are lovers to come and to take some of his tears (as if they were taking water from the "weeping" fountain he has just mentioned being possibly changed into). They should use "crystal vials" (perfectly clear and flawless) so that they can see and taste his tears in their purest state, just as one would "TRY" (test) wine: he, in fact, calls his tears "love's wine" that should be compared in

purity, clarity, and taste to the tears of the mistresses (the ladies
who are loved) of these men. If the ladies' tears do not taste like
the speaker's tears, then they are "false" tears (and from false
women whose love is false). The tears as wine ironically connects
with the motif of transubstantiation introduced earlier in the
poem. In the Eucharist the wine taken by the Christian
communicant is seen as actually transformed into Christ's blood,
and this blood is evidence of the great love of Christ shown
through sacrifice for humanity. But here we have a reversal or
parody of the Eucharist on a secular level. The partakers are
secular lovers, and they are to drink "wine" from this speaker who
sees himself as having sacrificed himself for his secular love. He
sheds tears, rather than blood, and this "love's wine" manifests his
role as the "Christ" of secular love. His "wine" is the ultimate test
for true secular love. Just as people of the Middle Ages and
Renaissance believed that the site of Calvary, of Christ's cross, was
on the same spot as the Garden of Eden (Christ being crucified
where Adam fell), so this speaker portrays himself becoming a
"senseless piece" in Twicknam Garden, which he has equated with
"true paradise." (For Donne's use elsewhere of the idea of Calvary
located on the site of Eden, see "HYMN TO GOD MY GOD, IN MY
SICKNESS.") Lines 23–25 indicate why the speaker feels that such
a test of a woman's tears is necessary: her eyes do not reveal what
is in her heart, and just seeing a woman weep does not reveal her
true thoughts (i.e., a woman commonly is hypocritical). He
cynically compares trying to judge her inner thoughts by her tears
to trying to determine what clothes she is wearing by looking
merely at the blur that is her shadow. Tears are similarly only
shadows of the reality of thoughts. The last two lines of the poem
complete the speaker's railing at the whole "perverse" female sex
that seems to have only one true woman (the one he has
unsuccessfully courted): even this true woman, he says, is only
true in order deliberately to show malice to the speaker. Her
"truth" indeed "KILLS" (in the PETRARCHAN sense) him. She is
"true" (faithful) to the one who already loves her and therefore
refuses to return the speaker's love: if the lady is indeed the
Countess of Bedford, then the one she is being "true" to is her
husband. In this light, the speaker's (or Donne's) sinful desire
earlier implied (in bringing the serpent) would be adultery on
both his and the Countess's parts. But what we must see is that
this obviously is a pose by Donne, not to be taken seriously as a
proposed affair. Rather, it is an ironic way to compliment the
Countess's character in being true. The wit in attributing her
faithfulness to a desire just to be cruel to Donne would be

appreciated as a joking paradox by the Countess. The courtly wit and flattery would not be lost on someone of her intellect and social perception.

Two Books of God. See BOOKS OF GOD.

Tympany. *Noun:* swelling or tumor.

Type. *Noun:* (1) a symbol or emblem; (2) a person, object, or event of the Old Testament that prefigures or foreshadows a person, thing, or event of the New Testament.

Tyran. Common spelling of "tyrant."

U

"Undertaking, The." One of the *SONGS AND SONNETS*. The poem was not titled in the 1633 edition, but it was given the usual title "The Undertaking" in 1635 and later editions. In some manuscripts, however, it is called "Platonic Love," a title which does indicate much about the poem's subject. In fact, the "one braver thing" referred to by the speaker in the first line is subscribing to the PLATONIC concept of love. As we see in the remainder of the poem, this "one braver thing" is variously referred to as finding "loveliness within" a woman and loving it (lines 13–14), seeing "virtue attired in woman" (line 18), and forgetting "the he and she" (line 20). So, the man speaking says that in his loving a woman platonically he has done something that is "BRAVER" (in multiple senses) than all of the supposedly greatest heroes of history (the WORTHIES) ever did. So, he implies that loving platonically is very difficult and unique. But he goes on to say in lines 3–4 that there is an even "braver" thing than loving platonically, and that is to keep that platonic love hidden (i.e., not to reveal it). It is rather ironic that hiding something is "braver," since one meaning of "brave" is showy. His hiding of it is from the "PROFANE" men referred to in line 22: they are men who would not understand the sacredness and spiritual mystery of this platonic love.

Stanzas two and three develop a METAPHYSICAL CONCEIT to explain why he does not reveal the secret of loving platonically. It would be madness to teach anyone the art or skill of how to cut SPECULAR STONE if there is no more of this stone in existence to be cut. Similarly, it would be ridiculous for the man speaking to teach anyone else how to love platonically if there is no more "stuff" (i.e., women that qualify!) to be loved platonically. So, the way people love would not be changed.

Just after the speaker has said that it is useless to tell about loving platonically, in the fourth stanza he tells about it! Anyone who finds the loveliness of a woman on the inside (in the intellect and spirit) and loathes the mere physical beauty, the "outward," does indeed know how to love platonically. The externals ("color" and "skin") are only like the "oldest clothes" covering the true beauty within, and someone who loves these old "clothes" is not loving platonically.

The last three stanzas tell the reader that if he (like the speaker) sees virtue within the woman, loves that virtue, forgets the male and female sexual love, hides that spiritual love from "profane" men who will either not even believe this kind of love or will ridicule ("deride") it, then the reader has done a "braver thing" than the Worthies and an even "braver" in keeping that platonic love hidden. So, the speaker implies that the reader can equal what the speaker has done: love platonically and hide that love. Ironically, the speaker says that he does this "brave" thing by not telling of his love, yet by the end of the poem he has told about it! He says it is hidden, but, by the end of the poem, it is no longer hidden!

Much of the meaning and irony depend on wordplay. For example, "BRAVE" as "courageous" or "heroic" or "glorious" or "showy" creates the irony that not boasting is more courageous than boasting! And it raises the question of whether boasting is more or less showy than not boasting! (Is this speaker making a show of not bragging, for example?) Also, the title "The Undertaking" has its ironies: it seems to imply a great heroic task or heroic undertaking to be accomplished (equal to those of the Worthies), but it also might point to the secret and to the key subject matter—"taking" what is "under" the external beauty of a woman as the true object of love.

Universal monarchy of wit. See CAREW, THOMAS.

Unobnoxious. *Adjective*: not exposed to harm or evil or injury.

Use. *Verb*: (1) to follow as a custom, (2) to be usual or customary, (3) to carry on an occupation or profession or function, (4) to spend time in a certain way, (5) to put into practice or carry into action, (6) to employ something for a certain purpose, (7) to make use of land by working or tilling or occupying, (8) to have sexual intercourse with, (9) to take or partake of as food or drink, (10) to do a thing customarily or by habit. *Noun*: (1) act of employing a thing for any purpose; (2) spending; (3) habit or custom; (4) distinctive ritual, liturgy, service, or worship in a particular church or ecclesiastical division.

Usufructuary. *Noun*: one who has the temporary use of an estate or property or office of another and benefits from its fruits or profits.

Usury. *Noun*: the lending of money at interest, especially large or excessive interest.

V

Vain. *Adjective*: (1) having no value, worth, or significance; (2) having no effect or power, futile, fruitless, useless; (3) empty; (4) foolish, silly, thoughtless. This word did *not* have the meaning of "proud" or "displaying personal vanity" in Donne's time.

Valediction. *Noun*: saying or bidding farewell to someone or something.

"Valediction: Forbidding Mourning, A." One of the *SONGS AND SONNETS*. This poem undoubtedly is the most famous and most quoted of all METAPHYSICAL poems: it usually is cited as the best example of what metaphysical poetry is, and it contains the most famous example of a METAPHYSICAL CONCEIT. WALTON says that Donne wrote the poem for his wife (ANN MORE) when he left for a journey to the continent with Sir ROBERT DRURY in 1611. But, since Walton commonly uses writers' works to help construct their biographies, many later biographers, critics, and scholars are doubtful about this occasion. It is a possible one for the writing, but Donne very well could have written it before or after this time, to his wife or to another lady, or could have created it around an imaginary or general occasion.

One can say that in the title "VALEDICTION" designates the occasion portrayed in the poem as a bidding of farewell. The speaker wishes to forbid any mourning and grieving at this parting and farewell, one may also assume. As the poem progresses, the reader does see that the speaker is leaving and will be away from the lady he is addressing for some period of time. To designate their proper attitude about this parting and ultimately to define the nature of their perfect love relationship, the speaker employs a series of four METAPHYSICAL CONCEITS that make up the entire poem.

The first conceit is developed in the first two stanzas. Just as "virtuous men" (implying those of strong faith in and assurance of life hereafter) die very calmly and unemotionally ("pass mildly away"), so should the speaker and his lady ("us") part calmly and unemotionally in such a way that they seem to "melt" in an almost imperceptible distancing from each other. We, he says, should be as unemotional and noiseless as the virtuous men that just whisper to their souls to part from the bodies. Donne also pictures in the first stanza the people around the bedsides of these dying men trying to determine the exact moment of death: some of them think that the breath has gone at one point, but other witnesses disagree and say, "No, he is still breathing." So, neither the dying men nor their friends are carrying on emotionally: this reminds us that, as the title implies, there is no "mourning" (i.e., the assured spiritual life of these dying virtuous men prevents grieving over the mere loss of physical life). Thus Donne transfers this lack of emotion and lack of noisy weeping at this death to the situation of the two lovers' parting (commonly related to DEATH). Just as a virtuous man does not weep at his physical death, so the two lovers should not at their physical parting (the implication being that they too should have confidence in a spiritual togetherness and life beyond mere physical separation—an implication to be more fully developed through the poem). He does not want them to display "tear-floods" (floods of tears) and "sigh-tempests" (storms of sighs) when they part: these are elements in a ridiculous PETRARCHAN and/or utterly physical love relationship. He implies to his lady that their love is far above this worldly level: if they were seen "mourning" their own parting in this way, their action would be denigrating and desecrating ("profanation") of their love and its higher, sacred, spiritual joys. If they were to display their love so emotionally, they would be lowering it to the level of the "laity," the laymen in love. The implications are that he and the lady are the clergy in love (with a love of spiritual mystery above the worldly and physical) and that the ordinary people with ordinary love are the laity that do not understand the spiritual mystery in true love.

With the sudden change in imagery beginning the third stanza, the second conceit begins: it extends through stanzas three, four, and five. This conceit, however, continues and expands the feelings about their love contrasted to that of ordinary worldly lovers. Stanza three presents a contrast between an earthquake ("moving of the earth") and a movement ("trepidation") in the Ptolemaic SPHERES. The speaker says that, when an earthquake occurs, it causes damages ("harms"), and men "reckon" (estimate or size up) the damage done ("what it did"). The earthquake also brings "fears": men are frightened by it and wonder what it "meant," whether or not it is divine punishment or warning, for example. But the movement or vibration or oscillation ("trepidation") attributed to the spheres, even though it is a far greater movement through the expanse of space as opposed to a mere earthquake on a limited portion of the earth, is "innocent" (i.e., harmless). Men do not look for damage, and they are not frightened by the "trepidation of the spheres." This contrast is applied by implication in stanzas four and five, and complete development of the conceit occurs thereby. Stanza four speaks of "SUBLUNARY" lovers—ordinary, earthly, worldly lovers (found literally below the moon in the realm of time, change, and death). They are "dull," earthbound, physical lovers: their soul is "sense"— their love only communicates through their five senses on the physical level, rather than on the intellectual and spiritual level. These lovers, by implication, are a contrast to the speaker and his lady. These ordinary lovers cannot "admit" absence from each other—i.e., they cannot even permit physical absence from one another in their relationship. If they allow partings and absences from each other, then there is no relationship at all, since it depends completely on their being together physically. Absence "doth remove those things which elemented it" ["it" being their love for each other]: absence takes away their physical parts and selves from each other, and these physical entities are the very things that made up ("elemented") their love. So, the speaker is implying that these ordinary physical lovers cannot stand to part from each other, but that he and his lady can do so easily without damage to their superior kind of love. Thus the analogy is made that the "sublunary" lovers' parting is like the earthquake: it is a parting of their earth (their bodies, their flesh), and it damages (even destroys) their relationship. They would be frightened at the prospect of parting (just as men are of an earthquake). They would be the ones to carry on emotionally and to be "mourning"— the very things that the speaker tells his lady that he and she should not do, since their love is on a level much higher than that of the "sublunary," earthly, physical, changeable type of love. This is why stanza five asserts the spiritual perfection of the love between the speaker and the lady he is addressing: their own love is "refined" (as opposed to the "dull" earthly love of those others just discussed). Their love is refined in its spiritual and intellectual nature that gives it purity above the earthly, physical kind of love. This implication, then, makes their love comparable to the celestial spheres, and their physical parting is a movement like the "trepidation of the spheres": it is "innocent," does no damage to their love, and should cause no fears to the partners. So, the conceit of stanzas three, four, and five is completed and may be stated simply in the analogy that an earthquake is to the trepidation of the spheres as the parting of sublunary lovers is to the parting of refined lovers. The refined love of the speaker and the lady is so perfect in its spiritual nature that they cannot even define it precisely (line 18). It is one in which their love is of mutual faith and assurance because of their intellectual and spiritual union with each other. Therefore, they do not need "eyes, lips, hands" (i.e., their physical, bodily elements) to be together to experience their love (in contrast to the "sublunary lovers").

After the preceding implications of their love being a spiritual one, the speaker asserts the fact quite directly in stanza six and expresses the idea through another analogy. This stanza makes up the third major conceit of the poem. He says that their two souls are one. Even though he must "go" (on his journey), their two souls nevertheless ("yet") do not experience ("endure") a breaking apart ("breach"). Instead, the spiritual bond between their souls expands over the physical distance between them: they are still together spiritually. He compares this expanding spiritual bond to the hammering out and expansion of a piece of gold (which is soft and can be beaten out in thin gold leaf). The conceit is ingeniously appropriate for the expansible, malleable quality of gold but also because gold connotes the ultimate in beauty, purity, and value that he thus transfers to their love relationship.

The fourth and climactic conceit (and the most famous in Donne's work and in all of metaphysical poetry) occurs in the last three stanzas of the poem. It employs draftsmanship to convey ideas and feelings about spiritual love: it is indeed ingenious in detail, farfetched, and perfectly appropriate in conveying these ideas and feelings. The speaker proposes that if "they" (the two souls of himself and the lady) are indeed "two," then they are two in a special way in which they are also one. To illustrate the truth of this paradox, he compares their two souls to "stiff twin compasses"—i.e., to a drawing compass or draftsman's compass that has two legs (or "feet," as Donne calls them). The two legs are connected at the top: this represents the spiritual bond between their souls, and the two legs represent their two souls. So, they are both separate and united in souls, just as the two legs of the drawing compass are both separate and united. At the bottom of the legs there is no connection, and the legs can be separated from each other to determine the distance desired before a circle is drawn: this separation of the legs when pulled apart on these ends, then, represents the physical distance between the speaker and his lady as he makes his journey—the important fact that he wants her to see, of course, is that they are still spiritually together by the bond between their souls that is comparable to the bond between the legs of the compass at its top. Even more explicitly, the speaker designates the "fixed foot" of the compass (the one that stays firmly in place while the other foot is drawn

outward from it) as analogous to the lady's soul: the logic in this is
that she indeed is the one who will be remaining in place while he
makes the journey away from her. His soul, then, is represented
by the "other" foot that "far doth roam" (i.e., roams far away
physically from the fixed one). He says that, while it remains
firmly in the center, the fixed foot does "lean and hearken" at the
top outward toward the moving foot: symbolically, her soul also
pulls toward and communicates attentively with his soul
spiritually over the physical distance. Upon his return home, the
tension is released as they come together (just as the two legs of
the compass). The final stanza emphasizes that her soul is like the
fixed foot and that it is her "firmness" that allows him to draw a
perfect circle, just as the fixed foot of the compass must stay
absolutely firm in its place for a perfect circle to be drawn by the
other foot. The "firmness" applied to her soul here is her
constancy, her fidelity: the speaker compliments her character
highly. In fact, she is at the center of their love relationship, just
as the fixed foot is at the center of the circle: the circle is the
symbol of their perfect love relationship, especially since a circle
traditionally represents infinity and something unending,
undying. Their spiritual love relationship is therefore perfect and
undying: it corresponds to the celestial circles of the infinite
SPHERES that he earlier compared their love to, in contrast to the
changeable, earthly, "sublunary" love. The man, then, can "end"
where he "began" through her firmness and their spiritual unity:
he can close the perfect circle of their love and also can return
home to one that he was only physically separated from, rather
than spiritually separated from, to begin with.

Their farewell, then, should have no mourning associated
with it, since it is a parting that is not really a parting at all, in the
most important sense. Just as the virtuous man's spirit does not
die in physical death and the spheres do not separate in their
movement and gold does not break in its expansion and the legs
of the compass do not separate when drawn apart, so do these two
lovers remain together spiritually in the face of any physical
parting. This kind of love is perfect and unending.

"Valediction: Of My Name in the Window, A." One of the
SONGS AND SONNETS. "VALEDICTION" in the title suggests that
the occasion is a bidding of farewell. For the contemplation of his
lady during the time that the two lovers are apart, the man
speaking leaves his name cut with a diamond into her window.

Stanza one implies that the hardness of the diamond that
engraved his name reflects his own "firmness" (i.e., faithfulness or

constancy to her).   In turn, he contends, the diamond's firmness and his own "firmness" have been transferred to the glass of the window, almost by means of magic or "charm."   The durability of his name, now unremovably engraved in the glass, symbolizes his fidelity and will remind the lady of it.   He flatters the lady by saying that her eye looking on the name in the glass will make the glass of more value than the finest of diamonds in the world ("diamonds of either rock").   (See "Selected Bibliography: Critical Studies, Poetry" for a 1962 note by Evans explaining the implications of this phrase [line 6] in Donne's time.   Apparently Donne means the two best kinds of oriental diamonds: his lady's look will make the value of the window glass put these diamonds to shame.)

In the second stanza the man tells her that it is significant that the glass is "through-shine" (i.e., transparent) and confesses all (nothing is hidden or obscured by this glass) because it symbolizes his own openness and honesty.   In addition, she can see her own face reflected in the glass ("it shows thee to thee" and "reflects thee to thine eye").   But he points out also that "here you see me," referring most obviously to seeing him in (1) his name engraved on the glass and (2) his own "firm" and "transparent" self in the glass.   However, his statement is made ambiguous by his final assertion that "I am you": i.e., she also sees him in (3) her own reflection, since he has identified them as two in one, as unified.   He flatters her in this argument by implying that she also sees herself in his name and in his qualities of constancy and honesty—with the man perhaps hoping that she does have these qualities in herself and will continue to illustrate them!

Stanza three says that not even a dot ("point") or dash in this engraved name will be washed out by rains and storms.   This fact is used to symbolize that he (like the name) will not be changed or lessened (in his devotion to her) by time (analogous to "showers and tempests").   He then suggests that she can complete this circle of devotion by reciprocating his constancy: he has made it easy for her to show this "entireness" because he has left her his durable name, which is the "pattern," the model, of absolutely permanent devotion to a lover.   She will always ("STILL") have it to look at and follow.

Stanza four presents the man assessing what he has made the name symbolize, and he self-consciously admits that the intellectual depth might be difficult to probe or might be excessively strained in philosophy.   However, I think we must see a bit of tongue-in-cheek humor as he says this, since it is ironic to say that a name that is only "scratched" (by definition, superficial) into the surface of the glass gives (punningly) "deep" learning! And for the man to make the lady recall the "hard" diamond and his own "hard" constancy and then to say that the idea is too "hard" shows him consciously and wittily making a playful pun! At any rate, he has two suggestions (each a METAPHYSICAL CONCEIT, in fact) about how to regard the name: it is a "death's head" (a skull or a representation of a skull—see MEMENTO MORI) to provide a lesson that all lovers die (i.e., it preaches a lesson of mortality). This conceit is doubly apt in this "VALEDICTION" because of lovers' parting regarded as one kind of DEATH. Or, he says, the "ragged bony name" (with its jagged, angular, minimally-scripted letters) can be interpreted as the man's skeleton (one meaning of ANATOMY), all of his bones remaining after DEATH.

In stanza five Donne develops this conceit into one assuming that man is a MICROCOSM: here specifically (lines 28–30) the speaker pictures himself as a house. The bones are the "rafters," and the rest of his body (muscles, sinews, veins) are the "tiles" (i.e., the mortal clay of man's body). Just as the parts of the body (bones and flesh) are reassembled at the Resurrection, so he says that he (the body he takes with him on his journey away from the lady) "will come again" after his journey to rejoin the "bones" of himself that he left with the lady in the form of the letters on her window. The house of himself will be formed again, ironically, at her literal house! He assures her that this return and reuniting of himself is destined to occur at her house because he has also left his "soul(s)" there within her (his whole life is in her). At Resurrection the soul and body will be rejoined, and this is analogous to his return (after his journey) with his body that will join with his "bones" (letters in the name) and with his "soul(s)" (deposited in the paradise of his lady). The speaker says "all my souls" (rather than "soul," as we would say today) because he is using a concept inherited from Scholastic Philosophy (see SCHOOLMEN) and ARISTOTLE that was still commonly alluded to in Donne's time. The "soul" many times was assumed actually to consist of three souls or three parts of the soul (the tripartite soul). The vegetative (or vegetable) soul is possessed by plants, animals, and humans, and it is responsible for growth and reproduction (note "grow" in the third line of the stanza). The sensitive (or sensible) soul is possessed by animals and humans, and it is responsible for the functioning of the five senses (note "see" in the third line of the stanza). The rational (or intellectual) soul is possessed by humans, and it is responsible for reason, understanding, and free will (note "understand" in the third line of the stanza). This third soul distinguishes humans from plants and animals, places humanity just below the angels and God in the hierarchy of creatures (see NATURAL ORDER), and makes humans potentially angelic and godlike.

Stanzas six and seven are integrally related, and one must see the circular structure of the two stanzas together to penetrate their complex argument. In the first two lines of stanza six, the speaker puzzlingly tells the lady to proceed to put his body back together before he returns. The solution of how this should be done is suspended until the end of stanza seven: her mourning daily for him while he is away will already be attracting, pulling him back. He will die daily (in being separated from her), and his return to her will be his resurrection, the fulfillment of the attracting power she already can exert on him through their unity and communication during absence. So, the end of stanza seven states the process, the means of what he has stated at the beginning of stanza six. Between these two points and connecting them is a METAPHYSICAL CONCEIT: just as (it was believed in astrology) certain stars convey their particular powers (when these stars are ascendant) into letters engraved at that time, so did "love" and "grief" (like the stars) pour their power and nature into the letters of the speaker's name when he engraved it into the glass of the window (i.e., "love" and "grief" were in the ascendant, at their peaks then, and his name will convey their "influence"). The speaker tells the lady not to attempt to shut off or avoid the name's influence. She should indulge herself in the love and grief that will flow from the name, and indeed she will be both more loving and more sad as she succumbs to the influence of his name on the window. This will cause her, then, to mourn: this mourning will be communicated to him in his absence, attract him back toward her, and already be serving to "repair" and "recompact" his scattered body.

Stanzas eight, nine, and ten develop the speaker's fear that another man might come to woo the lady during his absence, a fear that prompts him to use the name as a warning to her. If she opens the casement to look out upon this other man who is trying to impress and win her with his cleverness ("WIT") or wealth and property ("land"), then he wants her to think that his name is alive and is the speaker's guarding spirit ("GENIUS") that she is offending. If the maid who serves the lady "melts" (softens) to the cause of the potential wooer (because of his bribery of her with gold and of the appeal of his own male servant ["PAGE"]) and conveys the suitor's letter to the lady and argues with the lady on behalf of the suitor, the lady herself might warm ("thaw") to the words of the man in his letter. If this happens, the speaker wants his name on the window to replace the name of the suitor on the letter (at least to come to her mind?). The speaker also allows for the even more dangerous possibility that the lady's thought of "treason" (i.e., unfaithfulness to the speaker as her one and only love) might actually be put into action: if she writes a letter in return to the suitor, it will be "overt" treason. If this occurs, the speaker wants his own name to enter her thoughts as she is addressing the suitor in the letter and, instead of writing the suitor's name, to write the speaker's name unknowingly.

After letting his imagination range in all directions to show how his name scratched on the window will preserve their love, the speaker supposedly has more rational thoughts in the last stanza and supposedly retracts the extremity of his fears and warnings to the lady. He says that, upon cooler consideration, they must not rely on mere glass and lines engraved on it to keep their love firm. He claims that he is like a man close to "DEATH" (i.e., almost at the moment of parting from her) and that this irrationality comes from him just as it does from all men who are dying (in a coma before death). It would seem that he is ashamed that he has said all that he has to the lady and ends apologetically and with the feeling that he actually is quite assured of their "firm substantial love." He, then, apparently throws away the entire matter of the poem, along with the dismissal of his name in the window. But a possibility might be that the speaker really feels that he already has made his major points to the lady and has successfully caused her to ponder any potentially dangerous thoughts and actions and that now he can smooth feelings with a courtly excuse and then part amicably.

"Valediction: Of the Book, A." One of the *SONGS AND SONNETS*. "VALEDICTION" in the title implies that the occasion is a bidding of farewell when the speaker is leaving on a journey. He will be parted for some period from the lady he is addressing.

The first stanza blames the necessity for parting on "DESTINY": her (i.e., the goddess of destiny's) action has angered the lovers, but they will seek revenge by angering destiny in return. The speaker says that, even though destiny sends him far away ("she esloign me"), he has a means by which he can stay with the lady at the same time. And they will enable all posterity to know how they frustrated destiny. The speaker tells his lady that her (the lady's) glory (to be gained by the means that he will reveal) will exceed and outlast that of SIBYL (the prophetess who aided Aeneas), CORINNA (the poetess who taught PINDAR to write but also could take away from ["ALLURE"] his renown by outwriting him in poetic contests), Polla Argentaria (who helped her husband LUCAN to write better poetry), and the mythical Phantasia (who supposedly wrote the book that was the source used by HOMER for *The Iliad* and *The Odyssey*).

In the second stanza the man tells the lady to study the many letters that they have written each other: these are their "manuscripts," out of which the lady can compose their "annals," the history of their love. This composition will be the book that will (1) retain the man in her presence even though he is physically absent, (2) give her greater glory than that of all of those other female writers listed in the first stanza, (3) defeat destiny, and (4) contain all central truths about all learning, beliefs, arts, crafts, and skills. Rules and examples will be there that can teach all lovers, all whom the "subliming" (i.e., sublimating or purifying) fire of love enters. This book will be the divinely-dictated Bible of love in the religion of love: no bases of its faith will dare to be challenged by any SCHISMATIC. Love, the God of Love himself, has granted these two lovers the privilege of composing, preserving, using, and being Love's definitive records.

The third stanza asserts that this large book ("tome") is to have a life as long as that of the original ELEMENTS and form of the world, the words of which will permanently be engraved ("graved") in ancient "cypher" (cryptograph) or in some new code. (Donne seems to be playing on "grave" as buried, punning on "tome" as tomb, and suggesting in "cypher" the literally puzzling messages on ancient crypts.) He tells the lady to write the book in secret cypher or code because the message is only meant for the clergy of love, those who understand and can "read" its mysteries. So, even if the world were again invaded by the barbaric VANDALS and GOTHS, this book will be ignored in their destruction: they will not be able to understand it, since they are the ignorant opposites of love's clergy. So, all learning will be preserved in this book; therefore, this book is a MICROCOSM, a "universe" that can teach necessary knowledge to all levels of the created universe from schools of various learning on earth to the SPHERES and even to the angels.

The fourth stanza argues that the "divines" (i.e., clergy) of Love—any other people (like the speaker and the lady) who are privy to a full understanding of the mysteries of love—will be able to find all they wish to know about love just in this account of the couple's love. They can find spiritual love in which the lovers' souls seem to remove themselves from their bodies and to communicate on a level above the physical. On the other hand, they also can see love communicated physically and with the senses ("Something which they may see and use"): he says that love in this way descends from its aloof level of only the spiritual and stops bewildering ("amuse") a weak faith in love that needs its physical manifestation in order to be assured that love indeed exists (i.e., it convinces the doubting Thomases of the reality of love). The speaker justifies both the spiritual and physical in love in the last two lines of this stanza: the mind (embracing the spiritual and intellectual domain of the human MICROCOSM) is like a heaven in which true love rules like a god, and the beauty (seen in and expressed by the body) is like the earthly expression of this heaven. Beauty (bodily) is an earthly symbol ("TYPE") that does represent ("FIGURE") that heavenly love. (Donne here plays a bit with PLATONIC concepts regarding the physical as a mere hint of spiritual truth and beauty. While Platonists argued that the spiritual was, then, the only true reality and to be sought, Donne is justifying the equivalent combination of spiritual and physical in perceiving the fullness of love.)

Stanza five (lines 37–45) moves from the previous clergy ("divines") and what this book has for them to "lawyers" and what the book is able to provide them. The speaker says that this book is better than law books: here can be found the legal rights ("titles") to men's ladies as property, but also how women avoid being taken by men as such property by assuming that Love's special privileges ("PREROGATIVE") are transferred to the women, allowing them to make men "pay" exorbitant rents for the use of this property (i.e., the women). The payments ("subsidies") that a woman requires are taken from a man's "heart" and "eyes." The trusting man who gives all of these sighs and pains from his heart, as well as looks and tears from his eyes, to the woman, however, is then abused by his landlady: the woman does not complete her end of the bargain. She does not let the man use or enjoy the fruits of this property he has paid rental on: she refuses to honor the agreement by pleading that she must preserve her "HONOR" or "conscience." The speaker caustically labels these two supposed "causes" as "chimeras," as figments of imagination that are as "VAIN" as both the women and their so-called "PREROGATIVE" are.

Stanza six (lines 46–54) proceeds to what statesmen (politicians and/or leaders in government) can find useful to them in the lovers' book. The speaker says (satirically and critically) that even though some statesmen cannot read, those who can do so will find the basic principles ("grounds") upon which their own occupation is built. For example (lines 48–49), in both love and politics, one must act and not think about it: i.e., it is fatal to love, just as to politics, if one thinks before he acts! Next (lines 50–51), successful lovers and successful politicians are those who concentrate only on the present and its opportunities, without considering future consequences. Then (line 52), the speaker adds that those successful in both realms also either dupe or intimidate people in order to remain free of criticism from them. Finally (lines 53–54), the speaker asserts that in this book the politicians will see how politics is based upon nothing substantial, and neither is ALCHEMY. So, this book is like the Bible in being such an effective teaching tool that it can teach even the false bases of false arts! And the clearly satirical implication is that the politician will not give up politics when he discovers its falseness; on the contrary, he will learn even better how to use such low principles. Ambiguously (and adding to the complexity of interpretation), these last two lines also seem to suggest that just as alchemists find what they want to for their own benefit in the Bible (something that really is not there), just so will politicians find what they want to for their own benefit in this book (something that really is not there)—i.e., the alchemists and politicians both distort in interpreting these respective books, making something out of nothing.

The last stanza tells the lady, then, to put forth ("vent") her thoughts into this book about their love. While the man is abroad and thus separated from her he will "study" the lady (in the form of her writings or by mere contemplation of her during the separation). He begins a METAPHYSICAL CONCEIT by comparing this study of her at a distance to one who can precisely determine heights of things at a distance (by mathematical, trigonometric calculations involving the shadows cast). Their presence together as lovers, he says, shows them how large their love is; however, it is through their absence that the love is tested as to how "long" it will last (the length or the time that the love endures is compared, then, to the height of something that is calculated best at a distance). Absence of lovers tests ("tries") the durability of the love. To say it another way and add to the geographical and mathematical conceit, the speaker notes that one best determines "latitude" by the sun or stars at their brightest (comparable to the extreme brightness of the lady as a star or sun when he is in her presence, allowing him to calculate how "great" is their love). But to "conclude of" (i.e., calculate) "longitude," one must be at a distance to measure shadows ("ECLIPSES"): just so must the two lovers calculate their "longitude" (by playing on the word associated with lines of longitude on a map, he makes it symbolize also both lines of height and how "long" their love will last). This calculation is made by noting the shadows or "dark eclipses" of sadness and sorrow in their relationship while physically removed from each other. If they withstand these "eclipses," their love will endure. (For even more complexities possible in the geographical conceit, see many editors' speculations in the various editions listed in "Selected Bibliography: Works.") Thus the "valediction" will not matter: their love will endure, just as he supposes that the "book" of that love will be permanent.

"Valediction: Of Weeping, A." One of the *SONGS AND SONNETS.* "VALEDICTION" in the title implies that the occasion for the commentary on weeping is a parting, a bidding of farewell. Line 2, in fact, implies that the man speaking will be leaving soon: he says, "while I stay here." He is weeping as he stands before the lady he is saying farewell to ("Let me pour forth / My tears before thy face"). Beginning with line 3 Donne creates a series of METAPHYSICAL CONCEITs based on the tears. Lines 3–4 picture the tears as coins: the lady's face "coins" the tears in that his tears flow because of looking at her face before leaving—i.e., her face causes the tears to be produced. Like coins, the tears bear a stamp on them: her face is reflected on the tears in a way similar to a ruler's face being imprinted on the coins of a country. The speaker then (in line 4) compliments the lady highly by saying that her image on the tears gives them their high value, their "worth" (just as a ruler's image on coins makes them true, accepted money). Suddenly lines 5–7 make these tears comparable to a pregnant woman, creating the second conceit. The tear is pregnant, with the rounded tear like a rounded belly, and the lady's face reflected in the tear is like a baby in a woman's womb. The father is the "grief" at parting that the speaker feels: the tears are "fruits" (results) of this grief, and they are "emblems" (symbols) foreshadowing "more" (both more grief and more tears) to come after parting. The last two lines of stanza one assert that when a tear [of the speaker's] falls from his eyes to the ground or floor, then the woman (the "thou") that the tear ("it") carried ("bore") also falls: i.e., her face's reflection falls with his tear reflecting her face. His tear and her reflection fall into nothingness on the ground or floor between them, and the speaker argues that this symbolizes how "nothing" they will be when they are separated by a sea after he journeys to another land. The tears from his eyes falling between the two lovers thus (in another conceit) become a sea between them—one that foreshadows the real sea that will soon separate them.

The second stanza expands the geographical conceit of the tears as a sea into larger analogies of a tear as an earth and of the relationship between the two lovers as encompassing both earth and heaven. Lines 10–16 picture a workman taking a globe (which is "nothing" in itself), laying some maps on this globe, and thus making the globe a replica of the earth; therefore, the workman makes "all" out of "nothing," the whole world out of a blank globe. Each tear from the speaker is then made analogous to such a globe: the tear was blank (a "nothing") before the lady's face was reflected on it. Her face is the whole world (in importance to the speaker), and her reflection on the tear is like a map of the whole world laid on a globe. The conceit conveys his powerful feeling that the lady is his "all," everything of value in existence. The tear is a world, a MICROCOSM, containing his world, her. The lady now is like the Creator, like God, in forming a world. The speaker then (lines 17–18) implies that if she also were to weep as they part, her tears will mix with his tears: this is analogous to God sending down "waters" from heaven to flood the world he created (as in the Old Testament flood). She is "heaven dissolved" if she rains down tears. But also another implication is that if her tears dissolve his tears, they destroy both the world (his tear) and the heaven in that world (i.e., the lady's reflection). She is his world and his heaven, both symbolized in the tear. The man is trying to prevent the lady from weeping through his witty, exaggerated compliment.

The third stanza continues the idea of the lady as the heavens by developing her as analogous to a particular part of the heavens. She is like the moon, but, to do her justice, she is "more than moon." Her status as a world makes her greater than the moon, and her power to draw up seas and tides of tears to drown a world pictures the lady as exceeding the moon in power. The speaker explicitly does not want the lady to draw forth these seas of tears from herself (i.e., she should not weep). The man does not want to be drowned "in thy sphere" (line 20): the moon is embedded in its SPHERE, according to the PTOLEMAIC concept of the universe, and here the lady's arms encircling and embracing the man are equated with the sphere of the moon (a meaning made clear by the phrase "in thine arms" in line 21). Also, to encourage emotional restraint in her, the man asks her not to give a bad example that will illustrate what the sea might be able to do to the speaker on his journey. If she weeps him dead, the sea might take it as a model by which the sea can drown him. Similarly, if she sighs, then the wind might put forth its own destructive power in a storm at sea to destroy the speaker. She should neither weep nor sigh, then, as they part. To reinforce the importance of her not sighing, he argues from the assumption that he and the lady are unified: his life is in hers, and hers is in his. Since this is the case, if one sighs, it costs the breath of the other: the belief in Donne's time was that every sigh draws a drop of blood from the heart and shortens one's life. Her sighs, then, shorten his life (since the two are one). The last line of the poem makes sighing a cruelty to the other lover, hastening the end of his or her death: the man clearly wishes to imply to the lady that she would not want to be so cruel by being emotional at their parting.

Valentine, Saint. Bishop of Terni, Christian martyr of the 3rd century whose day is February 14 and is thought to be the person honored by St. Valentine's Day (although another individual is so named and proposed for the honor). Donne refers to him in "An Epithalamion, or Marriage Song on the Lady Elizabeth and Count Palatine being Married on St. Valentine's Day." Birds were thought to pair up on this day.

Vandal. *Noun*: one of a Germanic tribe that overran the Roman Empire in its latter stages, destroying many marks of its civilization, art, culture, and history. The word variously connotes anyone or anything barbaric, rude, uncivilized, lacking culture or taste, ignorant, passionate, violent, or destructive. Usually associated with GOTH.

Vapor(s). *Verb*: (1) to evaporate, to cause to ascend in vaporous form; (2) to cause to pass away in the form of vapor. *Noun*: (1) matter in the form of an imperceptible exhalation; (2) something insubstantial or worthless; (3) [in plural form] exhalations or hot HUMORS or SPIRITS (see NATURAL SPIRITS, VITAL SPIRITS, and ANIMAL SPIRITS) supposed to originate in bodily organs and to affect health adversely, most commonly thought to ascend from the stomach to the head and brain.

Vaughan, Henry (1621–1695). One of the major METAPHYSICAL poets. Born in Wales. After apparently studying law for a time in London, he returned to Wales where he eventually settled into a medical practice. His early works are secular and reflect more the influence of JONSON and the CLASSICAL strain in both subject matter and style. But about 1648–50 illness, war, death, and a reading of the poetry of GEORGE HERBERT led to a spiritual transformation in Vaughan. Thereafter he wrote the religious poetry on which his poetic reputation rests. The influences of Donne and Herbert are apparent, and generally METAPHYSICAL CONCEITS, colloquialisms, wordplay, and paradox dominate his work, although some of the classical style remains. Like Herbert and MARVELL, then, he is primarily metaphysical, but not exclusively. The quality of his poetry varies from poem to poem and line to line, and he is generally regarded as ranking fourth in the line of quality behind Donne, Herbert, and Marvell, as far as the major metaphysicals are concerned. Influences from ALCHEMY and mysticism combine with Christianity in Vaughan to create some unique spiritual beliefs and poems. His major book of poetry is *Silex Scintillans* (1650, expanded in 1655), and two of his best and most famous poems are "The Retreat" and "The World."

Vegetative (Vegetable) Soul. See discussion of stanza five in "A VALEDICTION: OF MY NAME IN THE WINDOW."

Velvet glass. *Noun*: a hand-mirror (GLASS) with velvet material as backing. But Donne seems to pun bawdily on "velvet" as the clitoris (a pun found in other Renaissance writers: see, for example, Partridge's notings in Shakespeare [see Partridge in "Selected Bibliography: General Background"] under the entries "piled for a French velvet" and "velvet leaves"). The "velvet" mirror, Donne suggests, was used in female masturbation: see "Elegy 2: The Anagram," lines 53–54.

Venite. Command meaning "come." Donne uses it (in line 44 of *THE SECOND ANNIVERSARY*) to refer to God's command at the Last Judgment.

Venus. (1) In mythology, Roman name for Greek goddess of love, Aphrodite. Known also as the goddess of beauty. Married to Vulcan (god of fire) but was unfaithful to him in having many lovers, resulting in many children by her. One of her sons was Cupid, god of love. Although primarily symbolic of physical beauty, love, and passion, she also is seen in some contexts as the principle of fertility and generative love; (2) the planet Venus; (3) the planet Venus as the morning star or evening star (also see HESPERUS).

Verse Letters. A group of poetic epistles apparently sent by Donne to individuals, just as he wrote and sent letters in prose to different people. Some editors group these poems under the heading *Letters to Several Personages*, rather than under *Verse Letters*. Depending upon each editor's classification, from thirty-seven to forty or more such poems exist. They can be dated from 1592 to 1614. Most of these letters are written (as far as can be ascertained) to the following individuals (addressed by full name or title or initials): 'CHRISTOPHER BROOKE (including "the Storm" and "The Calm"), SAMUEL BROOKE, ROWLAND WOODWARD, THOMAS WOODWARD, SIR HENRY WOTTON, and the COUNTESS OF BEDFORD.

    Although in this "Dictionary" there is no separate entry that discusses fully any one of these poems, some are briefly discussed in the entries concerning the persons to whom they are addressed. Also, the content of all of the *Verse Letters* has been examined for other important elements that are included as entries.

Verulam, Baron. See BACON, SIR FRANCIS.

Vesper. See HESPER.

Vicissitudinary. *Adjective*: coming alternately (i.e., by turns).

Villiers, George (1592–1628). Prepared by his family to be a courtier. Introduced to King JAMES in 1514 and given the office of cupbearer. The resentment and jealousy of ROBERT KER, Earl of Somerset, toward Villiers increasingly alienated the King and hastened the rise of Villiers as the new favorite of James. In 1615 James made Villiers gentleman of the bedchamber and knighted him. In 1616 he became Viscount Villiers and Baron Waddon, with an impressive grant of land. In 1617 he was made Earl of Buckingham. He later secured the unquestioned endorsement of King James when the King stated, "You may be sure that I love the Earl of Buckingham more than any one else" and "Christ had his John, and I have my George." Further titles, privileges, and income accumulated for Buckingham, including his appointment as Lord High Admiral, responsible for the navy. In 1623 he was created Duke.

    By the time James died, Buckingham was controlling foreign policy and continued to do so in the early years of the reign of CHARLES. His role as favorite (and practically king himself) increasingly disturbed the House of Commons, with England becoming involved in incompetent attempts at alliances and battles. Parliament impeached Buckingham in 1626, but Charles dissolved Parliament to prevent a trial. Misunderstandings with France increased, and by early 1627 war with France resulted.

Buckingham's leading of ships and men at the Isle of Rhé failed miserably with a loss of thousands of English soldiers. Parliament, in a remonstrance, designated Buckingham's power as the cause of England's troubles. He was condemned and hated publicly after this, a mood leading to his assassination in 1628 by a discharged naval officer who felt that his own act served England by ridding it of a tyrant.

Before 1621 Donne had begun to sue favors from Buckingham, whose influence on the King apparently was crucial to Donne being made Dean of ST. PAUL'S CATHEDRAL in that year. Donne wrote Buckingham a letter expressing his gratitude and continuing service. In 1623 Donne wrote Buckingham another letter, one of his most famous, in which he refers to "the Mistress of my youth, Poetry" and "the wife of mine age, Divinity," implying that he sees his own early interest in secular poetry (and its concerns) as an ephemeral love relationship, in contrast to his deeper dedication and "marriage" to a theological career.

Virtues. See (1) HIERARCHY, THE HEAVENLY; (2) CARDINAL VIRTUES.

Virtues, cardinal. See CARDINAL VIRTUES.

Vital spirits. Vapors believed to result from action in the heart (by heat and air from the lungs) upon NATURAL SPIRITS. Believed to carry life and heat through the arteries and to link body and soul. Associated with the SENSITIVE part of man's nature.

Vivary. *Noun*: a vivarium, a place in which live animals are kept under their normal conditions.

W

W., R. See WOODWARD, ROWLAND.

W., T. See WOODWARD, THOMAS.

Walkers in hot ovens. See CHILDREN IN THE OVEN.

Walton, Izaak (1593–1683). The evidence of Walton's trade(s) is a bit confusing: he may have been an ironmonger (a dealer in hardware—the same occupation as that of Donne's father) at one time (he belonged to the Ironmongers' Company), and he almost certainly was a linen draper (dealing in cloth and clothing), since there is evidence that he had such a shop in London. Later in life he was a writer of prose. Living on Fleet Street, he was a parishioner of ST. DUNSTAN'S-IN-THE-WEST while Donne was its vicar. Became a friend and admirer of Donne, as well as an acquaintance of other writers and clergymen of the time. Wrote the first biography of Donne, published in 1640 with *LXXX Sermons*. He added to it and published his *The Life of John Donne* separately in 1658. Then it was revised further and included as one of the *Lives* in 1670 and 1675 volumes (containing also those of HENRY WOTTON, GEORGE HERBERT, and Richard Hooker). Walton also wrote *The Compleat Angler* (first published in 1653), a book concerning fishing—but with comments on nature, pastoral ideals, theology, poets, and poetry mingled in it.

Although Walton's biographies have been severely challenged on many points of facts, chronology, accuracy of quotations, and completeness of character (see, for example, Novarr's *The Making of Walton's "Lives"* and Bald's *John Donne: A Life*, as well as others in the "Selected Bibliography"), he did write from some firsthand experiences and knowledge gathered from friends and letters. All later biographers of Donne are indebted to Walton, even though modern research has discovered records that correct many of his assertions. To some extent Walton imposed order and simplicity on his *Life of Donne* (and on his other lives, as well) by picturing his subject as the epitome of holiness and as symbolic of the best that the Church of England in its traditional and Royalist loyalties could offer, especially since Walton wrote through the decades in which the English Church was being attacked and changed by the Puritans and Nonconformists.

Walton went to CHELSEA, witnessed Donne's memorial sermon for MAGDALEN HERBERT, and bought a copy after its publication. He also was at the bedside shortly before Donne's death. Before the writing of his *Life of Donne* Walton contributed a poem ("An Elegy upon Dr. Donne") published with the 1633 edition of Donne's *Poems*, in which Walton calls himself Donne's "convert." He also says that Donne's great qualities and talents find a "living grave in good men's hearts."

Want. *Verb*: to lack or be without. *Noun*: (1) deficiency, shortage, or lack of something; (2) poverty or destitution.

Ward. Name of a pirate who plundered in the Mediterranean Sea.

Waste. *Verb*: (1) to devastate or ruin; (2) to suffer to fall into decay, deterioration; (3) to use up, diminish; (4) to consume or destroy by decay or sickness; (5) to diminish the goodness or virtue of; (6) to spend; (7) to employ uselessly; (8) to expend needlessly or to squander; (9) to spend or to pass unprofitably or idly.

Water. *Noun*: (1) one of the four ELEMENTS; (2) the liquid of which seas, lakes, ponds, and rivers are made; (3) liquid that falls as rain; (4) drink that sustains life; (5) in some contexts, liquid for washing, cleansing; (6) in some contexts, water of baptism that cleanses the spirit; (7) in some contexts, a reference to tears; (8) flood; (9) in some contexts, a reference to urine.

"What if this present were the world's last night?" First line of one of the *HOLY SONNETS*. The speaker is addressing his own soul, urging it to consider its chances for salvation if this very night ("this present night") happened to be the last night of earth's existence before the earth is destroyed and Christ returns for the Last Judgment. The soul was assumed to reside within man's heart, and the speaker says for the soul there to ponder intently the image of the crucified Christ who, through love, sacrificed himself for humanity. The speaker wants to emphasize that this denotes a loving God, not one that is wrathful, angry, and frightening. Thus, to quell any misgivings his soul has, the speaker is emphasizing the loving gentleness of God the Son, rather than the power and wrath of God the Father (see TRINITY).

Lines 4–8 present further evidence of this aspect of God. The tears of Christ obliterate any terrifying ("amazing") light burning out of the eyes of a wrathful God. The "frowns" also associated with the image of the wrathful, angry God are filled with (and transformed by) the blood of the crucified Christ. And he assures his soul that Christ surely will not condemn his soul to hell, since Christ even prayed for his enemies. The specific reference is to Luke 23:34: while being crucified, Christ said from the cross, "Father, forgive them; for they know not what they do." Donne makes "foes' fierce spight" convey a sense of loathsomeness by the heavy stresses and the "s" and "sp" sounds in the words, making the reader spit out the words with disgust. The conclusion implied, then, from the octave of this Italian SONNET is that God's love and mercy are paramount and make the soul's heavenly destiny almost a certainty. His soul should have no fear to face Judgment.

Then, in the sestet, he reinforces the same insistence in an analogy or METAPHYSICAL CONCEIT. The speaker compares Christ to a lover: the speaker says that in his IDOLATRY when he worshipped PROFANE mistresses, he would tell them that beauty is a sign of pity in someone and that foulness is a sign of rigor. In other words, as a seductive man, he would try to get a woman to respond to him, to yield to him (show him "pity" in a PETRARCHAN sense) by arguing that if she did show this compassion from her soul, it reflected her physical beauty externally. So, he makes it sound as if beautiful women respond with pity and ugly women (those with "foulness" externally) are the ones that show "rigor" (hardness and strictness in not yielding to a man). In using this argument he would hope, we assume, to convince the woman to yield, since she would rather be considered to be beautiful, rather than ugly. The speaker of the sonnet actually twisted (for his own seductive purposes) a PLATONIC argument about the direct relationships between external beauty and internal goodness and external ugliness and internal evil, the most famous expression of which is found in Castiglione's *THE COURTIER*, a work quite well known by Donne and others of his time. The essential argument is that internal goodness expresses itself externally as physical beauty, and thus external beauty signals internal goodness. Conversely, internal evil expresses itself externally as physical ugliness, and thus external ugliness signals internal evil. Now that the speaker has turned away from his frivolous period of idolizing secular lovers and has chosen God as his true lover, he strangely applies the same argument to convince his soul of the compassion of Christ and the consequent salvation of the soul that is the recipient of Christ's pity. So, he says that the "beauteous form" of the crucified Christ that he has just had the soul visualize is the external manifestation of that internal goodness in Christ's pitying nature. This is in contrast to a horrible shape signifying a wicked spirit within: this cannot be the shape and the nature of a loving God like Christ, he assures his soul.

"Will, The." One of the *SONGS AND SONNETS.* In the first five stanzas the speaker catalogs things and qualities he supposedly leaves as legacies to various groups and individuals in his will. The first six lines of each stanza list what he leaves, and the last three lines explain the general principle behind and common bond among the legacies just listed.   In general, the poem is quite satirical toward the groups and individuals he names as recipients, as well as toward a lady that has mistreated him by exemplifying the qualities he attributes to the recipients of his legacies.   The last stanza (the sixth) states an end to his legacies, prepares for his "death," and asserts what he hopes to accomplish through death, especially as a means to avenge himself on the lady and on love itself.

Stanza one introduces the "dying" speaker (apparently a variety of the PETRARCHAN man experiencing Petrarchan DEATH from treatment by a Petrarchan lady).   He is addressing "Love" (clearly implying CUPID).   He leaves his seeing eyes to ARGUS, who does not need any more, or, if his eyes are blind (i.e., they might be from the effects of love), he leaves them to Cupid who already is blinded.   To "FAME" (i.e., rumor) he leaves his tongue, of which there are already a sufficient number wagging to spread rumor.   He gives his ears to ambassadors, who already hear enough in their negotiations.   He leaves his tears either to women (who shed them profusely enough already) or to the sea (that already has enough salty liquid itself).   The caustic stab at Love and the lady then comes with the summary in the last three lines: Love taught him this principle of giving only to those who already had too much by making the speaker serve a lady who already had twenty suitors.

The second stanza presents the man giving his own "constancy" to the planets: the planets were regarded as inconstant "stars," compared to the fixed stars of the PTOLEMAIC system (and the Greek origin of the word *planet* implies wandering).   To those at Court he leaves his "truth," of which they have very little, he implies.   He leaves his "INGENUITY" (candidness, ingenuousness) and openness to JESUITS, who were regarded in Donne's time as hypocritical schemers and liars.   In the same vein, buffoons are not known for pensiveness, and travelers abroad are not known for reticence about their travels.

CAPUCHINS were vowed to poverty, had no pockets sewn on their clothing, and, therefore, could not even keep money on themselves (see Henderson's explication in "Selected Bibliography: Critical Studies, Poetry"). So, he gives qualities to those incapable of receiving them, because Love taught him to try to love a lady incapable of receiving that love.

In stanza three the speaker gives his faith to Roman Catholics, who emphasize salvation through good works, and his good works to SCHISMATICS of Amsterdam (extreme CALVINISTs), who emphasize only salvation through faith. His courtliness ("Courtship") and polish, manners ("civility") he gives to a university (characteristics perceived as lacking in and not even understood by the scholars of the time). To immodest, indecently-dressed soldiers he gives modesty, and to frenetic "GAMESTERs" he gives patience. (An additional satirical point is that he gives it to them to "share," something a gambler is not particularly versed in or desirous to do.) In the summary lines the speaker again accuses Cupid of teaching him to give to those who would be insulted or offended by gifts beneath their dignity, since Cupid forced him to love a lady who believed that there existed a disparity between his lowly love and her own high nature.

In stanza four he gives various things that actually were stimulated in him and could be said to have been given him by those to whom he is really returning (restoring) them. This stanza strangely combines apparent praise with criticism. Attributing his good(?) "reputation" to his friends seems on the surface to be complimentary, but one might consider if he also could be implying that his "reputation" is not good: if he has a bad reputation, it is attributed to those who (significantly) were his friends. The motivation to work hard because of enemies' detractions is quite caustic. His own befuddlement as a result of the philosophical mazes of the SCHOOLMEN is pointedly satirical, since they wanted to describe the nature of reality but (the speaker implies) raised more questions than they presented solutions. Quite satirically paradoxical is his giving back of his sicknesses to his physicians (i.e., they caused ills rather than cured them). But it is doubly satirical to blame his sicknesses on *either* the physicians *or* excesses (i.e., excesses of certain ELEMENTS and HUMORS in the body), since the statement implies that the two are equally bad as causes and that perhaps, rather than the speaker's excesses, the physicians' own excesses (excessive cures) are the causes of sicknesses. For the truths embodied in his verse, he gives credit to Nature (the source of those truths). Also in apparent humility he attributes his cleverness and talent for brilliant statement ("WIT") to other people in his social groups. In the summarizing lines, then, paradoxically he blames Love again while acknowledging, if not complimenting, the lady's power to stimulate the love in him that he simply is returning to her.

Stanza five presents the speaker leaving gifts that are inappropriate for the recipients: medical ("PHYSIC") books to a dying or dead person (see "PASSING BELL"), moral advice to the asylum for the insane (see "BEDLAM"), unspendable old bronze coins or commemorative medals ("brazen MEDALS") [see Mabbott and Keister explications in "Selected Bibliography: Critical Studies, Poetry"] to someone who is in lack ("WANT") of food, and the English language to those who will travel in foreign countries (where English is not understood). The use of "brazen" denotes "made of brass," but, significantly, the word has the figurative suggestion of "impudent" or "illustrating effrontery," a characteristic certainly present in one who would give such medals to starving people. The summarizing lines in this stanza are a bit exasperating in their ambiguity, even though the main point is clear. One will find that many critics and editors try to clarify the statement, but they disagree in the process. The questions essentially are these: (1) Is the speaker (regarding himself as young) saying that Cupid forced him to love a woman who only gives frustrating "friendship" (i.e., nonsexual love) to lovers "younger" than herself or simply "younger" in general? (2) Or is he (assuming that he is older than the lady or older than other lovers) saying that the lady responds with her "friendship" (including sexual love) only to lovers younger than herself or younger than the speaker? At any rate, his point is that the lady's "gift" to him is inappropriate to his own nature or desire or situation; therefore, he is making these particular gifts in his will also inappropriate (see "DISPROPORTION").

In the last stanza the speaker cuts off his list of legacies and ends the will. He says that he will die (again, especially implying that it is through the lady's rejection): since he regards himself as the epitome of love, love will die with him. In this way he will "undo the world," because all "beauties" (individual beautiful women of the world and the specific beautiful characteristics of his particular lady) will be worth nothing if there are no more people in the world capable of love and admiration of that beauty (analogous to gold in mines that has no one to take it out or to a sundial in the darkness of a grave). Ironically, then, the lady's rejection (killing) of him actually will lead to a killing of herself! In the concluding three lines, the man again says that he learned how to take this action because Love made him love a woman who killed with rejection both the man and love. So, in vengeance he will annihilate the lady ("her"), love ("thee"), and himself ("me"): he will thus annihilate "all three" by dying and thereby taking love with him and rendering the lady useless without admirers (i.e., she herself does this by living the role of the PETRARCHAN lady).

Will Conqueror. Phrase in line 26 of "Upon Mr. Thomas Coryat's Crudities" to refer to William the Conqueror (see CONQUEROR, WILLIAM THE).

Wingfield, Sir John (died 1596). Soldier. Served under and knighted by the Earl of Leicester in the 1580's. Sailed in the expedition against CADIZ under Robert DEVEREUX, Earl of Essex, in 1596. He was one of the first to enter the town and was shot in its marketplace. One of Donne's *EPIGRAMS* is entitled "Sir John Wingfield," in which Donne praises him as being a "fitter Pillar" (i.e., better than the "old PILLARS") that "our Earl (i.e., Essex) did bestow." See *EPIGRAMS* and PILLARS.

Wink. *Verb*: (1) to close the eyes, (2) to flicker or twinkle (said of a light or candle). *Noun*: (1) a closing of the eyes, (2) a glance, (3) a blink.

Wise politic horse. Reference (in line 80 of "Satire 1") to the horse (named Morocco) owned by a Mr. Banks. It was famous as a performing horse during the 1590's and is referred to by many writers of the time. Of its several tricks, it was said to bite and strike at a person who mentioned the king of Spain (see line 82 of "Satire 1").

Wit. *Noun*: (1) intelligence or understanding; (2) a person possessing intelligence or understanding; (3) cleverness or mental quickness; (4) talent for brilliant and amusing statement; (5) a learned, clever person; (6) quality of speech and writing that aptly associates thoughts, usually in a surprising or unexpected way.

"Witchcraft by a Picture." One of the *SONGS AND SONNETS*. This poem employs the belief that by witchcraft someone can kill another person by destroying a picture or other appropriate representation of the person. Donne plays on the PETRARCHAN implications of "KILL," "burning," and "drowned" through the poem.

In the first stanza the man speaking to the lady is looking into her eye and thus sees the reflection of his own face there. He imagines the lady "burning" his picture there, as a means by which this PETRARCHAN lady can KILL him. He also sees either the tear in her eye covering and drowning his image or a tear beneath her eye both containing and drowning his reflection, drowning being another way to destroy him. Her tear is "transparent" in the literal sense of being clear, but even more significant is the implication that it is easily seen through—i.e., he sees the falseness, insincerity, and lack of compassion behind her surface tear.

The second stanza presents the speaker having "drunk" her tears: he has seen his own mouth in his reflection taking in those tears, but apparently he has had similar tears from her in the past that he has been duped by. But now he sees them for what they are, and he can leave her despite her attempt to manipulate him further by weeping even more. As he removes himself from her presence, he also removes his image from her eye and tears, since his face is no longer in front of her to be reflected. So, this takes away any fear that she can use the "art" of witchcraft (also implying the "art" of that witch, the PETRARCHAN lady) to torture or KILL him any further. The only picture she has left of him is the one left in her heart because of his earlier being captivated by her, but he is sure that she will not practice the "malice" of witchcraft on this picture because she would also have to harm her own heart in the process.

Wittol. *Noun*: a man who is aware of and does not object to his wife's adultery.

Wolf. A special use of the word describes a type of cancer growing rapidly on the skin. Compare modern *lupus*, Latin for "wolf."

"Woman's Constancy." One of the *SONGS AND SONNETS*. The man speaking is a cynical, sarcastic lover addressing the woman whom he has known for a day—a day that is ended by sleeping together and experiencing sexual intercourse.

Donne violates normal metrical pattern in the first line to place heavy stresses on each syllable (i.e., on each word) of "one whole day." This technique adds length and enforces the sense that one day is a very long time for a relationship to last, the sarcastic joke being that it actually is a ridiculously short time. He is attributing to the lady, however, this attitude of thinking that loving an entire day is being constant in love. He is foreseeing that, after sexual intercourse that night, she will be ready to break off the relationship the next day ("tomorrow"). He is curious how she will rationalize or justify this action ("what wilt thou say?"). The speaker plays on "leav'st" (see LEAVE) to emphasize that he expects her both to stop loving him and to depart from him the next day. Significantly, the alliteration in "loved" (line 1) and "leav'st" (line 2) forces the reader to see the implied connection: to the lady, "loving" naturally leads to "leaving" soon thereafter, and this is indeed one level in the title of the poem, if it is regarded as sarcastic. The man (in lines 3–13) provides a series of five possible justifications and rationalizations that he expects the woman to choose from and to tell him tomorrow: (1) Will you now make some assertion about our relationship and pretend that you had said it before (i.e., "antedate" it)? [line 3]; (2) Will you say that we have changed and are not really the same people we were when we became lovers (even though it was only a day ago!)? [lines 4–5]; (3) Will you claim that any "oaths" (including lovers' vows) forced on one by the sheer power and terror of the God of Love (Cupid) may legitimately be forsworn (see FORSWEAR)? [lines 6–7]; (4) Will you claim that just as the actual physical deaths of marriage partners undo the marital knot, the marital vows (i.e., "till death us depart," as the *Book of Common Prayer* phrased it in Donne's time), so should sexual lovers' contracts which are the images of true marriages ("those") last only until "sleep" (euphemistically implying sexual intercourse) which is commonly seen as a symbol of death ("death's image") unties the lovers' knot? [lines 8–10] (In addition to the audacious analogy between marriages and unmarried lovers' sexual relationships, quite crucial to understanding the projected argument here is the play on "DEATH," as literal physical death and as sexual consummation.); (5) Will you (to justify your original aim or intention or goal ["end"] which was to be fickle and false) paradoxically choose falsehood (to me) in order to be true (to your original intention to be false!)? [lines 11–13]. The double irony in the title becomes apparent at this point: the woman's "constancy" is really inconstancy, as far as being faithful to him is concerned, but her "constancy" really is constancy, as far as her original intention to be unfaithful is concerned.

The last four lines are the man's rebuttal and victory over her "VAIN" (ineffectual) arguments and self. He calls her a "LUNATIC," implying not only that she is a bit mad or insane, but also that she literally is controlled by the moon (*luna*) and thus is indeed changeable: in the PTOLEMAIC universe everything in the

sublunary realm (below the moon) is subject to change
(inconstancy), and the moon's face also itself changes as it goes
through its phases each month.　Therefore, the moon is commonly
used as a symbol of inconstancy in Donne's time, and he
appropriately uses it as such in this poem.　The man forcefully
claims that, if he wished to, he could argue against and defeat all
of her "'scapes" (escapes, evasive assertions), those that he himself
has projected for her to use!　But he sneeringly and flippantly
says that he refuses even to waste effort doing it, because
tomorrow he "may think so too"—i.e., after their sexual pleasure he
may well be ready to end their relationship and thus acknowledge
its ephemeral nature also.　In addition, he may think and agree
with everything that he has imagined her saying to him.　The final
irony of the poem thus appears in the fact that the man says that
he is not even going to argue with the woman, but, in fact, the
whole poem is his argument with her.

Woodward, Rowland (1573–1637).　Friend to Donne from his
days at LINCOLN'S INN.　He was, at one time, imprisoned by the
Inquisition for spying.　After serving SIR HENRY WOTTON, he
complained to a friend that Wotton would not do much to help
and support him.　Donne wrote five of his *VERSE LETTERS* to
Woodward (four titled "To Mr. R. W." and one titled "To Mr.
Rowland Woodward").

Woodward, Thomas.　Brother of ROWLAND WOODWARD.
Probably the recipient of the four *VERSE LETTERS* titled "To Mr. T.
W.," but no one has proved this for a fact.　Donne addresses him as
a "sweet poet."

Word, the.　(1) Christ, (2) the Bible or a part of it.

Worm.　*Noun*: (1) maggot [especially the "worm" of the grave]; (2)
segmented earthworm; (3) snake; (4) larva or grub that destroys
wood; (5) metaphorically, a human as a miserable or pitiable
creature.

Worthies, The.　Designated also as the nine Worthies (or the nine
Nobles).　Famous individuals of ancient and medieval history and
legend composing a group of three Jews (Joshua, David, and Judas
Maccabaeus), three Gentiles (Hector, Alexander, and Julius Caesar),
and three Christians (Arthur, Charlemagne, and Godfrey of
Bouillon).

Wotton, Sir Henry (1568–1639).   Courtier, diplomat, minor writer of poetry and prose.   Was educated at Oxford, where he began a lifelong friendship with Donne.   In 1595 he became a secretary to ROBERT DEVEREUX, 2nd Earl of Essex, and through Wotton Donne may have secured service under Essex for the Cadiz and Azores Islands expeditions.   After the fall of Essex, Wotton stayed mainly in Italy until the death of Queen ELIZABETH.   In 1602, however, Wotton had warned King JAMES in Scotland of a possible attempt on the King's life, and, with the accession of James to the English throne, Wotton was welcomed back to England, knighted, and made an ambassador, choosing Venice as his post.   Despite short periods away from there, most of his service was spent in Italy until 1624 when he returned to England permanently.   He was made Provost of Eton in 1624, served in Parliament early in the reign of CHARLES, and took holy orders in 1627 (probably with hopes of advancement to a high position in the Church).   He remained at Eton, with some government pensions granted in support of his writing, until his death.   He was a good friend of WALTON: he actually had planned to write a life of Donne with some help from Walton in gathering material, but he had not done so before his own death, leaving Walton to carry out the project.

Donne wrote some of the *VERSE LETTERS* to Wotton (two entitled "To Sir Henry Wotton," another entitled "H. W. in Hibernia Belligeranti [i.e., H(enry) W(otton) fighting in Ireland]," and a fourth in 1604 entitled "To Sir H. W. at His Going Ambassador to Venice").   Some comments both in these verse letters and in many of Donne's prose letters to Wotton express disappointment in and contempt for some of the courtly life and its ways, themes reflected in a few of the *SATIRES* and *SONGS AND SONNETS*.

X

Xerxes (519?–465 B.C.). King of Persia from 486 to 465 B.C. The Biblical Ahasuerus, husband of Vashti and Esther. Invaded Greece and constructed a bridge across the Dardanelles. For Donne's treatment of the story of Xerxes and the LYDIAN plane tree, see lines 29–32 of "ELEGY 9: THE AUTUMNAL."

Y

Yield. *Verb*: (1) to give in, submit, surrender; (2) to give in to seduction; (3) to pay for, repay, reward.

Z

Zenith. *Noun*: (1) the highest point of the sky overhead as viewed from any one place on earth, (2) highest point or state of anything.

Zodiac, zodiak. *Noun*: (1) a circle in the celestial sphere in which the movements of the sun, moon, and planets were assumed to occur: the circle is divided into twelve parts or "signs"; (2) figuratively used to refer to a set of twelve.

SELECTED BIBLIOGRAPHY

I. WORKS [All of Donne's works are listed by editor.]

A. Poetry

Clements, A.L., ed. *John Donne's Poetry.* New York: W.W. Norton & Co., 1966.

Gardner, Helen, ed. *John Donne: The Divine Poems.* Oxford: Clarendon Press, 1978.

Gardner, Helen, ed. *John Donne: The Elegies and The Songs and Sonnets.* Oxford: Clarendon Press, 1965.

Grierson, Herbert J.C., ed. *The Poems of John Donne.* Oxford: Clarendon Press, 1912. 2 vols.

Manley, Frank, ed. *John Donne: The Anniversaries.* Baltimore, Maryland: The Johns Hopkins Press, 1963.

Milgate, W., ed. *John Donne: The Epithalamions, Anniversaries, and Epicedes.* Oxford: Clarendon Press, 1978.

Milgate, W., ed. *John Donne: The Satires, Epigrams and Verse Letters.* Oxford: Clarendon Press, 1967.

Patrides, C.A., ed. *The Complete English Poems of John Donne.* London: J.M. Dent & Sons, 1985.

Redpath, Theodore, ed. *The Songs and Sonets of John Donne.* 2nd ed. New York: St. Martin's Press, 1983.

Shawcross, John T., ed. *The Complete Poetry of John Donne.* Garden City, New York: Doubleday & Co., 1967.

Smith, A.J., ed. *John Donne: The Complete English Poems.* 1971. Reprint. Harmondsworth, Middlesex, England: Penguin Books, 1984.

B. Prose

Clebsch, William A., ed. *Suicide: "Biathanatos" Transcribed and Edited for Modern Readers.* Chico, California: Scholars Press, 1983.

Healy, T.S., S.J., ed. *John Donne: Ignatius His Conclave.* Oxford: Clarendon Press, 1969. [Both the Latin and the English texts]

Hester, M. Thomas, ed. *Letters to Severall Persons of Honour (1651).* Delmar, New York: Scholars' Facsimiles & Reprints, 1977. [Facsimile reproduction with an introduction by Hester]

Mueller, Janel M., ed. *Donne's Prebend Sermons.* Cambridge, Massachusetts: Harvard University Press, 1971.

Peters, Helen, ed. *Paradoxes and Problems.* Oxford: Clarendon Press, 1980.

Potter, George R., and Evelyn M. Simpson, eds. *The Sermons of John Donne.* Berkeley and Los Angeles: University of California Press, 1953–62. 10 vols.

Raspa, Anthony, ed. *Devotions Upon Emergent Occasions.* Montreal: McGill—Queen's University Press, 1975.

Rhodes, Neil, ed. *John Donne: Selected Prose.* Harmondsworth, Middlesex, England: Penguin Books, 1987.

Rudick, Michael, and M. Pabst Battin, eds. *Biathanatos: A Modern-Spelling Edition, with Introduction and Commentary.* New York: Garland Publishing, 1982.

Savage, Elizabeth, S.S.J., ed. *Devotions Upon Emergent Occasions.* Salzburg: Institut für Englische Sprache und Literatur, Universität Salzburg, 1975. 2 vols.

Simpson, Evelyn M., ed. *Essays in Divinity.* Oxford: Clarendon Press, 1952.

Sparrow, John, ed. *Devotions Upon Emergent Occasions.* Cambridge: Cambridge University Press, 1923.

Sullivan, Ernest W., II, ed. *Biathanatos.* Newark: University of Delaware Press, 1984.

Sypher, Francis Jacques, ed. *Pseudo-Martyr.* Delmar, New York: Scholars' Facsimiles & Reprints, 1974. [Facsimile reproduction with an introduction by Sypher]

C. Poetry and Prose

Coffin, Charles M., ed. *The Complete Poetry and Selected Prose of John Donne.* New York: Random House, 1952.

Craik, T.W., and R.J. Craik, eds. *John Donne: Selected Poetry and Prose.* London: Methuen, 1986.

II. BIBLIOGRAPHIES, CONCORDANCES, AND INDEXES

Combs, Homer Carroll, and Zay Rusk Sullens. *A Concordance to the English Poems of John Donne*. Chicago: Packard and Company, 1940.

Keynes, Geoffrey. *A Bibliography of Dr. John Donne*. 4th ed. Oxford: Oxford University Press, 1973. [Bibliography of Donne's works and Walton's "Life of Donne," with appendixes devoted to such matters as books from Donne's library and a check-list of biography and criticism from 1594 through 1971]

Reeves, Troy D. *Index to the Sermons of John Donne*. 3 vols. Salzburg: Institut für Anglistik und Amerikanistik, Universität Salzburg, 1979, 1980, 1981. [Vol. 1, "Index to the Scriptures"; Vol. 2, "Index to Proper Names"; Vol. 3, "Index to Topics"]

Roberts, John R. *John Donne: An Annotated Bibliography of Modern Criticism, 1912-1967*. Columbia: University of Missouri Press, 1973.

Roberts, John R. *John Donne: An Annotated Bibliography of Modern Criticism, 1968-1978*. Columbia: University of Missouri Press, 1982.

III. LIFE

Applebaum, Wilbur. "Donne's Meeting with Kepler: A Previously Unknown Episode." *Philological Quarterly* 50 (1971): 132-34.

Bald, R.C. *John Donne: A Life*. Edited by Wesley Milgate. New York and Oxford: Oxford University Press, 1970. [The standard biography: the most meticulous, scrupulous, and detailed in facts about Donne]

Bell, Ilona. "'Under Yᵉ Rage of a Hott Sonn & Yʳ Eyes': John Donne's Love Letters to Ann More." In *The Eagle and the Dove: Reassessing John Donne*, edited by Claude J. Summers and Ted-Larry Pebworth, 25-52. Columbia: University of Missouri Press, 1986. [Argues that three letters are the only extant correspondence between John Donne and Ann More and that they significantly add to our knowledge of the courtship and relate to some of the poems]

Bennett, R.E. "John Donne and the Earl of Essex." *Modern Language Quarterly* 3 (1942): 603-4.

Carey, John. *John Donne: Life, Mind and Art*. New York: Oxford University Press, 1981. [Read Bald's *Life* first to understand its extensions by Carey]

Clive, Mary. *Jack and the Doctor.* New York: St. Martin's Press,
1966. [A popularizing account, with interesting illustrations,
portraits, and photographs. Unfortunately, as Margaret
Maurer notes (in the *ELH* article cited below), the portrait
designated as the Countess of Bedford is, in fact, the
Countess's mother.]
Deas, M.C. "A Note on Rowland Woodward, the Friend of Donne."
Review of English Studies 7 (1931): 454–57.
Flynn, Dennis. "Donne and Hugh Broughton." *Seventeenth-Century
News* 37 (1979): 71–72. [Illustrates Donne's moderate
Anglicanism through his irony and wit in some letters]
Flynn, Dennis. "Donne the Survivor." In *The Eagle and the Dove:
Reassessing John Donne,* edited by Claude J. Summers and
Ted-Larry Pebworth, 15–24. Columbia: University of
Missouri Press, 1986. [Moderates some of Carey's
arguments]
Garrod, H.W. "Donne and Mrs. Herbert." *Review of English Studies*
21 (1945): 161–73.
Gosse, Edmund. *The Life and Letters of John Donne.* 2 vols.
London: William Heinemann, 1899. [Although increasingly
becoming outdated, the work is still a source for some facts,
especially about the letters.]
Larson, Deborah Aldrich. "John Donne and Biographical Criticism."
South Central Review 4 (1987): 93–102.
Le Comte, Edward. *Grace to a Witty Sinner: A Life of Donne.* New
York: Walker and Company, 1965.
Marotti, Arthur F. "John Donne and the Rewards of Patronage." In
Patronage in the Renaissance, edited by Guy Fitch Lytle and
Stephen Orgel, 207–34. Princeton, New Jersey: Princeton
University Press, 1981.
Maurer, Margaret. "The Real Presence of Lucy Russell, Countess of
Bedford, and the Terms of John Donne's 'Honour is so
Sublime Perfection.'" *ELH* 47 (1980): 205–34.
Novarr, David. *The Making of Walton's "Lives."* Ithaca, New York:
Cornell University Press, 1958. [Essential to determine
Walton's "truths" about Donne]
Ray, Robert H. "Herbert's Words in Donne's Mouth: Walton's
Account of Donne's Death." *Modern Philology* 85 (1987–88):
186–87.
Sellin, Paul R. "John Donne: The Poet as Diplomat and Divine."
Huntington Library Quarterly 39 (1975–76): 267–75.
[Documents a previously unrecognized high status accorded
Donne on the embassy in 1619 to Germany with Doncaster]

Sellin, Paul R. *So Doth, So Is Religion: John Donne and Diplomatic Contexts in the Reformed Netherlands, 1619–1620.* Columbia: University of Missouri Press, 1988.

Thomson, Patricia. "John Donne and the Countess of Bedford." *Modern Language Review* 44 (1949): 329–40.

Walton, Izaak. *The Lives of John Donne, Sir Henry Wotton, Richard Hooker, George Herbert, and Robert Sanderson.* The World's Classics. London: Oxford University Press, 1927. [Classic, original *Life of Donne* published first in 1640, revised in 1658, further revised in 1670, and revised to its final form in 1675 (the 1675 publication is the version reproduced in this 1927 edition)]

Whitlock, Baird W. "Donne's University Years." *English Studies* 43 (1962): 1–20.

IV. REPUTATION AND INFLUENCE

Alvarez, A. *The School of Donne.* New York: Pantheon Books, 1961.

Bald, R.C. *Donne's Influence in English Literature.* 1932. Reprint. Gloucester, Massachusetts: Peter Smith, 1965.

Drinkwater, D.J. "More References to John Donne." *Notes and Queries* 199 (1954): 514–15.

Duncan, Joseph E. *The Revival of Metaphysical Poetry: The History of a Style, 1800 to the Present.* Minneapolis: University of Minnesota Press, 1959.

Eldredge, Frances. "Further Allusions and Debts to John Donne." *ELH* 19 (1952): 214–28.

Gottlieb, Sidney. "*Elegies Upon the Author*: Defining, Defending, and Surviving Donne." *John Donne Journal* 2, no. 2 (1983): 23–38.

Granqvist, Raoul. *The Reputation of John Donne 1779–1873.* Stockholm: Almqvist and Wiksell, 1975.

Hannaford, Renée. "'Express'd by mee': Carew on Donne and Jonson." *Studies in Philology* 84 (1987): 61–79.

Haskin, Dayton. "Reading Donne's *Songs and Sonnets* in the Nineteenth Century." *John Donne Journal* 4 (1985): 225–52.

Keynes, Geoffrey. *A Bibliography of Dr. John Donne.* 4th ed. Oxford: Oxford University Press, 1973. [Appendix V is an annotated check-list of biography and criticism of Donne from 1594 through 1971.]

MacColl, Alan. "The Circulation of Donne's Poems in Manuscript." In *John Donne: Essays in Celebration,* edited by A.J. Smith, 28–46. London: Methuen, 1972.

Milgate, W. "References to John Donne." *Notes and Queries* 198 (1953): 421–24.

Nethercot, Arthur H. "The Reputation of the 'Metaphysical Poets' During the Age of Johnson and the 'Romantic Revival.'" *Studies in Philology* 22 (1925): 81–132.

Nethercot, Arthur H. "The Reputation of the 'Metaphysical Poets' During the Age of Pope." *Philological Quarterly* 4 (1925): 161–79.

Nethercot, Arthur H. "The Reputation of the 'Metaphysical Poets' During the Seventeenth Century." *Journal of English and Germanic Philology* 23 (1924): 173–98.

O'Connor, William Van. "The Influence of the Metaphysicals on Modern Poetry." *College English* 9 (1947–48): 180–87.

Ray, Robert H. "Another Perspective on Donne in the Seventeenth Century: Nehemiah Rogers's Allusions to the *Sermons* and 'A Hymne to God the Father.'" *John Donne Journal* 6 (1987): 51–54.

Ray, Robert H. "Unrecorded Seventeenth-Century Allusions to Donne." *Notes and Queries* 33 (1986): 464–65.

Roberts, John R. "John Donne's Poetry: An Assessment of Modern Criticism." *John Donne Journal* 1 (1982): 55–67.

Sharp, Robert Lathrop. *From Donne to Dryden: The Revolt Against Metaphysical Poetry*. Chapel Hill: University of North Carolina Press, 1940.

Smith, A.J., ed. *John Donne: The Critical Heritage*. London: Routledge and Kegan Paul, 1975. [Presents and comments on allusions to and criticisms of Donne from about 1598 to 1889. Emphasizes references to Donne's poetry, including references to the prose only when they also bear upon the poetry]

Summers, Joseph H. *The Heirs of Donne and Jonson*. New York: Oxford University Press, 1970.

Tillotson, Kathleen. "Donne's Poetry in the Nineteenth Century (1800–72)." In *Elizabethan and Jacobean Studies*, edited by Herbert Davis and Helen Gardner, 307–26. Oxford: Clarendon Press, 1959.

Williamson, George. *The Donne Tradition: A Study in English Poetry from Donne to the Death of Cowley*. 1930. Reprint. New York: The Noonday Press, 1961.

V. CRITICAL STUDIES

A. Background

Allen, Don Cameron. "John Donne's Knowledge of Renaissance Medicine." *Journal of English and Germanic Philology* 42 (1943): 322–42.

Barkan, Leonard. *Nature's Work of Art: The Human Body as Image of the World.* New Haven, Connecticut: Yale University Press, 1975.

Bradshaw, Graham. "Donne's Challenge to the Prosodists." *Essays in Criticism* 32 (1982): 338–60.

Clark, Ira. *Christ Revealed: The History of the Neotypological Lyric in the English Renaissance.* Gainesville, Florida: University Presses of Florida, 1982. [Chapter 3 is "Explicating the Heart and Dramatizing the Poet: Seventeenth-Century Innovations by English Emblematists and Donne."]

Coffin, Charles Monroe. *John Donne and the New Philosophy.* Morningside Heights, New York: Columbia University Press, 1937.

Cragg, Gerald R. *Freedom and Authority: A Study of English Thought in the Early Seventeenth Century.* Philadelphia: The Westminster Press, 1975.

Doggett, Frank A. "Donne's Platonism." *Sewanee Review* 42 (1934): 274–92.

El-Gabalawy, Saad. "Aretino's Pornography in the Later Renaissance." *English Miscellany* 25 (1975–76): 97–119. [Includes Donne's references to Aretine]

Eliot, Thomas Stearns. "Donne in Our Time." In *A Garland for John Donne, 1631–1931,* edited by Theodore Spencer, 3–19. Cambridge, Massachusetts: Harvard University Press, 1931. [Moderates some of the statements in his 1921 essay "The Metaphysical Poets"]

Eliot, Thomas Stearns. "The Metaphysical Poets." *[London] Times Literary Supplement,* October 20, 1921, pp. 669–70. [A famous and influential essay, reprinted frequently in collections of essays and in anthologies]

Freeman, Rosemary. *English Emblem Books.* London: Chatto & Windus, 1948.

Galdon, Joseph A., S.J. *Typology and Seventeenth-Century Literature.* The Hague and Paris: Mouton, 1975.

Halewood, William H. *The Poetry of Grace: Reformation Themes and Structures in English Seventeenth-Century Poetry.* New Haven, Connecticut: Yale University Press, 1970.

Johnson, Samuel. *Johnson's Lives of the Poets: A Selection*, ed. J.P. Hardy. Oxford: Oxford University Press, 1971. [Contains the "Life of Cowley," a famous and influential commentary on metaphysical poetry and Donne that was originally published in 1779]

Lewalski, Barbara Kiefer. "Typological Symbolism and the 'Progress of the Soul' in Seventeenth-Century Literature." In *Literary Uses of Typology from the Late Middle Ages to the Present*, edited by Earl Miner, 79–114. Princeton, New Jersey: Princeton University Press, 1977.

Martines, Lauro. *Society and History in English Renaissance Verse*. Oxford: Basil Blackwell, 1985.

Moloney, Michael Francis. *John Donne: His Flight from Mediaevelism*. Urbana: University of Illinois Press, 1944.

Mulder, John R. *The Temple of the Mind: Education and Literary Taste in Seventeenth-Century England*. New York: Pegasus, 1969.

Murray, W.A. "Donne and Paracelsus: An Essay in Interpretation." *Review of English Studies* 25 (1949): 115–23.

Nicolson, Marjorie Hope. *The Breaking of the Circle: Studies in the Effect of the "New Science" upon Seventeenth-Century Poetry*. Revised ed. New York: Columbia University Press, 1960.

Parfitt, George. *English Poetry of the Seventeenth Century*. London: Longman, 1985.

Parry, Graham. *Seventeenth-Century Poetry: the Social Context*. London: Hutchinson, 1985. [Chapter 2 is "John Donne: patronage, friendship and love."]

Peterson, Douglas L. *The English Lyric from Wyatt to Donne: A History of the Plain and Eloquent Styles*. Princeton, New Jersey: Princeton University Press, 1967.

Rivers, Isabel. *Classical and Christian Ideas in English Renaissance Poetry: A Students' Guide*. London: George Allen & Unwin, 1979.

Tuve, Rosemond. *Elizabethan and Metaphysical Imagery: Renaissance Poetic and Twentieth-Century Critics*. Chicago: University of Chicago Press, 1947.

Williamson, George. "Mutability, Decay, and Seventeenth-Century Melancholy." *ELH* 2 (1935): 121–50.

B. General: Poetry and Prose

Aers, David, and Gunther Kress. "Vexatious Contraries: A Reading of Donne's Poetry." In *Literature, Language and Society in England 1580–1680*, edited by David Aers, Bob Hodge, and Gunther Kress, 49–74. Dublin: Gill and Macmillan, 1981.

Asals, Heather. "John Donne and the Grammar of Redemption." *English Studies in Canada* 5 (1979): 125–39. [Some relationships between Donne's *Sermons* and the *Holy Sonnets*, particularly in the concern with the Divine Word and men's words]

Baker-Smith, Dominic. "John Donne's *Critique of True Religion*." In *John Donne: Essays in Celebration*, edited by A.J. Smith, 404–32. London: Methuen, 1972. [Discusses the quest for true religion, emphasizing "Satire 3," the *Anniversaries, Pseudo-Martyr*, and *Sermons*]

Bozanich, Robert. "Donne and Ecclesiastes." *PMLA* 90 (1975): 270–76.

Bullough, Geoffrey. "Donne: The Man of Law." In *Just So Much Honor: Essays Commemorating the Four-Hundredth Anniversary of the Birth of John Donne*, edited by Peter Amadeus Fiore, 57–94. University Park: The Pennsylvania State University Press, 1972. [Comments on the legal training of Donne reflected in his works, especially in *Satires, Biathanatos, Pseudo-Martyr, Essays in Divinity*, and *Sermons*]

Colie, Rosalie L. *Paradoxia Epidemica: The Renaissance Tradition of Paradox*. 1966. Reprint. Hamden, Connecticut: Archon Books, 1976. [Chapter 3 is "John Donne and the Paradoxes of Incarnation."]

Evans, Gillian R. "John Donne and the Augustinian Paradox of Sin." *Review of English Studies* 33 (1982): 1–22.

Fiore, Peter Amadeus, ed. *Just So Much Honor: Essays Commemorating the Four-Hundredth Anniversary of the Birth of John Donne*. University Park: The Pennsylvania State University Press, 1972.

Geraldine, Sister M. "John Donne and the Mindes Indeavours." *Studies in English Literature, 1500–1900* 5 (1965): 115–31. [Examines *Satire 3*, portions of the *Sermons*, and *Ignatius His Conclave* to argue Donne's belief that intellectual energy precedes and determines the good man's virtuous choices and that shallow thinking underlies much evil]

Gilman, Ernest B. "'To adore, or scorne an image': Donne and the Iconoclastic Controversy." *John Donne Journal* 5 (1986): 62–100.

Gransden, K.W. *John Donne.* Revised edition. Hamden, Connecticut: Archon Books, 1969.

Guibbory, Achsah. *The Map of Time: Seventeenth-Century English Literature and Ideas of Pattern in History.* Urbana: University of Illinois Press, 1986. [Chapter III is "John Donne: The Idea of Decay."]

Henricksen, Bruce. "Donne's Orthodoxy." *Texas Studies in Literature and Language* 14 (1972–73): 5–16.

Hughes, Richard E. *The Progress of the Soul: The Interior Career of John Donne.* New York: William Morrow and Company, 1968.

Jackson, Robert S. *John Donne's Christian Vocation.* Evanston, Illinois: Northwestern University Press, 1970. [Discusses several poems and prose works in the context of Donne's development toward a Christian vocation in the Anglican Church]

Klause, John L. "Donne and the Wonderful." *English Literary Renaissance* 17 (1987): 41–66.

Klinck, Dennis R, "John Donne's 'knottie Trinitie.'" *Renascence* 33 (1980–81): 240–55. [On uses of "Trinity," both word and concept, in the prose and poetry]

Kremen, Kathryn R. *The Imagination of the Resurrection: The Poetic Continuity of a Religious Motif in Donne, Blake, and Yeats.* Lewisburg, Pennsylvania: Bucknell University Press, 1972. [Chapter 2 is "The First Resurrection in Donne's Religious Prose and Poetry: The Whole 'World's Contracted Thus.'"]

Mahood, M.M. *Poetry and Humanism.* 1950. Reprint. New York: W.W. Norton & Company, 1970. [Chapter IV is "Donne: The Progress of the Soul," and Chapter V is "Donne: The Baroque Preacher."]

Mazzeo, Joseph A. "Notes on John Donne's Alchemical Imagery," *Isis* 48 (1957): 103–23.

McGrath, Lynette. "John Donne's Apology for Poetry." *Studies in English Literature, 1500–1900* 20 (1980): 73–89.

Nardo, Anna K. "John Donne at Play in Between." In *The Eagle and the Dove: Reassessing John Donne,* edited by Claude J. Summers and Ted-Larry Pebworth, 157–65. Columbia: University of Missouri Press, 1986. [Donne's play and wit in both poetry and sermons]

Novarr, David. *The Disinterred Muse: Donne's Texts and Contexts.* Ithaca, New York: Cornell University Press, 1980.

Partridge, A.C. *John Donne: Language and Style.* London: André Deutsch, 1978.

Roberts, Donald Ramsay. "The Death Wish of John Donne." *PMLA* 62 (1947): 958–76.

Rugoff, Milton. *Donne's Imagery: A Study in Creative Sources.* New York: Corporate, 1939.

Shami, Jeanne. "Anatomy and Progress: The Drama of Conversion in Donne's Men of a 'Middle Nature.'" *University of Toronto Quarterly* 53 (1983–84): 221–35.

Shaw, Robert B. *The Call of God: The Theme of Vocation in the Poetry of Donne and Herbert.* Cambridge, Massachusetts: Cowley Publications, 1981. [Chapter II is "John Donne."]

Sherwood, Terry G. *Fulfilling the Circle: A Study of John Donne's Thought.* Toronto: University of Toronto Press, 1984.

Slights, Camille Wells. *The Casuistical Tradition in Shakespeare, Donne, Herbert, and Milton.* Princeton, New Jersey: Princeton University Press, 1981.

Sloane, Thomas O. *Donne, Milton, and the End of Humanist Rhetoric.* Berkeley: University of California Press, 1985. [Chapter III is "Donne's Rhetoric."]

Smalling, Michael. "Donne's Medieval Aesthetics and His Use of Morally Distant *Personae*: Two Questions, One Answer." In *New Essays on Donne*, edited by Gary A. Stringer, 74–109. Salzburg: Institut für Englische Sprache und Literatur, Universität Salzburg, 1977.

Smith, A.J., ed. *John Donne: Essays in Celebration.* London: Methuen & Co., 1972.

Smith, A.J. "No Man Is a Contradiction." *John Donne Journal* 1 (1982): 21–38. [Argues for Donne's consistency regarding the interdependence of body and soul]

Smith, Julia J. "Donne and the Crucifixion." *Modern Language Review* 79 (1984): 513–25.

Spencer, Theodore, ed. *A Garland for John Donne, 1631–1931.* Cambridge, Massachusetts: Harvard University Press, 1931.

Stein, Arnold. *The House of Death: Messages from the English Renaissance.* Baltimore, Maryland: The Johns Hopkins University Press, 1986. [Chapter Three is "Donne's Pictures of the Good Death," and Chapter Seven is "Imagined Dyings: John Donne."]

Stein, Arnold. "Voices of the Satirist: John Donne." In *English Satire and the Satiric Tradition*, edited by Claude Rawson, 72–92. Oxford: Basil Blackwell, 1984. [Discusses narrator and persona in both poetry and prose]

Stringer, Gary, ed. *New Essays on Donne*. Salzburg: Institut für
    Englische Sprache und Literatur, Universität Salzburg, 1977.
Summers, Claude J., and Ted-Larry Pebworth, eds. *The Eagle and
    the Dove: Reassessing John Donne*. Columbia: University of
    Missouri Press, 1986.
Waller, G.F. "John Donne's Changing Attitudes to Time." *Studies in
    English Literature, 1500–1900* 14 (1974): 79–89.
Warnke, Frank J. *John Donne*. Boston: Twayne Publishers, 1987.
White, Helen C. *The Metaphysical Poets: A Study in Religious
    Experience*. New York: The Macmillan Co., 1936. [Chapter IV
    is "The Conversions of John Donne," and Chapter V is "The
    Divine Poetry of John Donne."]
Winny, James. *A Preface to Donne*. Revised ed. London: Longman,
    1981.

C. Poetry

1. The Anniversaries

Anselment, Raymond A. "'Ascensio Mendax, Descensio Crudelis':
    The Image of Babel in the *Anniversaries*." *ELH* 38 (1971):
    188–205. [Emphasizes the ultimate lesson of humility
    through the poems]
Bellette, Antony F. "Art and Imitation in Donne's *Anniversaries*."
    Studies in English Literature, 1500–1900 15 (1975): 83–96.
Colie, Rosalie L. "'All in Peeces': Problems of Interpretation in
    Donne's Anniversary Poems." In *Just So Much Honor: Essays
    Commemorating the Four-Hundredth Anniversary of the
    Birth of John Donne*, edited by Peter Amadeus Fiore, 189–
    218. University Park: The Pennsylvania State University
    Press, 1972.
Elliott, Emory B., Jr. "Persona and Parody in Donne's *The
    Anniversaries*." *Quarterly Journal of Speech* 58 (1972): 48–
    57. [Argues that Donne uses the mask of a Puritanical
    speaker to parody Puritan preaching in *The First
    Anniversary* and the mask of a mystic to parody Jesuit
    mysticism in *The Second Anniversary*]
Fox, Ruth A. "Donne's *Anniversaries* and the Art of Living." *ELH*
    38 (1971): 528–41. [Emphasizes the importance of Elizabeth
    Drury's death on Donne himself and on the role of the poet]
Gill, Roma. "Hesper/Vesper—and Phosphor." *Notes and Queries* 27
    (1980): 318–19. [Comments on Donne's apparent confusion
    concerning "Hesper" as the morning star in *The Second
    Anniversary*]

Goldberg, Jonathan. "Hesper—Vesper: Aspects of Venus in a Seventeenth-Century Trope." *Studies in English Literature, 1500–1900* 15 (1975): 37–57. [Includes a discussion of lines 197–98 of *The Second Anniversary* and their symbolic import in the seventeenth century]

Hardison, O.B., Jr. *The Enduring Monument: A Study of the Idea of Praise in Renaissance Literary Theory and Practice.* 1962. Reprint. Westport, Connecticut: Greenwood Press, 1973. [Chapter VII ("The Idea of Elizabeth Drury") discusses the two poems as praise and proposes structural schemes for each]

Hughes, Richard E. "The Woman in Donne's *Anniversaries.*" *ELH* 34 (1967): 307–26. [Regards as central the associations of Elizabeth Drury with St. Lucy and her implications]

Kelly, Kathleen. "Conversion of the Reader in Donne's *Anatomy of the World.*" In *The Eagle and the Dove: Reassessing John Donne,* edited by Claude J. Summers and Ted-Larry Pebworth, 147–56. Columbia: University of Missouri Press, 1986. [Argues that the reader of *The First Anniversary* is converted to the poet's world and joins in celebrating both Elizabeth Drury and one's own hopes for a spiritual life]

Kreps, Barbara I. "The Serpent and Christian Paradox in Donne's *First Anniversary.*" *Revista di Letterature Moderne e Comparate* 24 (1971): 198–207.

Lebans, W.M. "Donne's *Anniversaries* and the Tradition of Funeral Elegy." *ELH* 39 (1972): 545–59. [Argues that the two *Anniversaries* should be read in conjunction with "A Funeral Elegy" and in the context of *Epicedes and Obsequies*]

Lewalski, Barbara Kiefer. *Donne's "Anniversaries" and the Poetry of Praise: The Creation of a Symbolic Mode.* Princeton, New Jersey: Princeton University Press, 1973. [Discusses the two poems in the context of poetry of praise and compliment, Protestant meditation, and funeral sermons]

Love, Harold. "The Argument of Donne's *First Anniversary.*" *Modern Philology* 64 (1966–67): 125–31.

Mahony, Patrick. "The *Anniversaries*: Donne's Rhetorical Approach to Evil." *Journal of English and Germanic Philology* 68 (1969): 407–13.

Mahony, Patrick J. "The Heroic Couplet in Donne's *Anniversaries.*" *Style* 4 (1970): 107–17.

Mahony, Patrick. "The Structure of Donne's *Anniversaries* as Companion Poems." *Genre* 5 (1972): 235–56.

Manley, Frank. "Formal Wit in the *Songs and Sonnets.*" In *That Subtile Wreath: Lectures Presented at the Quatercentenary*

Celebration of the Birth of John Donne, edited by Margaret
W. Pepperdene, 5–27. Atlanta: Agnes Scott College, 1973.

Mann, Lindsay A. "The Typology of Woman in Donne's
Anniversaries." Renaissance and Reformation 23 (1987):
337–50. [Sees Elizabeth Drury as a complex symbolic figure
of Biblical significance, pointing to ultimate fulfillment and
perfection only in the next life]

Martz, Louis L. "Donne's *Anniversaries* Revisited." In *That Subtile
Wreath: Lectures Presented at the Quatercentenary
Celebration of the Birth of John Donne,* edited by Margaret
W. Pepperdene, 29–50. Atlanta: Agnes Scott College, 1973.
[Modifies somewhat his earlier views (especially in *The
Poetry of Meditation*), seeing now *The First Anniversary* as
successful in terms of satire]

Martz, Louis L. *The Poetry of Meditation: A Study in English
Religious Literature.* Revised ed. New Haven, Connecticut and
London: Yale University Press, 1962. [Chapter 6 ("John
Donne in Meditation: The *Anniversaries*") analyzes the
structure of each poem as it reflects Roman Catholic stages
in meditations]

Maud, Ralph. "Donne's *First Anniversary." Boston University
Studies in English* 2 (1956): 218–25. [Finds successful unity
that Martz (see above) does not]

Morris, June. "A Study of Humor in Donne's *Anniversaries*: 'How
Witty's Ruin?'" *English Miscellany* 28–29 (1979–80): 157–70.

Nicolson, Marjorie Hope. *The Breaking of the Circle: Studies in the
Effect of the "New Science" upon Seventeenth-Century
Poetry.* Revised ed. New York: Columbia University Press,
1960. [Chapter 3 ("The Death of a World") interprets *The
First Anniversary*, viewing Elizabeth Drury as a complex of
symbols, including the idea of Woman, Queen Elizabeth, and
the Virgin Mary]

Parrish, Paul A. "Poet, Audience, and the Word: An Approach to
the *Anniversaries."* In *New Essays on Donne,* edited by Gary
A. Stringer, 110–39. Salzburg: Institut für Englische Sprache
und Literatur, Universität Salzburg, 1977. [Argues that
Donne is in the role of poet and prophet, is a disciple of St.
Augustine, and celebrates faith, grace, and virtue as
embodied in Elizabeth Drury]

Pollock, Zailig. "'The Object and the Wit': The Smell of Donne's *First
Anniversary." English Literary Renaissance* 13 (1983): 301–
18. [Contends that Donne implies the corruption of man's
fallen intellect through the poet's own indecorous wit, the
lack of decorum being deliberate and an artistic virtue]

Quinn, Dennis. "Donne's *Anniversaries* as Celebration." *Studies in English Literature, 1500-1900* (1969): 97–105.

Rowland, Daniel B. *Mannerism—Style and Mood: An Anatomy of Four Works in Three Art Forms.* New Haven, Connecticut and London: Yale University Press, 1964. [Chapter 3 ("John Donne: Mannerist Style in the Meditative Genre") discusses the style of *The First Anniversary* in terms of metrics, metaphors, and structure]

Sicherman, Carol M. "Donne's Timeless *Anniversaries.*" *University of Toronto Quarterly* 39 (1969–70): 127–43.

Stanwood, P.G. "'Essentiall Joye' in Donne's *Anniversaries.*" *Texas Studies in Literature and Language* 13 (1971–72): 227–38. [Emphasizes religion, Christianity, and grace in the two poems]

Tourney, Leonard D. "Joseph Hall and the *Anniversaries.*" *Papers on Language and Literature* 13 (1977): 25–34. [Discusses Hall's prefatory poems as the most perceptive contemporary criticism and response to *The Anniversaries*]

Voss, A.E. "The Structure of Donne's *Anniversaries.*" *English Studies in Africa* 12 (1969): 1–30.

Willard, Thomas. "Donne's Anatomy Lesson: Vesalian or Paracelsian?" *John Donne Journal* 3 (1984): 35–61. [Explores the extent of Donne's medical knowledge from Paracelsus and Vesalius and its use in the *Anniversaries*]

Williamson, George. "The Design of Donne's *Anniversaries.*" *Modern Philology* 60 (1962–63): 183–91.

2. Divine Poems, Excluding Holy Sonnets

Archer, Stanley. "The Archetypal Journey Motif in Donne's *Divine Poems.*" In *New Essays on Donne*, edited by Gary A. Stringer, 173–91. Salzburg: Institut für Englische Sprache und Literatur, Universität Salzburg, 1977.

Baumgaertner, Jill. "'Harmony' in Donne's 'La Corona' and 'Upon the Translation of the Psalms.'" *John Donne Journal* 3 (1984): 141–56.

Chambers, A.B. "Goodfriday, 1613. Riding Westward: The Poem and the Tradition." *ELH* 28 (1961): 31–53.

Chambers, A.B. "*La Corona*: Philosophic, Sacred, and Poetic Uses of Time." In *New Essays on Donne*, edited by Gary A. Stringer, 140–72. Salzburg: Institut für Englische Sprache und Literatur, Universität Salzburg, 1977.

Dubinski, R.R. "Donne's 'La Corona' and Christ's Mediatorial Office." *Renaissance and Reformation* 16 (1980): 203–8.

Duncan, Joseph E. "Donne's 'Hymne to God my God, in my sicknesse' and Iconographic Tradition." *John Donne Journal* 3 (1984): 157–80. [Illustrates how visual art preceding and during Donne's lifetime supports the tradition of the two Adams and of the connection between the Tree of Knowledge and the Cross]

Finnegan, Robert Emmett. "Donne's 'A Hymn to God the Father,' 13–18." *The Explicator* 39 (Fall 1980): 38–39.

Friedman, Donald M. "Memory and the Art of Salvation in Donne's Good Friday Poem." *English Literary Renaissance* 3 (1973): 418–42.

Glaser, Joe. "'Goodfriday, 1613': A Soul's Form." *College Literature* 13 (1986): 168–76.

Goldberg, Jonathan. "Donne's Journey East: Aspects of a Seventeenth-Century Trope." *Studies in Philology* 68 (1971): 470–83. [Primarily concerns "Good Friday, 1613. Riding Westward" and its theological and typological backgrounds]

Kirkpatrick, Hugh. "Donne's 'Upon the Annunciation and Passion Falling Upon One Day. 1608.'" *The Explicator* 30 (1971–72): Item 39.

Leigh, David J., S.J. "Donne's 'A Hymne to God the Father': New Dimensions." *Studies in Philology* 75 (1978): 84–92. [Discusses puns on Ann More's name in this and other poems, some of which are also noted by Morris's 1973 article (see below, under "Miscellaneous and More Than One Type of Poem")]

Lisbeth, Terrence L. "Donne's 'Hymne to God My God, in My Sicknesse.'" *The Explicator* 29 (1970–71): Item 66.

Maurer, Margaret. "The Circular Argument of Donne's 'La Corona.'" *Studies in English Literature, 1500–1900* 22 (1982): 51–68.

Malpezzi, Frances M. "Christian Poetics in Donne's 'Upon the Translation of the Psalmes.'" *Renascence* 32 (1979–80): 221–28.

McNees, Eleanor. "John Donne and the Anglican Doctrine of the Eucharist." *Texas Studies in Literature and Language* 29 (1987): 94–114.

Nania, John, and P.J. Klemp. "John Donne's *La Corona*: A Second Structure." *Renaissance and Reformation* 14 (1978): 49–54.

O'Connell, Patrick F. "'La Corona': Donne's *Ars Poetica Sacra*." In *The Eagle and the Dove: Reassessing John Donne*, edited by Claude J. Summers and Ted-Larry Pebworth, 119–30. Columbia: University of Missouri Press, 1986.

O'Connell, Patrick F. "'Restore Thine Image': Structure and Theme in Donne's 'Goodfriday.'" *John Donne Journal* 4 (1985): 13–28.

Owens, Robert R. "Donne's South-West Discoverie." *Notes and Queries* 24 (1977): 142–43. [Notes some sixteenth-century accounts of the Strait of Magellan that probably lie behind Donne's "Hymn to God My God, in My Sickness"]

Pollock, John J. "Donne's 'Hymne to Christ.'" *The Explicator* 38 (Summer 1980): 21–22.

Pritchard, Allan. "Donne's Mr. Tilman." *Review of English Studies* 24 (1973): 38–42. [Facts and documents concerning the person addressed in "To Mr. Tilman after He Had Taken Orders"]

Severance, Sibyl Lutz. "Soul, Sphere, and Structure in 'Goodfriday, 1613. Riding Westward.'" *Studies in Philology* 84 (1987): 24–43.

Sullivan, David M. "Riders to the West: 'Goodfriday, 1613.'" *John Donne Journal* 6 (1987): 1–8. [Argues that an allusion to riding west to Tyburn (or Tyburn tree), the famous place of execution in London, adds to the poem the dimension of following Christ to crucifixion on his tree]

Svendsen, Kester. "Donne's 'A Hymne to God the Father.'" *The Explicator* 2 (1943–44): Item 62.

Wolfe, Ralph Haven, and Edgar F. Daniels. "Donne's 'A Hymn to God the Father,' lines 13–14." *The Explicator* 40 (Summer 1982): 13–14.

3. *Elegies*

Armstrong, Alan. "The Apprenticeship of John Donne: Ovid and the *Elegies*." *ELH* 44 (1977): 419–42.

Bedford, R.D. "Ovid Metamorphosed: Donne's *Elegy XVI*." *Essays in Criticism* 32 (1982): 219–36.

Bowers, Fredson T. "An Interpretation of Donne's Tenth Elegy." *Modern Language Notes* 54 (1939): 280–82.

Bueler, Lois E. "The Failure of Sophistry in Donne's Elegy VII." *Studies in English Literature, 1500–1900* 25 (1985): 69–85.

Deitz, Jonathan E. "Donne's 'To His Mistress Going to Bed,' 33–38." *The Explicator* 32 (1973–74): Item 36. [Interprets "Atlanta's balls" as a bawdy allusion to breasts]

Dixon, Peter. "Donne's 'To His Mistress Going to Bed, Lines 7–12,'" *The Explicator* 41 (Summer 1983): 11.

French, Roberts W. "Donne's 'Elegie XVIII (Loves Progress),' 38." *The Explicator* 34 (1975–76): Item 5.

Gill, Roma. "*Musa Iocosa Mea*: Thoughts on the *Elegies*." In *John Donne: Essays in Celebration*, edited by A.J. Smith, 47–72. London: Methuen, 1972.

Gregory, E.R., Jr. "The Balance of Parts: Imagistic Unity in Donne's 'Elegie XIX.'" *The University Review* 35 (1968–69): 51–54.

Hester, M. Thomas. "Donne's (Re)Annunciation of the Virgin(ia Colony) in *Elegy XIX.*" *South Central Review* 4 (Summer 1987): 49–64.

Hurley, C. Harold. "'Covering' in Donne's 'Elegy XIX.'" *Concerning Poetry* 11 (Fall 1978): 67–69.

LaBranche, A. "'Blanda Elegeia': The Background to Donne's 'Elegies.'" *Modern Language Review* 61 (1966): 357–68.

Lewis, E. Glyn. "An Interpretation of Donne's 'Elegie—The Dreame.'" *Modern Language Review* 29 (1934): 436–40.

Love, Harold. "Donne's 'To His Mistris Going To Bed,' 45." *The Explicator* 26 (1967–68): Item 33. [Notes the importance of the ecclesiastical courts' orders for penance in white sheets for adulterers and prostitutes]

Rockett, William. "John Donne: The Ethical Argument of *Elegy III.*" *Studies in English Literature, 1500–1900* 15 (1975): 57–69.

Schwartz, Elias. "Donne's 'Elegie X (The Dreame).'" *The Explicator* 19 (1960–61): Item 67.

Thumboo, Edwin. "Donne's 'The Bracelet (Elegie XI),' 113–114." *The Explicator* 27 (1968–69): Item 14.

Wiggins, Peter De Sa. "The Love Quadrangle: Tibullus 1.6 and Donne's 'lay Ideot.'" *Papers on Language and Literature* 16 (1980): 142–50. [Concerns "Elegy 7"]

Young, R.V. "'O my America, my new-found-land': Pornography and Imperial Politics in Donne's *Elegies.*" *South Central Review* 4 (Summer 1987): 35–48.

4. *Epicedes and Obsequies*

Kolin, Philip C. "Donne's 'Obsequies to the Lord Harrington': Theme, Structure, and Image." *Southern Quarterly* 13 (1974–75): 65–82.

Lebans, W.M. "The Influence of the Classics in Donne's *Epicedes and Obsequies.*" *Review of English Studies* 23 (1972): 127–37.

Sherwood, Terry G. "Reason, Faith, and Just Augustinian Lamentation in Donne's Elegy on Prince Henry." *Studies in English Literature, 1500–1900* 13 (1973): 53–67.

Tourney, Leonard D. "Convention and Wit in Donne's *Elegie on Prince Henry.*" *Studies in Philology* 71 (1974): 473–83.

Wallerstein, Ruth. *Studies in Seventeenth-Century Poetic.* 1950. Reprint. Madison: University of Wisconsin Press, 1965.

[Chapter 3 discusses the death of Prince Henry, including extensive comments on Donne's memorial poem.]

5. *Epigrams*

Hester, M. Thomas. "Donne's Epigrams: A Little World Made Cunningly." In *The Eagle and the Dove: Reassessing John Donne*, edited by Claude J. Summers and Ted-Larry Pebworth, 80–91. Columbia: University of Missouri Press, 1986.

Hester, M. Thomas. "*Genera Mixta* in Donne's 'Sir John Wingfield.'" *English Language Notes* 16 (1978–79): 202–206.

Hester, M. Thomas. "Reading Donne's Epigrams: 'Raderus'/'Ralphius.'" *Papers on Language and Literature* 21 (1985): 324–30.

Shawcross, John T. "The Source of an Epigram by John Donne." *English Language Notes* 21 (1983–84): 23–24. [Cites a prose account of 1589 as the source of "Fall of a Wall"]

6. *Epithalamions*

Dubrow, Heather. "'The Sun in Water': Donne's Somerset Epithalamium and the Poetics of Patronage." In *The Historical Renaissance: New Essays on Tudor and Stuart Literature and Culture*, edited by Heather Dubrow and Richard Strier, 197–219. Chicago: University of Chicago Press, 1988. [Argues that the poem is subtle, that it is not as simplistic and blatant in praise and flattery as previous critics have interpreted it. Says, in fact, that Donne embodies symbolism of the number "11," signifying trespass and sin, on the part of the couple and possibly on Donne's own part in violating his moral dictates with his praise. Also argues that Allophanes and Idios may represent the two sides of Donne caught in conflict]

Dubrow, Heather. "Tradition and the Individualistic Talent: Donne's 'An Epithalamion, Or mariage Song on the Lady Elizabeth . . . .'" In *The Eagle and the Dove: Reassessing John Donne*, edited by Claude J. Summers and Ted-Larry Pebworth, 106–16. Columbia: University of Missouri Press, 1986.

McClung, William A., and Rodney Simard. "Donne's Somerset Epithalamion and the Erotics of Criticism." *Huntington Library Quarterly* 50 (1987): 95–106. [Traces the extrapoetic judgments about Donne's poem from his time to the present,

focusing especially on associations with the sexual and
political nature of the Somerset scandal and with Donne's
desire for patronage]

McGowan, Margaret M. "'As Through a Looking-glass': Donne's
Epithalamia and their Courtly Context." In *John Donne:
Essays in Celebration*, edited by A.J. Smith, 175–218. London:
Methuen, 1972.

Novarr, David. "Donne's 'Epithalamion Made at Lincoln's Inn':
Context and Date." *Review of English Studies* 7 (July
1956): 250–63. [Argues that the poem is a parody or mock-
epithalamion, possibly written for the Midsummer revels at
Lincoln's Inn in 1595]

Ousby, Heather Dubrow. "Donne's 'Epithalamion made at Lincolnes
Inne': An Alternative Interpretation." *Studies in English
Literature, 1500–1900* 16 (1976): 131–43. [Disagrees with
Novarr (see preceding entry) that the poem is parodic. Sees
it instead as Donne's attempt to imitate Spenser's
"Epithalamion" after its publication in 1595 and not
succeeding in harmonizing Spenser's qualities with his own
distinctive ones]

7. Holy Sonnets

Archer, Stanley. "Meditation and the Structure of Donne's 'Holy
Sonnets.'" *ELH* 28 (1961): 137–47.

Bedford, R.D. "Donne's Holy Sonnet, 'Batter My Heart.'" *Notes and
Queries* 29 (1982): 15–19. [Summarizes much of the critical
debate on the sonnet and proposes a new emphasis on the
conceit of God as a potter to explain much of the poem]

Blanch, Robert J. "Fear and Despair in Donne's *Holy Sonnets*."
American Benedictine Review 25 (1974): 476–84.

Bond, Ronald B. "John Donne and the Problem of 'Knowing Faith.'"
Mosaic 14 (Winter 1981): 25–35. [Explicates "Thou hast
made me, and shall thy work decay" in light of Biblical and
doctrinal background]

Brooks, Cleanth, and Robert Penn Warren. *Understanding Poetry.*
3rd ed. New York: Holt, Rinehart and Winston, 1960.
[Explicates "If poisonous minerals, and if that tree" on pp.
355–61]

Carlson, Norman E. "Donne's *Holy Sonnets*, XIX." *The Explicator* 32
(1973–74): Item 19. [Explicates lines 5–8 of "Oh, to vex me,
contraries meet in one"]

Clements, Arthur L. "Donne's Holy Sonnet XIV." *Modern Language
Notes* 76 (1961): 484–89. [Explicates "Batter my heart, three-

personed God, for you" in terms of major analogies and
numerous Biblical associations]

Cornelius, David K. "Donne's 'Holy Sonnet XIV.'" *The Explicator* 24
(1965–66): Item 25. [Explicates "Batter my heart, three-
personed God, for you," relating Donne's treatment of the
Trinity in his sermons to this sonnet]

Daniels, Edgar F. "Donne's *Holy Sonnets* VI." *The Explicator* 31
(1972–73): Item 12. [Explicates "This is my play's last scene,
here heavens appoint," particularly lines 6–7]

Delany, Paul. "Donne's 'Holy Sonnet V,' Lines 13–14." *American
Notes and Queries* 9 (1970–71): 6–7. [Concerns "I am a little
world made cunningly"]

Dubinski, Roman. "Donne's Holy Sonnets and the Seven Penitential
Psalms." *Renaissance and Reformation* 22 (1986): 201–16.

Fenner, Arthur. "Donne's 'Holy Sonnet XII.'" *The Explicator* 40
Summer 1982): 14–15. [Explicates "Why are we by all
creatures waited on," noting its argumentative structure]

Grant, Patrick. "Augustinian Spirituality and the *Holy Sonnets* of
John Donne." *ELH* 38 (1971): 542–61.

Grenander, M.E. "Donne's *Holy Sonnets*, XII." *The Explicator* 13
(1954–55): Item 42. [Explicates "Why are we by all creatures
waited on," emphasizing the paradoxes, the sense of wonder,
and the assumption of a chain of being]

Grenander, M.E. "Holy Sonnets VIII and XVII: John Donne." *Boston
University Studies in English* 4 (1960): 95–105. [Explicates
"If faithful souls be alike glorified" and "Since she whom I
loved hath paid her last debt"]

Handscombe, Richard. "Donne's Holy Sonnet VI: A Problem of
Plainness." *Language and Style* 13 (Spring 1980): 98–108.
[Explicates "Death, be not proud, though some have called
thee"]

Herman, George. "Donne's *Holy Sonnets*, XIV." *The Explicator* 12
(1953–54): Item 18. [Argues for a conceit of a besieged and
occupied woman-town in "Batter my heart, three personed
God, for you"]

Hester, M. Thomas. "Re-signing the Text of the Self: Donne's 'As
due by many titles.'" In *"Bright Shootes of Everlastingnesse":
The Seventeenth-Century Religious Lyric*, edited by Claude J.
Summers and Ted-Larry Pebworth, 59–71. Columbia:
University of Missouri Press, 1987.

Kerrigan, William. "The Fearful Accommodations of John Donne."
English Literary Renaissance 4 (1974): 337–63. [Primarily
concerns "Batter my heart, three-personed God, for you" and

"Show me, dear Christ, Thy spouse so bright and clear,"
  commenting on the motif of God's sexuality]
Knox, George. "Donne's *Holy Sonnets*, XIV." *The Explicator* 15
  (1956–57): Item 2. [Explicates "Batter my heart, three-
  personed God, for you," emphasizing the role of the Trinity]
Levenson, J.C. "Donne's *Holy Sonnets*, XIV." *The Explicator* 11
  (1952–53): Item 31. [Suggests a conceit of God as tinker and
  Donne as pewter vessel in "Batter my heart, three-personed
  God, for you"]
Levenson, J.C. "Donne's *Holy Sonnets*, XIV." *The Explicator* 12
  (1953–54): Item 36. [Defends his views and elaborates on
  the conceits of "Batter my heart, three-personed God, for
  you"]
Linville, Susan. "Donne's *Holy Sonnets* IX." *The Explicator* 36
  (Summer 1978): 21–22. [Explicates "If poisonous minerals,
  and if that tree," especially the last few lines]
Malpezzi, Frances M. "The Weight/lessness of Sin: Donne's 'Thou
  hast made me' and the Psychostatic Tradition." *South Central
  Review* 4 (Summer 1987): 71–77.
Mueller, William R. "Donne's Adulterous Female Town." *Modern
  Language Notes* 76 (1961): 312–14. [Explains some Biblical
  images in "Batter my heart, three-personed God, for you"]
O'Connell, Patrick F. "The Successive Arrangements of Donne's
  'Holy Sonnets.'" *Philological Quarterly* 60 (1981): 323–42.
Parish, John E. "No. 14 of Donne's *Holy Sonnets*." *College English* 24
  (1962–63): 299–302. [Explicates "Batter my heart, three-
  personed God, for you"]
Patrick, J. Max. "Donne's *Holy Sonnets* VI." *The Explicator* 31
  (1972–73): Item 12. [Explicates "This is my play's last scene,
  here heavens appoint," particularly lines 7 and 11–14]
Peterson, Douglas L. "John Donne's *Holy Sonnets* and the Anglican
  Doctrine of Contrition." *Studies in Philology* 56 (1959): 504–
  18.
Pritchard, R.E. "Donne's Angels in the Corners." *Notes and Queries*
  33 (1986): 348–49. [Identifies the four angels assumed by
  Donne in "At the round earth's imagined corners blow" and
  their importance in the principle of four operating in the
  sonnet: four elements, four humors, and four types of death]
Ricks, Don M. "The Westmoreland Manuscript and the Order of
  Donne's 'Holy Sonnets.'" *Studies in Philology* 63 (1966): 187–
  95.
Rollin, Roger B. "'Fantastique Ague': The Holy Sonnets and
  Religious Melancholy." In *The Eagle and the Dove:
  Reassessing John Donne*, edited by Claude J. Summers and

Ted-Larry Pebworth, 131–46. Columbia: University of Missouri Press, 1986.

Romein, Tunis. "Donne's 'Holy Sonnet XIV.'" *The Explicator* 42 (Summer 1984): 12–14. [Proposes that "Batter my heart, three-personed God, for you" pictures God as a glass blower]

Ruotolo, Lucio P. "The Trinitarian Framework of Donne's Holy Sonnet XIV." *Journal of the History of Ideas* 27 (1966): 445–46. [Concerns "Batter my heart, three-personed God, for you"]

Simpson, Arthur L., Jr. "Donne's *Holy Sonnets*, XII." *The Explicator* 27 (1968–69): Item 75. [Explicates "Why are we by all creatures waited on," noting the importance of several Biblical allusions]

Stachniewski, John. "John Donne: The Despair of the 'Holy Sonnets.'" *ELH* 48 (1981): 677–705.

Summers, Claude J. "The Bride of the Apocalypse and the Quest for True Religion: Donne, Herbert, and Spenser." In *"Bright Shootes of Everlastingnesse": The Seventeenth-Century Religious Lyric*, edited by Claude J. Summers and Ted-Larry Pebworth, 72–95. Columbia: University of Missouri Press, 1987. [Discusses "Show me, dear Christ, Thy spouse so bright and clear"]

Wall, John N., Jr. "Donne's Wit of Redemption: The Drama of Prayer in the *Holy Sonnets*." *Studies in Philology* 73 (1976): 189–203.

Yearwood, Stephenie. "Donne's *Holy Sonnets*: The Theology of Conversion." *Texas Studies in Literature and Language* 24 (1982): 208–21.

Young, R.V. "Donne's Holy Sonnets and the Theology of Grace." In *"Bright Shootes of Everlastingnesse": The Seventeenth-Century Religious Lyric*, edited by Claude J. Summers and Ted-Larry Pebworth, 20–39. Columbia: University of Missouri Press, 1987.

Zitner, S.P. "Rhetoric and Doctrine in Donne's Holy Sonnet IV." *Renaissance and Reformation* 15 (1979): 66–76. [Concerns "At the round earth's imagined corners blow"]

8. *Metempsychosis (The Progress of the Soul)*

Corthell, Ronald J. "Donne's *Metempsychosis*: An 'Alarum to Truth.'" *Studies in English Literature, 1500–1900* 21 (1981): 97–110. [Argues that the poem depends heavily on paradox, is open-ended, invites the reader to answer Donne's interpretation of the soul's progress, and is self-referential to the extent that it might be Donne's own soul planned as the final manifestation in 1601]

Mueller, Janel M. "Donne's Epic Venture in the *Metempsychosis.*" *Modern Philology* 70 (1972–73): 109–37. [Argues that the poem is an Ovidian epic]

Murray, W.A. "What was the Soul of the Apple?" *Review of English Studies* 10 (1959): 141–55. [Argues that *Metempsychosis* essentially is about the Fall of man and moral choice in a fallen world]

Smith, M. van Wyk. "John Donne's *Metempsychosis.*" *Review of English Studies* 24 (1973): 17–25, 141–52. [Argues for Robert Cecil as the ultimate recipient of the corrupt soul and as the primary butt of political satire in the poem]

Tepper, Michael. "John Donne's Fragment Epic: 'The Progresse of the Soule.'" *English Language Notes* 13 (1975–76): 262–66. [Argues that the poem actually is a finished work]

Wentersdorf, Karl P. "Symbol and Meaning in Donne's *Metempsychosis* or *The Progresse of the Soule.*" *Studies in English Literature, 1500–1900* 22 (1982): 69–90. [Notes the importance of vegetal, animal, and human symbolism in the poem's journey through the hierarchy of creation]

Williamson, George. "Donne's Satirical *Progresse of the Soule.*" *ELH* 36 (1969): 250–64.

9. Satires

Andreason, N.J.C. "Theme and Structure in Donne's *Satyres.*" *Studies in English Literature, 1500–1900* 3 (1963): 59–75.

Baumlin, James S. "Donne's Christian Diatribes: Persius and the Rhetorical Persona of 'Satyre III' and 'Satyre V.'" In *The Eagle and the Dove: Reassessing John Donne*, edited by Claude J. Summers and Ted-Larry Pebworth, 92–105. Columbia: University of Missouri Press, 1986.

Baumlin, James S. "Donne's 'Satyre IV': The Failure of Language and Genre." *Texas Studies in Literature and Language* 30 (1988): 363–87.

Bellette, A.F. "The Originality of Donne's *Satires.*" *University of Toronto Quarterly* 44 (1974–75): 130–40.

Bradbury, Nancy Mason. "Speaker and Structure in Donne's *Satyre IV.*" *Studies in English Literature, 1500–1900* 25 (1985): 87–107.

Corthell, Ronald J. "'Coscus onely breeds my just offence': A Note on Donne's 'Satire II' and the Inns of Court." *John Donne Journal* 6 (1987): 25–31.

Corthell, Ronald J. "Style and Self in Donne's Satires." *Texas Studies in Literature and Language* 24 (1982): 155–84.

Dubrow, Heather. "'No man is an island': Donne's Satires and Satiric Traditions." *Studies in English Literature, 1500–1900* 19 (1979): 71–83.

Eddy, Y. Shikany, and Daniel P. Jaeckle. "Donne's 'Satyre I': The Influence of Persius's 'Satire III.'" *Studies in English Literature, 1500–1900* 21 (1981): 111–22.

Elliott, Emory. "The Narrative and Allusive Unity of Donne's *Satyres.*" *Journal of English and Germanic Philology* 75 (1976): 105–16.

Hester, M. Thomas. "'All our Soules Devotion': Satire as Religion in Donne's *Satire III.*" *Studies in English Literature, 1500–1900* 18 (1978): 35–55.

Hester, M. Thomas. "'Carelesse Phrygius': Donne's Separatist Sectarian." In *A Fair Day in the Affections: Literary Essays in Honor of Robert B. White, Jr.*, edited by Jack D. Durant and M. Thomas Hester, 87–99. Raleigh, North Carolina: The Winston Press, 1980. [Speculates on possible interpretations of Phrygius in "Satire 3"]

Hester, M. Thomas. *Kinde Pitty and Brave Scorn: John Donne's "Satyres."* Durham, North Carolina: Duke University Press, 1982.

Hester, M. Thomas. "The Satirist as Exegete: John Donne's *Satyre V.*" *Texas Studies in Literature and Language* 20 (1978): 347–66.

Johnson, S.F. "Donne's *Satires, I.*" *The Explicator* 11 (1952–53): Item 53. [Interprets "Satire 1" as a version of debate between body and soul]

Kerins, Frank. "The 'Businesse' of Satire: John Donne and the Reformation of the Satirist." *Texas Studies in Literature and Language* 26 (1984): 34–60.

Lauritsen, John R. "Donne's *Satyres*: The Drama of Self-Discovery." *Studies in English Literature, 1500–1900* 16 (1976): 117–30.

Lein, Clayton D. "Theme and Structure in Donne's *Satyre II.*" *Comparative Literature* 32 (1980): 130–50.

Moore, Thomas V. "Donne's Use of Uncertainty as a Vital Force in *Satyre III.*" *Modern Philology* 67 (1969–70): 41–49.

Newton, Richard C. "Donne the Satirist." *Texas Studies in Literature and Language* 16 (1974–75): 427–45.

Sellin, Paul R. "The Proper Dating of John Donne's 'Satyre III.'" *Huntington Library Quarterly* 43 (1979–80): 275–312. [Presents evidence arguing for a date of 1620, rather than in the 1590's]

Shawcross, John T. "All Attest His Writs Canonical: The Texts, Meaning and Evaluation of Donne's Satires." In *Just So Much Honor: Essays Commemorating the Four-Hundredth Anniversary of the Birth of John Donne*, edited by Peter Amadeus Fiore, 245–72. University Park: The Pennsylvania State University Press, 1972.

Smith, Hallett. *Elizabethan Poetry: A Study in Conventions, Meaning, and Expression*. 1952. Reprint. Ann Arbor: University of Michigan Press, 1968. [Chapter IV discusses English satire, including comments on Donne's five *Satires*]

Wall, John N., Jr. "Donne's *Satire IV* and the Feast of the Purification of Saint Mary the Virgin." *English Language Notes* 23 (September 1985): 23–31.

Zivley, Sherry. "Imagery in John Donne's *Satyres*." *Studies in English Literature, 1500–1900* 6 (1966): 87–95.

10. *Songs and Sonnets*

Allen, D.C. "Donne on the Mandrake." *Modern Language Notes* 74 (1959): 393–97.

Andrews, Michael Cameron. "Donne's 'The Ecstasy.'" *The Explicator* 39 (Summer 1981): 5–6.

Anthony, J. Philip. "Donne's 'The Relique.'" *The Explicator* 44 (Winter 1986): 13–15.

Armstrong, Ray L. "Donne's 'A Jeat Ring Sent.'" *The Explicator* 30 (1971–72): Item 77.

Ball, Lee, Jr. "Donne's 'The Canonization.'" *The Explicator* 8 (1949–50): Item 44.

Banerjee, Chinmoy. "Metaphysical Concreteness: John Donne's Better Hemispheres." *Notes and Queries* 28 (1981): 39–40. [Interprets lines 15–18 of "The Good-Morrow" as primarily referring to the eyes as hemispherical maps, with a contrast to the distortions found in literal maps of the time]

Beale, Walter H. "On Rhetoric and Poetry: John Donne's 'The Prohibition' Revisited." *Quarterly Journal of Speech* 62 (1976): 376–86.

Bell, Ilona. "The Role of the Lady in Donne's *Songs and Sonets*." *Studies in English Literature, 1500–1900* 23 (1983): 113–29.

Bentley, Greg. "Donne's 'Witchcraft by a Picture.'" *The Explicator* 42 (Spring 1984): 15–17. [Notes possible ambiguities, double meanings, and multiple interpretations of the poem not previously recognized in criticism]

Brooks, Cleanth. *The Well Wrought Urn: Studies in the Structure of Poetry.* New York: Reynal & Hitchcock, 1947. [The first chapter includes an explication of "The Canonization."]

Brown, Meg Lota. "'In that the world's contracted thus': Casuistical Politics in Donne's 'The Sunne Rising.'" In *"The Muses Common-Weale": Poetry and Politics in the Seventeenth Century,* edited by Claude J. Summers and Ted-Larry Pebworth, 23–33. Columbia: University of Missouri Press, 1988.

Brumble, H. David, III. "John Donne's 'The Flea': Some Implications of the Encyclopedic and Poetic Flea Traditions." *Critical Quarterly* 15 (1973): 147–54.

Carlson, Norman E. "The Drama of Donne's 'The Indifferent.'" *South Central Review* 4 (Summer 1987): 65–69.

Chambers, A.B. "The Fly in Donne's 'Canonization.'" *Journal of English and Germanic Philology* 65 (1966): 252–59.

Chambers, A.B. "Glorified Bodies and the 'Valediction: forbidding Mourning.'" *John Donne Journal* 1 (1982): 1–20.

Clair, John A. "Donne's 'The Canonization.'" *PMLA* 80 (1965): 300–302. [Relates the poem to the process of canonization in the Roman Catholic Church]

Cognard, Roger A. "Donne's 'The Dampe.'" *The Explicator* 36 (Winter 1978): 19–20. [Notes the importance that various meanings of "damp" and "die" have in the poem]

Collmer, Robert G. "Another Look at 'The Apparition.'" *Concerning Poetry* 7 (Fall 1974): 34–40.

Cowan, S.A. "Donne's 'The Legacie.'" *The Explicator* 19 (1960–61): Item 58. [Explains the significance of "colors" and "corners"]

Cross, K. Gustav. "'Balm' in Donne and Shakespeare: Ironic Intention in 'The Extasie.'" *Modern Language Notes* 71 (1956): 480–82.

Cunnar, Eugene R. "Donne's 'Valediction: Forbidding Mourning' and the Golden Compasses of Alchemical Creation." In *Literature and the Occult: Essays in Comparative Literature,* edited by Luanne Frank, 72–110. Arlington, Texas: The University of Texas at Arlington, 1977.

Cunnar, Eugene R. "Donne's Witty Theory of Atonement in 'The Baite.'" *Studies in English Literature, 1500–1900* 29 (1989): 77–98.

Daiches, David. "A Reading of 'The Good-Morrow.'" In *Just So Much Honor: Essays Commemorating the Four-Hundredth Anniversary of the Birth of John Donne,* edited by Peter Amadeus Fiore, 177–88. University Park: The Pennsylvania State University Press, 1972.

Daniels, Edgar F. "Donne's 'A Jeat Ring Sent.'" *The Explicator* 30 (1971–72): Item 77.

Daniels, Edgar F., and Ralph Haven Wolfe. "Donne's 'The Canonization,' 32." *The Explicator* 39 (Fall 1980): 46–47.

Dolan, Kathleen H. "*Materia in Potentia*: The Paradox of the Quintessence in Donne's 'A Nocturnall Upon S. Lucies Day.'" *Renascence* 32 (1979–80): 13–20.

Durr, R.A. "Donne's 'The Primrose.'" *Journal of English and Germanic Philology* 59 (1960): 218–22.

Empson, William. *Seven Types of Ambiguity*. 2nd ed. London: Chatto and Windus, 1947. [Explicates "A Valediction: Of Weeping" on pp. 139–45]

Estrin, Barbara. "Donne's Injured 'I': Defections from Petrarchan and Spenserian Poetics." *Philological Quarterly* 66 (1987): 175–93. [Notes some ways in which "The Broken Heart" and "A Valediction: Of Weeping" negate some Petrarchan and Spenserian poses and formulas]

Evans, G. Blakemore. "Donne's 'Subtile Knot.'" *Notes and Queries* 34 (1987): 228–30. [Physiological and philosophical background for lines 61–68 of "The Ecstasy" provided from a work contemporary with Donne]

Evans, G. Blakemore. "Two Notes on Donne: 'The undertaking'; 'A Valediction: of my name, in the window.'" *Modern Language Review* 57 (1962): 60–62. [Explains lines 1–4 in "The Undertaking" and lines 5–6 in "A Valediction: of my Name, in the Window"]

Freccero, John. "Donne's 'Valediction: Forbidding Mourning.'" *ELH* 30 (1963): 335–76.

Freedman, William. "Donne's 'Lovers Infiniteness.'" *The Explicator* 31 (1972–73): Item 6.

Gallant, Gerald, and A.L. Clements. "Harmonized Voices in Donne's *Songs and Sonets*: 'The Dampe.'" *Studies in English Literature, 1500–1900* 15 (1975): 71–82.

Gardner, Helen. "The Argument about 'The Ecstasy.'" In *Elizabethan and Jacobean Studies*, edited by Herbert Davis and Helen Gardner, 279–306. Oxford: Clarendon Press, 1959.

Gleckner, Robert F., and Gerald Smith. "Donne's 'Love's Usury.'" *The Explicator* 8 (1949–50): Item 43.

Grennen, Joseph E. "Donne on the Growth and Infiniteness of Love." *John Donne Journal* 3 (1984): 131–39. [Explicates portions and difficult words and phrases in "Lovers' Infiniteness" and "Love's Growth"]

Guss, Donald L. *John Donne, Petrarchist: Italianate Conceits and Love Theory in "The Songs and Sonets."* Detroit, Michigan: Wayne State University Press, 1966.

Hamilton, Lynn. "Donne's 'The Bait.'" *The Explicator* 46 (Spring 1988): 11–13. [Comments on the subtleties of the poem, in presenting both male and female as pursuing and being pursued, devouring and being devoured]

Henderson, Hanford. "Donne's 'The Will.'" *The Explicator* 7 (1948–49): Item 57. [Explains associations of "Capuchin," as perceived by Donne's contemporaries]

Hoover, L. Elaine. *John Donne and Francisco de Quevado: Poets of Love and Death.* Chapel Hill: University of North Carolina Press, 1978.

Johnstone, Peggy Ruth Fitzhugh. "Donne's 'Love's Growth.'" *The Explicator* 47 (Spring 1989): 8–10. [Argues for the centrality of new discoveries about the planet Venus in both the title and the poem]

Keister, Don A. "Donne's 'The Will,' 40–41." *The Explicator* 8 (1949–50): Item 55. [Explains "brazen medals" as commemorative medals]

Kennedy, Richard F. "Donne's 'The Canonization.'" *The Explicator* 42 (Fall 1983): 13–14.

Kolin, Philip C. "Love's Wealth in 'The Sunne Rising.'" *The South Central Bulletin* 43 (1983): 112–14.

Kronenfeld, Judy Z. "The Asymmetrical Arrangement of Donne's 'Love's Growth' as an Emblem of Its Meaning." *Concerning Poetry* 9 (Fall 1976): 53–58.

Labriola, Albert C. "Donne's 'The Canonization': Its Theological Context and Its Religious Imagery." *Huntington Library Quarterly* 36 (1972–73): 327–39.

Legouis, Pierre. *Donne the Craftsman: An Essay upon the Structure of the "Songs and Sonnets."* 1928. Reprint. New York: Russell & Russell, 1962.

Levine, Jay Arnold. "'The Dissolution': Donne's Twofold Elegy." *ELH* 28 (1961): 301–15. [Argues that the poem must be interpreted primarily on an erotic, sexual level, and only secondarily on the more commonly accepted funereal one]

Lewalski, Barbara K. "A Donnean Perspective on 'The Exstasie.'" *English Language Notes* 10 (June 1973): 258–62.

Linden, Stanton J. "Compasses and Cartography: Donne's 'A Valediction: forbidding Mourning.'" *John Donne Journal* 3 (1984): 23–32. [Notes the significance of Renaissance maps (with compasses portrayed on them) as inspiration for Donne]

Lockwood, Deborah H. "Donne's Idea of Woman in the *Songs and Sonets.*" *Essays in Literature* 14 (1987): 37–50.

Louthan, Doniphan. "The *Tome-Tomb* Pun in Renaissance England." *Philological Quarterly* 29 (1950): 375–80. [Argues particularly for the validity of the pun in "A Valediction: Of the Book"]

Low, Anthony. "The Compleat Angler's 'Baite'; or, The Subverter Subverted." *John Donne Journal* 4 (1985): 1–12. [Comments on the great differences between "The Bait" and either of its precursors by Marlowe and Raleigh, on how Walton's treatment of the three poems in his *The Compleat Angler* also implies its separateness, and on some of the sexuality and mockery in Donne's poem]

Mabbott, T.O. "Donne's 'The Will,' 40–41." *The Explicator* 8 (1949–50): Item 30. [Explains "brazen medals" as Roman bronze coins, of interest to coin collectors]

MacColl, Alan. "A Note on Donne's 'Loves Growth.'" *English Studies* 56 (1975): 314–15. [Explanation of lines 15–18]

Madison, Arthur L. "Explication of John Donne's 'The Flea.'" *Notes and Queries* 4 (1957): 60–61.

Mann, Lindsay A. "Radical Consistency: A Reading of Donne's 'Communitie.'" *University of Toronto Quarterly* 50 (1980–81): 284–99.

Mauch, Katherine. "Angel Imagery and Neoplatonic Love in Donne's 'Air and Angels.'" *Seventeenth-Century News* 35 (1977): 106–11.

McCanles, Michael. "Distinguish in Order to Unite: Donne's 'The Extasie.'" *Studies in English Literature, 1500–1900* 6 (1966): 59–75.

McKevlin, Dennis J. *A Lecture in Love's Philosophy: Donne's Vision of the World of Human Love in the "Songs and Sonets."* Lanham, New York and London: University Press of America, 1984.

McLaughlin, Elizabeth. "'The Extasie'—Deceptive or Authentic?" *Bucknell Review* 18 (Winter 1970): 55–78.

Middleman, Louis I. "Another Canon in Donne's 'Canonization.'" *English Language Notes* 22 (June 1985): 37–39.

Milgate, Wesley. "'Aire and Angels' and the Discrimination of Experience." In *Just So Much Honor: Essays Commemorating the Four-Hundredth Anniversary of the Birth of John Donne,* edited by Peter Amadeus Fiore, 149–76. University Park: The Pennsylvania State University Press, 1972. [Detailed reading of the poem]

Miller, C. William, and Dan S. Norton. "Donne's 'The Apparition.'" *The Explicator* 4 (1945–46): Item 24. [Notes that "quicksilver sweat" alludes to the common treatment for syphilis in Donne's time]

Mitchell, Charles. "Donne's 'The Extasie': Love's Ŝublime Knot." *Studies in English Literature, 1500–1900* 8 (1968): 91–101.

Moody, Peter R. "Donne's 'A Lecture Upon the Shadow.'" *The Explicator* 20 (1961–62): Item 60.

Morillo, Marvin. "Donne's 'Farewell to Love': The Force of Shutting Up." *Tulane Studies in English* 13 (1963): 33–40.

Murray, W.A. "Donne and Paracelsus: An Essay in Interpretation." *Review of English Studies* 25 (1949): 115–23. [Notes influences of Paracelsus on Donne's uses of alchemy and medicine in "Love's Alchemy" and "A Nocturnal Upon St. Lucy's Day"]

Okerlund, Arlene N. "The Rhetoric of Love: Voice in the *Amoretti* and the *Songs and Sonets.*" *Quarterly Journal of Speech* 68 (1982): 37–46.

Otten, Charlotte F. "Donne's Manna in 'The Primrose.'" *English Language Notes* 13 (1975–76): 260–62.

Perrine, Laurence. "Donne's 'Confined Love.'" *The Explicator* 39 (Fall 1980): 34–36.

Pinka, Patricia Garland. *This Dialogue of One: The "Songs and Sonnets" of John Donne.* University, Alabama: University of Alabama Press, 1982.

Pomeroy, Elizabeth. "Donne's 'The Sunne Rising.'" *The Explicator* 27 (1968–69): Item 4.

Pope, Myrtle Pihlman. "Donne's 'A Jeat Ring Sent.'" *The Explicator* 34 (1975–76): Item 44.

Pritchard, E.F. "Donne's 'Aire and Angels.'" *The Explicator* 41 (Fall 1982): 16–20. [Notes the importance of sounds, rhyme, and wordplay—particularly regarding "air," "hair," "inhere," and "sphere"—in the poem's progression and structure]

Pritchard, R.E. "Dying in Donne's 'The Good Morrow.'" *Essays in Criticism* 35 (1985): 213–22.

Rajan, Tilottama. "'Nothing Sooner Broke': Donne's *Songs and Sonets* as Self-Consuming Artifact." *ELH* 49 (1982): 805–28.

Rauber, D.F. "Donne's 'Farewell to Love': A Crux Revisited." *Concerning Poetry* 3 (Fall 1970): 51–63.

Richards, Bernard. "The 'bed's feet' in Donne's 'A Nocturnal upon St. Lucy's Day.'" *Notes and Queries* 36 (1989): 28–29. [Argues that the phrase is an apparently plural noun describing a singular object, the foot of the bed]

Richards, Bernard. "Donne's 'Twickenham Garden' and the *Fons Amatoria.*" *Review of English Studies* 33 (May 1982): 180–83. [Argues that the fountain image unites the poem and notes related secular parodies of Christian associations]

Rickey, Mary Ellen. "Donne's 'The Relique,' 27–28." *The Explicator* 22 (1963–64): Item 58.

Ringler, Richard N. "Donne's Specular Stone." *Modern Language Review* 60 (1965): 333–39. [Particularly concerns the reference in "The Undertaking"]

Rooney, William J. "'The Canonization'—The Language of Paradox Reconsidered." *ELH* 23 (1956): 36–47.

Ruffo-Fiore, Silvia. "Donne's 'Parody' of the Petrarchan Lady." *Comparative Literature Studies* 9 (1972): 392–406. [Includes comments on "Woman's Constancy," "Community," and "The Indifferent"]

Ruffo-Fiore, Silvia. *Donne's Petrarchism: A Comparative View.* Florence: Grafica Toscana, 1976.

Sackton, Alexander. "Donne and the Privacy of Verse." *Studies in English Literature, 1500–1900* 7 (1967): 67–82. [Notes Donne's value of privacy in writing, as exemplified in "The Triple Fool" and other poems]

Salomon, Willis. "Donne's 'Aire and Angels.'" *The Explicator* 46 Summer 1988): 12–14. [Emphasizes that the last six lines assert the dynamic quality of active courtship after twenty-two lines of "tortuous metaphysical invention"]

Sharp, Robert L. "Donne's 'Good-Morrow' and Cordiform Maps." *Modern Language Notes* 69 (1954): 493–95.

Shawcross, John T. "Donne's 'A Nocturnall Upon S. Lucies Day.'" *The Explicator* 23 (1964–65): Item 56. [Argues that the poem was written about December 12, 1617, and concerns the death of Ann More]

Shelston, Alan. "A Note on 'The Canonization.'" *Critical Quarterly* 24 (Summer 1982): 81–83.

Sleight, Richard. "John Donne: 'A Nocturnall Upon S. Lucies Day, Being the Shortest Day.'" In *Interpretations: Essays on Twelve English Poems,* edited by John Wain, 31–58. London: Routledge and Kegan Paul, 1955.

Sloan, Thomas O. "A Rhetorical Analysis of John Donne's 'The Prohibition.'" *Quarterly Journal of Speech* 48 (1962): 38–45.

Smith, A.J. "The Dismissal of Love Or, Was Donne a Neoplatonic Lover?" In *John Donne: Essays in Celebration,* edited by A.J. Smith, 89–131. London: Methuen, 1972. [Treats the general topic of the essay in relation to both literary background and Donne, with particular emphasis on "Farewell to Love"]

Smith, A.J. "The Metaphysic of Love." *Review of English Studies* 9 (November 1958): 362–75. [A reading of "The Ecstasy"]

Smith, A.J. "Two Notes on Donne." *Modern Language Review* 51 (1956): 405–7. [Explicates portions of "Air and Angels," especially the last six lines]

Stewart, Jack F. "Image and Idea in Donne's 'The Good-Morrow.'" *Discourse* 12 (1969): 465–76.

Stewart, Jack F. "Irony in Donne's 'The Funerall.'" *Discourse* 12 (1969): 193–99.

Stringer, Gary A. "Donne's 'The Primrose': Manna and Numerological Dalliance," *Explorations in Renaissance Culture* 1 (1974): 23–29.

Swinden, Patrick. "John Donne: 'Air and Angels.'" *Critical Quarterly* 21 (Spring 1979): 51–54.

Thomason, T. Katharine. "Plotinian Metaphysics and Donne's 'Extasie.'" *Studies in English Literature, 1500–1900* 22 (1982): 91–105.

Tjarks, Larry D. "Donne's 'Loves Usury' and a Self-Deceived Persona." *The Southern Quarterly* 14 (1975–76): 207–13.

Traister, Barbara. "Donne's 'Loves Growth.'" *The Explicator* 34 (1975–76): Item 60.

Walker, Julia M. "'Here you see mee': Donne's Autographed Valediction." *John Donne Journal* 4 (1985): 29–33. [Argues that "A Valediction: Of My Name in the Window" is explicitly autobiographical in presenting Donne and Ann More, with clues to their names embodied in the poem through a system in which letters of the alphabet are assigned numerical equivalents]

Walker, Julia M. "Donne's 'The Extasie' as an Alchemical Process." *English Language Notes* 20 (September 1982): 1–8.

Warren, Austin. "Donne's 'Extasie.'" *Studies in Philology* 55 (1958): 472–80.

Wertenbaker, Thomas J., Jr. "Donne's 'A Jeat Ring Sent.'" *The Explicator* 35 (Summer 1977): 27–28.

Wiggins, Peter De Sa. "'Aire and Angels': Incarnations of Love," *English Literary Renaissance* 12 (1982): 87–101.

Williamson, George. "Donne's 'Farewell to Love.'" *Modern Philology* 36 (1938–39): 301–3.

Williamson, George. *Seventeenth Century Contexts*. Chicago: University of Chicago Press, 1961. [Chapter 3 is the essay "The Convention of 'The Extasie.'"]

Wilson, Scott W. "Process and Product: Reconstructing Donne's Personae." *Studies in English Literature, 1500–1900* 20 (1980): 92–103.

11. *Verse Letters*

Aers, David, and Gunther Kress. "'Darke Texts Needs Notes':
Versions of Self in Donne's Verse Epistles." In *Literature,
Language and Society in England 1580–1680*, edited by
David Aers, Bob Hodge, and Gunther Kress, 23–48. Dublin:
Gill and Macmillan, 1981.

Bald, R.C. "Donne's Early Verse Letters." *Huntington Library
Quarterly* 15 (1951–52): 283–89.

Bauer, Robert J. "Donne's Letter to Herbert Re-Examined." In *New
Essays on Donne*, edited by Gary A. Stringer, 60–73. Salzburg:
Institut für Englische Sprache und Literatur, Universität
Salzburg, 1977. [Examines "To Sir Edward Herbert, at Juliers"
as a statement of moral principles and of a poet's role]

Beck, Joyce S. "Donne's Scholastic *Ars Dictaminis* in a Verse Epistle
to the Countess of Bedford." *Explorations in Renaissance
Culture* 8/9 (1982–83): 22–32. [Analyzes a five-part
structure in the verse letter beginning "(Madam,) You have
refined me"]

Bennett, R.E. "John Donne and Everard Gilpin." *Review of English
Studies* 15 (1939): 66–72.

Byard, Margaret M. "The Trade of Courtiership: The Countess of
Bedford and the Bedford Memorials; a family history from
1585 to 1607." *History Today* 29 (1979): 20–28. [Provides
background for Donne's verse letters to the Countess by
presenting records of her financial and social position]

Cameron, Allen Barry. "Donne's Deliberative Verse Epistles."
English Literary Renaissance 6 (1976): 369–403. [Classifies
and discusses seven verse letters as deliberative,
emphasizing the rhetorical conventions behind them and
Donne's high opinion of such verse]

Collins, Dan S. "Donne's 'To the Countess of Bedford' ('T' have
written . . .')." *The Explicator* 31 (1972–73): Item 19.

Finkelpearl, P.J. "Donne and Everard Gilpin: Additions, Corrections,
and Conjectures." *Review of English Studies* 14 (1963): 164–
67.

Jacobsen, Eric. "The Fable Is Inverted or Donne's Aesop." *Classica
et Mediaevalia* 13 (1952): 1–37. [Use of the fable of King Log
and King Stork in "The Calm"]

Jordan, John. "The Early Verse-Letters of John Donne." *University
Review* 2 (1962): 3–24.

Lein, Clayton D. "Donne's 'The Storme': The Poem and the
Tradition." *English Literary Renaissance* 4 (1974): 137–63.

Maurer, Margaret. "John Donne's Verse Letters." *Modern Language Quarterly* 37 (1976): 234–59. [Argues that Donne's conscious artistry and dramatic self-presentation are central in the *Verse Letters*]

Maurer, Margaret. "The Real Presence of Lucy Russell, Countess of Bedford, and the Terms of John Donne's 'Honour is so Sublime Perfection.'" *ELH* 47 (1980): 205–34.

Mizejewski, Linda. "Darkness and Disproportion: A Study of Donne's 'Storme' and 'Calme.'" *Journal of English and Germanic Philology* 76 (1977): 217–30.

Nellist, B.F. "Donne's 'Storm' and 'Calm' and the Descriptive Tradition." *Modern Language Review* 59 (1964): 511–15.

Palmer, D.J. "The Verse Epistle." In *Metaphysical Poetry*, edited by Malcolm Bradbury and David Palmer, 73–99. London: Edward Arnold, 1970. [Discusses Donne's *Verse Letters* in the context of others in the late 16th and early 17th centuries]

Pebworth, Ted-Larry, and Claude J. Summers. "'Thus Friends Absent Speake': The Exchange of Verse Letters between John Donne and Henry Wotton." *Modern Philology* 81 (1983–84): 361–77.

Reeves, Carolyn H. "Donne's 'The Calme,' 3–4." *The Explicator* 32 (1973–74): Item 3. [Argues that "the fable is inverted" calls attention to Donne's own inversion of calm and storm, the capriciousness of Fortune, Aesop's fable, and the capriciousness of deity]

Sackton, Alexander. "Donne and the Privacy of Verse." *Studies in English Literature, 1500–1900* 7 (1967): 67–82. [Primarily concerns the sense of privacy in the *Verse Letters*]

Stapleton, Laurence. "The Theme of Virtue in Donne's Verse Epistles." *Studies in Philology* 55 (1958): 187–200.

DeStefano, Barbara L. "Evolution of Extravagant Praise in Donne's Verse Epistles." *Studies in Philology* 81 (1984): 75–93.

Storhoff, Gary. "Metaphors of Despair in Donne's 'The Storme' and 'The Calme.'" *Concerning Poetry* 9 (Fall 1976): 41–45.

Storhoff, Gary P. "Social Mode and Poetic Strategies: Donne's Verse Letters to His Friends." *Essays in Literature* 4 (1977): 11–18.

Thomson, Patricia. "Donne and the Poetry of Patronage: The *Verse Letters*." In *John Donne: Essays in Celebration*, edited by A.J. Smith, 308–23. London: Methuen, 1972.

Tourney, Leonard D. "Donne, the Countess of Bedford, and the Petrarchan Manner." In *New Essays on Donne*, edited by Gary A. Stringer, 45–59. Salzburg: Institut für Englische

Sprache und Literatur, Universität Salzburg, 1977.
[Emphasizes the verse letters to the Countess of Bedford]
Yoklavich, John. "Donne and the Countess of Huntingdon."
    Philological Quarterly 43 (1964): 283–88. [Cites the date of
    Elizabeth Stanley's birth as 1587 (from Derby household
    records), notes Donne's very brief acquaintance with her in
    her childhood, and thus speculates on the date of one of the
    verse letters to her]

12. Miscellaneous and More Than One Type of Poem

Altizer, Alma B. *Self and Symbolism in the Poetry of
    Michelangelo, John Donne, and Agrippa d' Aubigné.* The
    Hague: Martinus Nijhoff, 1973. [Chapter III is "John Donne."]
Andreason, N.J.C. *John Donne: Conservative Revolutionary.*
    Princeton, New Jersey: Princeton University Press, 1967.
Bellette, Antony F. "'Little Worlds Made Cunningly': Significant
    Form in Donne's *Holy Sonnets* and 'Goodfriday, 1613.'"
    Studies in Philology 72 (1975): 322–47.
Bennett, Joan. *Four Metaphysical Poets: Donne, Herbert, Vaughan,
    Crashaw.* Cambridge: Cambridge University Press, 1934.
    [Chapter II is "John Donne, 1573–1631," and Chapter III is
    "Donne's Technical Originality."]
Brodsky, Claudia. "Donne: The Imaging of the Logical Conceit." *ELH*
    49 (1982): 829–48.
Brower, Reuben Arthur. *The Fields of Light: An Experiment in
    Critical Reading.* New York: Oxford University Press, 1951.
    [Contains comments on and readings of "The Ecstasy" and
    two of the *Holy Sonnets* ("Show me dear Christ" and "At the
    round earth's")]
Bryan, Robert A. "John Donne's Use of the Anathema." *Journal of
    English and Germanic Philology* 61 (1962): 305–12. [Treats
    "The Curse," "Elegy 11: The Bracelet," and "Elegy 15: The
    Expostulation"]
Cathcart, Dwight. *Doubting Conscience: Donne and the Poetry of
    Moral Argument.* Ann Arbor: University of Michigan
    Press, 1975.
Crawshaw, Eluned. "Hermetic Elements in Donne's Poetic Vision."
    In *John Donne: Essays in Celebration*, edited by A.J. Smith,
    324–48. London: Methuen, 1972. [Hermeticism and alchemy
    in Donne's poetry]
Daniels, Earl. *The Art of Reading.* New York: Rinehart and
    Company, 1941. [Explicates "A Valediction: Forbidding

Mourning" and "A Valediction: Of Weeping" (pp. 214–19), as well as "Death be not proud" (pp. 275–78)]

Docherty, Thomas. *John Donne, Undone.* London: Methuen, 1986.

Duncan, Edgar Hill. "Donne's Alchemical Figures." *ELH* 9 (1942): 257–85. [Notes many of Donne's references to and adaptations of elements from alchemy]

Estrin, Barbara L. "Framing and Imagining the 'You': Donne's 'A Valediction of My Name in the Window' and 'Elegy: Change.'" *Texas Studies in Literature and Language* 30 (1988): 345–62.

Evett, David. "Donne's Poems and the Five Styles of Renascence Art." *John Donne Journal* 5 (1986): 101–31.

Ferry, Anne. *All in War with Time: Love Poetry of Shakespeare, Donne, Jonson, Marvell.* Cambridge, Massachusetts: Harvard University Press, 1975. [Chapter 2 is titled "Donne" and presents readings of several poems.]

Ferry, Anne. *The "Inward Language": Sonnets of Wyatt, Sidney, Shakespeare, Donne.* Chicago: University of Chicago Press, 1983. [Chapter 5 is titled "Donne" and comments on parts of *Songs and Sonnets, La Corona*, and *Holy Sonnets.*]

Gilman, Ernest B. *Iconoclasm and Poetry in the English Reformation.* Chicago: University of Chicago Press, 1986. [Chapter 5 is "Donne's 'Pictures Made and Mard.'"]

Herz, Judith Scherer. "'An Excellent Exercise of Wit that Speaks So Well of Ill': Donne and the Poetics of Concealment." In *The Eagle and the Dove: Reassessing John Donne*, edited by Claude J. Summers and Ted-Larry Pebworth, 3–14. Columbia: University of Missouri Press, 1986. [Argues that the speaking voice in Donne's poems is a "calculated illusion"]

Hunt, Clay. *Donne's Poetry: Essays in Literary Analysis.* New Haven, Connecticut: Yale University Press, 1954. [Close readings of "The Blossom," "The Canonization," "Elegy 19," "The Good-Morrow," "Hymn to God, My God, in My Sickness," "The Indifferent," and "Love's Alchemy"]

Hunter, Jim. *The Metaphysical Poets.* London: Evans Brothers Limited, 1965. [General introduction to this group of poets, with Chapter 6 titled "John Donne"]

Kamholtz, Jonathan Z. "Imminence and Eminence in Donne." *Journal of English and Germanic Philology* 81 (1982): 480–91. [Donne's uses of "states of time" in confrontation with other imminent states of time]

Leishman, J.B. *The Metaphysical Poets: Donne, Herbert, Vaughan, Traherne.* 1934. Reprint. New York: Russell & Russell, 1963. [First major section is "John Donne"]

Leishman, J.B. *The Monarch of Wit: An Analytical and Comparative Study of the Poetry of John Donne.* London: Hutchinson University Library, 1951.

Lewalski, Barbara Kiefer. *Protestant Poetics and the Seventeenth-Century Religious Lyric.* Princeton, New Jersey: Princeton University Press, 1979. [Chapter 8 is "John Donne: Writing after the Copy of a Metaphorical God."]

Louthan, Doniphan. *The Poetry of John Donne: A Study in Explication.* New York: Bookman Associates, 1951.

Low, Anthony. *Love's Architecture: Devotional Modes in Seventeenth-Century English Poetry.* New York: New York University Press, 1978. [Chapter 3 is "John Donne: Liturgy, Meditation, and Song" and discusses much of the religious poetry.]

Low, Anthony. "The 'Turning Wheele': Carew, Jonson, Donne . . . Law of Motion." *John Donne Journal* 1 (1982): 69–80.

Marotti, Arthur F. *John Donne, Coterie Poet.* Madison: University of Wisconsin Press, 1986.

McGuire, Philip C. "Private Prayer and English Poetry in the Early Seventeenth Century." *Studies in English Literature, 1500–1900* 14 (1974): 63–77. [Notes the influence of private prayer on "Thou hast made me, and shall thy work decay," "A Hymn to God the Father," and "A Hymn to Christ"]

Miner, Earl. *The Metaphysical Mode from Donne to Cowley.* Princeton, New Jersey: Princeton University Press, 1969.

Morris, Harry. "John Donne's Terrifying Pun." *Papers on Language and Literature* 9 (1973): 128–37. [Argues that Donne puns on Ann More's name in "A Hymn to God the Father," "A Hymn to Christ," "Since she whom I loved," "The Canonization," and "A Valediction: Of Weeping"]

Nelly, Una. *The Poet Donne: A Study in His Dialectic Method.* Cork, Ireland: Cork University Press, 1969.

Nicolson, Marjorie Hope. *The Breaking of the Circle: Studies in the Effect of the "New Science" upon Seventeenth-Century Poetry.* Revised ed. New York: Columbia University Press, 1960.

Nye, Robert. "The body is his book: the poetry of John Donne." *Critical Quarterly* 14 (1972): 345–60.

Parrish, Paul A. "'A Funerall Elegie': Donne's Achievement in Traditional Form." *Concerning Poetry* 19 (1986): 55–66.

Pebworth, Ted-Larry. "John Donne, Coterie Poetry, and the Text as Performance." *Studies in English Literature, 1500–1900* 29 (1989): 61–75.

Radzinowicz, Mary Ann. "'Anima Mea' Psalms and John Donne's Religious Poetry." In *"Bright Shootes of Everlastingnesse": The Seventeenth-Century Religious Lyric,* edited by Claude J. Summers and Ted-Larry Pebworth, 40–58. Columbia: University of Missouri Press, 1987.

Revard, Stella P. "Donne and Propertius: Love and Death in London and Rome." In *The Eagle and the Dove: Reassessing John Donne,* edited by Claude J. Summers and Ted-Larry Pebworth, 69–79. Columbia: University of Missouri Press, 1986.

Rieke, Alison R. "Donne's Riddles." *Journal of English and Germanic Philology* 83 (1984): 1–20. [Notes the qualities of riddles and enigmas in certain of the *Songs and Sonnets* and *Epigrams*]

Roberts, John R., ed. *Essential Articles for the Study of John Donne's Poetry.* Hamden, Connecticut: Archon Books, 1975.

Roston, Murray. *The Soul of Wit: A Study of John Donne.* Oxford: The Clarendon Press, 1974.

Rudnytsky, Peter L. "'The Sight of God': Donne's Poetics of Transcendence." *Texas Studies in Literature and Language* 24 (1982): 185–207.

Sanders, Wilbur. *John Donne's Poetry.* London: Cambridge University Press, 1971.

Shawcross, John T. "The Arrangement and Order of John Donne's Poems." In *Poems in Their Place: The Intertextuality and Order of Poetic Collections,* edited by Neil Fraistat, 119–63. Chapel Hill: University of North Carolina Press, 1986.

Shawcross, John T. "A Consideration of Title-Names in the Poetry of Donne and Yeats." *Names* 31 (1983): 159–66.

Shawcross, John T. "Poetry, Personal and Impersonal: The Case of Donne." In *The Eagle and the Dove: Reassessing John Donne,* edited by Claude J. Summers and Ted-Larry Pebworth, 53–66. Columbia: University of Missouri Press, 1986.

Sicherman, Carol Marks. "Donne's Discoveries." *Studies in English Literature, 1500–1900* 11 (1971): 69–88.

Sicherman, Carol Marks. "The Mocking Voices of Donne and Marvell." *Bucknell Review* 17 (May 1969): 32–46.

Stampfer, Judah. *John Donne and the Metaphysical Gesture.* New York: Funk & Wagnalls, 1970.

Stein, Arnold. *John Donne's Lyrics: The Eloquence of Action.* Minneapolis: University of Minnesota Press, 1962.

Summers, Claude J., and Ted-Larry Pebworth, eds. *"Bright Shootes of Everlastingnesse": The Seventeenth-Century Religious Lyric.* Columbia: University of Missouri Press, 1987. [Several of the essays, in whole or in part, concern Donne]

Unger, Leonard. *Donne's Poetry and Modern Criticism.* Chicago:
     Henry Regnery Co., 1950.
Walker, Julia M. "Donne's Words Taught in Numbers." *Studies in
     Philology* 84 (1987): 44–60. [Discusses the importance of
     numerology in "Love's Growth" and "Elegy 11: The Bracelet"]
Wanamaker, Melissa C. *Discordia Concors: The Wit of
     Metaphysical Poetry.* Port Washington, New York: Kennikat
     Press, 1975. [Chapter 2 is "John Donne: Yoking of Opposites."]
Wiggins, Elizabeth Lewis. "Logic in the Poetry of John Donne."
     Studies in Philology 42 (1945): 41–60.
Williamson, George. *Six Metaphysical Poets: A Reader's Guide.*
     New York: Farrar, Straus & Giroux, 1967. [Two chapters
     concern Donne and present general paraphrases of some
     poems]
Wilson, G.R., Jr. "The Interplay of Perception and Reflection:
     Mirror Imagery in Donne's Poetry." *Studies in English
     Literature, 1500–1900* 9 (1969): 107–21.
Zunder, William. *The Poetry of John Donne: Literature and Culture
     in the Elizabethan and Jacobean Period.* Brighton, England:
     The Harvester Press, 1982.

D. Prose

1. *Biathanatos*

Williamson, George. "The Libertine Donne." *Philological Quarterly*
     13 (1934): 276–91.

2. *Devotions Upon Emergent Occasions*

Andreason, N.J.C. "Donne's *Devotions* and the Psychology of
     Assent." *Modern Philology* 62 (1964–65): 207–16.
Cooper, Robert M. "The Political Implications of Donne's
     Devotions." In *New Essays on Donne,* edited by Gary A.
     Stringer, 192–210. Salzburg: Institut für Englische Sprache
     und Literatur, Universität Salzburg, 1977.
Cox, Gerard H., III. "Donne's *Devotions*: A Meditative Sequence on
     Repentance." *Harvard Theological Review* 66 (1973): 331–51.
Friederich, Reinhard H. "Expanding and Contracting Space in
     Donne's *Devotions.*" *ELH* 45 (1978): 18–32.
Friederich, Reinhard H. "Strategies of Persuasion in Donne's
     Devotions." *Ariel: A Review of International English
     Literature* 9 (January 1978): 51–70.

Goldberg, Jonathan. "The Understanding of Sickness in Donne's *Devotions*." *Renaissance Quarterly* 24 (1971): 507–17. [Examines the work in the context of contemporary devotional books and commonplaces of the time, emphasizing sickness as sin, but with the joy of implicit salvation]

Harding, D.W. "The *Devotions* Now." In *John Donne: Essays in Celebration*, edited by A.J. Smith, 385–403. London: Methuen, 1972. [Notes timeless themes and feelings in the *Devotions*, regardless of one's personal religious faith]

Lander, Clara. "A Dangerous Sickness Which Turned to a Spotted Fever." *Studies in English Literature, 1500–1900* 11 (1971): 89–108. [Argues that the disease Donne describes in *Devotions* is typhus, that the twenty-three devotions represent the days of the sickness, and that the tripartite division of each devotion reflects the morning, afternoon, and evening behavior of the typhus sufferer]

Morrisey, Thomas J. "The Self and the Meditative Tradition in Donne's *Devotions*." *Notre Dame English Journal* 13 (1980–81): 29–49.

Mueller, Janel M. "The Exegesis of Experience: Dean Donne's *Devotions Upon Emergent Occasions*." *Journal of English and Germanic Philology* 67 (1968): 1–19. [Discusses the importance of the Bible in the *Devotions* and of the links with the *Sermons*]

Shapiro, I.A. "Walton and the Occasion of Donne's *Devotions*." *Review of English Studies* 9 (1958): 18–22. [Argues that Donne's illness in 1623 was relapsing fever, not typhus, and notes that Walton's *Life of Donne* confuses his illness of 1623 with that of 1625]

Shuger, Debora. "The Title of Donne's *Devotions*." *English Language Notes* 22 (June 1985): 39–40. [Finds puns suggesting allusions to baptismal rebirth and to Christ's Crucifixion and Resurrection]

Smith, Don Noel. "The Artistry of John Donne's Devotions." *University of Dayton Review* 10 (Summer 1973): 3–12.

Van Laan, Thomas F. "John Donne's *Devotions* and the Jesuit Spiritual Exercises." *Studies in Philology* 60 (1963): 191–202.

3. *Essays in Divinity*

[A dearth of criticism and scholarship exists on this work.]

4. *Ignatius His Conclave*

Anglo, Sydney. "More Machiavellian than Machiavel: A Study of the Context of Donne's *Conclave*." In *John Donne: Essays in Celebration*, edited by A.J. Smith, 349–84. London: Methuen, 1972.

Hassel, R. Chris, Jr. "Donne's *Ignatius His Conclave* and the New Astronomy." *Modern Philology* 68 (1970–71): 329–37.

Korkowski, Eugene. "Donne's *Ignatius* and Menippean Satire." *Studies in Philology* 72 (1975): 419–38.

Raspa, Anthony. "Theology and Poetry in Donne's *Conclave*." *ELH* 32 (1965): 478–89.

Sadler, Lynn Veach. "'Meanes blesse': Donne's *Ignatius His Conclave*." *College Language Association Journal* 23 (1980): 438–50.

5. *Juvenilia: or Certain Paradoxes and Problems*

Siegel, Paul N. "Donne's *Paradoxes and Problems*." *Philological Quarterly* 28 (1949): 507–11. [Argues that these works must be read in light of Donne's wit, irony, and delight in wickedness and presents examples]

Simpson, Evelyn M. "Donne's *Paradoxes and Problems*." In *A Garland for John Donne, 1631–1931*, edited by Theodore Spencer, 21–49. Cambridge, Massachusetts: Harvard University Press, 1931.

6. *Letters*

Bennett, R.E. "Donne's Letters from the Continent in 1611–12." *Philological Quarterly* 19 (1940): 66–78.

Bennett, R.E. "Donne's *Letters to Severall Persons of Honour*." *PMLA* 56 (1941): 120–40.

Corthell, Ronald J. "'Frendships Sacraments': John Donne's Familiar Letters." *Studies in Philology* 78 (1981): 409–25. [Treats style, tone, and persona in some of Donne's letters]

Maurer, Margaret. "The Poetical Familiarity of John Donne's Letters." *Genre* 15 (1982): 183–202. [Discusses Donne's powers to dramatize and to create an image of himself as a letter-writer]

Patterson, Annabel. "Misinterpretable Donne: The Testimony of the Letters." *John Donne Journal* 1 (1982): 39–53.

7. *Pseudo-Martyr*

Raspa, Anthony. "Time, History and Typology in John Donne's *Pseudo-Martyr.*" *Renaissance and Reformation* 11 (1987): 175–83.

8. *Sermons*

Carrithers, Gale H., Jr. *Donne at Sermons: A Christian Existential World.* Albany: State University of New York Press, 1972.

Chamberlin, John S. *Increase and Multiply: Arts-of-Discourse Procedure in the Preaching of Donne.* Chapel Hill: University of North Carolina Press, 1976.

Davies, Horton. *Like Angels from a Cloud: The English Metaphysical Preachers, 1588–1645.* San Marino, California: Huntington Library, 1986. [Isolates and discusses over forty preachers considered to be "metaphysical," with Donne as the best]

Davis, Walter R. "Meditation, Typology, and the Structure of John Donne's Sermons." In *The Eagle and the Dove: Reassessing John Donne,* edited by Claude J. Summers and Ted-Larry Pebworth, 166–88. Columbia: University of Missouri Press, 1986.

Dees, Jerome S. "Logic and Paradox in the Structure of Donne's Sermons." *South Central Review* 4 (Summer 1987): 78–92.

Doebler, Bettie Anne. *The Quickening Seed: Death in the Sermons of John Donne.* Salzburg: Institut für Englische Sprache und Literatur, Universität Salzburg, 1974.

Fish, Stanley. *Self-Consuming Artifacts: The Experience of Seventeenth-Century Literature.* Berkeley: University of California Press, 1972. [Pp. 43–77 make up a subsection titled "Donne: The Word As All," in which Donne's last sermon ("Death's Duel") is read as a "self-consuming artifact."]

Gifford, William. "Time and Place in Donne's Sermons." *PMLA* 82 (1967): 388–98.

Hall, Michael L. "Circles and Circumvention in Donne's Sermons." *Journal of English and Germanic Philology* 82 (1983): 201–14.

Hall, Michael L. "Searching the Scriptures: Meditation and Discovery in Donne's Sermons." In *New Essays on Donne,* edited by Gary A. Stringer, 211–38. Salzburg: Institut für Englische Sprache und Literatur, Universität Salzburg, 1977.

Harland, Paul W. "Dramatic Technique and Personae in Donne's Sermons." *ELH* 53 (1986): 709–26.

Harland, Paul W. "Imagination and Affections in John Donne's Preaching." *John Donne Journal* 6 (1987): 33–50.

Hayward, John. "A Note on Donne the Preacher." In *A Garland for John Donne, 1631–1931*, edited by Theodore Spencer, 73–97. Cambridge, Massachusetts: Harvard University Press, 1931.

Heatherington, Madelon E. "'Decency' and 'Zeal' in the Sermons of John Donne." *Texas Studies in Literature and Language* 9 (1967–68): 307–16.

Henricksen, Bruce. "Donne's Orthodoxy." *Texas Studies in Literature and Language* 14 (1972–73): 5–16.

Henricksen, Bruce. "The Unity of Reason and Faith in Donne's Sermons." *Papers on Language and Literature* 11 (1975): 18–30.

Hickey, Robert L. "Donne's Art of Memory." *Tennessee Studies in Literature* 3 (1958): 29–36.

Hickey, Robert L. "Donne's Art of Preaching." *Tennessee Studies in Literature* 1 (1956): 65–74.

Husain, Itrat. *The Dogmatic and Mystical Theology of John Donne.* London: Society for Promoting Christian Knowledge, 1938.

Lowe, Irving. "John Donne: The Middle Way. The Reason—Faith Equation in Donne's Sermons." *Journal of the History of Ideas* 22 (1961): 389–97.

Merchant, W. Moelwyn. "Donne's Sermon to the Virginia Company, 13 November 1622." In *John Donne: Essays in Celebration*, edited by A.J. Smith, 433–52. London: Methuen, 1972. [Discusses the sermon printed as no. 10 in Volume IV of Potter and Simpson edition]

Merrill, Thomas F. *Christian Criticism: A Study of Literary God-Talk.* Amsterdam: Rodopi, 1976. [Chapter Nine is "The Sermon as Sacrament," and Chapter Ten is "Performative Preaching."]

Mueller, William R. *John Donne: Preacher.* Princeton, New Jersey: Princeton University Press, 1962.

Ní Chuilleanáin, Eiléan. "Time, Place and the Congregation in Donne's Sermons." In *Literature and Learning in Medieval and Renaissance England: Essays Presented to Fitzroy Pyle*, edited by John Scattergood, 197–215. Dublin: Irish Academic Press, 1984.

Quinn, Dennis. "Donne's Christian Eloquence." *ELH* 27 (1960): 276–97.

Quinn, Dennis B. "John Donne's Principles of Biblical Exegesis." *Journal of English and Germanic Philology* 61 (1962): 313–29.

Schleiner, Winfried. *The Imagery of John Donne's Sermons.* Providence, Rhode Island: Brown University Press, 1970.

Sellin, Paul R. *John Donne and "Calvinist" Views of Grace.* Amsterdam: V U Boekhandel, 1983.

Sennhenn, Carl Braun. "John Donne, Poet in the Pulpit." In *New Essays on Donne*, edited by Gary A. Stringer, 239–60. Salzburg: Institut für Englische Sprache und Literatur, Universität Salzburg, 1977.

Shami, Jeanne M. "Donne on Discretion." *ELH* 47 (1980): 48–66. [On Donne's discussions and applications of discretion in his *Sermons*]

Shami, Jeanne M. "Donne's Protestant Casuistry: Cases of Conscience in the *Sermons*." *Studies in Philology* 80 (1983): 53–66.

Shami, Jeanne. "Kings and Desperate Men: John Donne Preaches at Court." *John Donne Journal* 6 (1987): 9–23.

Shapiro, I.A. "Donne's Sermon Dates." *Review of English Studies* 31 (1980): 54–56.

Stapleton, Laurence. *The Elected Circle: Studies in the Art of Prose.* Princeton, New Jersey: Princeton University Press, 1973. [The first chapter is "John Donne: The Moment of the Sermon."]

Thompson, Sister M. Geraldine. "'Writs Canonicall': The High Word and the Humble in the Sermons of John Donne." In *Familiar Colloquy: Essays Presented to Arthur Edward Barker*, edited by Patricia Bruckmann, 55–67. Ontario: Oberon Press, 1978.

9. Miscellaneous and More Than One Type of Prose Work

Mann, Lindsay A. "The Marriage Analogue of Letter and Spirit in Donne's Devotional Prose." *Journal of English and Germanic Philology* 70 (1971): 607–16.

Simpson, Evelyn M. *A Study of the Prose Works of John Donne.* 2nd ed. Oxford: Clarendon Press, 1948. [Summaries and general assessments of the prose]

Webber, Joan. *Contrary Music: The Prose Style of John Donne.* Madison: University of Wisconsin Press, 1963.

Webber, Joan. *The Eloquent "I": Style and Self in Seventeenth-Century Prose.* Madison: University of Wisconsin Press, 1968. [Donne's style is discussed particularly in Chapter II.]

VI. GENERAL BACKGROUND

Cirlot, J.E. *A Dictionary of Symbols*. New York: Philosophical
    Library, 1962.
Heninger, S.K., Jr. *A Handbook of Renaissance Meteorology, With
    Particular Reference to Elizabethan and Jacobean Literature*.
    1960. Reprint. New York: Greenwood Press, 1968.
Meadows, A.J. *The High Firmament: A Survey of Astronomy in
    English Literature*. Leicester: University of Leicester Press,
    1969.
Partridge, Eric. *Shakespeare's Bawdy*. Revised ed. New York: E.P.
    Dutton & Co., 1969. [Much of Shakespeare's use of bawdy
    language also applies to Donne's use.]
Ruthven, K.K. *The Conceit*. London: Methuen, 1969.
Tillyard, E.M.W. *The Elizabethan World Picture*. London: Chatto &
    Windus, 1943.